The Science of Change

The Science of Change

Discovering Sustained, Desired Change from Individuals to Organizations and Communities

Richard E. Boyatzis

OXFORD
UNIVERSITY PRESS

Oxford University Press is a department of the University of Oxford.
It furthers the University's objective of excellence in research, scholarship,
and education by publishing worldwide. Oxford is a registered trade mark of
Oxford University Press in the UK and in certain other countries.

Published in the United States of America by Oxford University Press
198 Madison Avenue, New York, NY 10016, United States of America.

Library of Congress Cataloging-in-Publication Data
Names: Boyatzis, Richard E., author.
Title: The science of change : discovering sustained, desired change from
individuals to organizations and communities / Richard E. Boyatzis.
Description: New York : Oxford University Press, [2024]
Identifiers: LCCN 2024019126 (print) | LCCN 2024019127 (ebook) |
ISBN 9780197765111 (hardback) | ISBN 9780197765135 (epub)
Subjects: LCSH: Change (Psychology) | Organizational change. |
Social change.
Classification: LCC BF637.C4 B69 2024 (print) | LCC BF637.C4 (ebook) |
DDC 155.2/4—dc23/eng/20240627
LC record available at https://lccn.loc.gov/2024019126
LC ebook record available at https://lccn.loc.gov/2024019127

DOI: 10.1093/9780197765142.001.0001

Printed by Sheridan Books, Inc., United States of America

This book is dedicated to
Max Boysen
David Kolb
David McClelland
and
Sandra Boyatzis

Contents

Acknowledgments   ix

1. The Quest for Sustained, Desired Change   1

2. Dreams, Shared Vision, and Purpose as the Driver of Change
    (Principle 1)   27

3. Tipping Points to Transitions: PEA and NEA (Principles 2 and 3) 64

4. The Real Self: Who Am I? Who Are We? (Principle 4)   106

5. A Path to My/Our Dreams: Joyful Planning and Preparation
    (Principle 5)   146

6. Exploring Possibilities: Experimenting and Practice to Mastery
    (Principle 6)   169

7. Resonant Relationships Are the Context for Change (Principle 7) 192

8. Leading Change at Multiple Levels (Principles 8, 9, and 10)   214

9. What Next? The Call to Study Change   237

Appendix   253
References   279
Index   321

Acknowledgments

This is a book about my life's work. It is dedicated to four people who have and continue to shape my thinking and life. Of course, this is in addition to my parents, Sophia and Kyriakos Boyatzis.

Max Boysen was my physics teacher in high school. He initiated the spark of curiosity and began me thinking like a scientist. His gentle provocations but persistent insistence on analyzing important phenomenon carefully reverberates within me today.

David Kolb turned me from an aerospace engineer and scientist into a psychologist. He became a lifelong friend and guide. His invitation to help with his data set while I was an undergraduate at MIT started me on the path I still follow. The work with him was the beginning of the theory on which this book and my professional work are based.

David McClelland began to guide and cajole me when he was skeptical of what I could offer. His perseverance and faith in me grew, as did our relationship from professor to advisor to colleague to friend. Dave sculpted me into a social scientist with a drive to incorporate insights and study many fields, from clinical and personality psychology to sociology and anthropology. His boldness in tackling social challenges that others avoided and creativity to formulate and refine new ways to measure elusive phenomenon is my model of an intellectual provocateur, a great scientist.

Sandy is the love of my life. She is my guide to being human. As my best friend, lover, co-conspirator, and adventurer, for over half a century she has been my muse and caring companion. She has tolerated my emotional absence during prolonged periods of research and writing, my mental visits to dimensions not clearly here on earth. I am looking forward to as many more years of laughter and loving together. I would also like to thank my son Mark Scott for believing in me, his patience and forgiving me for decades of being an absent and frequently preoccupied father, and his guidance on writing and social media.

Although many, many others have caringly played a major or minor role in my development, these four are the fountains of my spirit and motivation. They have at various times and throughout our relationships kept me going, helped me to survive, enticed me to thrive, and challenged me to be a better person. They are not responsible for the outcome, but they tried!

Many other faculty at MIT and Harvard helped me develop over time or sometimes in dramatic moments of transition. Ed Schein was a mentor and guide, and introduced me to adult socialization and the ways in which our interpersonal and cultural environment shape us. John and Bea Whiting sparked an appreciation for the vast array of cultures and their mythology. Freed Bales taught me how to understand group and team development in three dimensions, and coalitional dynamics. Robert Rosenthal sensitized me to research nuances that helped or hindered validity. Herb Kelman and Thomas Pettigrew brought me into a world of influence and the struggle against racial discrimination. Everett Hagen made psychoanalytic interpretation and psychohistorical analysis a deeper dimension of understanding others. John Schlein helped me to understand how to use Carl Rogers's recommended style in psychotherapy. Warren Bennis reappeared in my life at almost every inflection point and helped guide and champion me to the next great adventure. Chris Argyris encouraged and fostered an irreverence and willingness to challenge the accepted wisdom for something greater in our work. Other faculty I wish to thank include Paul Costa, Matina Horner, and Richard Hackman, and fellow doctoral students before and after me David Winter and Abbey Stewart.

A group of colleagues from MIT became close friends. They guided me through the world of consulting: David Berlew, Irv Rubin, Jim McIntyre, Fritz Steele, and Mike McCaskey.

Colleagues along the many stages of my 58-year journey in the social sciences were and are a constant source of insight and support. Dan Goleman began as a sympathetic compatriot in our quest to decipher how people change in our doctoral seminars at Harvard. In later years, Dan taught me how to write for professionals and practitioners. Together, our work in emotional intelligence, renewal, and change has enabled thousands of other scholars to see people and our relationships with new hope. Annie McKee began as a doctoral student and emerged as a caring, provocative, and insightful co-author and co-creator of the LEAD course, competency development longitudinal research, and later a series of books and articles to bring our messages to audiences that would not otherwise have heard of the ideas or research. Annie and Dan were the colleagues who reminded me to be more emotionally intelligent—not just write about it—with their style and advice.

During my years with McBer and Company (part-time from 1969 to 1972 and full-time from 1972 to 1987), my colleagues and some salient experiences sparked further curiosity into phenomenon of social concern, such as alcoholism, alcohol abuse and aggression, competencies, competency development, organizational climate, managerial style, coaching, and leadership.

The weekly interactions with my colleagues enhanced and reinforced a spirit of scientific empiricism with the typical phrase, "Let's collect data and see." We also had an iconoclastic approach to measurement inspired by David McClelland. In my years at McBer and Company, Jim Burruss was a partner in hundreds of interventions, and a few dozen research projects that shed light on effective alcoholism counselors, managerial style, efficacy, and career dynamics. Lyle Spencer Jr. was a true co-creator who would boldly take on projects that seemed too large to work and create new measures and ways to assess everything from organizational development interventions to project and account management in consulting. Murray Dalziel was and is a fount of innovative thinking about diverse aspects of our organizations, from introducing me to catastrophe theory (I had learned nonlinear dynamics at MIT in aerospace courses, but the escalation of the phenomenon to a different epistemology was a game changer), and years later as a highly innovative Dean of the School of Management at the University of Liverpool. David Miron guided me through learning how to involve others and be the type of manager and leader I wanted to be, as well as from his inspirational work in entrepreneurial development. Mary Esteves brought our work into new realms and showed how outstanding project and account management mattered to us and our clients. Warren Sawyer began as a board member and over decades of friendship taught me about grace and how faith can be operationalized into caring and innovative relationships with others and organizational designs. Others I wish to thank for a wide range of engaging and comforting conversations at McBer include Kris Amiralis (at The Hay Group), Jack Burns, Bernie Cullen, Chuck Daily, Susan Ennis, Ginny Flynn, Mary Fontaine, David Hoff, Ruth Jacobs, Steve Kelner, George Klemp, Corky Litwin, Mark Munger, Susan Munger (nea Mills), Tomas Perez, Paul Pottinger, Larry Rossini, Bob Ryan, Fabio Sala, Nell Slawson, Wayne Smevog, Signe Spencer, Tom Thomson, Steve Williamson, Steve Wolff, and Bernie Zimlicki.

The years I spent with Yankelovich, Skelly & White as COO were eye-opening, not just in learning about market research and the advertising industry, but because of the ever-caring and developmental Florence Skelly. Her insights created new fields within market research and her wisdom and style as a leader of YSW over the decades taught me so much about how to work with and lead professionals.

Along the way, certain faculty colleagues became close friends, co-researchers, co-authors, can co-creators of courses and development programs. Professor Melvin Smith helped to define our distinctive approach to coaching called "coaching with compassion," and its more typical but less effective counterpart "coaching for compliance." Melvin's incisive theoretical precision was a guiding light. His magnetic charisma enabled thousands to get inspired by emotional intelligence and leadership.

Professor Ellen Van Oosten began as an MBA student, then a doctoral student, and helped to create a corporate university for custom programs, founding the Coaching Research Lab with Melvin Smith, Angela Passarelli, Scott Taylor, and myself. She also kept provoking and guiding doctoral students and colleagues to study coaching in various forms and generate a steady stream of research publications. Melvin, Ellen, and I created a MOOC that hundreds of thousands have watched and enjoyed, and wrote *Helping People Change*. Melvin and Ellen also became more personal coaches, reminding me to be positive and avoid what Ellen called my "Greek male" disposition.

Professor Anthony (Tony) Jack approached me with a mutual interest in the impact of interpersonal interactions after a seminar I presented. It began a highly creative and productive 15-year process of conducting a series of fMRI studies as well as conducting other research and providing a series of articles on neuroscience, coaching, and leadership. Tony inspired me to learn more than I thought I could about neural functioning and neuroimaging. He has been my teacher and guide in the process. His unique theory of opposing domains (in his terms, Opposing Poles of Reason) and his truly transdisciplinary thinking about human functioning and beliefs continues to humble me.

Others have played a key role in developing and nurturing the Coaching Research Lab and were also long-time researcher collaborators, namely Professors Angela Passarelli and Scott Taylor. Angela was the project manager and main co-researcher on all of my fMRI studies, as well as conducting her own breakthrough hormonal studies of coaching and being a key researcher in a series of our longitudinal studies of the development of emotional and social intelligence competencies. She, along with Ellen, Anita Howard, and Suzanne Healy, helped me to design, create, and launch the Inspiring Leadership Through Emotional Intelligence MOOC, which together with the coaching MOOC has had about 1,500,000 visitors and learners from over 215 countries since 2013.

Professor Scott Taylor worked with me on the first longitudinal and cross-sectional studies, after the baseline studies with which Annie McKee had helped. Scott's perseverance at data collection, ingenuity in data analysis, and smooth and clear writing style make him a natural thinking and writing partner to this day.

In later years, Kylie Rochford and Udayan Dhar each provoked intellectual adventures and building on earlier ideas to improve them, make them more precise, and update them to the latest theories and research. Because of these insightful colleagues and friends, dozens of key articles were written and published advancing elements of ICT. In the most recent years, Han Liu, Maria Volkova-Feddeck, Roman Terehkin, and Sharon Ehasz have taken the mantle and are creating new studies and papers contemporaneously with this book.

I wish to thank many colleagues at Case Western Reserve University and Weatherhead School of Management for helping, supporting, and collaborating on research on ICT and sustained, desired change over the years. Besides Dave Kolb with waves of new topics, I wish to thank Scott Cowen, Dave Bowers, Mohan Reddy, Richard Osborne, Kalle Lytinnen, Gary Previts, Danny Solow, Mike Meserovich, Eric Baer, Dave Aron, JB Silvers, Stan Cort, Dave Campbell, Bob Mason, Dale Flowers, Kamlesh Mather, Ham Emmons, Fran Cort, Marian Hogue, Dori Coffey, Deb Bibb, Michael Devlin, Fred Collopy, Tim Fogerty, Bob Knight, Leonard Lynn, Larry Parker, Jim Rebeitzer, Peter Ritchken, Matt Sobel, Betty Vandenbosch, Sayan Chatterjee, David Cooper, Julia Grant, Betty Vandenbosch, George Vairaktarakis, Rob Widing, Bill Laidlaw, Bill Braesemale, Carol Musil, Cyrus Taylor, Joyce Kirkpatrick, Ed Hundert, Barbara Snyder, Eric Kaler, Cleve Gilmore, Doug Detterman, and Heath Demaree,

Within my department, I wish to thank Don Wolfe, Eric Neilson, Bill Pasmore, David Cooperrider, Ron Fry, Susan Case, Lisa Berlinger, Barbara Bird, Tracey Messer, Poppy McLeod, JP Stephens, Corinne Coen, Jamie Stsoller, Dave Aron, Harlow Cohen, Mike Manning, Chris Lazlo, Retta Holdorf, Pat Petty, Louella Hein, Lila Robinson, Frank Barrett, Vanessa Druskat, Diane Bergeron, Sandy Piderit, Hillary Bradbury, Melvin Smith, Ellen Van Oosten, and Anita Howard.

Of the faculty within the Department of Organizational Behavior and Weatherhead School of Management, I would like to thank the following for being co-researchers and co-developers of new courses and exec ed programs, and the MOOCs: Diana Bilimoria, Poppy McLeod, Anita Howard, Vanessa Druskat, Suzanne Healy, Angela Passsarelli, Scott Taylor, Lorraine Thompson, Deb O'Neil, Miggy Hopkins, David Leonard, Ken Rhee, Jane Wheeler, Babis Mainemelis, Udayan Dhar, Ray Massa, Terry Brizz, Steve Miller, Brigette Rapisarda, Mohamed Farraq, Dereck Faulkner, Brian Moran, Roman Terehkin, and Avi Turetsky.

Many of the doctoral students and faculty helped by participating in the monthly meetings of various study groups formed and which I chaired over the years at WSOM: Adult Learning and Change with Dave Kolb in the 1980s and 1990s; Coaching in the 2000s to 2010, and 2011–2017; ICT 2018–2023;

and Peer Coaching in Groups from 2019 to 2023. The Consortium for Research on Emotional Intelligence (CREIO) became an intellectual oasis for almost 30 years. Professor Cary Cherniss was a brilliant chair and co-founder with Dan Goleman, now chaired by Professor Rob Emmerling. Others in the founding group and regular attendees at our semiannual meetings were always a source of support and constructive feedback on research projects. In particular, I would like to thank Professor Kathy Kram, Doug Lennick, Marilyn Gowing, Professor Vanessa Druskat, Professor Scott Taylor again, and Lyle Spencer.

My 20 years as an Adjunct Faculty at Escola Superior d'Administració i Direcció d'Empreses (known worldwide as ESADE, part of Ramon Lull University) in Barcelona was exciting, produced research in new areas, and spread the pedagogy of the LEAD course based on ICT to thousands of undergraduate and graduate students of ESADE in many programs from throughout Europe, Latin America, and the Middle East. Professor Ricard Serlavos was my faculty partner and coach in how to adapt LEAD to these audiences, and the most effective educational institutional innovator I have ever met. His soft-spoken but relentless insight and ability to win even recalcitrant academics over to the importance of emotional and social intelligence competency development was awe-inspiring. The third of the Three Musketeers at ESADE, with Ricard and myself, was Professor Joan Manuel Batista. Joan Manuel became the champion for research on EI, coaching, competency development, competency assessment, and team development. His vast knowledge of how to use statistical methods and how to innovate with them was humbling to anyone who witnessed him teaching. Along the way, he, his wife Merce and his family, and my wife and I became close personal friends. He taught me to be an avid FC Barca fan and understand Catalan culture, and I reawakened the psychologist within him.

Many others at ESADE were essential to the continuing development of the ideas and research described in this book. Notably, the former Managing Director, Professor Carlos Losada, and Dean Xavier Mendoza, convinced me to join their faculty and expanded my portfolio at every opportunity. Professor Ceferi Soler was department chair at the time I began. He and I became co-authors through our "dining club" with which we sought to explore the most innovative restauranteurs in Catalonia every year. This led us to vineyards and the amazing brothers who reinvented Mas Doix and gave life in the midst of a failing economy to the Priorato vineyards. Others who took up the challenge and continued to innovate and spread the LEAD course and ICT pedagogy were Professors Carlos Royo, Rob Emmerling (a long-standing colleague from CREIO), and Professor and Dean Marc Correa. I cannot name all of the doctoral students and faculty who joined us along the way in our monthly seminars of the GLEAD research study group that continues under the leadership of Professor Laura Guillen, but feel grateful to each and every one.

A sequence of professors and their doctoral students who became professors at Ca' Foscari (part of the University of Venice) advanced competency research, competency development, and eventually created a Competency Centre. They were Professors Arnaldo Camuffo, Anna Comacchio, Fabrizio Gerli, Sara Bonesso, and Laura Cortelazzo. I continue to enjoy our work together.

Friends and colleagues at London Business School and Institue Européeno d'Administration des Affaires (known worldwide as INSEAD) have been a constant source of insight, provocative ideas, and reality testing. I would like to thank Lynda Gratton, Rob Goffee, Herminia Ibarra, and Manfred Kets de Vries. Similarly, friends and colleagues from Εργαστήριο Ελευθέρων Σπουδών (known worldwide as ALBA) in Athens, now part of the American University of Greece, have and continue to be sources of support and guidance. I would like to thank Nikos Ebeglou, Nikos Travlos, Babis Mainemelis yet again, Olga Epitropaki, Hari Tsoukas, and Erato Paraskevi.

Some colleagues became friends and worked with me and supported me during various transitions. I would like to thank Professors Kim Cameron, Warner Burke, Terrence Maltbia, Jonathan Passmore, James Quick, Ron Riggio, and Jay Conger. Other colleagues in Greece helped me spread the messages to colleagues in my ancestral land, notably Antonia Kassoulieri and Michelis Boussias.

I would like to deeply thank each and all of my co-authors, listed in alphabetical order: Kleo Akrivou, Emily Amdurer, B. Appleby, N. Asgswarwal, James Bailey, Ron Ballou, Joan Manuel Battista, Alim Beveridge, Nancy Blaize, Diana Bilimoria, Ann Black, Nancy Blaize, Sara Bonesso, Dave Bowers, Terry Brizz, G. Casadesus, Kevin Cavanagh, Cary Cherniss, Dave Clancy, G. Coenders, Phil Cola, Laura Cortellazzo, Scott Cowen, J. Cummings, Henry Cutter, Udayan Dhar, Sharon Ehasz, Rob Emmerling, Mary Esteves, Mary Fambrough, B. Ferré-Rosell, Xavier Fernandez-I-Marin, Eric Foley, Shannon French, Cindy Frick, Jonathan Friedman, Anna Galloti, Fabrizio Gerri, James Gaskin, Lindsey Godwin, Dan Goleman, Darren Good, Laura Guillen, Janet Harvey, Jim Hazy, Suzanne Healy, Miggy Hopkins, Anita Howard, Alicia Hullinger, Anthony (Tony) Jack, Fran Johnston, Steve Kelner, Masud Khawaja, Katherine Koenig, Dave Kolb, John Kotter, Kathy Kram, P. Kroutter, Gina Leckie, David Leonard, Alan Lerner, Tony Lingham, Frances Lissimore, Han Liu, Mark Lowe, Greg Lunceford, Ed Mahon, Babis Mainemelis, Hector Martinez, Ray Massa, Blessy Mathews, Dave McClelland, Poppy McLeod,

Cecilia McMillen, Annie McKee, Angela Murphy, JK Osiri, Angelas Passarelli, C. Pazzaro, George Perry, Bob Petersen, Mike Phillips, Frances Pinafore, Joann Quinn, Brigette Rapisarda, Franco Ratti, M. Refillable, Ken Rhee, Kylie Rochford, S. Rodriguez, Juric Safar, Chris Seal, M. Sjatoivic, Wilhelmina Saris, Argun Saatcioglu, Fabio Sala, Richard Serlavos, Florence Skelly, Amy Smith, Melvin Smith, Ceferi Soler, Lyle Spencer, Brigette Steinheider, Jamie Stoller, Liz Stubbs, W. Surewicz, Lora Swartz, Gabriela Topa, Dave Taylor, Scott Taylor, Silvia Tassarotti, Kiki Thiel, Margarita Truninger, Ellen Van Oosten, F. Velasco-Morena, Kristi Victoroff, Maria Volkova-Feddeck, Y. Want, Hongguo Wei, T. Westward, Jane Wheeler, BA White, Peter Whitehouse, Lauris Woolford, Baubeck Yeganeh, and Kira Zwygart.

Teams of students in my courses found and initiated comparisons of sustained, desired change at levels greater than dyads. They were doing research assignments in my course in the Master of Business Administration, Executive Master of Business Administration, Master of Positive Organizational Development, Doctorate in Management, Doctor of Business Administration, and Doctor of Philosophy programs in both Management and Organizational Behavior. I thank them for their ingenuity and depth of analysis (listed with their teams): David Garrett, Kevin Races, Mark Sands, and Mike Walasinski; Chris Bibbo, Sue Burbank, Kirsten Cronlund, and Bobbi Kahler; Brian Abraham, Al Chiaradonna, Susan Johnson, and Ellen Schmidt-Devlin; Judith Charleston, Rebecca Gadsden, Kara Homikel, and Michelle Patella; Amanda Blake, Terry Carter, and Alexis Rittenberger; Jessica Greenfield, Debra Holloway, Meredith Adkins, Christopher O'Donnell, and Natalie Zuniga; Regina Chandler, Kim Claszynaki, Madeline Gorman, and Jennifer Raleigh; Dominic Buccilli, Kristen Bishop, Shelly Wilson, Leah Weiss, and Veda Tare; Gail Garland; Joanna Camp, Elizabeth Madigen, Laurie Minott, Mickey Scherer, and Meghan Walsh; Adam Evans, Jill Fowler, Kristine Urban, and Christina Vellios; Juergen Bosch, Iman Joshua, Catherine Pizarro, Brant Silvers, and Mat Sinclair; Tony Stallion, Monica Colbert, Jeff Smith, and Jency John; Jon Coleman and Brian Newton; David Blaise, Ramona Hood, Steven Fulop, Alvin Serrano, and Alex Rodriguez; Cindy Fischer, Sarah Haacke, Vicki Nicholson, Catherine Shew, and JoEllen Thurman; Thomas Dunn, Kelly Somers, Lisa Waters, and Natalie Zuniga; Abe Joseph, Camilla Celati, Clara Steele, Emil Grimes, Irene Conklin, Joehanna Martinez Bugles, and Matthew Mazur; and any others to whom I apologize for forgetting.

Although they bear little responsibility for any errors or omissions in this book, a set of my colleagues helped in reviewing and commenting on earlier drafts. They include Melvin Smith, Ellen Van Oosten, and Anita Howard from Case Western Reserve University; Angela Passarelli from the College of

Charleston; Scott Taylor from Babson College; Kylie Rochford from University of Utah; Babis Mainemelis from ALBA; Nicky Terblanche from University of Stellenbosch; Fabrizio Gerri, Sara Bonesso, and Laura Cortelazzo from Ca' Foscari at the University of Venice; Joan Manuel Batista from ESADE; David Aron from Case Western Reserve University (CWRU and the Veterans Administration Hospital; Margaret Hopkins from the University of Toledo; and Deborah O'Neill from Bowling Green State University. Amy Salapski helped me transform my rudimentary visuals into sparkling figures and enhance the conceptual messages offered in this book.

Richard E. Boyatzis
Boston, Massachusetts

1

The Quest for Sustained, Desired Change

Change can be ephemeral, if it occurs at all. This book is about change that sticks, change that lasts. It is about sustained, desired change. The word "sustained" is used to capture the durability of change. The word "desired" refers to the end result or outcomes intended from any change process.

Change gives life. Without adaptation, learning, and growth, a human being atrophies or dies. Of course, the wrong change could be as disastrous as no change. The atrophy might be physical, psychological, or spiritual, causing a person to lose joy and hope. The same is true for dyads (i.e., any pair or couple relationship), teams, organizations, communities, and countries. Change determines the sustainability of the species, our relationships, and the durability of our human collectives (Wilson, 2000).

Change is hard. Our lives are filled with maxims proclaiming the evils of change. How many times have you heard someone say "If it ain't broke, don't fix it," "Leave well-enough alone," "That's not the way we do it here," or "Don't rock the boat?" And yet we do change and adapt. Some of us do so more than others. Some of our collectives—such as teams, organizations, or communities—do so more than others.

Our Ambivalence to Change

Change frightens us, and yet it is inevitable and necessary for survival. It is often perceived as a threat. And yet we often hear that we live in unique times. Never before, it is said, in the history of civilization has change been so rampant, and the speed and velocity of change so fast. Although some scholars have claimed that major scientific breakthroughs are not occurring as fast as they had in the past (Park, et al., 2023), change in almost every aspect of how we live and shop, how we work, with whom we live, how we see and refer to others, our political views, the search for information, and more is occurring at a pace that is often difficult to comprehend.

The Science of Change. Richard E. Boyatzis, Oxford University Press. © Richard E. Boyatzis 2024.
DOI: 10.1093/9780197765142.003.0001

Sometimes we feel that change is happening so fast that it is difficult to understand. Our reaction to this degree of change is not new, and at various times in the history of civilization, people have felt the same. In commenting about technological change, it has been said that "there is no greater danger for the devout soul than idleness." The quote goes on to say that new technology results in things that are not as permanent, will constrain access, and are aesthetically less attractive. The old ways benefit future generations by preserving learning and wisdom, while the user of new technologies "only sees what is [new] and contributes nothing to the edification of future generations." Further, "writing on good subjects is the very act introduced in a certain measure into the knowledge of the mysteries and greatly illuminated in his innermost soul; for those things which we write we more firmly impress upon the mind." These quotes and thoughts were repeated often in a series of books, lectures, and sermons by Abbott Johannes Trithemius in 1492 warning of the evils of movable type and the printing press (Trithemius, 1492, quotes from pp. 45 and 65; Brann, 1981).

It is difficult for us to contemplate the belief shattering revelations of the 100 years around 500 BCE when several major religions formed and social upheaval was occurring all around the world. Similarly, 1450–1550 were times in which almost every domain of human endeavor was subject to discoveries, changing assumptions, and beliefs. Today, anxiety and fear feed the belief that our destiny is on the cataclysmic path toward oblivion. This pervasive angst is evident in the frequency of apocalyptic books and movies. The current era has witnessed a resurgence of stories of superheroes, such as those that appeared in the early 1930s during the Great Depression. And yet we are still here.

When we feel change is happening to us, we become victims. We react and tend to feel placed in a defensive position. That is neither the healthiest nor most practical response. It is often not even a realistic assessment of the situation. This emotional position makes us vulnerable.

In this context, we seek solace amid the doomsayers. We seek hope while protesting current practices that are harming people and the planet. We seek interpretation and comfort from advisors, mentors, coaches, teachers, therapists, experts, clerics, and in our early years, from our parents and grandparents.

Change is required for survival. Such change is often not merely adapting to existing conditions, but also changing the causes as well as the consequences. Those seeking change must heed what Machiavelli said: "It must be remembered that there is nothing more difficult to plan, more doubtful of success, nor more dangerous to manage than the creation of a new system. For the initiator has the enmity of all who would profit by the preservation of the old institution, and merely lukewarm defenders in those who would gain by the new ones" (Machiavelli, 1502, cf. Black, 2022).

People raised in cultures that have low risk aversion (Hofstede, 1984) or high tolerance for uncertainty (Maddi, 1969) are disposed to seek novelty, and do not suffer the discomfort of anticipating change. People may seek novel experiences when feeling liminal or during a mid-life crisis (more on this in the next chapter). When in the midst of change, the rest of us are thrust into territory that often evokes fear of the unknown. In our collectives, like organizations, we often seek consistency and conformity as an assurance of future performance, quality, or service. These forces squelch innovation and shun change. As with the more typical fears of change and the unknown, stability and predictability provide comfort, especially in troubling times.

Humility Amid Hope

The quest for sustained, desired change does not work most of the time, or is not sustained (Osman, et al., 2020). Relative to the billions of dollars spent and effort devoted every year to change, it is surprising how little of it occurs and lasts.

The focus of "will" or volition seems to be needed; intention is essential (Wilson, et al., 2014). But intention is not enough. Wanting to change one's personality traits can be facilitated through intentional treatment (Roberts, et al., 2017). On the other hand, meta-analyses suggest that aging and maturation can also account for just as much change in some personality traits (Damian, et al., 2018). While intentionality seems important, it does not appear to be sufficient for sustained and lasting change (Hudson & Farley, 2015).

At the individual level, the evidence is humbling despite billions spent on education, training, and healthcare each year. A national survey of 2,073 adults in the United States conducted by the American Psychological Association in association with Harris Interactive Polling (Bethune & Brownawell, 2010) asked about New Year's Eve resolutions made in relation to improving health and well being. The percentage of those achieving their desired outcomes was appalling: only 20% succeeded at losing weight, only 15% succeeded at starting an exercise program, only 10% succeeded at eating a healthier diet, and only 7% succeeded at reducing stress.

A top 20 ranked Master's in Business Administration program in the US assessed retention of learning from their first required course in accounting for the 28-year-old full-time MBAs. The MBAs could only produce half of what they had produced on the same final exam taken six and a half weeks earlier (Specht & Sandlin, 1991). When comparing value-added outcomes of graduates of full- and part-time MBA programs (assessing them at graduation versus when they entered the program) on behavioral evidence of learning the emotional, social, and cognitive intelligence competencies that predict effectiveness in management and professional jobs, the average impact was a 4% improvement over one to two years (Boyatzis, et al., 2002; Pfeffer & Fong, 2002).

Earlier competency outcome studies of thousands of graduates of four-year undergraduate programs in the US showed that including measures of various forms of cognitive reasoning, as well as emotional and social intelligence competencies needed in most jobs to be effective, the median number of competencies on which there was significant value added was one (Winter, et al., 1981). That was over four years. Of course, other outcome studies have shown a wide variety of effects, but with regard to competencies, these studies were humbling to academics (Astin, 1993; Pascarella & Terrinzini, 1991; Pfeffer & Fong, 2002).

The impact of leadership training programs in government and industry don't fare much better. The documented impact of such training is about an 11% improvement over the three weeks to three months following training (Boyatzis, 2008). Sadly, these numbers deteriorate quickly after what is called the "honeymoon period" of training (Campbell, et al., 1970; Boyatzis, 2008). In healthcare, treatment adherence means the degree to which patients do what their physicians and nurses tell them to do post-surgery or to treat various diseases. Treatment adherence is typically only between 20% and 50%, which results in prolonged difficulties and progressive deterioration or disease (Khawaja, 2010; Siris, et al., 2011; Kulik, et al., 2013).

The efficacy of psychotherapy has been a puzzle for decades. In his classic review of the literature, Hans Eysenck (1952) concluded that "roughly two thirds of a group of neurotic patients will recover or improve to a marked extent within about two years of the onset of their illness, whether they are treated by means of psychotherapy or not" (p. 319). He showed how being on the waiting list for treatment was just as beneficial as psychotherapy. Of course, practices have advanced in recent decades, but the efficacy of outcomes is still in question (Osman, et al., 2020). The effectiveness of some forms of psychotherapy have been documented, with cognitive behavior therapy showing the most benefit (Barkham, et al., 2021).

In their exhaustive review of behavioral interventions, Osman and colleagues (Osman, et al., 2020) concluded that the types of failures included the following: no treatment effects, backfiring, positive treatment effects offset by negative side effects, no treatment effects but with positive side effects, and only proxy changes. Examples of studies they cited included the failure to reduce water consumption in droughts, increase tax compliance among corporations, increase physical fitness and exercise, reduce total caloric consumption, reduce drinking of sugary and carbonated beverages, support for a carbon tax, an increase in organ donation, and utilizing bike-sharing programs in cities.

Although divorce may not be a failure of a couple, it is a statement about two people not wanting to continue a relationship that began with high hopes of a sustaining relationship. During the COVID-19 pandemic, the divorce rate in the US rose from 10% to 14% in 2019 to 24% in 2020 and 34% in 2021 (Halt, 2022). In Europe, as of 2020 the number of registered divorces equaled half the number of registered marriages (Eurostat, 2022). This is in addition to the observation that in many countries, the number of divorces exceeds the number of marriages. Other forms of dyadic relationships fare no better. The leadership and management literature is replete with statements that people do not leave organizations, they leave bosses (Buckingham, 1999).

At the team level, any review of professional or collegiate sports teams or the longevity of music groups reveals a typical lack of intentional development or improvement. Among organizations, growth and development are elusive despite legions of consultants and experts trying to help them. Beer and Nohria (2000) claimed that 70% of organizational change efforts fail. Spencer (1988) reported a major review of organizational effectiveness improvement programs in the US Army; over a two-year period, 80% of the projects never achieved their objectives. He also showed that the 20% of projects that did succeed had a benefit-to-cost payback that paid for the entire army-wide program multiple times over initial costs. Among mergers and acquisitions, it is reported that over 80% fail or result in reduced asset value (Clayton, 2014). Competition neglect is cited as a cause for many organizations missing what their competitors or the market are doing, thereby losing their business base. As with team change, when it works, the effect is amazing, but it does not work often.

At the community level, examining changes in economic development, homelessness, and crime also add to other community attempts to foster a better life and environment. It is often the exceptional city or community that succeeds on such efforts—again, despite billions in government assistance, taxes spent, consultants employed, policy analysts writing papers, and academics studying urban change. At the country level, the same dynamic can be observed about increasing the health, education, and housing of the population, including disadvantaged minorities and indigenous populations.

As will be examined in this book, there are ample examples of failure to achieve desired change at all levels of human endeavor—but there is hope. We can also find brilliant examples where such efforts succeeded and desired results were obtained. Sustained, desired change can work if you do it correctly.

The Courage to Change

This book is about finding the courage to change and sustain the change. It uses research and theories from many fields to help us understand the process of sustained, desired change, including those of the author as well as colleagues and graduate students over the past 58 years. The research has been behavioral, psychological, neurological, hormonal, educational, medical, dental, and at times sociological and anthropological. The insight from these studies and others' research from various fields should provide hope that sustained, desired change is possible. These insights help guide us in how to study change, as well as how to provoke, inspire, or lead it in others.

Amid the fear of change, we can find hope from evidence of successful change efforts. They are successful in that they are desired and sustained. A desired change is one that is neither random nor happens to you, like a hurricane. It is something you wish or want to occur as an event, new state, or condition. In our collectives, desired change is those events or conditions that are desired by many if not most of the people involved at that level, whether a team, organization, community, or country. It is not merely something that others in authority positions have told you is to be desired or valued. In Chapter 2, the nature of imposed change will be addressed as parts of an Ought Self—the person someone else has told you to be.

Curiosity and Awe

Imagine the array of thoughts and feelings of Lieutenant Bouchard as he brushed sand from the large block of stone his soldiers found in Rashid, Egypt, in 1799 (Dolnick, 2021). He might have yawned and thought about how hot the day was, and the challenge of shipping yet another massive stone back to France. Or he might have realized that he had opened ancient history to the modern world in discovering a decoder for ancient forms of writing (what is now known as the Rosetta Stone). Was he curious, and did he think about the possibilities of his find? Did he appreciate the tremendous change he was about to unleash upon the world?

A prophetic moment engages a sense of mystery. It can be uplifting and even liberating. It is reminiscent of an anticipatory assurance written by F. Scott Fitzgerald about Dick Diver, the protagonist in his story in *Tender is the Night*, where he tells the reader, "without the satisfaction of knowing that the hero, like Grant lolling in his general store in Galena, is ready to be called to an intricate destiny. Best to be reassured, Dick Diver's moment now began" (Fitzgerald, 1934, Book II, Chapter 1, p. 92).

Moments of discovery, if appreciated, invoke awe. They are exciting. They may feel transcendent. Moments of discovering a change can be described as realizations entering conscious awareness. They might bring a smile, a sigh of relief, or cause you to jump for joy. Using complexity theory concepts, these can be called moments of emergence when something pops into your consciousness.

Intentional Change Theory

This book aims to use the vast array of research to propose and articulate a theory of sustained, desired change. It is called Intentional Change Theory (ICT). When this theory is turned into practice, dramatic results occur. The dynamics of the theory reverberate at all levels of human endeavor to learn, grow, and develop.

Sustained, desired change typically occurs through a series of moments of emergence. They do not feel gradual or evolutionary, but revolutionary. They seem to be a radical departure from what was thought or believed previously to that moment. James (1892) believed that sustained action was a function of attention over time; more conscious attention would result in perpetuated action. His explanations of what caused or aided conscious attention over time was fuzzier, and devolved into his exhortation of "other factors."

Sadly, many people are not ready to be aware. They are closed off. Technically, their perceptions and field of vision are limited, and as a result, they miss things. They miss discoveries. They miss awe. They miss changing.

The same psychological and physiological states that close people off to noticing and being aware are aroused by stress and defensiveness. It can be due to the fear of the unknown, past experiences, ego defense mechanisms, or the burdens of responsibility. These moments of stress may be mild, annoying stress, like your cell phone dropping a call, or major stress, like being fired during a pandemic. The stress could come from expectations of parents, imposed performance targets of managers, or norms of a social group to which you wish to belong.

A unique feature of ICT is that it is a fractal theory for all levels of human effort, from individual change to country change (i.e., a multileveled theory). That is, ICT explains and predicts sustained, desired change at each of these levels with the same phases, tipping points, and dynamics. Like the visual surprise when studying fractals in nature, the discovery of the fractal nature of ICT occurred as a set of awe-inspiring moments that came in waves. The first moment occurred to me when the isomorphism was noted for sustained, desired change at the individual, small group, and organization levels in the early 1970s. Later, this realization about ICT occurred for dyads and communities. Lastly, this awareness expanded to country-level change. The awareness that this is truly a fractal theory and not merely isomorphism occurred decades later when teaching ICT and complexity theory in an engineering graduate course. Building from these moments of awe, the efforts at sustained, desired change at each level will be described and explained in subsequent chapters.

Emergent of Moments of Discovery: The Process and Principles of ICT

Sustained, desired change may occur when five phases of emergence are experienced. The five phases of ICT create an iterative process of change. The movement from one phase to the next, which is actually a conscious realization of the next phase, often surprises us, which is an adaptation of a property of complex systems called emergence. A graphical portrayal of the process of ICT to achieve sustained, desired change appears in Figure 1.1.

In addition to the process of sustained, desired change, ICT is a comprehensive theory of change best described by 10 principles, which include the five phases and tipping points. For a conceptual overview, the 10 principles that constitute ICT are shown in Table 1.1. The chapters of this book are organized around the five phases and tipping points (i.e., the process of change) and incorporate the additional principles within each chapter. Special emphasis on the last three principles of ICT—those explaining sustained, desired change at and across the various levels (fractals) of sustained, desired change,

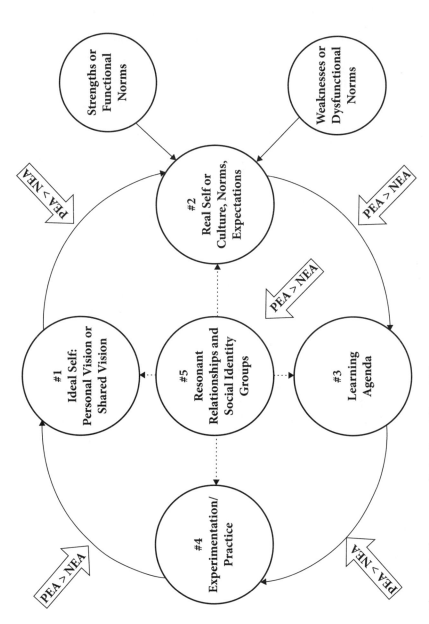

Figure 1.1 The process of Intentional Change Theory
Source: Boyatzis (2008, 2015).

Table 1.1 10 Principles of Intentional Change Theory (ICT)

1. The first phase of ICT is the driver of sustained, desired change—the Ideal Self or personal vision, and at the collective levels, a shared vision.

2. Being in the PEA allows a person or human system to be open to new ideas, other people, and emotions, and scanning their environment. It is a tipping point into the next phase of Intentional Change Theory. The psychophysiological states called the Positive Emotional Attractor and Negative Emotional Attractor are described with three axes: Parasympathetic versus Sympathetic Nervous System arousal, neural activation of the Default Mode versus Task Positive Networks, and positive versus negative affect.

3. Sustained, desired change in humans and human systems is most often discontinuous and nonlinear.

4. The second phase of ICT is realization of the Real Self. At the individual level, this is one's strengths and weaknesses relative to their Ideal Self. In human collectives, it is the norms, values, and culture of the specific human system that are strengths or weaknesses relative to their shared vision.

5. The third phase of ICT is articulation of a learning agenda and plan to use one's strengths to move closer to the Ideal Self, while possibly working on developing 1–2 weaknesses. Collectively, it is a shared learning agenda and plan. For best progress and sustainable effort, the weaknesses chosen should be closest to the tipping point into becoming strengths.

6. The fourth phase of ICT is the sequence of repeated experimentation with the new feelings, thoughts, attitudes, or behavior, and then moving into repeated practice to the point of mastery (beyond the point of comfort).

7. The fifth phase of ICT is the establishment and maintenance of resonant relationships.

8. As a fractal theory, ICT describes sustained, desired change at all levels of human endeavor from the individual to dyads, teams, organizations, communities, countries, and global processes.

9. Resonant leadership relationships facilitate moving information and emotions within and across levels of human systems, facilitating sustained, desired change.

10. Social identity groups facilitate the enduring quality of sustained, desired change by helping or hindering progress toward one's Ideal Self (vision) or a group's shared vision and moving information and emotions within and across levels of human systems, facilitating sustained, desired change.

including dyads, teams, organizations, communities, and countries—appears in Chapter 8. The principles of ICT to achieve sustained, desired change are shown in Figure 1.2.

Legend

Human systems are dyads, teams, organizations, communities, countries, and global networks.

Pertinent research from many fields and diverse domains will be reviewed for each ICT phase and principle. Because ICT is a complex system, some exploration of each phase's impact on sustained, desired change at levels other than individual will use narratives, and, when possible, comparative narratives (Tsoukas & Hatch, 2001). Narratives are useful because they fill in gaps in the entire process of change, not just one phase, and increase the sensitivity to context and initial conditions within which a change process is occurring (Aikan, et al., 2019).

Dreams, Shared Vision, and Purpose

Principle 1: The first phase of ICT is the driver of sustained, desired change—the Ideal Self, or personal vision and at the collective levels, a shared vision.

The first phase of ICT is the discovery of a person's Ideal Self or personal vision, addressed in Chapter 2. This captures a person's sense of purpose or calling, their personal and social identities, their core values, and operating philosophy (Boyatzis, 2006b, 2008; Boyatzis & Akrivou, 2006; Boyatzis & Dhar, 2021). These components merge to enable prospection and dreaming. When modified by hope, this becomes a person's Ideal Self.

Chapter 2 will examine the Ideal Self and how it changes and then examine shared vision in our collectives, with specific explanations of shared vision helping sustained, desired change in dyads, teams, organizations, communities, and countries.

It was shared vision that motivated the pursuit of the highest and lowest points on Earth. Two expeditions attempted the frozen, low-oxygen summit of Mount Everest, which is around 29,000 feet. The Allegra Expedition, which included Erik Weihenmayer, a blind mountain climber, had 19 of their members reach the summit with everyone returning safely even after the risks of hanging on ice walls and delicately crossing ladders over crevasses. Meanwhile, the Adventure Consultants Expedition had only three of their 19

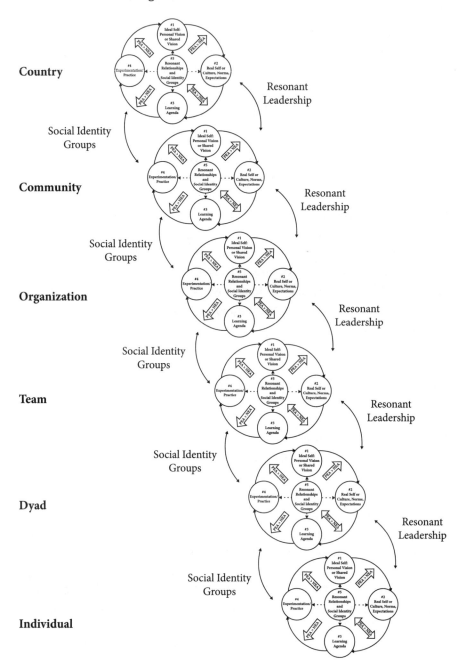

Figure 1.2 The 10 principles of Intentional Change Theory including fractals
Source: Boyatzis (2008, 2015).

members reach the summit and had four of the members of their team die during their return.

Among the dark, wet, freezing world of deep-caving, two teams have been competing to reach the lowest depth from the Earth's surface outside of an ocean. The Krubera Team, led by Alexander Klimchouk, completed a several week trip during which they set the record, and continued pushing past their own records under the surface of Abkhazia, Georgia, to depths below 7,188 feet. Meanwhile, the Cheve Team, led by Bill Stone, has attempted this feat many times in Oaxaca, Mexico. They have gotten close to breaking the record, but the Krubera Team continues to beat them. In addition, the Cheve Team has had a death and injuries during their expeditions. Throughout this book, these two sets of teams will be examined in terms of how they handled many of the phases of ICT.

At a community level, the success and popularity of bicycling and bike-sharing programs in the Netherlands, Paris, and Amsterdam will be compared to the relative lack of success in cities in the US, Canada, and elsewhere. Differences in how a shared vision was developed, and among which parts of their respective communities the vision was shared, will reveal major causal factors predicting what would happen in their pursuit of a sustained, desired change in travel and transportation in cities.

Tipping Points to Transitions: Positive Emotional Attractor and Negative Emotional Attractor

Principle 2: Being in the PEA allows a person or human system to be open to new ideas, scanning their environment, other people, and emotions. It is a tipping point into the next phase of ICT. The psychophysiological states called the PEA and NEA are described with three axes: Parasympathetic versus Sympathetic Nervous System arousal, neural activation of the Default Mode versus Task Positive Networks, and positive versus negative affect.

Moments of emergence occur when a tipping point is reached. It is the boundary between two conditions. Thirty-two degrees Fahrenheit or zero degrees Centigrade is a tipping point for liquid water to become solid ice. In human change and ICT, two tipping points are called the Positive Emotional Attractor (PEA) and the Negative Emotional Attractor (NEA), and are addressed in Chapter 3. They occur in terms of three axes. One is when a person's hormonal system moves into the state where the Sympathetic Nervous System (SNS) or Parasympathetic Nervous System (PNS) is dominant. These can be called stress and renewal, respectively. At any moment in time, a person's body has one of these systems dominating and resulting in dramatically different cognitive, emotional, and perceptual conditions (Boyatzis, et al., 2021; Boyatzis, et al., 2015).

A second axis is the activation of one or the other of two specific neural networks. One is the Task Positive Network (TPN), what Tony Jack calls the Analytic Network (Jack, 2024), and the other is the Default Mode Network (DMN), or what Tony Jack calls the Empathic Network (Jack, 2024). The TPN allows us to focus, solve problems, and make decisions, while the DMN allows us to be open to change, new ideas, people, and emotions. The challenge is that these two networks are antagonistic—they suppress each other (Jack, et al., 2013; Jack, 2024). The third axis is whether a person's emotional state is predominantly described by positive or negative adjectives and emotions. While each of these systems are useful, together they create a PEA tipping point and usher us into the next phase of sustained, desired change.

How the PEA and NEA spread among people will be examined in terms of emotional and social contagion. Swarming will be discussed as an alternative to how change occurs rather than rational, strategic planning. These dynamics will be explored in terms of how protests might change to riots, how the hope of the Arab Spring was crushed, or how using PEA was able to rally national efforts for renewable sources of energy in Iceland but not in the UK. At the community level, the efforts to reduce homelessness are discussed that appeared to work well in Houston and Boston, but not in Washington, DC or San Diego.

Change Is Discontinuous and Often in Power Curves

Principle 3: Sustained, desired change in humans and human systems is most often discontinuous and nonlinear.

Human change, individually or in our collectives, does not appear as a "normal" distribution (i.e., mathematically it is called a Gaussian distribution). Instead, more often than not it appears as either a power curve or a discontinuity. These features of complexity theory help us understand how the PEA and NEA, as well as emotional and social contagion and swarming, work to produce or inhibit sustained, desired change. The regressive forces that push humans and our groups tend to enact power curves.

The Real Self: Who Am I? Who Are We?

Principle 4: The second phase of ICT is the realization of the Real Self. At the individual level, this is one's strengths and weaknesses relative to their Ideal Self.

In human collectives, it is the norms, values, and culture of the specific human system that are strengths or weaknesses relative to a shared vision.

The second major emergence needed for sustained, desired change to proceed and develop is the realization of how a person affects and is experienced by others, as discussed in Chapter 4. In collectives, this is the culture (i.e., shared norms and values) of the relationships, teams, organizations, communities, or countries. This is called the Real Self.

In the moment of realization of how others are experiencing a person's behavior, comparisons are made—often unconsciously—with one's Ideal Self. When the two are consistent, these behaviors, thoughts, feelings, attitudes, and mindset can be considered strengths. When they are not, they can be called weaknesses. In this sense, the second emergence allows for creation of a personal balance sheet. Borrowing from the field of accounting, this is a compilation of a person's assets (those resources or capabilities they have and can help them toward a desired future) and liabilities (those debts or characteristics that would hold a person back from desired change or move them in the opposite direction). In collectives, the comparison of the existing culture and the shared vision would create a comparable assessment for the group, organization, or community.

For decades, scholars and practitioners thought that the discrepancies between the Real and Ideal Selves created the driving power for change. While this might help some people, Chapters 2 and 4 will explain why the Ideal Self is a much more potent and sustainable driver of sustained, desired change than these discrepancies. The power of focusing on one's strengths will also be examined.

In Chapter 4, contributions to developing a Faux Self (a false image of oneself) from social desirability, ego defense mechanisms, and past experiences will be explored. Since the essence of the Real Self in ICT is how others experience or observe a person, the behavioral level within a personality is the most important to examine. For this, competencies are reviewed and explained as emotional, social, and cognitive intelligence capabilities. How they can be developed in adults will be reviewed, along with the many longitudinal studies, neuroimaging, and hormonal studies showing how the internal mechanism of PEA versus NEA affect a person's behavior.

In our collectives, this phase is the realization of the norms and values that describe how we act and make choices. In this way, the Real Self in our teams, organizations, communities, and countries is a description of our culture, our norms, and shared beliefs. Examples mentioned will be discussed from the perspective of norms within the Everest and deep-caving teams. In various organizations norms can help them innovate, adapt, grow, and develop—like Netflix did, when shifting from DVD rentals to streaming—or atrophy and cease to function, like Blockbuster.

Again, the experience of the PEA will be a tipping point into the next phase of ICT.

A Path to My/Our Dreams: Joyful Planning and Preparation

Principle 5: The third phase of ICT is articulation of a learning agenda and plan to use one's strengths to move closer to the Ideal Self, while possibly working on developing one to two weaknesses. Collectively, it is a shared learning agenda and plan. For best progress and sustainable effort, the weaknesses chosen should be closest to the tipping point of becoming strengths.

The third emergence on the path to sustained, desired change is discovery of a learning agenda, as examined in detail in Chapter 5. In sharp contrast to a performance improvement plan, which arouses NEA, a learning agenda is a joyful exploration of possibilities. It is focused on getting closer to one's vision and Ideal Self using one's strengths, and may be working on development of a weakness or two.

In our collectives, this phase is our shared agenda or plans. But to be shared, they must reflect a consensus of all subgroups and not be imposed by a few on the many. To be sustainable, it must be a plan that excites and engages us, and not merely something we "should" do. Sadly, in collectives there may not be a shared learning agenda or plan, often because there is no shared vision or culture comparison, nor PEA tipping points to move the collective through swarming, which then may move the collective ahead in the phases of sustained, desired change.

In Chapter 5, goal setting will be examined as to when it is helpful in a change process and when it hurts. In this sense, specific, measurable goals too early in the process inhibit further change precisely because it helps the person focus rather than remain open to possibilities. This will expose the fallacy of strategic planning as a motivating device for change. If there is more to learn or options or possibilities to consider, focusing during an early stage in change is premature and denies options. It causes people to miss important possibilities. One source of SMART goals, McClelland's Need for Achievement, is explored in detail, as are the insights from the learning versus performance goal orientation research. Different approaches to planning, namely domain and direction planning, are reviewed along with the power of goal intention.

Examples of this phase in teams are explored, to include the deep-caving teams as well as Incident Commanders at Level 1 of the US Forest Fire Fighting

Service. The effective and ineffective efforts to reduce homelessness in several cities will also be reviewed.

If the PEA is experienced, the fourth phase arrives.

Exploring Possibilities: Exploring and Practice to Mastery, Not Comfort

Principle 6: The fourth phase of ICT is the sequence of repeated experimentation with the new feelings, thoughts, attitudes, or behavior, and then moving into repeated practice to the point of mastery (beyond the point of comfort).

The fourth phase of ICT is the period of experimenting with new thoughts, feelings, and behavior, as explained in Chapter 6. To help make progress closer to one's personal vision, a person may continue to practice the new thoughts, feelings, or behavior until they become a part of their repertoire. In collectives, these experiments and efforts to socialize and institutionalize people's behavior to the new shared practices would result in a form of culture change. In our collectives, this is exploring and institutionalizing new norms and values.

In this chapter, visualizing will be examined as a type of practice establishing new neural pathways. Other approaches to make experimentation and practice more effective include new thoughts, feelings, or behavior in safe settings; using awareness of your preferred learning styles; practicing to mastery; and the concept of deliberate practice. The myth of 10,000 hours will be debunked, and the context for determining how much practice and for how long will be explored in terms of rhythm and dosage. Stealth learning will be shown to enable practice but minimize additional stress. Nudges and nagging will be differentiated as techniques for reminders. The role of habits, feedback, and training will be discussed, along with perhaps the lowest cost but most enduring form of practice to promote sustained, desired change of being in peer coaching groups.

The difference in sustainability of various music groups, both in terms of their longevity and ability to adapt genres, will be explained in terms of the ideas of this phase of ICT. How have U2 and Green Day kept themselves creative and popular over decades, while Van Halen, Oasis, ABBA, and myriad other groups have ceased to perform or create new music? Two organizations that began in the same mail order business, Amazon and Sears, have had different trajectories in the last 30 years. ICT and in particular the experimentation and practice phase will explain the difference. At the community level, the dramatic work of Akhtar Hameed Khan in East Pakistan (now Bangladesh) in the late 1950s helped poor and uneducated farmers triple food production and save their families and villages following the ICT process of using experimentation and practice. Meanwhile, at this same time, a geographic neighbor to the East of Comilla, China, used a centralized, top-down approach to planning and resource allocation that created conditions in which it is estimated that over 30 million people died of starvation. Khan repeated this amazing feat in the poorest neighborhoods of refugees in Karachi 25 years later to create safe, healthy, and vibrant neighborhoods.

Another PEA tipping point can begin the next iteration in the ICT process and return to the first emergence for adaptation and morphing of the Ideal Self and personal vision, or a new shared vision for a collective.

Relationships Are the Context for Change

Principle 7: The fifth phase of ICT is the establishment and maintenance of resonant relationships.

Our relationships are the agar agar of the petri dish of life. They are context for anything that occurs in life or work, and the context for any attempt at sustained, desired change. Throughout the ICT process, a PEA tipping point can allow emergent awareness in appreciating one's caring and trusting relationships, as explained in Chapter 7. Key features of relationships that enable us to be in sync with others and to resonate with each other are the degrees of shared vision, shared compassion, and shared energy. Through shared vision, we experience hope. Through shared compassion, we experience caring. Through shared energy, we activate and vibrate to the same frequency as others. These three qualities of our key relationships enable us to move through each phase of ICT. Conversations with people with whom we share a trusting relationship enable PEA tipping points to occur and new discoveries to emerge. The next iteration of the ICT cycle begins and is sustained by these new PEA experiences.

The impact of resonant relationships on sustained, desired change will be examined through examples of its presence or negative effects of dissonant relationships. A mine disaster in Chile is used to illustrate how resonant relationships at many levels saved 33 miners trapped 2,000 feet below the surface for 69 days in 2010. The president of Chile, executives and engineers from various government, and private mining companies came together and formed close relationships with a shared vision, cared for the miners and their families, and accomplished an amazing feat of engineering while the world watched and prayed. This event will be contrasted with the horrendous lack of resonant relationships involved in the worst man-made oil spill in history at the Deepwater Horizon drilling platform in the Gulf of Mexico in 2010. The impact of a lack of resonant relationships and the presence of dissonant relationships will also be examined through the death and destruction during and in the wake of Hurricane Katrina in New Orleans in 2005 and the surrounding area.

Examples of using resonant relationships in creative ways to inspire and support sustained, desired change are also examined. For example, the activation of "grandmother power" in Zimbabwe with what is called "friendship benches" is spreading throughout sub-Saharan Africa and to other countries. Another example is the training of psychiatric aides in Topeka State Hospital to be friends with patients and in basic relationship-building skills. The chronic schizophrenics in these wards faced years of incarceration, but with this experiment in relationship-building showed remarkable results and almost doubled the rate of patients returning to nursing homes and independent lives outside of the wards.

Leading Change at Multiple Levels

Principle 8: As a fractal theory, ICT describes sustained, desired change at all levels of human endeavor from individual to dyads, teams, organizations, communities, countries, and global processes.

ICT contends that the process of sustained, desired change at all levels— from individuals to dyads to teams to organizations to communities to countries—is the same. The process uses PEA tipping points to advance or NEA tipping points to inhibit along a nonlinear, discontinuous process. The multilevel fractal nature of ICT will be explained in each chapter in the context of the specific phase of ICT, and its specific features are examined in Chapter 8.

A complex system also has a property called scale dependence. Scale dependence means that the system has multiple levels observed in a hierarchy. Each level should be distinct to be considered an independent level, but that does not imply that the levels do not affect or more accurately cannot affect each other. Multilevelness is not just a function of aggregation or disaggregation (Rousseau, 1985), but that each level can function on its own.

A complex system will not only have multiple levels that are fractals of each other (like various possible focal planes in observing the same phenomenon), but will also contain factors that move information across levels. In human systems, a key aspect of information is emotional. In ICT, it is proposed that two factors move information and emotions across levels: resonant leadership and social identity groups (SIGs). These are the vehicles of contagion or cross-level interaction.

Cross-level communication is a transfer or transmission of information and emotion (Baer, et al., 1987). Miller's (1978, 1995) proposal is that cross-level communications can be in the form of matter, energy, or information. In ICT, being in a PEA state makes the boundaries more permeable. Like sensitizing neural synapses, this may mean that being in the PEA at one level means that the person or people are more open to sensing, noticing, or tuning in to the offered transmissions from other levels. This may also mean that they may be more susceptible or vulnerable to being influenced by such transmissions. Transmissions can go in both directions across levels. One of the ways that resonant leaders or SIGs effect cross-level transmissions are through the PEA and NEA tipping points.

Principle 9: Resonant leadership relationships facilitate moving information and emotions within and across levels of human systems facilitating sustained, desired change.

Principle 10: Social identity groups facilitate the enduring quality of sustained, desired change by helping or hindering progress toward one's Ideal Self (vision) or a group's shared vision, and moving information and emotions within and across levels of human systems to facilitate sustained, desired change.

In Chapter 8, resonant leadership will be examined in terms of leader–follower relationships and how they capture the hearts and minds of those around them. Mrs. Nomusa Zikhali, founding principal of the Nkomo Primary School in Kwa-Zulu Natal in South Africa, is a resonant leader who crossed many levels with her infectious smile, passion, and hope. She was the only teacher assigned to the school, along with 60 children from these communities and four trees in 1998. Today, Nkomo Primary School has over 1,000 students, 24 teachers, 8 staff, and 19 concrete classrooms (concrete classrooms being how the government of South Africa authorizes the number of teachers to be paid), and a special program for over 70 AIDS orphans. Other resonant leaders whose presence and speeches reverberate across many levels and time—notably the Reverend Martin Luther King Jr. and Nelson Mandela—will also be discussed.

The development and use of social identity groups is a potent aspect of ICT working across levels. Examples to be discussed include how the Antarctica Treaty has been so endurably successful, and why many if not all attempts at climate change accords have paled in comparison. Senior women partners at Coopers & Lybrand formed an informal SIG that stood the test of time in a male-dominated firm and field. Backup singers like Lisa Fischer and Darlene

Love, who created the most memorable sounds of hit songs, were proud to identify as backup singers. Another example is how Coach Herb Brooks quickly turned a collection of hockey players from different colleges and universities into a surprise Gold Medal–winning team in the 1980 Olympics. Apple approached their customers through a different SIG than SONY, and was successful in terms of market dominance when they started in comparable technologies. The National Park Service is described as one of the most successful national programs to conserve nature and help people appreciate and enjoy it by managing many SIGs.

In higher education, development of new SIGs helped propel The PhD Project, which inspired African Americans into PhD programs and the professoriate of business and management schools; it's still going strong almost 30 years later, spreading the creation of spin-off SIGs for faculty. A new Massive Open Online Course (MOOC) launched in 2013 surprised everyone involved with its popularity and spawned dozens of SIGs to meet on their own to advance their learning. The tension between elitism and inclusiveness will be examined in the creation and support of SIGs as part of the process of sustained, desired change.

A Unique Fractal, Multilevel Theory of Change

Various theories and streams of research on change will be examined in certain chapters when the benefits or differentiation of ICT from these other theories are most poignant.

Individual, Dyad, and Team Levels

At the individual level, these will include self-determination theory (Deci & Ryan, 2000), broaden and build theory (Fredrickson, 2001), process model (Prochaska, et al., 1992), social learning theory (Bandura, 1981), motivation change theory (McClelland, 1965), immunity to change theory (Kegan & Lahey, 2009), nudge theory (Thaler & Sunstein, 2008), the theory of reasoned action (Fishbein, 1979), and attitude change (Kelman, 1961). At the dyad level, other theories of change and research will include Gottman, et al. (2002). Theories and research on team change will also be examined, such as Bennis and Shepard (1956), Bales (1970), Gersick (1991), Tuckman (1965), and Akrivou, et al. (2006).

Organizational Level

At the organizational level of change, a range of theories and research will be discussed. Organizational developmental has been defined as "a system-wide application and transfer of behavioral science knowledge to the planned development, improvement, and reinforcement of the strategies, structures, and processes that lead to organizational effectiveness" (Cummings & Worley, 2015, p. 2). One cluster of theories have been categorized as structural, sociotechnical systems and organizational design (Burke & Noumair, 2015; Neuman, et al., 1989; Flores, 2023), culture and climate (Lawrence & Lorsch, 1967; Schneider & Barbara, 2014), and job design (Hackman & Oldham, 1980), as well as business process re-engineering (Hammer & Champy, 1993).

Another approach has been "planned change" (Bennis, et al., 1962; Lippitt, et al., 1958; Kotter, 1995; Nadler & Tushman, 1977) and the theoretical roots coming from these scholars as well as Kurt Lewin and Ed Schien. Some approaches were a stylistic attempt to merge task and people orientations, like Blake and Mouton (1964). Some theories are based on survey or needs assessment diagnosis, like Likert (1967), Weisbord (1976), Tichy (1983), and Burke-Litwin (1992). Other theories appeal to openness in questioning purpose and organizational learning, like Argyris (1985) and Senge (1990). Some theories or approaches to organizational operations or functioning, like the McKinsey 7-S model, will not be addressed because they do not focus on change (Waterman, et al., 1980; Rothwell, 2015).

There are theories based on looking ahead, like Future Search conferences and summits (Weisbord, 1992) and Appreciative Inquiry (Cooperrider & Srivastvsa, 1987). There are dynamic theories such as Golembiewski (1986) or Lambert, et al. (2020), as well as the many organizational development theories (Burke, 2014; Burke & Nooumair, 2015; Beckhard & Harris, 1987; Bradford & Burke, 2005). Specialized theories focusing on topical domains within organizational change include ways to improve diversity, equity, and inclusion (Flores, 2023), and commitment, engagement, and competency based human resource systems (Flores, 2023). Continuous improvement became a major trend in the 1970s as quality circles, then morphed into self-managing work teams, LEAN, and Agile (Flores, 2023). These approaches focused on maximizing efficiency, minimizing waste, and increasing the quality to customers (Matusky, 2023).

It has been observed that change management is often a top-down process, while organizational development is a bottom-up process (Rothwell, 2015). The meta-analyses have reported that "OD interventions were situationally specific and, in general, did not significantly effect attitudes" (Neuman, et al.,

1989, p. 468). Some studies showed that attitudes of satisfaction improved toward other people, the job, and organization with moderate effects, but the impact was not sustained or durable, and often likely a part of the honeymoon effect mentioned earlier. Another meta-analysis made several observations about organizational change. Armenakis and Bedeian (1999) explained that external changes did not necessarily convert to organizational change, with older organizations less likely to change than younger ones. They showed that size did not matter and that organizations were more likely to repeat previous changes than to venture into new areas. Armenakis and Bedeian (1999) reported that product and market strategies did not necessarily contribute to market failure, and that success of any effort was often less about the approach and more a function of the degree of inertia experienced in the organization.

Some of the methods that involve the use of teams and small groups, quality improvement, and self-managing approaches will be addressed as a part of team-level change. Similarly, when theories have primarily focused on management, leadership development, or talent management, they will be discussed as part of individual level of change.

Community and Country Levels

Communities have been defined as "places where people live and work, though not necessarily in the same place" (DeFilippis & Saegert, 2012, p. 1). The definition used in ICT and this book is expanded to go beyond places to include communities of practice (i.e., like-minded people with a shared cause, purpose, or values, Garber, 1995), as well as church or faith organizations, military affiliations, councils of elders, economic elite, subcultures (DeFilippis & Saegert, 2012), tribal affiliations or identification, and regions of the world.

Community-level change literature has evolved with a shifting focus, from the early days of social planning to community organizing in the 1960s, and community development and radical approaches (DeFilippis & Saegert, 2012; Sites, et al., 2007). Special interest advocacy and economic development followed, with a later emphasis on social services. The most recent focus has been community-building with an emphasis on strengthening social connections and building on common values (Traynor, 2012).

The field has progressive roots, with advocacy and embedded antagonism at its core (O'Connor, 1999), focused predominantly on power redistribution. The subsets of community development have been urban planning and development. They have typically further defined themselves as focusing on issues like eliminating poverty and homelessness, or stimulating economic development and jobs (DeFilippis & Saegert, 2012). The theories labeled as more radical, such as those of Saul Alinsky (1971), sought more fundamental change in the structure and culture of communities, to mobilize people and power and change the society of which they were a part.

Community development has often been dependent on state and federal policies and funding (O'Connor, 1999). In the US, the Great Society programs of the 1960s and the creation of the Office of Economic Opportunity in the early 1970s gave rise to funding community development corporations (CDCs) as local nonprofits. The CDCs have shown a lack of impact, with 25% showing some increase in community pride and 50% showing some progress in empowering new leadership (Stoecker, 1997). In the 1970s it gave rise to legions of consultants and graduate students writing proposal after proposal to participate in the funding programs. My argument is not that CDCs have been doing bad things, or operate with an evil intent. As Lenz (1998, p. 25) notes, CDC practitioners "are good people with bad theory" (Stoecker, 1997, p. 362). More recent efforts at community-building have resulted in greater effectiveness (Traynor, 2012), and both successful and unsuccessful community-level change projects will be reviewed in the coming chapters of this book.

Country-level change literature has either focused on leadership (Hagen, 1962) or specific, diverse domains of economic development, environmental sustainability, social justice, social upheaval (Brinton, 1952), or political philosophy. As a result, there are few general theories of national- or country-level change that have been examined in a scholarly way.

Community- and country-level change approaches will not be examined or explored in as much depth as the individual, dyadic, and team change research for several reasons. Organizational change studies and literature is examined less than individual, dyadic, and team levels, but more than community and country levels of change. As a psychologist and social psychologist, my reading and updating of the literature on change has been more focused on individual, dyadic, team, and organizational development.

It is also my impression that quantitative research on change at the organizational, community, and country levels are less abundant. This often occurs because the literature is preoccupied with practical applications, where consulting on change has far outpaced the energy and time devoted to rigorous research. But this also reveals a need for future work on sustained, desired change at these levels to be explored in Chapter 9. Organizational, community, and country change will be examined in each chapter with a narrative, extreme case analysis approach, as is typical in the literature.

ICT is unique. No other theory of change embraces complexity theory other than Gottman's and Fredrickson's (Gottman, et al., 2002; Fredrickson, 2001). No other theory integrates psychological, physiological, and behavioral factors other than Fredrickson's (2001). No other theory predicts multilevel fractals in the change process and cross-level transmission of information and emotion. Only Henderson and Boje (2016) have explored many levels within organizations as fractals using complex adaptive systems theory.

In management research most studies and theories focus on only one level, but multilevel theories are needed (Hitt, et al., 2007). Hackman (2003) emphasized learning from brackets of levels above and below a targeted phenomenon. Based on evolutionary psychology and therapy models, Wilson, et al. (2014) explained how intentional change needs a multilevel approach.

What Next?

In Chapter 9, possible research questions and topics for ICT will be explored. These will include a discussion of how to measure change and the nature of the dependent variables in such studies. If the research continues to support this theory and its components, various possibilities will be discussed as to applications.

The Possibilities

Sustained, desired change can transport us to new possibilities. It might be something as mundane as finding a faster way to get to work. But it can also transform us to a new and better life. Seeing what others have not or may not have dreamt is at the heart of sustained, desire change. ICT is about seeing possibilities. Humphrey Repton (1803), a famous eighteenth-century landscape designer in the United Kingdom, would reflect for hours after reviewing a plot of land and explain to his clients that he was seeking something awesome—a "certain degree of magnificence." Another famous eighteenth century landscape designer, "Capability" [Lancelot] Brown, was so named for looking at an expanse of land and proclaiming, "This has capabilities" (McKenna, 2016). Both saw possibilities where others had not. Both inspired hope and beauty with their vision, while also transforming land into landscapes, parks, gardens, and places of tranquility.

To Explore Uncharted Territory

Except for parts of space beyond our closest planetary neighbors and the deepest oceans, humans have gone to many places. Geographically, to go where no one has gone before is quite rare. In terms of psychological, sociological, and anthropological ventures to create better lives, to go where others have tried and failed is common.

There are several ways to read this book. Within each chapter, the distinctions of ICT are examined with references to the many fields and research clarifying and supporting these concepts. They are examined as to how they may be different from those commonly believed or perceived. The following sections of the chapters then examine that component of ICT at various levels of human collectives. As explained, these explorations will be more narrative and example based, citing statistical studies and meta-analyses where possible. The chapters can be read in sequence or out of sequence, depending on the reader's specific interests. The reader is also invited to jump back and forth between the different levels within a particular concept.

If you are an advanced professional but not currently involved in research, this book should help you be a better consumer of research on change. It can help you be skeptical of slick claims. The ideas and critique in each chapter will equip you with a lens of the possible, while also adding the rigor of knowing what to look for when reading research on change and learning.

"A Certain Degree of Magnificence"

This research and theory is offered with the hope that in continuing to seek the wisdom of how to create, initiate, and foster sustained, desired change, we can make the world a better place for all. We can engage people's better angels and work together to create hope, compassion, and the energy to help others move ahead to more responsible and fulfilling families, organizations, communities, and countries—a human degree of magnificence.

2

Dreams, Shared Vision, and Purpose as the Driver of Change (Principle 1)

Principle 1: The first phase of ICT is the driver of sustained, desired change—the Ideal Self, or personal vision and at the collective levels, a shared vision.

If you want to build a ship, don't herd people together to collect wood and assign them tasks and work, but rather teach them to long for the endless immensity of the sea.

—Antoine de Saint-Exupéry

Humans are purposive beings. William James brought the concept of teleos, our sense of purpose, from Aristotle and ancient Greek philosophers into psychology (James, 1892). He claimed that we are imbibed with the ability to exert conscious volition in the path of our lives. This has also been called "free will." As a contrast to the determinism of the past in some religions and psychoanalytic thought, or the leap from consciousness to the automaticity of behaviorism, free will allows us to create a new context for current decisions and a desired future (Seligman, et al., 2013).

While these ideas have been argued from philosophical approaches to our purpose for living, it remained a topic of debate until psychology and neuroscience research could enlighten us as to the emotional and cognitive processes involved. That is, the internal neural and hormonal mechanisms of how our sense of purpose and construction of a future (desired Ideal Self of life and work) was shown to affect us. The way an image of our desired future might guide our current behavior and decisions is clearer now than it has been for several thousand years.

The conclusion of this chapter asserts that our hopes, dreams, and deep sense of purpose are the drivers of *sustained* change and learning (see Figure 2.1). They provide the big picture as to why someone is engaged in learning or change

The Science of Change. Richard E. Boyatzis, Oxford University Press. © Richard E. Boyatzis 2024.
DOI: 10.1093/9780197765142.003.0002

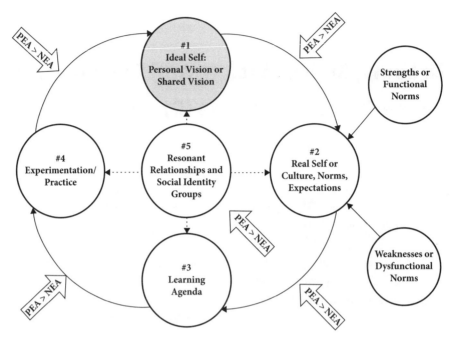

Figure 2.1 This chapter in the process of Intentional Change Theory
Source: Boyatzis (2008, 2015).

as explained in this chapter and the next. They stimulate psychophysiological processes that replenish a person's energy, openness, and desire to change. Ideas in this chapter have been updated and developed but relied on earlier papers, notably Boyatzis and Akrivou (2006) and Boyatzis and Dhar (2021).

We can say that the Ideal Self *is* our personal vision. It is an aspiration or dream. It may be wanting to be our best, possible self. It might be how we feel when we are the person we wish to be and are behaving consistently with our values. Our Ideal Self or shared vision with others invokes hope, and with it the power of possibility. It is called many things, such as our North Star, guiding light, calling, noble purpose, and dharma, as well as the Ideal Self.

The Ideal Self or personal vision is a combination of our sense of purpose, calling, meaning, core values, operating philosophy, and personal and social identities. They combine to form a person's dream or prospection. Moderated by hope, this becomes the Ideal Self, as shown in Figure 2.2. One's Ideal Self morphs over one's life and career eras, as a result of salient experiences and socialization (Boyatzis & Dhar, 2021). It is also adversely affected by ought selves: the future self others wish, expect, or demand from us.

The positive impact of our Ideal Self in our life and how it affects others around us may be less evident than the loss of it. Numerous surveys

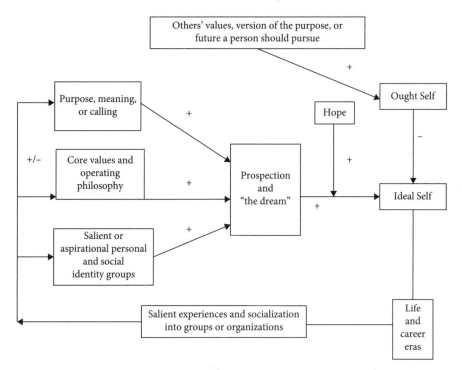

Figure 2.2 The components of the Ideal Self and the iterative process of how they change. The plus and minus signs denote an additive/multiplicative or subtractive/ respective relationship. No sign means that the impact of the process varies by type of experience.
Source: Slightly adapted from Boyatzis & Dhar (2021), which was modified based upon Boyatzis & Akrivou (2006).

throughout the industrialized world have shown extremely low levels of engagement in work. This is frighteningly and suggests that people bring little of their talent to work (Harter, 2020). But the lack of an Ideal Self and sense of purpose also manifests itself as identity conflict (Gibson, et al., 2020), mental health problems (Stolzer, 2016), restlessness, and disaffection (Higgins, et al., 1985; Higgins, 1987; Higgins, et al., 1990; Hardin & Lakin, 2009), among other undesirable states. In developing an updated, nuanced concept of free will, Baumeister (2023) described the range of possibilities evoked when a person exercises forms of free will.

Among the many possibilities, there are at least four different ways of dealing with or preparing for the future. One is the tradition-based model, using the past and present as the descriptive context for the future. Related is another approach, the forecasting model, which attempts to predict the future based on the most likely trends from the recent past and present.

This approach could assign confidence limits of high and low possibilities to the most likely trend. Another approach is a developmental model that incorporates what is often called metacognition, or learning how to learn. This involves thinking about how you learn and attempting to continue in the same manner. Continuing education in many professions is built on a developmental model. The last approach is aspirational—how we would wish or love to be in the future. While all models can be useful, ICT focuses on the aspirational model to create a desired, comprehensive (i.e., holistic), and compelling future.

The Ideal Self

In philosophy and religion, we often contemplate and possibly articulate what it means to be a good person. Attributed to Eleanor Roosevelt is the observation that "the future belongs to those who believe in the beauty of their dreams" (Roosevelt, 1957, p. 4). Other the concept of the ego ideal in the view of Freud and contemporaries, the examination of the Ideal Self in psychology, management, or social sciences was framed as part of the motivating effect of internal conflict between the way we are (our Real Self) and the way we wish to be (our Ideal Self), and the way others think we should be (the Ought Self) (Higgins, 1987). Or, it appeared as the internal conflict among these and other possible selves (Markus & Nurius, 1986; Obodaru, 2012).

The role of the Ideal Self in facilitating or motivating personal change was introduced earlier by Kolb and Boyatzis (1970a). Their stream of research that followed focused primarily on the process of self-directed and sustaining change and not on the discrepancies between the Ideal Self and Real Self. In later years, the focus shifted to the nature of the Ideal Self and how to elicit it (Boyatzis & Akrivou, 2006; Boyatzis, 2008).

Work in organizational psychology examined the tensions and conflicts and labeled them as identity development and change (Dukerich, 2001; Dutton, et al., 2010; Ibarra, 1999). But the Ideal Self is distinct from and more than identity, because it is also aspirational and is anchored in one's values. Further, the Ideal Self incorporates concepts like calling, sense of purpose, and the act of prospection (Boyatzis & Dhar, 2021). It also explains the interactions among the various components of the Ideal Self.

Another popular approach in organizational psychology has been the "reflected best self" (Roberts, et al., 2005). But here again, the Ideal Self is different because it focuses on aspirations for the future, not experiences in one's past. Although the reflected best self might reveal insight into episodes when a person's ideal and real selves overlap, it does not allow for the possibilities emerging from prospection, dreams, and fantasies of a different and more desired future.

The Ideal Self can be the integrating force motivating development of a coherent self (Taylor, et al., 2019). A clearer, more coherent, and comprehensive Ideal Self predicts well-being, engagement, and organizational citizenship among Latin American mid-level managers (Martinez, et al., 2021). In their integration of ICT with Self-Determination Theory (SDT), Taylor, Passarelli, and Van Oosten (2019) explained how the Ideal Self is central to the activation of autonomy, which was defined as "act[ing] freely, with a sense of volition and choice" (Deci & Flaste, 1995, p. 89). SDT further enhances free will as not just an option but as a key motivating force and essential component of intrinsic motivation.

Beyond possibility, the Ideal Self can feel more mysterious and even elusive. It could be finding and exploring what William Shakespeare had Hamlet pose as the "undiscover'd country" (Shakespeare, *Hamlet*, Scene 1, Act III). Hamlet pondered what is left after death and the life that could have been if not stolen from our spirit. The inspiration a person may derive from their Ideal Self or personal vision feels transcendent and provokes a sense of well-being (Thrash, et al., 2010). The presence of a dream has even been shown to predict life satisfaction among 28-year-olds (Schiller, 1998).

In a marvelous integration of psychological and neuroscience literature, Dahl, Wilson-Mendenhall, and Davidson (2020) proposed that there are four "pillars of psychological well-being": sense of purpose, vision, and an Ideal Self; connection with others with caring and compassion; insight from self-knowledge; and increased awareness of self, others, and the environment. Other related outcomes from future thinking shown in multiple studies include execution of purposive intent, goal accomplishment, increased health outcomes, and decreased risk-oriented behavior (Kooij, et al., 2018).

Desire Versus Drive

In their prophetic article "Navigating into the Future or Driven by the Past," Seligman, Railton, Baumeister, and Sripada (2013) claim that thinking about a desired future is a motivating force. As will be examined in the next section, it conjures up images of a sense of purpose, meaning, and calling as the context for what our lives could be. Prospection (Gilbert & Wilson, 2007) brings dreams or images of a desired future into consciousness and considers the possible futures a person might or could have.

Many theories of motivation in psychology have postulated drive or need reduction as a motivating force. The drive is to alleviate discomfort or deprivation of the past or present. In realizing a discrepancy between what is (or has been) and what might be, the human acts to reduce the apparent discrepancy. It is proposed that this becomes a motivating force for change.

There are four major problems with a "drive" theory of motivation to change. First, change requires effort and exercise of self-control. As will be explained in the next chapter, these actions engage neural networks and hormonal systems that limit functioning and eventually exhaust the person. The durability or sustainability of change efforts is therefore limited beyond what is likely needed for the change to occur and continue. A drive motivation may work for short-term changes, just as the effect that avoidance motivation has been shown to have (McClelland, 1985).

Second, a drive motivation may encourage people to create new habits. If these behaviors or thought patterns become "habituated" and used excessively, they may become new addictions. The very nature of their automatic engagement moves the person into routinized action, which may lose the other benefits or meaning of the new thoughts, feelings, or behavior.

Third, approach motivation inherent in a "desire" may take longer to effect, but appears to last longer (McClelland, 1985). The desire provides a vision, calling, or purpose that becomes a greater context for the future. The Ideal Self becomes a positive motivating force for change. The benefit of approach versus avoidance motivation for sustainable change has been documented widely (McClelland, 1985).

Fourth, a large discrepancy between the ideal and real or ought selves may squelch any effort to change. The magnitude of the perceived gap may be too great to overcome and the need for change is abandoned (Boldero & Francis, 1999).

In their pivotal work on level of aspiration, which built on work with Jerome Frank, colleagues Lewin, Dembo, Festinger, and Sears (1944, p. 335) claimed that a level of aspiration is a "level of future performance in a familiar task." It becomes an ideal goal or part of the Ideal Self. A more perfunctory aim than level of aspiration was called an action goal and limited a person's future accomplishment, innovation, and performance.

Prospection and the Dream

> All people dream, but not equally. Those who dream by night in the
> dusty recesses of their minds, wake in the day to find that it was vanity.

But the dreamers of the day are dangerous people, for they may act
their dreams with open eyes to make it possible.

—**T. E. Lawrence**

The act of visualizing and experiencing future events was called prospection
by Gilbert and Wilson (2007). It involved simulating and evaluating possible
future events (Bulley & Schacter, 2020). Prospection can be fantasies of a
desired future (Oettingen & Mayer, 2002) and include trying to make sense
of them and the possible experience (Vazeou-Nieuwenhuis, et al., 2017). The
process may involve exploring many possible dreams and sorting those that fit
into a coherent Ideal Self (Reay, et al., 2017). Visualizing a desired future has
been shown to be a potent form of practice for Olympic athletes preparing for
competition (McCall, et al., 2023).

In contrast to prospection, forecasting is based on the Real Self. Forecasting
considers trends of past experiences. It is an analytic task that uses the neural
Task Positive Network (Jack, Dawson, et al., 2013). Prospection about a possible desired future uses the lateral visual cortex and part of the default mode
network (DMN) (Jack, Dawson, et al., 2013), as will be examined in the
next section. Because prospection has been linked to elements of the DMN
(Seligman, et al., 2013) and the recognition that these two neural networks
suppress each other, forecasting or planning details will likely inhibit the
ability to consider the possibilities and dream, and create an Ideal Self. As
Hershfield and Bartels (2018) argue, prospection may result from a failure of
imagination, or distancing one's current self from a possible future self.

There are various neurological disorders that can make thinking about the
future less likely. Aphantasia is a condition associated with inhibition of visual
imagery, and therefore less ability to construct images of a desired future
(Dawes, et al., 2022).

Neural Basis of Thinking of the Future

Considering future outcomes has been called a future time perspective, and
was questioned as a dispositional trait (Kooji, et al., 2018). Integration of various streams of neuroimaging studies has offered a dramatically different perspective. The consideration of the future desired possible living, work, and
self, as well as the possible future outcomes, involves thinking of trade-offs
among various possibilities (Bulley & Schacter, 2020). Building on the concept of prospection (Gilbert & Wilson, 2007) to mentally imagine or represent
a future, "the capacity to imagine or stimulate experiences that might occur in

one's personal future" was called episodic future thinking (Bulley & Schacter, 2020, p. 239).

Creating and imaging a desired future appears to rely on the activation of recognized brain areas that include many parts of the default mode network (Bulley & Schacter, 2020), which Tony Jack of Case Western Reserve University calls the Empathic Network (discussed in the next chapter; Jack, Dawson, et al., 2013; Jack, 2024). This was further confirmed in a meta-analysis, which also showed that activation of the DMN and episodic future thinking was negatively related to the onset of neurodegenerative disease (Ward, 2016). Future episodic hypothesized events stimulate networks with autobiographical memory retrieval or salient event retrieval from the past (Addis, et al., 2007). Personal and more self-reflective thoughts activate the medial prefrontal cortex (mPFC), which is a part of the DMN. The medial orbito-frontal cortex appeared central to episodic memories and imagined future events, and was more pronounced for those imagining in the far future (Dixon, et al., 2017)

The DMN appears key to both remembering and prospection or any form of self-projection (Buckner & Carroll, 2007), as further shown in meta-analysis of studies (Spreng, et al., 2008). In fact, both autobiographical remembering and prospection activated the same regions of the brain as are in the DMN (Spreng & Grady, 2010).

The neural network appears particularly relevant to a person's thinking about their own life and not merely thinking about the future. Exploring plausible personal future events activated the ventromedial prefrontal cortex (vmPFC) and posterior cingulate cortex (PCC), both key components of the DMN (D'Argembeau, et al., 2009, 2010), as compared to nonpersonal future events. These same two regions of the brain appear to enable future states of the self that are desired (Ideal Self) and capture a person's desire to attain them more poignantly than mere fantasizing or wishful thinking about nonpersonal future events.

Construction of desired future events invokes other key regions into a network, including the anterior hippocampus, inferior frontal gyrus, PCC and temporal cortices, the medial temporal lobe, and cerebellum (Addis, et al., 2009). Prospective memory or intentions to carry out future actions also invoke other elements of this network and are related to emotional processing of positive events, like the amygdala, ventral medial prefrontal cortex, rostral anterior cingulate cortex (rACC), and dorsal medial prefrontal cortex (dmPFC) (Schacter, et al., 2008). In terms of activating this network, implementation intentions were a better predictor of actual behavior than goal intentions (Schacter, et al., 2008).

Invoking prospection or stimulations of future desired events may delay discounting (Bulley & Schacter, 2020). Jack, Dawson, et al. (2013) showed that asking people to develop a vision of their ideal future not only cues prospection, but does so by activating the lateral visual cortex and components of the DMN, notably the orbitofrontal cortex (OFC), nucleus accumbens, and PCC. In a latter study (Jack, et al., 2023; Passarelli, et al., 2018), talking about one's vision with a coach (a person trained to elicit such cues) activated the ventral medial prefrontal cortex with two or more brief conversations. This study further revealed that merely asking a person to reflect and write a vision did not have the same activation effect. This is a key part of the potency of invoking the Positive Emotional Attractor (PEA), as discussed in the next chapter (Boyatzis, et al., 2015).

Purpose, Meaning, and Calling

In moments of contemplation, we are often drawn to something bigger than ourselves. Such moments may but do not often occur when cowering in a defensive posture responding to a threat. People are often quoted as wondering about the meaning of life at momentous occasions, like the death of a parent or the birth of a child, the joy of discovery, and looking into the eyes of a deeply loved person. This something bigger is a deeper and more meaningful sense of purpose (Kashdan, et al., 2023). This is not a goal, which is often a specific objective (see Chapter 5 for a full discussion of the role of goals in sustained, desired change).

Although not everyone can express their deep purpose or the meaning of life, many people find inspiration in such discoveries or recognition. Sense of purpose can be said to be a stable intent to do something meaningful and of benefit to others beyond yourself (Damon, et al., 2003). It may emerge from core values and have a mission-like appeal (Steger, et al., 2009). It can feel spiritual. It reveals and articulates what is meaningful to the person.

Calling is a form of passion that drives long-term, career-long commitment and sustainable effort (Riza & Heller, 2015). Calling, like purpose, is an intrinsic motivation and quite different from instrumental reasons such as working for pay (Dik & Duffy, 2009). Studying 196 managers and professionals from two large organizations, it was found that people saw their work either as a job, part of a career with future expectations, or a calling in about equal percentages (Wrzesniewki, et al., 1997). Those who saw their work as an expression of a calling had higher career and life satisfaction, tended to seek more formal education, and have higher-status roles and higher pay than others. The differences held even when controlling for only those in administrative positions.

Faith or a spiritual practice can provide a deep sense of purpose. Besides commitment to a moral code of values, faith can stimulate caring for others and social responsibility (Jack, et al., 2016). The social relationships developed within a faith or spiritual community reinforce the shared sense of calling.

Whether a function of the effort we expend at work (number of hours per week) or the desire for *more* than extrinsic rewards from work, people today may seek more purpose, meaning, and calling than in previous eras (Blustein, 2008). Surveys of Millennials suggest a worldwide shift toward seeking organizations and jobs with a sense of purpose (American Express, 2017; Manpower, 2016). Studies on the changing nature of work, expectations about it, and an evolving sense of unease were manifest in what has been called the Great Resignation or "quiet quitting" following several years of COVID-related disruption, social isolation, and virtual work (Smith, 2023; Bamboo.com, 2023). Such studies identified and continue to call for work with a greater sense of purpose.

The benefits experienced by having a sense of purpose in life extend to dramatically improved cardiovascular health (Kim, et al., 2019) and living longer (Hill & Turiano, 2014). A meta-analysis of ten studies involving 136,265 people showed that having a higher purpose in life was predictive of reduced mortality and fewer damaging cardiovascular events (Cohen, et al., 2016). Sense of purpose has been empirically shown to be a predictor and causal factor in a sense of well-being and other benefits of purpose, as well as a moderator revealing catalytic moments when purpose produces desirable benefits (Kashdan, et al., 2023).

Having a sense of purpose in life occurs through enhancement of a variety of psychological and physiological resources that provide direct and indirect paths from overwhelming stress (Kim, et al., 2019). Researchers explained that people seemed to be able to exert more self-control when in service of a purpose in life (and higher purpose) than others. They had better sleep patterns, could reframe and reduce the intensity of negative experiences, and used more coping behaviors than others (Kim, et al., 2019). These increased coping behaviors, which will be referred to as renewal in the next chapter, included restorative processes through better nutrition, exercise, and social interaction, and even better mental health (Kim, et al., 2019; Gamble, et al., 2021).

Age and experience may contribute to one's openness to a sense of purpose. Older people appear more willing to expend resources and effort to help others at least equally significant as efforts to help themselves (Lockwood, et al., 2021). The act of formally retiring seems to invoke a greater sense of purpose in life, even among those in jobs classified as lower status and those who were dissatisfied with their jobs (Yemiscigil, et al., 2021).

Some dispositional characteristics may make it easier to find and articulate one's sense of purpose and calling, like having a growth mindset (O'Keefe, et al., 2018). A growth mindset enabled those in five studies to explore new meaning and purpose, and to integrate them into their personal Ideal Self. A mechanism possibly allowing discovery of purpose or calling was called "goal shielding" (Belanger, et al., 2013). These studies suggested that an intense or "obsessive passion" could preclude consideration of new possibilities, while more "harmonious passion" would allow for adaptation and emergent purpose. Vallerand (2008, 2015) proposed that "harmonious passion" was an autonomous drive that had been internalized into one's identity. It enabled a person to be more adaptive and to learn and change, likely due to the activation of the Positive Emotional Attractor (PEA) (see Chapter 3; Curran, et al., 2015). On the other hand, "obsessive passion" was a fixation that was an uncontrollable response. It was experienced as more rigid and was likely to arouse the Negative Emotional Attractor (NEA) (see Chapter 3).

As will be discussed in Chapter 5, a predominant focus on passion or purpose in one's work can have undesirable side effects (Cech, 2021). Beyond the balancing effect of considering social responsibility so that a person's personal passion does not become egocentric, the sense of purpose and Ideal Self should be more comprehensive than just work. It should include a person's spiritual and physical health, quality of relationships intimate and otherwise, and contributions to the community. For some, work is a means to provide for life's needs or a lifestyle. Work can also provide meaning in and of itself. Work can help a person move closer to their Ideal Self both inside and outside of work.

Passion for work can be exploited and damage a person's options (Cech, 2021). Similar to an occurrence in many purpose-driven nonprofits, executives of the UN World Food Program lamented the pressure placed on their country managers. They mentioned people who could not visit their families every six weeks as was allowed and encouraged because of the perceived needs of those they were serving, which included pressure from their own staff. A result was disruption to families, divorces, and mental health problems (personal communication, 2004). The healthiest approach is to contemplate, develop, and refresh a holistic Ideal Self with careful attention to social responsibilities as well as personal sustainability.

Core Values and Operating Philosophy

Purpose and calling are an expressions of personal meaning. Meaning is an expression of one's values and way of determining value or operating philosophy. Values are a method of evaluating our current worth because they reflect elements of our ego ideal (Schwartz, et al., 2010). They help us determine the extent to which we are being a "good person" or if we are living "a good life" (Haybron & Tiberius, 2012). They contribute to our personal identity and what type of work we deem appropriate (Dose, 1997), as well as guide us in making decisions (Schlegel, et al., 2011). When our aspirations are compatible with our values, we experience an increase in our sense of well-being and happiness (Lyubomirsky, et al., 2005). Beliefs, which are sets of values, are thought to interact and support change when perceived control is present (i.e., the change is perceived as consciously intentional) (Ajzen, 1991). Our values may be adopted from a religious or spiritual moral code, or socialization in early childhood by one's family.

An operating philosophy is the basis for assigning value to activities or experiences. It is the lens through which we view experiences and assess the worthiness or attractiveness of an action, experience, event, or another person (Boyatzis, et al., 2000). In sorting the multitude of possible operating philosophies, Boyatzis, Murphy, and Wheeler (2000) categorized them as one of three types: pragmatic, intellectual, and humanistic. The person with a dominant pragmatic operating philosophy assesses the world through a cost-benefit analysis. It is a utilitarian approach that determines if the ends justify the means. A person with a dominant intellectual operating philosophy assesses the world through a lens of conceptual meaning and clarity. They seek a model, theory, or abstract code to determine the worth of an act, experience, or event. A person with a dominant humanistic operating philosophy assesses the world through the impact of actions and events on those specific individuals with whom they have a close, personal relationship.

Both our values and operating philosophy contribute to the framing and articulation of our sense of purpose, meaning, and calling. A person who values novelty and has a dominant pragmatic operating philosophy may find meaning in being a serial entrepreneur in business, a program innovator in universities, or a process innovator in healthcare. A person who values caring for others and compassion and has a dominant humanistic operating philosophy may find meaning in being a personal, life, career, or health coach to others. Once they discover this vocation, it may feel like they have found their calling.

Salient Aspirational Personal Identity and Social Identity Groups

While values and operating philosophy exist in the context of alternate ideas and ways of viewing the world, our social context contributes to formulation of our personal identity (or identities) and our social identities (social identity groups to which we belong or aspire to belong).

Personal identity, also called self-identity, is an integration of various ways in which a person values or aspires to think, feel, and act. It is how they assess meaning to themselves (Gecas, 1982). We use our personal identity to determine individual choices. It may help distinguish ourselves from others through a social comparison or evaluative process (Ashforth & Mael, 1989; Tajfel, 1974).

When the identity and social comparisons allow us to join or find meaning in identification with a group, then it becomes a social identity. They may be aspirational, like a doctoral student seeking to become a professor and academic or medical student seeking to become a physician. Once a social identity is formed, the person adopts the group's shared values, norms, and symbols in signaling to others that they are a member of and belong to a specific group (Stets & Burke, 2000; Tajfel, 1982). Social identity confers a sense of belonging and differentiation from others (Sluss & Ashforth, 2007), but also influences individual aspirations (Ostrove, et al., 2011). Social identity groups contribute to our superego.

Spiritual beliefs and faith, even a religion, can be a shared vision and part of a person's Ideal Self. It can lift us out of this world to the one we wish to be in as a manifestation of core values (Jack, et al., 2016). For some, the experience of a religion and religious practices feel imposed and are part of an Ought Self.

A high-valence Ideal Self can also have a deleterious effect on performance when conditions or context change (DiBenigno, 2022). When attached to a social identity group, a person may ignore cues that a change in behavior is needed to address current performance.

Social roles, like being a mother or father, will likely be an expression of one's personal identity. But unless a person joins specific mother or father groups, like Mothers Against Drunk Driving, it does not become a social identity group as well. A social identity group provides, as was said, a sense of belonging, but also reinforces a set of norms and values, including using symbols of membership that both signal inclusion but also differentiation from other groups. Social identity groups can help a person move closer to their dream if the groups are part of their desired future. They can also hold a person back from changing behavior and style to suit the aspirant social identity group by maintaining symbols, modes of speech, and practices of a social identity group that is part of their older self, or even have become part of their Ought Self (to be discussed more in the following section and in Chapter 8).

Hope

> Hope is the thing with feathers
> That perches in the soul,
> And sings the tune without the words,
> And never stops at all.
> **—Emily Dickinson**

> We judge a person's wisdom by his hope.
> **—Ralph Waldo Emerson**

Hope is an emotion. It is a positive expectation of a valued or desired future state or experience. It enables a person to believe a dream or prospection is possible or feasible. In this sense, it moderates the prospection or dream and helps it become an Ideal Self or personal vision.

The most referenced approach, theory, and research about hope is that of C. R. Snyder (2000). But in the definition used, agency, pathways, and goals may have confused the concept by contaminating the measurement. Akrivou (2005) showed that measures of hope (e.g., the PANAS), optimism (Scheier's Life Orientation Scale), and internal control of reinforcement (Rotter's IE Scale) contained a common theme of achievement and goal-striving. By removing that common conceptual element from the variables and their measures, it may be possible to better clarify three distinctive and important concepts.

As a primary emotion, hope becomes an effective driver of the possible and change (Boyatzis & Akrivou, 2006; Boyatzis & Dhar, 2021). For example, Jim Johnson of the University of North Carolina would bring high school students from disadvantaged neighborhoods to the business school to learn about how to find and get a job (Salter, 2000). In the program he taught study skills, etiquette, and how to interview. But he also exposed them to mentors who were just like them in background but had made it to college, graduate school, and entered professions. He was intent on creating a sense of hope of new possibilities that they might not consider in their neighborhoods and existing social identity groups. The program worked wonders, as is evident in the number of participants who completed college and went on to complete professional degrees and returned to the program to counsel new participants.

Hope plays a key role in motivating women in STEM to remain in their careers (Buse & Bilimoria, 2014). For these professional and executive women, hope both as a basic emotion and as part of their personal vision combined to create an engine driving continued engagement in their work and believing in a desired future. In contemplating one's financial future while nearing retirement, Lunceford (2017) showed that the Ideal Self predicts well-being, particularly among women. Hope had the same impact on engagement in their work organizations among mid-level Latin American managers (Martinez, et al., 2021).

Within a larger cultural context, Dukhaykh (2019) showed that professional women in Saudi Arabia who persisted in what were nontraditional careers in their culture were driven by hope. Her structural equation model showed that self-efficacy and optimism contributed to feeling hope for the future. As part of their Ideal Self and personal vision, hope came from support of their family and amplified the effect on career commitment and career satisfaction. A great deal of family support for their career showed how this social identity group enabled more autonomy and individual volition than was typical for professional women in Saudi Arabia.

An important distinction regarding the power of hope for change is that the hope should be feasible in some way (Groopman, 2003). If the hope was for something unlikely to ever occur, it could be setting the stage for the person to feel betrayed and deflected from any sustained effort at change.

Nemesis of the Ideal Self: The Ought Self

The antithesis of the Ideal Self, and often its nemesis, is the Ought Self, or more correctly the many ought selves imposed on us from others (Higgins, 1987; Freitas & Higgins, 2002). Often well-meaning parents, teachers, or managers tell us what we should become or do. In the process, they become helping bullies. Collectivist cultures reinforce the obligation to conform to authority's views and surrender one's dreams. This makes it exceedingly difficult for a person to access their Ideal Self. For people in this situation, they may realize or become aware of their Ideal Self and its components following their next mid-life crisis.

The Ought Self is a version of a future imposed or coming from external sources to the person. Often, these other people are in authority roles (such as parents, teachers, managers). It constitutes an obligation to seek the future others want for you, or how they want you to be. The discrepancy between the Ideal Self and the Real Self will be addressed in Chapter 4. Here, the discrepancy between the Ideal Self and Ought Self or Selves is a focal point for internal conflict and deflection from pursuing one's dream or vision. The arousal of the NEA is a result of social, evaluative comparisons, regardless of whether the person sees themselves as more positive or negative than others (Obodaru, 2012). Another source of NEA arousal is the realization that one is living an "undesired self," whether the Ought Self was the source or not (Ogilvie, 1987).

The Ought Self or parts of it can be introjected, but it is still an external source and therefore part extrinsic motivation—pleasing others or being conscientious. Over time, the feelings about this Ought Self will likely change. At some point, like a mid-life crisis, the person awakes and feels betrayed by people with whom they have had relationships for possibly misdirecting them for what may have been years, and causing excess guilt. In social collectives, this shifting of Ought and Ideal Self may occur the same way.

The Ought Self can be a force for good, especially when socializing children. Consider how a child learns the value of oral hygiene or courtesy and manners. The initial experiences may begin as Ought Self. If they can later morph into parts of their Ideal Self, then they have contributed to the development of a healthier and better citizen. The same can be said of beliefs and practices of a faith. But when the practices are continued into later life without critical thought, they remain in the more negative aspect of imposed, obligatory expectations. At the extreme, it can be the basis for socializing someone into extreme positions, like a cult and not an act of free will.

The time lag in experiencing the conflict between the Ideal Self and the Ought Self was eloquently described by a highly successful business executive and later author and scholar, Charles Handy. In *The Hungry Spirit: Beyond Capitalism: A Quest for Purpose in the Modern World*, he wrote, "I spent the early part of my life trying hard to be someone else. At school I wanted to be a great athlete, at university an admired socialite, afterward a businessman and, later, the head of a great institution. It did not take me long to discover that I was not destined to be successful in any of these guises, but that did not prevent me from trying, and being perpetually disappointed with myself. . . . The problem was that in trying to be someone else, I neglected to concentrate on the person I could be. That idea was too frightening to contemplate at the time. I was happier going along with the conventions of the time, measuring success in terms of money and position, climbing ladders which others placed in my way, collecting things and contacts rather than giving expression to my own beliefs and personality" (Handy, 1997, p. 86).

Socialization into a work or social organization will communicate and show role models of an Ought Self to the newcomers or initiates. The seduction of joining social identity groups and adopting their aspirations can be Ought Self in service of feeling like you belong to some group. Social identity groups can, in this fashion, literally hold a person back from moving toward their dream by maintaining a strong hold on their past and present identifications.

In many work organizations, professionals, managers, and executives are repeatedly trained to engage in prospection for their organization. They are encouraged to create a shared vision and mission as part of strategic planning. The forces of socialization are strong and may bleed into an Ought Self. But it is surprising that few of the same people engage in developing and articulating their own personal vision or Ideal Self (Berg, 2016).

In her study of executives of purpose-driven companies, Berg (2016) showed that having a personal Ideal Self and vision predicted engagement, life satisfaction, and organizational commitment. Shared vision with others with whom an executive worked helped to amplify the effect on engagement and organizational commitment. A similar discovery was made of engineers in the research division of a major international manufacturing company (Boyatzis, Rochford, et al., 2017). The engineer's perception of the degree of shared vision with their project teammates accounted for 27% of the unique variance in how engaged they felt about their work.

The power and frequency of ought selves imposed on people is the largest factor as to why some people do not have a clear personal vision or dream. Another reason is fear of being disappointed. In some totalitarian regimes, dreaming is forbidden and violations are met with severe punishments. For some, they do not dream because they have not witnessed or observed adults around them dreaming of a better life. But dreams change.

Morphing of the Ideal Self

It is no failure to fall short of realizing all that we might dream. The failure is to fall short of dreaming all that we might realize.

—Dee Hock, founding CEO of VISA, creator of Chaordic Organizations.

Although change in one's dreams dreaming may occur as a result of many forces or situations in life, three of the most profound are eras in our life and careers, also known as life and career stages; particularly salient experiences and socialization; and the quality of our close relationships.

Life and Career Eras

Age affects our bodies and minds. With age, varied and more experience may occur. But it doesn't always. Some people live in cyclical repetition of the same or similar experiences. They spend time with the same people, do the same things, and get exposed to the same perspectives. Hopefully that is rare, and new experiences and exposure to more and varied people comes with age. This may invite wisdom and other changes in what and how we dream. For example, our sense of purpose may change, as well as the meaning we perceive in events (Kashdan & McKnight, 2009; Steger, et al., 2009).

Beyond age, the rhythm of our lives reveals an amazingly consistent cycle. These cycles have been called life or career stages. The poignant moments of transition have been called various mid-life crises (Levenson, et al., 1978). While conceptualizing a person's progress through life as a developmental process has been explored by numerous scholars, Erickson's (1985) effort has been one of the more comprehensive attempts to capture this rhythm throughout life, not just our early years. His theory is truly a stage model in that growth or development is forward movement, and conflicts within a stage can cause backsliding and regression.

Levinson, et al.'s (1978) model was more of a sequence theory separated by periods of transition or crisis. They went so far as to predict that the periodicity is about seven to nine years, followed by a three- to five-year transition period. They felt that the twenties were a time of testing oneself against the world, which might extend into the thirties. The often clichéd forties mid-life crises were the realization that mastery or success in one's efforts or life left gaps, and often ushered in a period of exploring meaning and wanting to even out the ways in which life is meaningful. This rhythm continued until death, with each transition creating new challenges of meaning (Frazier, et al., 2000), values (Gouveia, et al., 2015), and personality (Kitayama, et al., 2020). It is easy to see how such periods or transitions would affect a person's purpose, meaning, values, identity, and social identity groups. It is also easy to see how changes in these components would change a person's prospection and Ideal Self. An up-to-date conceptualization of life and career eras for professional women integrated opportunities and current frustrations with continued effects of sexism on sense of progress (O'Neil & Bilimoria, 2005).

Some of these changes were documented by Dhar (2022a). He showed that MBA students in their twenties often wrote vision essays about their desired future in terms of career and professional desires and aspirations. The lack of family or relationships was stunning. By the time EMBAs around 40 were writing personal vision essays, they included work–life balance and family as additional themes. When 50-year-olds in an executive doctorate program wrote their visions and talked with a coach, they added contributions to the community and society, as well as a new level of fervor in work, life, and family balance.

Sheehy (1995) reframed the sequence as more of an accordion, with major life experiences easily expanding or contracting the period or trauma expanding the period of a transition. Birth of a child, death of a parent, major surgery, and events from outside of the person like a terrorist attack, war, or natural disaster could expand or contract the period. Almost any form of trauma, like being a victim of violence, can provoke a new era or, at excessive levels, inhibit any progress or change (Mangelsdorf, et al., 2018). Witnessing birth or death will often invoke questions about the meaning of life. For some, these questions may invite a wave of reflection and changes in one's desired future.

A fourth approach to life and career eras is that of Boyatzis and Kolb (1999). They proposed that we go through three iterative modes in our lives and careers: performance, learning, and development modes. In the performance mode, a person is preoccupied with mastery and proving to themselves and others that they can achieve desired levels of performance. They compare themselves against superior performers (i.e., benchmarks) and seek feedback to improve.

In the learning mode, a person is preoccupied with novelty and experiencing new and different things. They look for new opportunities, different roles and jobs, and alternate experiences. They compare their experiences against their own prior experiences. In the development mode, a person is preoccupied with meaning, seeking to "give back" to the community, others, and society. People are often in each of these modes for up to seven years and then shift into the next mode. Once a semblance of mastery has been achieved, the person seeks something else, something different. Once a variety of new things have been experienced, the person questions the meaning of it all and seeks something bigger as a purpose in life. Our theory contended that a person goes through each of these modes and recycles the sequence, but usually about different themes or values.

A comparable rhythm occurs in careers. Dalton and Thompson (1986) created a stage model of careers, with the similar one-way path to development as Erikson's life development theory. Super's (1984) and Schein's (1978) theories of career development had the sequential properties of a Levinson-type theory. The most dramatic depiction of the sequence and cyclical nature of careers was described by Michael Driver (1982). He postulated that professionals had spiral careers. Professors, physicians, nurses, engineers, and lawyers may stay in the same field and practice their profession the same way (teaching classes, seeing patients, handling trusts and litigation), but the career era changes become evident in the content of what they work on or find exciting.

Transitions and Liminal Periods

> Our children may learn about the heroes of the past. Our task is to make ourselves architects of the future.
> **—Jomo Kenyatta, Kenya's first president**

Major changes in one's roles in life or work begin long before the change appears in their behavior or Ideal Self. These changes often begin with a restlessness and vague desire for something different or novel (Ibarra & Barbulescu, 2010). Being "in-between" captures the feeling of being in transition (Dhar & Boyatzis, 2024). Too often people act out these vague unsettled sensations and engage in dysfunctional explorations.

When the person is reflective and considers the possibilities, they may be consciously considering changes to their Ideal Self. Responses can include adaptation of current activities (Whittman, 2019); reconciliation of apparent discrepancies with one's desires (Reay, et al., 2017), personal identity, or social identities (Ladge, et al., 2012; Shepherd & Williams, 2018); or changes in or experimentation with possible ideal selves.

Ibarra and Petriglieri (2010) called this identity play. Formally, this identity play may be the fourth phase of ICT: experimentation and practice with possible new thoughts, feelings, or behavior (discussed in Chapter 6). Video games provide an opportunity for people to try out new selves and identities (Przybylski, et al., 2012). These can be powerful developmental moments in part because they have no real consequences or costs at that moment.

Another approach to providing opportunities to explore new possibilities include when organizations experiment with creating task forces to address real problems, but assign the leadership of the task forces to those exploring management and leadership positions. By providing a temporary setting in which a person can explore a possible future work self, the organization allows a person to examine the possible salience of such a career move before actually making it (Strauss, et al., 2012). It also provided opportunities to practice the new role and see if it felt like an exciting part of the person's future. The potency and relevance of a desired future self will sustain the emotional valence and curiosity, but a "fading effect" has been documented when the person is experiencing anxiety (Montijin, et al., 2021). The presence of the anxiety brings the NEA, with the closing down of perceptual fields and openness discussed in the next chapter.

Salient Experiences and Socialization

Whether a part of a transition period, liminal moment, or episodic event, there are experiences in life and work that can profoundly affect a person's values, identity, purpose, or hope about future possibilities. Examples include childbirth (Malacrida & Boulton, 2012), role transitions (Dukerich, 2001), and telecommuting (Thacher & Zhu, 2006), even before the worldwide pandemic forced it upon us and disturbed our way of approaching life and work. If they are associated with conversations with others—whether peers, social identity groups, or coaches—that invoke reflection, it brings to consciousness these feelings. Awareness of changes in any of the Ideal Self components may happen gradually, or arrive in a person's consciousness like a sudden wave.

A new framing of high-valence experiences has been described as post-traumatic and post-ecstatic growth (Mangelsdorf, et al., 2018). In studying 122 longitudinal samples (154 independent samples representing 98,436 people), Mangelsdorf, Eid, and Luhmann (2018) claimed that intense or high-salience experiences can invoke growth, whether the original experience was negative or positive. ICT would predict, as explained in the next chapter, that negative experiences may create a perceptual wake-up call to capture a person's conscious attention. But unless that is converted to a positive aspiration, the sustainability of a change effort will be compromised.

Every time a person joins a new organization, whether work, community, or social, they are exposed to a series of experiences to help them learn the norms and values of that organization (Van Mannen & Schein, 1979). These may invoke changes in a person's aspirations for the future and their sense of belonging (Sneed & Whitbourne, 2003; Pratt, et al., 2006). A person's desire to belong results in the values and behavior of the new group being integrated into their own repertoire (Burke, 2006).

As described in the previous chapter, our experiences do not occur on a blank slate. Any of these prior socialization or salient experiences can create lingering identities that can hold back change (Whittman, 2019). As with the process of changing an Ideal Self, people can respond through negotiated adaptation, identity substitution, or creation of an identity quite different from the earlier ones (Whittman, 2019). Several key experiences and socialization may occur simultaneously or in succession before a tipping point.

Shared Vision in Our Key Relationships

Our relationships affect us in many ways. As will be discussed in depth in Chapter 7, certain qualities of relationships are powerful stimulation of changes to the Ideal Self. But perhaps the most powerful is the quality of our relationships—that is, the degree to which we share a sense of purpose, values, identity, and vision with others. The juncture of personal vision and social responsibility was described by noted author, Nobel Laureate, Holocaust survivor, and humanitarian Elie Weisel, who said at a Case Western Reserve University Commencement Address in 2004, "Your purpose is to pursue your dreams, as long as your dream is not someone else's nightmare."

The degree of a shared vision of people in a relationship—whether a dyad, team, organization, community, or country—has been shown to be one of the most statistically significant predictors of leadership effectiveness, engagement, citizenship, and innovation (Boyatzis, et al., 2015; Boyatzis & Rochford, 2020) (see Figure 2.3). Shared vision is the articulation and realization of the Aristotelean dream of shared telos or shared purpose.

Shared vision must truly reflect all of the people involved, not just a coalition of powerful people in the organizational hierarchy. With diversity of thought may come diversity of views of a desired vision. Disagreement requires dialogue and personal reflection to reconcile. "The answer is that moral reflection is not a solitary pursuit but a public endeavor. It requires an interlocutor—a friend, a neighbor, a comrade, a fellow citizen. Sometimes the interlocutor can be imagined rather than real, as when we argue with ourselves. But we cannot discover the meaning of justice or the best way to live through introspection alone" (Sandel, 2009, p. 28).

A shared vision in our various collectives (pairs, teams, organizations, communities, and countries), as said above, will emerge from a degree of shared values, identities, and sense of purpose. These will percolate from various experiences without consciousness, necessarily. For example, in a major study of leader–follower pairs in Egypt, Farraq (2022) showed that the degree of shared vision, compassion, and energy, as viewed by the followers, mediated the leader's Ideal Self and vision's impact on the effectiveness and

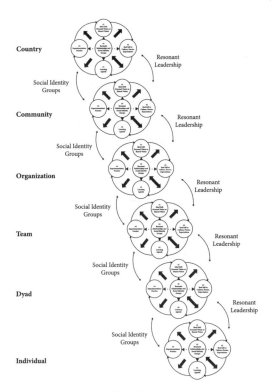

Figure 2.3 The multilevel fractals of shared vision within Intentional Change Theory

Source: Boyatzis (2008, 2015).

engagement of the leader as well as their followers. Well-being of couples was mediated by their degree of shared vision (Lunceford, 2017).

A shared vision drives sustained, desired change at many levels of human collectives and enables cross-level transmission of emotions and ideas. In this way, a shared vision becomes one piece of evidence of the multilevel fractal nature of ICT, to be discussed in Chapter 8. By expressing a shared vision, a leader can invoke comparable emotions in many people at many levels across the globe at the same time.

For example, consider the enduring impact of two specific moments when two organizational and social movement leaders articulated a shared vision to people within their respective countries: Nelson Mandela and the Reverend Martin Luther King Jr. In his Presidential Inaugural Celebration Address in 1994, Mandela said, "We have triumphed in the effort to implant hope in the breasts of the millions of our people. We enter into a covenant that we shall build the society in which all South Africans, both black and white, will be able to walk tall, without any fear in their hearts, assured of their inalienable right to human dignity—a rainbow nation at peace with itself and the world" (Mandela, 1994). At the Lincoln Memorial in 1963, King said, "When we let freedom ring, when we let it ring from every village and every hamlet, from every state and every city, we will be able to speed up that day when all of God's children, black men and white men, Jews and Gentiles, Protestants and Catholics, will be able to join hands and sing in the words of the old Negro spiritual, 'Free at last! Free at last! Thank God Almighty, we are free at last!'" (King, 1963). The videos and phrases from these two speeches continue to invoke and evoke strong emotions and elements of a shared dream for many people in their organizations, movements, communities, and countries around the world. Even key phrases like Mandela's "rainbow nation" or King's "free at last" arouse a shared vision, PEA, and hope (Howard & Coombe, 2006).

Social identity groups continuously remind their participants of their shared purpose, values, and norms. Creating memorable and often repeated phrases is another way in which social identity groups are a powerful force for change in one's Ideal Self—or in hindering any progress.

As mentioned earlier, spiritual beliefs and faith, if shared, *are* a shared vision. "Where there is no vision, the people perish" (*King James Bible*, Proverbs, 29:18). The consequence of loss of faith and an increasingly secular world is the loss of a traditional source of one's sense of purpose and meaning (Cates, 2015).

When studying MBAs with an average age of about 28 in a major European management school who had developed and articulated their personal vision (Ideal Self), it was found that talking about it with a coach predicted positive changes in each subscale of the measure of the Ideal Self (Mosteo, et al., 2016). The Ideal Self test (Boyatzis, Buse, et al., 2010) used in this research appears in the appendix of this book.

Shared Vision as a Driver of Collective Desired Change

Principle 8: As a fractal theory, ICT describes sustained, desired change at all levels of human endeavor from individual to dyads, teams, organizations, communities, countries, and global processes.

ICT claims that not only does realization and articulation of a personal vision or Ideal Self drive openness to desired change and determine the durability of any change or learning effort, but in our social collectives, our shared vision has the same effect. To be clear, a shared vision is not merely the chair of a team, CEO of a company, mayor of a city, or dominant coalition declaring a vision. To be shared, a vision must have an inspiring and compelling effect on those involved.

In other words, it must be shared as a dream among those involved. It may not be shared by every person, but it has to be a motivating force for everyone in a dyad, most of a team, and a critical mass of people in an organization, community, or country. Again, shared vision is bigger than a shared goal, as discussed in depth in Chapter 5. Critical mass is a statistical majority (over 50%). But an old rule of thumb from organizational development projects says that if a vision was shared among one-third or more of the opinion leaders or network nodes and influential people in an organization, it has probably achieved critical mass. At the community level, the rule of thumb might be a commitment and excitement about the shared vision from most of the social identity groups and subcultures within the community. It would require support from the key leaders of all of the groups, or at least acquiescence from those not championing the shared vision. What is shared of the vision might be all of the components of the shared ideal, like the values, the dream, or the personal and social identities, but not necessarily all of them.

In a lecture on positive resiliency to the Consortium on Research on Emotional Intelligence in Organizations, Richard Davidson of the University of Wisconsin, the noted neuroscientist expert on meditation and compassion, made an important observation. He reminded the audience that in his stirring speech on the National Mall, Reverend Martin Luther King Jr.'s reverberating refrain was "I have a dream," not "I have a nightmare." For most of us who share an uplifting reaction to hearing that refrain and remembering or listening to the speech at the time or later, the stimulating effect was not conditional on whether we felt similar on each of the elements of King's dream (Howard & Coombe, 2006).

It was the overall image and the aspirational sense of hope and possibility that moved and often still moves us. In the following sections of this chapter, the effect of shared vision on dyads, teams, organizations, communities, and countries will be explored. The mechanism for emotional and social contagion that makes this sharing possible will be examined in the next chapter.

Vision Driving and Helping Change in Pairs or Dyads

Shared vision or the lack thereof affects our pair or dyadic relationships. The mate selection literature of the 1970s showed that value congruence predicted stability of caring, intimate relationships over time more than any other characteristic (Rubin, 1973). The dramatic increase in the divorce rate mentioned in the first chapter is often accompanied with reports that people "don't have much in common any longer." Current activities, priorities, and daily choices are in the context of what one wants out of life and a longer-term view—our vision.

At work, it is said that people do not leave organizations, they leave managers (Buckingham, 1999). Buse and Bilimoria (2014) reported that professional women remaining in STEM careers was a function of the quality of their relationships to their immediate manager and the degree of hope and purpose in their personal vision. Female succession in family businesses, when there was an alternative among the next-generation family members, was shown to be a function of the daughter's sense of efficacy and the degree of shared vision she had with the family business founder, which was often her father (Overbeke, et al., 2015).

Another startling statistic reported in the first chapter was poor treatment adherence. It has been suggested that the state of health and the cost of healthcare in our societies would be far better if people followed instructions or recommendations of their physicians and nurses after contracting a disease, having surgery, or as a preventative approach (Khawaja, 2010). Khawaja reported that although many factors affected treatment adherence for patients diagnosed with Type II diabetes, they were all mediated (i.e., partially or fully transformed in their positive effect) by the patient's perception of the degree to which they and their physician had a shared vision for their health. It is important to note that these were not shared goals, but shared big-picture, future vision.

A prolific history of research on manager–subordinate or leader–follower relationships from Leader Member Exchange Theory (Graen & Uhl-Bien, 1995; Riggio, et al., 2008; Farrag, 2022) cited many aspects of their interactions. Work on the perceived qualities of the relationship continued to show that shared vision (not goals) was a major—if not *the* major—predictor of engagement and perceived effectiveness of the manager or leader (Docherty, 2020; Warr, 2018). Further studies on leader–follower responses showed that a compelling vision expressed by the leader resulted in increases in adaptive and proactive behavior of others (Griffin, et al., 2010).

A prominent approach to coaching has been called "solution-focused coaching" (Cavanagh & Grant, 2018). This approach chooses to focus on desired aims instead of problems. It might be a goal or aspiration, but could be the same as a personal vision or Ideal Self.

The research on coaching has gone beyond the one-way discussion of the client's vision, as discussed in more detail in the following chapter from our fMRI studies, to examine the quality of the coach–client relationship. One approach has shown that forming an "alliance" works wonders (De Hann, et al., 2020). Ellen Van Oosten showed that when top executives of a major bank developed a relationship with shared vision with their coach, their growth and use of their emotional and social intelligence dramatically affected their perceived effectiveness and engagement (Van Oosten, et al., 2019).

The mechanism for this dyadic effect is more than emotional contagion and the usual verbal and nonverbal cues. The affirmation and perceptions of a close relationship has been called the Michelangelo effect (Drigotas, et al., 1999). In a wide variety of ways, the research shows that a partner or another person in the dyad communicates their perception to the other person. Not only is there an affirmative component, but it often focuses on the person's Ideal Self and their progress toward it. They also create opportunities for the person to show the desired behavior. When it is working, the behavior is often reciprocal and mutually supporting movement toward their ideal selves. All of this results in affecting their well-being and relationship. Of course, the effect could be away from the other person's Ideal Self and have a negative impact on both members of the dyad.

Another possible source of difficulty in developing and maintaining a shared vision can occur when multiple roles are involved. For example, if a coach was supervising or advising another coach, the two roles of being a coach and a supervisor might conflict. The two roles could, at times, surface a dialectical tension in the demands and responsibilities of each role (Dhar, 2022b). If the supervisor believes the coach is getting too emotionally involved with a client, they would want to somehow warn the client. But if the client is also a coach, they expect the supervisor to use effective coaching behavior and not just give advice.

If the client feels strongly about their relationships with their own client, any advice about ethical limits or possible confusion being created could cause the person being supervised to shut down and ignore the advice. Dhar (2022b) suggested that being able to maintain a "paradoxical mindset" in such situations would allow the supervisor to deal with what might seem to be directly conflicting things to say to their client. A clear, shared vision between the supervisor and client could be the basis for communicating these seemingly paradoxical demands when simultaneous roles create such conflicts.

Vision Driving and Helping Change in Teams

Shared vision has a profound impact on increasing engagement among members in knowledge worker teams in research and development or consulting (Mahon, et al., 2014; Boyatzis, et al., 2017). The effect of the shared vision can bring people together and last for a long time. For example, early in their relationships, the Beatles were suffering and kept boosting their spirits by claiming they were going to the top. As their creative muses emerged, John

Lennon and Paul McCartney shared a vision of creating new music (Kozinn, 1995). Added to a variety of factors, including wanting to avoid the stress and strain of public appearances and touring, they retreated to the studio to create and record their music. At about the same time, the Rolling Stones expressed a shared vision of playing music together (Jagger, et al., 2003). Despite fighting among themselves, the Stones admitted that once they jumped on stage, they came together to perform. Within ten years of achieving notoriety and fame, the forces of creating new music contributed to tearing the Beatles apart. John, Paul, and George in particular wanted to create different kinds and genres of music. Meanwhile, the Rolling Stones continue performing and touring over 50 years later.

Perhaps one of the more dramatic examples of the dangers of setting and committing to a goal without a vision is found in comparing two teams climbing Mount Everest (Kayes, 2006). Adventure Consultants assembled a group of expert climbers in 1996 to achieve the summit of Mount Everest. It was a commercial trip for which eight clients paid $85,000 each to make it to the top of the world. Their party consisted of 15 climbers. Despite recommendations, and later insistence by their watchers at base camp, they did not heed warnings about the incoming weather, nor did they listen to the lead guide, Rob Hall, and turn around when their time to return to camp was safely exceeded. Only three of the clients reached the summit, while two clients and two of their guides died on the attempted return. As one of the members said, "I felt disconnected from the climbers around me—emotionally, spiritually, physically—to a degree I hadn't experienced on any previous expedition. We were a team in name only, I'd sadly come to realize. Although in a few hours we would leave camp as a group, we would ascend as individuals, linked to one another by neither rope nor any deep sense of loyalty. Each client was in it for himself or herself, pretty much" (Krakauer, 1997). Their lack of shared vision neither prepared them to handle the adversity of the climb, nor was it a common reference on which they could rely in airing differences of opinion as to what to do next.

Not long after, another expedition surpassed many firsts in reaching the summit of Everest (Weihenmayer, 2001). With the mission of showing that blind people are fully capable of dramatic human feats, the Allegra Expedition, supported by the National Federation of the Blind, wanted to change the world's view of blindness. With 21 climbers and eight sherpas, the expedition had 19 people achieve the summit (a new record), including Erik Weihenmayer, who was blind. They trained for over a year together and had a clear vision: "Every member of the team was there for the sole purpose of getting Erik to the summit and back down safely" (Pierce, 2001). While they were all there for the purpose of Erik reaching the summit, there was the greater purpose of inspiring others who are blind and globally changing perceptions. The team's shared vision clarified their purpose and was a basis for communicating with each other during the hazardous and frenzied moments on Everest.

Vision Driving and Helping Change in Organizations

A shared vision within an organization creates a compelling sense of purpose and motivating force. It provides a constant big picture and purpose that invokes motivational processes within individuals, teams, departments, and people. A shared vision appears more durable and sustaining than a strategic plan, goals, and performance targets. As explained earlier in this chapter, expressing shared values and a deep sense of purpose creates imagery of what and how an organization can function. It also shows how they can contribute to society, their people, customers, suppliers, and the community (Carton, et al., 2014).

Many prominent organizational development (OD) theories emphasized the driving, motivating force of shared vision, such as Beckhard and Harris (1987). Kotter (1995) saw it as empowering others to act. Tichy (1983) saw "mission" as the initiating topic, while Weisbord (1976) saw diagnostic work on the nature of the vision and culture as important first steps in any effort. The distinction of the focus on vision, identity, and values, not objectives, is clear in the Burke-Litwin theory (1992).

In contrast, many approaches to organizational development and other theoretical models focused on needs assessment and organizational diagnosis as the starting point of OD (Burke & Noumair, 2015). Such an approach appears more efficient and focused to the practitioner and clients, but emphasizes differences between the current organizational functioning and what it should or ought to be. Efforts using these theories or approaches would likely arouse more Ought Self issues and the NEA. A major meta-analysis of OD projects and their effects on attitude change found that the efforts focused on organizational norms before vision, if vision and purpose were involved at all (Neuman, et al., 1989). They further claimed that "human process interventions" were more effective in stimulating attitude change than sociotechnical approaches, possibly because they allowed or encouraged people to discuss values, purpose, and vision and not just assume everyone had the same vision.

Other approaches to OD addressed the degree of shared vision in a variety of ways. Argyris (1985) challenged people to probe their values and assumptions rather than proceed toward assumed course corrective actions. He called the process "double loop" versus "single loop" learning. Senge (1990) argued a similar dynamic, but based on a systems view of the organization and the degree to which the practices encouraged learning new and different ways to act. Work and job redesign efforts, like Hackman and Oldham (1980), purported to help people in organizations find or design jobs that were more closely aligned with their own values and purpose.

In the emotionally intense environment of family businesses, a shared vision moves people beyond the assumption of stability and long-lasting existence of the family business itself. It predicts financial performance over five years (Neff, 2015). A shared vision not only affects and predicts succession (Overbeke, et al., 2015), but also development of the next generation of business leaders (Miller, 2014, 2023). In part, it achieves the potent results by placing the bonds beyond familial obligation and longevity to purpose and mission. In a major study of entrepreneurial firms, the imagery within a vision predicted growth, especially when that imagery involved benefits and purpose for their full range of stakeholders and a growth orientation (Baum, et al., 1998).

In companies, a shared vision predicts championing behavior about a merger or acquisition, which in turn is a major predictor of mergers and acquisitions that work (Clayton, 2014). But it also interacts with the shared social identity of those within the company and their appeal to their customers and investors. The startling differences between the leaders of Netflix and Blockbuster serve as an example. Netflix saw themselves as bringing entertainment to customers, whereever they were. Blockbuster saw their purpose as building brick-and-mortar shops where prospective viewers could browse and rent or purchase videotapes and later DVDs. Netflix adapted and became a driving force for video streaming and a savior to many families during the COVID pandemic. Blockbuster went out of business. An odd coda to this story is that the leaders of Netflix offered to sell their fledgling company to Blockbuster, who turned them down because they were "in a different business" (Randolph, 2019).

Future Search and Appreciative Inquiry

A popular technique for achieving a shared vision is Appreciative Inquiry, first developed by colleagues of the author at Case Western Reserve University,

David Cooperrider, Ron Fry, and Suresh Svivastva (Cooperrider & Srivastva, 1987; Barrett & Cooperrider, 1990; Cooperrider, et al., 2008). To find the "life giving force" within the organization, people are brought together to tell each other stories of moments they felt proud and effective in their organization. These stories are shared and themes are identified that become components of a compelling vision. In one powerful application to Roadway, the combination of the Appreciative Inquiry process and training in ICT and emotional intelligent leadership resulted in dramatic changes in functioning from executive to driver and dock loader levels. These in turn resulted in major financial performance improvements and outpacing their competitors (Van Oosten, 2006; Boyatzis, et al., 2003).

A more broadly used technique for large groups within organizations, communities, or across communities is the Future Search Conference or Summit first noted in the 1990s (Weisbord, 1992). The process was based on the organizational models of Fred Emery and Eric Trist, and visioning meetings promoted by Ron Lippitt and Eva Schindler-Rainman (Schindler-Rainman & Lippitt, 1992). The approach emphasized the power of bringing many if not most of the people in an organization or community together to re-experience the entire system (Baburolgu & Garr, 1993). The conversations stimulate the widespread sharing of ideas and emotions and are egalitarian in involving a wide spectrum of people, not just the elite or leadership (Weisbord, 1992).

Future Search and Appreciative Inquiry summits bring people together and discover shared purpose, values, and aspirations. It helps to create the themes that can be molded into a widely inspiring shared vision. It can also help the participants coalesce into task and action groups with new energy to move the organization or community to a better future.

Remembering the Core Purpose

A shared vision within hospital organizations included many images of a desired future and core values and was found to boost performance in 151 hospitals studied (Carton, et al., 2014). This was part of the approach taken by Thomas Strauss, when he took over as president and CEO of Summa Health Systems in Akron, Ohio. He used focus groups and task forces to engage as many people who worked at the hospital to think about their purpose and vision. They then had numerous groups meet to discuss the exact wording and make changes over many weeks and months.

The result was a powerful vision that people at Summa carried with them as wallet-size cards. "You Are Summa. You are what people see when they arrive here. Yours are the eyes they look into when they're frightened and lonely. Yours are the voices people hear when they ride the elevators and when they try to sleep and when they try to forget their problems. You are what they hear on their way to appointments that could affect their destinies. And what they hear after they leave those appointments. Yours are the comments people hear when you think they can't. Yours is the intelligence and caring that people hope they find here. If you're noisy, so is the hospital. If you're rude, so is the hospital. And if you're wonderful, so is the hospital. No visitors, no patients, no physicians or coworkers can ever know the real you, the you that *you* know is there—unless you let them see it. All they can know is what they see and hear and experience. And so we have a stake in your attitude and in the collective attitudes of everyone who works at the hospital. We are judged by your performance. We are the care *you* give, the attention *you* pay, the courtesies *you* extend. Thank you for all you're doing" (Strauss, 2003). It reminded people that they did not exist to fill hospital beds or make budget, but to heal people. In the years following, Summa grew to nine hospitals and seven outpatient clinics.

In a different type of nonprofit organization, a symphony orchestra, vision can work the same way. George Szell, musical director of the Cleveland Symphony Orchestra, told his musicians, board members, members, patrons, and donors that he was in search of a "clean, perfect sound" (Rosenberg, 2000). The musicians understood what he meant without words. It was music that was transcendent and uplifting. The orchestra went on to be among the top five symphonies, if not number one in the US for decades.

It is said that nonprofit organizations are mission- and vision-driven (i.e., purpose-driven) more than other forms of organizations in society. The Young Men's Christian Organization, known to most as the YMCA, was founded in London in 1821 and then brought to the US in 1851. It has continued to serve communities in many ways and sustain itself. It created a vision that was to serve the entire community's needs, with flexibility and adaptability to different needs. Later it adopted the Kampala Principles (circa 1973) to claim service to God through equal opportunity and justice for all (Muukkonen, 2015). Their adaptability and continuing commitment to their shared purpose and core values motivated and continues to motivate their leadership and members to this day. Many organizations and social service agencies created to serve communities have come and gone without leaving a lasting legacy of hope and positive social impact. Often, they frame their vision as a limited one and fail to achieve true shared claim to the vision among their various stakeholders.

Vision Driving and Helping Change in Communities and Countries

Developing a shared vision becomes increasingly complex as the size and scope of the human collectives increases. Creating, developing, and sustaining a truly shared vision in an organization is difficult. It is more complex and difficult within communities and countries because they are composed of many different groups, organizations, subcultures, and broader cultures. The tendency is that a powerful coalition declares a vision for the people that they or their followers represent (DeFilippis, 2004). More often than not, this leaves out many others. Community development has often suffered from battling visions between board members of community organizations and the people they are meant to serve (Stoecker, 1997; O'Connor, 1999). Sometimes this conflict is between the community organizations and the foundation boards or funding agencies within a government (Brown, et al., 2003).

Within communities and countries there are many groups with varied views and experiences of life, and varied desires. These emerge from different socioeconomic groups, different ethnicities and races, and faith-based groups, neighborhoods, political parties, gender orientations, and issue-based advocacy groups. These can become communities of choice with shared purpose (Garber, 1995). Joseph Bower has observed that the "art of private sector management is using unlimited resources to achieve a limited set of objectives, while public sector management is using limited resources to achieve an infinite set of objectives" (Bower, 1977). The same applies to creating a vision among the widespread diversity of aspirations, values, and detonating issues fueling the desire for social action, and the perception as to what constitutes prosperity and a "good life."

ICT provides a template and guide for understanding what will comprise a vision and a shared vision. It cannot be assumed that a vision is shared because it feels compelling to one group. Errors in the process of seeking community change and development are often to blame for lack of progress rather than the original intent of the participating organizations (Stoecker, 1997). The communitarian movement within community development often assumes a shared vision that is not there (De Filippis, 2004). Sharing the vision requires, first and foremost, talking about the core values, aspirations, dreams, and identities to which all present can aspire. They exist within the context of individuals, their families, and their past experiences with social identity groups.

Diversity within a collective requires more dialogue to find mutually compelling dreams than when homogeneity is present. Past injustice haunts attempts for people to come together and seek a common dream. Some communities and some countries do move forward to create a better life and better conditions for their populace. One often cited characteristic of those moments is that the people involved have a vision that has become "a common narrative that can be repeated and customized to different audiences" (Katz & Nowack, 2017, p. 236). The more recent emphasis on "community-building" rather than development has encouraged a dialogue approach to discussing and recognizing shared vision (Traynor, 2012).

Examining several efforts to help communities be healthier and safer places to live, work, and recreate might help us understand sustained, desired change at the community level and the country level.

Bicycling in Cities

While bicycling may be a favorite sport to watch during the Tour de France or Olympics, or a fond childhood memory, the bicycle could play a major role in our future health. Ever since automobiles, motorcycles, and scooters became popular, air pollution and smog, as well as deterioration of building surfaces, has become an issue in cities around the world. Efforts have been made to reduce congestion and traffic. Although bicycles have been around for almost 200 years and are a major mode of transportation in placed like the Netherlands and Japan, their presence on city streets in many other countries did not become a frequent sight until 2007, when bike-sharing programs were launched. Is this the promise of the future or another fad?

The use of bicycles in cities was proposed to address—if not resolve—a variety of problems. There would be less car traffic, congestion, fumes, and smog, and possibly healthier citizens. "Riding a bike once a week for a whole year instead of using a car saves half a ton of CO_2" (PBSC, 2022). Since 40% or as much as half of our trips are less than three miles from home, using a bicycle is an alternative for many. Those with physical mobility challenges or certain elderly individuals may not find this a help. But for most citizens, riding a bicycle could help themselves and others.

During the 1960s, bike-sharing programs were introduced to Europe. Although not the first in France, the program in Paris, called Vélib', became a model. Today, they have over 20,000 bicycles and 1,200 stations throughout the city (Hikes, 2022b). The program appealed to giving Parisians independence and freedom. Translated, their slogan was "Paris Breathes." The city planners and company projected an image of a better lifestyle: a healthier and better quality of life. They appealed to professionals as well as to others who were environmentally conscious. They capitalized on the Tour de France fever, and are also an option for the more than 44 million tourists that visit Paris each year (Hikes, 2022a).

The early years were a challenge, with significant theft and vandalism. The advocates used a variety of media, from local newspapers and blogs, to an appeal to make their city beautiful again and build a widely shared vision (Coles, et al., 2012). Employers were encouraged to provide membership as a benefit with an annual fee of 19 euros. They gave out "green awards" to users as a function who used the bicycles frequently. They created bike cafes, organized bicycle get-togethers at cocktail hour, and named bicycle stations in honor of key users.

While groups in Paris used many efforts to engage and excite people within the city, early efforts in Montreal were not so thoughtful. Although Montreal launched their program, Bixi, around the same time as Paris, the mayor sponsored the initiative and began with a plan to export their model to other cities. They appealed to the "bo-bo's" (the bohemian bourgeois), which left most Montreal citizens on the sidelines (Gagnon, 2009). Despite learning from the initial problems with Paris Vélib', designing for Montreal's weather, and using new anti-vandalism technology (Montagne, 2014), they did not make efforts to ingrain the program as part of the community, even emphasizing bicycling as a leisure activity rather than a necessary and convenient mode of transportation and independence. With a focus on the innovation, technology, and the prospects of selling software and program features to other cities, the promoters did not create a shared vision among the people of Montreal.

Good ideas and potential innovations for communities are often hijacked by the lure and the analytics of system design (Yuan, et al., 2019). The new effort becomes a design challenge instead of a shared, user-driven vision challenge. They focus on the systems engineering or budgets instead of the dream, or how to emotionally engage more coalitions and social identity groups within the community (the latter point will be examined in Chapter 8 on social identity groups). By 2018, when Bixi relaunched in Montreal, they changed the pricing of their program and use social media to appeal to the "young and attractive" professionals. By 2022, they are an active part of the city.

While it is not surprising to see thousands of bicycles riding along the streets of various Chinese cities, many people are amazed at the prevalence in other major cities around the world. When you approach the main train station in Amsterdam, a visitor from the US would be surprised to not see massive automobile parking lots. But moored to the wharf on the river side of the station are barges with two floors and multiple levels of bicycles hooked onto rails—a massive bicycle parking lot.

Amsterdam appealed to safety and became what is called the bicycle capital of the world in 2018 (Van der Zee, 2015; Ton, et al., 2019). With rising traffic casualties and the memory of 400 children killed in traffic accidents in 1972, streets were closed to cars and trucks on certain days like car-free Sundays. This rallied mothers behind the push for bicycles (Van der Zee, 2015). Protests groups mobilized and advocated for a wide variety of benefits, from safety to cleaner air to a more beautiful city. By 2018, there were 881,000 bicycles in the city and an estimated 38% of all trips are made by bicycle (Van der Zee, 2018). Many different groups were enlisted in the effort, and a shared vision emerged (Veldhoven, 2020).

The effort in Amsterdam was part of a national identity that went back decades. Bicycles were not merely for sport or recreation, as they are often viewed in the US; they were a vital aspect of mobility and transportation. In the Netherlands, during the world wars, bicycles were often a way to move within and between cities during foreign occupations. Health and environmental benefits were always a priority, and bicycling helped address both themes. The oil embargo of the early 1970s further fueled bicycling benefits and independence from foreign forces (Van der Zee, 2015). Various leaders helped, like former Prime Minister Mark Rutte, who bicycled to work every day, or King Willem-Alexander, when he acceded to the throne in 2013 and rode a bicycle.

Meanwhile, many in the US still view bicycling as something done on a Peloton with a video trip, while cycling in a health club or your living room. That is hardly a vision that will be shared by sufficient groups and people to become a driving force for sustained change for increased bicycling in the US. Evidence for the consequences of lacking a shared vision in most cities within the US is that the bike-sharing programs are foundering and some closing, with few if any making sufficient funds to survive ("Slow Puncture," *The Economist*, p. 19).

Concluding Thought

The articulation of an Ideal Self, and in our social collectives a shared vision, can be the driver of sustained, desired change. It is not the only emergent experience that is needed. For that, we need the entire ICT process. However, an exciting Ideal Self or personal vision and a shared vision can be a major motivating force when supported by repeated return to PEA throughout the process of change. It can provide the inspiration for movement and guidance as to adjustments in behavior, thoughts, and feelings along the way. The Ideal Self is only the beginning of sustained, desired change.

3

Tipping Points to Transitions: PEA and NEA (Principles 2 and 3)

Principle 2: Being in the PEA allows a person or human system to be open to new ideas, scanning their environment, other people, and emotions. It is a tipping point into the next phase of ICT. The psycho-physiological states called the PEA and NEA are described with three axes: Parasympathetic versus Sympathetic Nervous System arousal, neural activation of the Default Mode versus Task Positive Networks, and positive versus negative affect.

Principle 3: Sustained, desired change in humans and human systems is most often discontinuous and nonlinear.

Desired change is often sudden. To be more specific, the *awareness* of a desired change occurring or having occurred is often sudden. These moments are called tipping points in complexity theory. The Positive Emotional Attractor (PEA) and Negative Emotional Attractor (NEA) describe the two most potent and prevalent sources of tipping points in sustained, desired change at all levels, as shown in Figure 3.1. Delving into the constituent components of the PEA and NEA helps us to understand the processes and mechanisms that accompany, precipitate, and in that sense cause a sudden change in awareness, thoughts, feelings, attitudes, and behavior. Parts of this chapter have been updated and developed but relied on earlier papers, notably Boyatzis, Rochford, and Taylor (2015) and Boyatzis, Goleman, Dhar, and Osiri (2021).

A tipping point is the moment at which the state or condition in a system changes. It is a moment of transition. For individuals, a tipping point is a moment of conscious awareness which may be the moment of change or occur soon after a change has begun. For collectives, it is the degree of shared awareness of the change that may follow the actual transition, which often requires a number of the people in the collective to have had the moment of awareness occur before the realization that it is being experienced by others.

The Science of Change. Richard E. Boyatzis, Oxford University Press. © Richard E. Boyatzis 2024.
DOI: 10.1093/9780197765142.003.0003

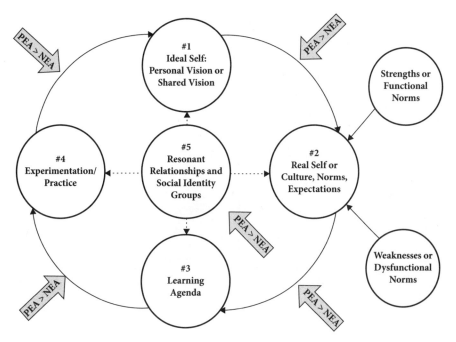

Figure 3.1 The PEA and NEA tipping points in the process of Intentional Change Theory
Source: Boyatzis (2008, 2015).

The Moment of Awareness

As mentioned in Chapter 1, strange attractors pull like a magnet, but unlike a magnet, the approaching states are caught in an orbit around the center. As described first by Ed Lorenz (1963), the orbit is around a centroid. In contrast, limit point cycle attractors pull states into their center, like the gravitational pull of a black hole in space (Casti, 1994; Erdi, 2008). A strange attractor is in perpetual motion, as a magnetic attraction and in keeping a state within the sphere of influence of the type of attractor. A limit point cycle attractor pulls a person or collective into it and then the force and state disappear (i.e., metaphysically it may reappear in another dimension, but exploration of this effect requires more than this chapter can address).

The PEA and NEA are strange attractors for the emerging process of sustained, desired change. In this sense, people do not resist change, but the lack of change is likely due to being attracted to the NEA and seeking predictability and safety. But the intensity of the PEA or NEA is not calculated as the square of the distance from the centroid. It is determined by the degree of arousal along the three axes that constitute the PEA and NEA, as shown in Figure 3.2.

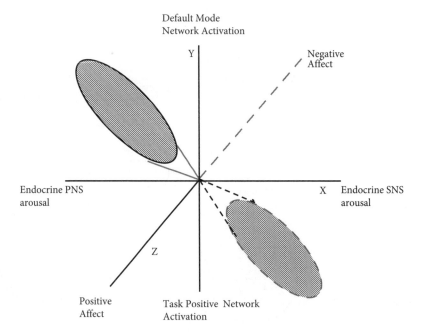

Figure 3.2 Positive Emotional Attractors (PEA) and Negative Emotional Attractors (NEA) in Intentional Change Theory. The dotted part of the z axis and the NEA ellipse are behind the visual plane of the paper.
Source: Boyatzis, et al. (2015)

The graphic portrayal shows that a person or a human collective may be aroused mildly and be in the attractor close to the zero point of the three axes. Or, a person or collective might be strongly aroused in the PEA or NEA and be described with their location further along on each of the three axes (closer to the extremity of either ellipse). As will be explained in the next sections, whether mild or strong in arousal, the costs and benefits of being in the PEA or NEA state are the same, but vary in degree of intensity.

Tipping into the PEA will serve three major purposes regarding change. First, it entices and invokes the next phase of ICT and the process of sustained, desired change. Second, when it occurs within a phase, it allows for greater awareness of new ideas, recognition of others, and emotions relevant within that phase of ICT. Tipping into the NEA has the reverse effect. It inhibits changes in state and awareness. Third, as will be described in the next sections, being in the PEA is typically experienced as energizing and restorative. Meanwhile, being in the NEA is typically experienced as draining and deflating. As a result, the motivation to continue in a learning and change process is sustained by the PEA and stifled by the NEA.

The tipping points into PEA are essential for the iterative nature of ICT to create and maintain sustained, desired change. The tipping points into the NEA act as brakes, slowing or stopping the growing awareness, requiring more and more effort to continue, and possibly cease the actual changes in a state or condition. There are moments in the change process in which the tasks require the narrower focus provided by the NEA and may be inherently stressful, but are necessary (Passarelli & Taylor, 2023).

Being in a liminal state (a state of being in between and in transition) will make a person and a collective more vulnerable to the pull of a PEA or NEA. As described in the reasons for power curves and discontinuous distributions later in this chapter, moments of opportunity for change are more likely to become moments of restraint and surrender to the NEA. Negative emotions are stronger than positive ones (Baumeister, et al., 2001), and with the defensive negativity bias (Rozin & Royzman, 2001), the pull of the NEA is robust.

The PEA and NEA

Change occurs through a process of states and transitions. As just stated, the moments of transition can be called tipping points, or trigger points. Within the individual and our collectives, the two most profound tipping points are the PEA and NEA. They are psychophysiological states that become a "force around one's thinking, feeling, and behaviors" (Passarelli, 2014, p. 20), as shown in Table 3.1.

A more accurate depiction of the two attractors is made through the three axes that constitute each state. One dimension, or axis, is arousal of the Sympathetic Nervous System (SNS, stress) or the Parasympathetic Nervous System (PNS, renewal). A second dimension is activation of either of two neural networks: the Default Mode Network (DMN, what Anthony Jack calls the Empathic Network) or the Task Positive Network (TPN, what Anthony Jack calls the Analytic Network) (Jack, et al., 2012; Boyatzis, et al., 2015). The third dimension is the emotional state of positive or negative affect. These are graphically portrayed in Figure 3.2. Each dimension of the PEA or NEA contributes different power and effect to the state. Each state is a self-reinforcing condition until other stimuli or experiences change one or more of the constituent components (one or more of the continua portrayed as axes).

Self-regulating systems are inherently homeostatic. Over time, if the system is perfectly efficient, it will maintain itself. But humans are not efficient, and are exposed to input from myriad others and events (Ferber, 1999). Therefore,

Table 3.1 Components and Indicators of the Positive and Negative Emotional Attractors

	Positive Emotional Attractor (PEA)	Negative Emotional Attractor (NEA)
Physiological	Greater parasympathetic influence;	Greater sympathetic influence;
	Release of oxytocin and vasopressin associated with social bonding; Healthy immune system functioning	Release of epinephrine and norepinephrine to mobilize defenses; release of cortisol;
	Decreased blood pressure;	Increases pulse, blood pressure, and rate of breathing; compromised immune system
	Higher heart rate variability	Lower heart rate variability
Neurological	Default Mode Network (DMN); neurogenesis	Task Positive Network (TPN); Inhibited neurogenesis
Emotional	Positive affect: hope, joy, amusement, elation, compassion, caring, gratitude	Negative affect: defensiveness, guilt, shame, fear, anxiety
Cognitive	Enhanced working memory and perceptual openness;	Decreased executive functioning; Limited field vision and perception;
	Global attention;	Local attention;
	Promotion focus;	Prevention focus;
	Learning orientation	Performance orientation
Orientation	Possibilities, dreams, optimism	Problems, expectations, pessimism
Focal Capabilities	Strengths	Weaknesses
Primary Self Focus	Ideal Self or shared vision	Real Self or Ought Self
Learning Agenda	Excited about trying something	Should do, performance improvement plan
Experimentation/ Practice	Novelty, experiments Practice to mastery	Supposed to do Practice to comfort
Relationships	Resonant (in tune with each other)	Dissonant (out of sync or distant)

Source: Adapted from Boyatzis (2008) and Passarelli (2014).

in the course of normal events, and unless the PEA is actively maintained over time, a deterioration of the PEA state will cause a tipping point into the NEA state because of the relative strength of negative emotions and the necessity of defensive positions for survival (Baumeister, et al., 2001).

The actual moment of a tip between the two attractors is not likely to be experienced or consciously acknowledged as a continuous occurrence. It is more likely to be experienced as a discontinuous jump in state. A tip into the

PEA will often be experienced as energizing and adding to one's psychological resources. A tip into the NEA will often be experienced as deflating and draining resources, as described in ego depletion or conservation of resources theories (Hobfoll, 1989; Baumeister, et al., 1998; Fredrickson, 2001).

The process may emerge over time or be sudden. For example, when in an NEA state, the accumulation of events that are mildly PEA may eventually be sufficient to invoke a tipping point. The NEA may subside in intensity and move closer to the zero point in the graph, allowing one additional somewhat mild PEA experience to tip the person into a PEA state. A sudden but intense typically PEA event, such as the birth of a child, may also invoke a large shift into the PEA state. Triggering or invoking a tipping point can occur through any of the components of the PEA and NEA. Milkman (2021) contended that the best time to start a change is when you have an opportunity for a fresh start, often signaled by an event in ICT terms that tips a person into the PEA.

Sympathetic versus Parasympathetic Nervous System (Stress versus Renewal)

The Autonomic Nervous System has three parts: sympathetic, parasympathetic, and enteric (Insel, 1997; Schulkin, 1999). The sympathetic (SNS) is also known as the body's stress response. The parasympathetic (PNS) can be called the renewal response, and has the opposite effects on the human body and mind. The Enteric Nervous System (ENS) is the system of nervous, hormonal, and endocrine secretions for the set of nerves from your brain stem to your gut. Its functions are being studied and understood anew as current research emerges. It may, in the future, help us to understand what "gut instinct" really is.

The SNS aids the human with its defense against threats and specific functions of adaptation, like decision-making and problem solving (Sapolsky, 2004). It is also our response to negative experiences or emotions. The SNS immobilizes aspects of a human's functioning in order to reallocate resources to those areas needed for protection and to ensure continued functioning. For example, the SNS suppresses our ability to engage in effective communication due to limiting facial expression, eye gaze, hand gesture, and listening abilities (Porges, 2003). In contrast to the health benefits associated with positive emotions and PNS arousal, prolonged periods of negative emotion and SNS arousal can be harmful to our health and well-being (McEwen, 1998).

In humans, the SNS is aroused when we feel that we are in danger, when we feel something is important, when something is uncertain, or when we are being evaluated (Segerstrom & Miller, 2004). Oddly, such experiences or events do not have to occur to arouse the SNS. Merely anticipating any of them can do it (Segerstrom & Miller, 2004; Sapolsky, 2004). Some of the experiences invoke a mild SNS activation and others can be acute, while some are of brief duration and others are chronic (Segerstrom & Miller, 2004), but they all activate the SNS. The practical definition of stress is said to be the activation of the SNS or its main physiological components.

Arousing a person's obligations, or what was called Ought Selves in the previous chapter, almost certainly arouses the SNS. Whether by stimulating awareness of one's obligations or expectations of others, an Ought Self invokes stress. In this way, it may inhibit forward progress toward a personal vision or dream, or openness to learning and change. It is the dynamic underlying the dysfunctions caused by specific goal setting as documented in the performance versus learning goal orientation research (VanderWalle, et al., 1999). Even something as normal as problem solving evokes cortisol and the SNS response in young adults (Gilbert, et al., 2017).

Current life and work demands on a person at work and at home, and societal events (such as war, terrorism, pandemics), create an overload of stress. The chronic presence of mild stressful (i.e., annoying) experiences results in compromising our immune system (Sapolsky, 2004; Igic, et al., 2017), limiting our perceptual ability and awareness of events (Boyatzis, et al., 2006), and impairs our creativity and cognitive functioning (Sapolsky, 2004), which makes us feel poorly (Boyatzis, et al., 2006).

The most significant challenge lay in the dosage of stress a person experiences. The accumulation creates a positive feedback loop in which events may be interpreted as threatening when in fact they are not. The frequency and consistency (i.e., lack of variety) of stress experiences contribute to strain that perpetuates the effects on a person's cognitive, emotional, and perceptual performance (Gianaros & Jennings, 2018).

Typical experiences that invoke SNS include:

Intrapersonal experiences
- Sleep disruption or insufficient sleep (Brosschot, et al., 2007)
- Delays in getting to or returning from work (Koslowsky, et al., 2013)
- Malfunctioning technology (Tarafdar, et al., 2007)
- Feeling sick or ill, a pandemic (Selye, 1974)
- Worrying that something will not turn out well (Pieper, et al., 2007)

Interpersonal experiences

- Helping family members get ready for the day and other similar moments at home (Bolger, et al., 1989; Randall & Bodenmann, 2009)
- Arguing with a spouse or partner at home (Bolger, et al., 1989)
- Unpleasant conversations or emotions expressed at a family meal (Story & Neumark-Sztainer, 2005)
- Conflict and frustrating experiences at work (Friedman, et al., 2000)
- Performance pressures at work or school, as well as having others watching you or evaluating you at school or work (McIntyre, et al., 2008; Caplan & Jones, 1975)
- Being angry at someone (Motowidlo, et al., 1986)
- Someone yelling or shouting at you (Keashly, 1997)
- Automobile accidents (Murray, et al., 2002)
- Work role conflict (Morris & Koch (1979)

Acute stress is aroused by life-threatening events, being in the midst of a natural disaster (a hurricane, monsoon, or tornado), being physically attacked, witnessing mob violence, the death of a loved one, a financial crisis, or the loss of a job. For most, acute stress experiences are not everyday occurrences.

Activation of the PNS ameliorates and reverses the effects of the SNS. The PNS has been shown to stimulate renewal by improving the functioning of a person's immune system (Boyatzis, et al., 2006), stimulating neurogenesis (i.e., growing new neurons from selected stem cells in the adult human brain) (Erikson, et al., 1998), and enhancing cognitive functioning (Sapolsky, 2004). Arousal of the PNS is associated with an increase in vagal tone (Kok, et al., 2013). Taken together, the PNS and SNS are a negative feedback system (Janig, 2006) within a hierarchy, where one is relatively dominant at any one point in time (Gianaros & Jennings, 2018). Either system operates in homeostasis (Gianaros & Jennings, 2018), so a trigger event or tipping point is needed to shift to the other hormonal system.

The PNS supports what has been called our "rest and digest" functions, immune system, cardiovascular health, and the parts of the neuroendocrine system (Uchino, et al., 1996). The PNS also supports social engagement. Arousal of the PNS arouses the vagus nerve and consequently triggers the release of a number of hormones, including oxytocin in women and vasopressin in men (Insel, 1997; Schulkin, 1999; Kemp & Guastella, 2011). It is the secretion of these hormones at this dosage level that is largely responsible for the health benefits commonly associated with positive emotions, including general well-being (Heaphy & Dutton, 2008), improved immune system functioning (Mahoney, et al., 2002), faster physical recovery following surgery (Carver & Scheier, 1993), lower risk of angina and heart attacks (Kubzansky, et al., 2001), and lower risk of depression (Davis, et al., 1998). Increases in vagal tone will help positive social connections and increase autonomic flexibility (Kok, et al., 2013; Kok, et al., 2013). Given these effects, the PNS is literally a renewal process for the person, and, as we shall illustrate, for our collectives (Boyatzis, et al., 2006; Boyatzis & McKee, 2005; Boyatzis, et al., 2019).

Male and female behavioral responses to stress may appear different, in part as a result of the hormones aroused (Taylor, et al., 2000). It has been observed that societal sexist practices, like expecting females to be caretakers of young children, may dispose females to seek others or provide comfort to others in times of stress (Taylor, et al., 2000). The primary hormone responsible for this "tending and befriending" is oxytocin (Taylor, et al., 2000).

Oxytocin also plays an important role in learning and neural plasticity (Doidge, 2007). It encourages bonding with others and stimulates the nucleus accumbens (Ross, et al., 2009). This can result in an increased feeling of trust in others (Insel, 1997; Kosfeld, et al., 2005) by the above-mentioned process, and interrupting or extinguishing avoidance and negative affective connections. The latter appears to be enhanced by secretion of the Brain Derived Neurotropic Factor (BNDF) and Nerve Growth Factor (NGF) in the hippocampus (Doidge, 2007; Hennigan, et al., 2007).

The nature of openness invoked by the PNS is not the trait of openness, but a state of being increasingly aware of one's surroundings, including other people. It is a noticing and awareness of others, new ideas, and perceptions. It is aided by the expansion of one's peripheral vision. In this sense, it is openness as a willingness to consider alternatives.

Some techniques, like cognitive reappraisal, can invoke a tipping point by changing the perception of the experience—that is, recode the threat and not invoke the SNS, or not arouse it as severely. Such reappraisals take time and repetition to learn and adapt. Knowing and understanding which day-to-day experiences arouse the SNS can help in determining when and how often a renewal activity could engage the PNS and reduce the allostatic load (i.e., wear and tear on the human).

Experiences that invoke renewal (PNS) include:

Intrapersonal experiences
- Walking in nature (Park, et al., 2010; Bratman, et al., 2015; Capaldi, et al., 2014)
- Gardening, such as an allotment garden in a community-dwelling (Hawkins, et al., 2013)

- Meditating (Good, et al., 2015; Goleman & Davidson, 2017)
- Prayer (Ferguson, et al., 2010; Koenig, 2012; Galanter, et al., 2016)
- Modest physical exercise, including yoga and tai chi (Wall, 2005; Bijlani, et al., 2005; Blumenthal, et al., 2005)

Interpersonal experiences
- An enjoyable meal with family (Story & Neumark-Sztainer, 2005; Fruh, et al., 2011)
- Helping someone or volunteering (Boyatzis, et al., 2006; Kram & Hall, 1989)
- Caring for others and feeling cared for (Insel, 1997; Sapolsky, 2004; Goleman, 2003)
- Caring for and playing with pets (Miller, et al., 2015; Powell, et al., 2019)
- Reflecting upon, or discussing one's greater purpose in life (Schaefer & Coleman, 1992; Steger, 2012).
- Laughter with others (Greene, et al., 2017; Sliter, et al., 2014; Wijewardena, et al., 2017)
- Quality time and being in love with spouses or partners (Lapp, et al., 2010; Berry & Worthington, 2001)
- Playing with a child, and in general, being playful (Qian & Yarnal, 2011; Magnuson & Barnett, 2013).

The intensity of a person's stress arousal is dependent on the intensity of the stressful experiences and degree of threat perceived, not necessarily the real threat. Similarly, the intensity of the renewal arousal is dependent on the intensity of the experiences and the frequency. The intensity, duration, and timing of either can be thought of as dosage. When the dosage of renewal exceeds the dosage of stress, a person feels more engaged, has a greater sense of well-being, is more resilient and more empathic, less anxious and depressed, and more satisfied with life and their work as assessed with the Personal Sustainability Index (Boyatzis, et al., 2021; see Boyatzis, et al., 2021 for the test or the Personal Sustainability Index in the appendix of this book).

Furthermore, since the moments of renewal have their major benefit in the interruption of the hormonal secretions of the stress experiences, more frequent, briefer doses of renewal will more likely help a person balance their state during any given day. The growing research on micro-breaks at work has shown that they lead to more engagement (Kim, et al., 2018; Kim, et al., 2022). The key to renewing regularly may be 10- to 15-minute moments spread throughout a day. This is the process that enables triggers of renewal to sustain effort at change (Goldsmith & Reiter, 2015).

The frequency of renewal can also be understood from theoretical perspectives of conservation of resources theory (Hobfoll, 1989), ego depletion theory (Baumeister, et al., 1998), and effort recovery theory (Meijman & Mulder, 1998). In each of these theories, the degree of renewal needed is determined by the degree of stress activated. The result is that the person has resources and energy in relationships, work, and life to feel more engaged, excited, and satisfied.

The experience of gratitude and compassion not only activates the PEA (Boyatzis, et al., 2019; Boyatzis, Smith & Beveridge, 2013), but actually replenishes internal resources (Schabram & Heng, 2022). Compassion becomes a natural antidote to negative and destructive emotions, as described in detail in a marvelous series of conversations between Daniel Goleman and the Dalai Lama (Goleman, 2003). Furthermore, self-focused compassion helps with the experience of exhaustion, while other-focused compassion ameliorates cynicism (Schabram & Heng, 2022).

In a series of studies, it was shown that the variety of renewal experiences in a given week, as contrasted to the variety of stress experiences, had the same effect on engagement, satisfaction, sense of well-being, empathy, and resilience, and lowered depression and anxiety (Boyatzis, et al., 2021). Maybe, as the saying goes, variety really is the spice of life. The variety may create a sense of novelty and increase interest and excitement in life or work (Schweizer, 2006). If the intensity of renewal and stress experiences is low, there is not likely to be much variety or much impact of variety. In addition, if a person repeatedly chooses or experiences one type of activity as a renewal arousal, there is not merely less variety, but it may become a habit and lose some of its beneficial effect as well as be more difficult to change in the future (Kanfer & Goldstein, 1991).

In summary, arousal of the PNS (renewal) has many functions. It stimulates growth, openness, thriving and flourishing, higher cognitive functioning, neurogenesis, and higher immune functioning. Meanwhile, arousal of the SNS (stress) stimulates focus, helps decision-making and meeting deadlines, and survival, but also increased defensiveness and reduced peripheral vision, and the opposite of all of the beneficial effects of renewal.

Neural Networks: DMN and TPN

Of the many neural networks in our brain that enable a human to function from the motor neuron network, mirror neuron network, salience network, frontoparietal control network, and so forth, there are two that affect many of the activities in which we engage at home and at work: the Default Mode Network (DMN) and the Task Positive Network (TPN) (Jack, et al., 2013). The DMN is activated when a human engages in creative thought and openness to new ideas (Andrews-Hanna, et al., 2010; Raichle, et al., 2001; Mars, et al., 2012; Van Overwalle, 2011; Raichle & Snyder, 2007). It is also crucial to emotional self-awareness (Ochsner, et al., 2005; Schilbach, Eickhoff, et al., 2008) and social cognition (Jack, et al., 2012; Mars, et al., 2012; Schilbach, et al., 2008; Lieberman, 2013; Eisenberger & Cole, 2012). The DMN includes the simultaneous activation of the medial prefrontal cortex (mPFC), the medial parietal cortex (MPC), posterior cingulate cortex (PCC), and the right temporoparietal junction (rTPJ) (Jack, et al., 2012; Buckner, et al., 2008; Corbetta, et al., 2005).

Activation of the DMN is thought to be directly linked to arousal of the PNS through one of its constituent components, the ventromedial prefrontal cortex (vmPFC, Eisenberger & Cole, 2012). Neural networks are a set of regions of the brain that are co-activated. Hormonal systems such as the SNS and PNS are part of the nervous system, as mentioned earlier, but involve secretion of hormones and other organs of the body, not just the brain. This is why Anthony Jack refers to it as the Empathic Network (Jack, 2024). In a follow-up replication study of Jack, et al. (2012), the vmPFC was significantly activated in a random effects analysis by two or three half-hour PEA coaching sessions, in contrast to one or no PEA coaching session (Jack, et al., 2023). In a meta-analysis of 43 studies, Beissner, Meissner, Bär, & Napadow (2013) showed that the TPN was engaged in cognitive tasks and had direct links to SNS arousal. Meanwhile, they also showed that in affective and somatosensory tasks, the PNS was aroused. The effects noted were significant but not completely overlapping, so as to suggest that activation of the TPN and DMN were not the same as arousal of the SNS and PNS.

Meanwhile, the TPN enables a human to analyze things, manipulate abstract symbols such as numbers, solve problems, make decisions, and focus attention. This is why Anthony Jack refers to it as the Analytic Network (Jack, 2024). It is comprised of parts of the dorsal attention system (Fox, et al., 2005; Jack, et al., 2013), the frontoparietal control network (Vincent, et al., 2008), and the ventral attention network (Fox, et al., 2006, Kubit & Jack, 2013). The TPN is activated when an activity or tasks require focused attention, working memory, logical reasoning, mathematical reasoning, and causal and mechanical reasoning (Duncan & Owen, 2000; Fox, et al., 2005; Owen, et al., 2005; Shulman, et al., 1997; Van Overwalle, 2011).

These two neural networks are antagonistic (Buckner, et al., 2008; Raichle & Snyder, 2007; Corbetta, et al., 2005; Jack, et al., 2013; Jack, 2024; Uddin, et al., 2009); that is, they suppress each other. The challenge to someone needing to use both networks is to learn how to toggle or switch between the networks easily, and appropriately to the situation at hand (Jack, et al., 2013; Boyatzis, et al., 2014).

The relationship between the SNS and the TPN appears to be less clear-cut than that between the PNS and the DMN. While there tend to be few instances (if any) when a person would be in the SNS and the DMN, we do believe it is possible to experience positive emotions and PNS arousal associated with tasks that require the TPN (e.g., data analysis, solving equations). While the relationship between the NEA and TPN has not yet been systematically tested, there is a growing body of evidence that these two constructs are tightly coupled (Matthews, et al., 2004). For example, negative emotions have been found to enhance memory accuracy (Kensinger, 2007), a task associated with the TPN. Negative emotions have been linked to paying greater attention to detail and focusing on the task at hand (Luce, et al., 1997), which are also functions of the TPN.

The neurological distinctions shown in Table 3.1 have been validated in two fMRI studies (Jack, et al., 2013; Jack, et al., 2023), as have the hormonal distinctions in two other studies (see Howard, 2015 and Passarelli, 2015). The cognitive process distinctions listed in Table 3.1, with the exception of memory and field of vision, were supported by Jack, Passarelli, and Boyatzis (2023). The relationship distinctions listed in Table 3.1 were supported in Boyatzis, et al. (2012) in a study of neural activations from follower–leader relationships.

In summary, when the DMN or the Empathic Network is activated, it enables a person to scan their environment and be open to new ideas, to others, and to emotions (Jack, et al., 2013; Jack, 2024). Meanwhile, when the TPN or the Analytic Network is activated, it enables a person to be abstract, use symbolic logic, make rational decisions, focus, and solve specific problems (Jack, et al., 2013; Jack, 2024). Jack's theory is called Opposing Domains or Opposing Poles of Reason (Jack, 2024). It offers a clearer distinction about these antagonistic processes in the brain than Kahneman's (2011) dual process theory. As Jack points out (2024), Analytic Networks can be fast or slow, just as emotional networks can be. Although proposed as an alternate way of conceptualizing these processes, many parts of Porges's et al. (1994) and Proges's (2003) polyvagal theory have not been tested, even though the vagal nerve clearly plays a crucial role in the PNS.

Positive Versus Negative Emotions

Emotions have been defined as "multicomponent response tendencies that unfold over relatively short time spans . . . [resulting in a] cascade of response tendencies [that] manifest across loosely coupled component systems, such as subjective experience, facial expression, cognitive processing, and physiological changes" (Fredrickson, 2001, p. 218). They create a tone or color the perception of people and events. Positive emotion refers to discrete emotions that we use to describe or express our response to a pleasant or desirable experience. Examples of positive emotions include joy, interest, amusement, and love (Fredrickson, 2001, 2009). Examples of negative emotions are fear, anxiety, sadness, anger, disgust, contempt, frustration, jealousy, envy, and despair (Levenson, 1992; Fredrickson, 2001, 2009). For a more complete discussion of emotions, Heaphy and Dutton (2008) offer a review of a broad array of emotions.

Positive feelings and the related experience of optimism have strong effects on the body and interaction with the other axes of the PEA and NEA. For example, in a study of 124 first-year law students at a major university, the researchers assessed their positive feelings about the law program five different times during the year (Segerstrom & Sephton, 2010). They found that as the law students' positive feelings rose, so did the functioning of their immune system as measured through cell-mediated immunity, and the reverse was associated with a decrease in immune system functioning. Further, randomized control group studies of invoking positive emotions through loving kindness meditation showed profound effects on a person's physical health (Kok, et al., 2013). Consistent with results of previous meta-analyses, positive affect predicts job performance and organizational citizenship behavior, while negative affect predicts counterproductive work behavior (Kaplan, et al., 2009)

Baumeister, et al. (2001) argued that this is a necessary function of human beings because negative emotions allow humans to be highly adaptable and facilitate human survival. Without surviving, there can be no thriving (Boyatzis, et al., 2021). The distinctions being made here are not that one end of each axis is good and the other is bad, but each are necessary, and each have different effects on change and its durability (Passarelli & Taylor, 2023). When a person adopts a negative view of events or people, their negativity becomes a trait-like characteristic (Shackman, Tromp, et al., 2016). The negativity becomes a perceptual habit. Experiencing positive affect proportionally opens a person's attentional spectrum and reduces selective filtering (Rowe, et al., 2007).

It is worth noting that while some scholars claim that positive and negative affect are two separate dimensions (Cacioppo & Bernsten, 1994), other scholars contend that positive and negative emotions can be treated as polar opposites. For example, in the circumplex model of emotions (Posner, et al., 2005), emotions consist of arousal and valence. Arousal represents the vertical axis and valence represents the horizontal axis. The center of the model shows zero valence and medium levels of arousal. Meanwhile, the evaluative space model of emotions, which is offered as a counterproposal to the circumplex model, also contends "that positivity and negativity have antagonistic effects. Positivity fosters approach; negativity fosters avoidance. . . . Though positivity and negativity may often be characterized by reciprocal activation, they may also be characterized by uncoupled activation, co-activation, or co-inhibition" (Larsen, et al., 2001, p. 686). The same authors went on to summarize that "most of our data are consistent with the circumplex prediction that polar opposite emotions are mutually exclusive" (Larsen, et al., 2001, p. 693.)

An alternative view was offered by Russell and Carroll (1999). They argued that an orthogonal dimension of degree of activation was needed in affective models. Their position was supported by Posner, Russell, and Peterson (2005) with the development of the circumplex model of emotions and was a similar contention by Gottman, et al. (2002) in the creation of a mathematical model of strange attractors describing the emotional states of married couples.

The field of positive psychology has capitalized on the benefits and focuses on positive emotions. Attributes of positive emotion that appear to be particularly relevant to the PEA include higher levels of optimism about the future (Bower & Forgas, 2001), greater perceptual openness (Fredrickson & Branigan, 2005; Talarico, et al., 2009), and openness to behavior change (Janig & Habler, 1999), as well as openness to new experiences and people (Fredrickson, 2009). Additionally, positive emotional states increase the likelihood of altruistic, helpful, cooperative, and conciliatory behavior (Barsade & Gibson, 2007; Insel, 1997) and improved decision-making (Chuang & Lin, 2007).

Alternatives or Antagonistic States

Taken together, these three axes or dimensions of the PEA and NEA provide differing states and resulting experiences of a person or the collection of people in them. They appear in much of the research and theorizing as antagonistic conditions where one chases out, precludes, or suppresses the other. It does seem from the research that a person cannot experience both ends of any of the three dimensions at the same moment. Therefore, it is likely that people cannot experience PEA and NEA at the same time. They appear to be ends of a dialectical tension. Each needs the other, like a yin–yang relationship.

The also means that each state has beneficial and deleterious effects on a person's functioning (Passarelli & Taylor, 2023). While PEA helps a person be more open to new ideas and change, the NEA helps a person focus on cognitive tasks, problem solving, and making decisions. The PEA enables us to scan the environment and be aware of our context, while the NEA enables us to identify a deficit and move quickly to remedy it.

In her earlier work on positivity, Fredrickson used team advocacy versus inquiry and self versus other as two axes (Fredrickson & Losada, 2005). Although the mathematics in that article was later criticized, Fredrickson's continuing work on positivity, as part of her broaden and build theory of change, has earned substantial support from legions of studies (Fredrickson, 2009). Gottman, et al. (2002) used positive and negative affect and intensity of expression as two dimensions to their model of change. They also had congruence of influence styles of a dyadic couple (husbands and wives in his studies) as a third dimension.

This duality appears to replicate in a wide variety of theories with substantial research. The PEA and NEA are remarkably similar to Higgins's (1997) promotion versus prevention self-regulatory focus. A prevention focus invokes self-control, the TPN, and becomes an energy-deflating experience in the NEA (Higgins, 1997), as they appear compatible with Dweck's (2006) growth versus fixed mindset. The seemingly perpetual models of relational or interpersonal interaction versus task or individual activity are further confirmation that although various scholars may not have made the leap or connections to neural networks or hormonal systems, these theories or models reflect the underlying differences inherent in the PEA and NEA (Boyatzis, et al., 2015).

The challenge is how to toggle or cycle between these states, whether for the leader, helper, or parent wanting to invoke or stimulate a PEA in someone or in a group that is in the NEA. Given any situation, there is also the issue of which state might be needed or more appropriate to the situational demands, tasks, or conditions. In a budget crisis, PEA of a management team is needed to create hope and open their cognitive abilities to identify options. But NEA is needed to help them do the analysis and sort through the options to find the best alternative.

Conceptualizing the sustainability of people at work led a set of scholars to consider a larger framework of sustainable work organizations and systems (Barnes, et al., 2023). They claimed that entropic forces are threats to survival. Many of the NEA and in particular the SNS experiences listed in this chapter were cited as examples. They created "restricted employee sustainability theory" to encapsulate the alternative to entropic forces which they classified as maintenance, growth and generative activities. The balancing of these three types of activities allows for coping and recovery, as well as growing beyond a current state and therefore sustainability enterprises. This theory emerged from a comprehensive meta-analysis and applies a resource allocation perspective to PEA versus NEA activities. The entropic forces deplete a person's energy or shared energy in collectives like the NEA state. The maintenance, growth, and generative activities enhance and add to a person's or collective's energy like the PEA state.

Creating Tipping Points to Sustained, Desired Change

> *Principle 8: As a fractal theory, ICT describes sustained, desired change at all levels of human endeavor from individual to dyads, teams, organizations, communities, countries, and global processes.*

Although the phenomenon is the same, stimulating, invoking, or inspiring a tipping point into the PEA will seem different at the various levels of human collectives. Examining the effect of PEA and NEA at various levels of human collectives supports the nature of ICT as a multilevel fractal theory of sustained, desired change, as shown in Figure 3.3.

Invoking the PEA Tipping Points in Leadership, Coaching, and Healthcare Dyads

To increase the efficacy of healthcare and reduce the cost, physicians and nurses chase the desired outcome of treatment adherence. That is, does the patient do the activities, take the drugs, change habits and lifestyle appropriately to speed recovery from the surgery or illness, or better maintenance of a chronic condition? Khawaja (2010) showed that beyond the many factors medical science has identified that help treatment adherence, it is still painfully low. It is about 50% for Type II diabetics worldwide, 50% for patients following orthopedic surgery, and a similar 50% for those having had coronary bypass surgery. Khawaja (2010) found that the patient's perception of the degree to which they and the physician have a shared vision (i.e., sense of purpose), not treatment goals, mediated the effects of all other factors in improving or increasing treatment adherence. The perception of the shared vision helped

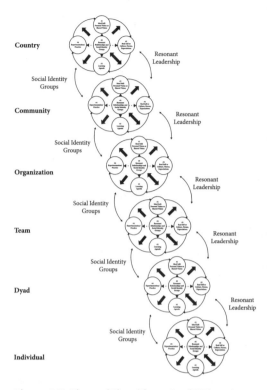

Figure 3.3 The multilevel fractals of PEA and NEA within Intentional Change Theory
Source: Boyatzis (2008, 2015).

the patient experience a PEA state in the midst of trying to deal with Type II diabetes for the rest of their lives.

The specific behaviors—what might be termed micro-actions—of a medical student diagnosing various presenting conditions in "standardized patients" in their third year of medical school revealed a clear benefit of PEA acts (Dyck, 2018). Dyck (2018) developed a code for PEA and NEA actions during the 15- to 20-minute sessions with standardized patients. Standardized patients are people paid to enact a specific malady or condition for hundreds of medical students in their third year. They become quite good at acting their role and condition. The standardized patient then writes an evaluation of the medical student following the session. A supervising physician reviews the standardized patient's summary and writes their own evaluation of the session.

With the benefit of high-definition video recordings of these sessions, Dyck (2018) created a code from one cohort of medical students and then applied it to the following year's cohort. Examples of PEA actions were smiling at the patient, placing a gentle hand on the patient's shoulder, and asking if they were cold and needed a blanket. Examples of NEA actions were facing the computer while taking the patient's history (such as typing and not looking at the patient), asking abrupt questions, and showing impatience and the need to hurry things along. In a multivariate analysis (a structured equation model), the standardized patients' evaluation of the medical student was significantly predicted by the number of PEA versus NEA acts during a session. The NEA actions were not predictive. The supervising physician's evaluation was predicted by both the PEA and the NEA actions independently. An interesting side point: the medical student's entrance exam, the MCAT, showed a significant negative prediction to the standardized patient's evaluation of effectiveness.

In coaching or helping others to be open to learning and change, two fMRI studies and two hormonal studies made it clear that certain actions of the coach can invoke the PEA in the client (Jack, et al., 2012; Jack, et al., 2023; Howard, 2015; Passarelli, 2015). In these two hormonal studies, coaches created a PEA stimulation by asking the clients in 60- to 90-minute sessions about their "ideal life and work, if everything were perfect, 10–15 years in the future." Howard's (2015) subjects were 49-year-old dentists and dental professionals, such as periodontists or endodontists. The question about their ideal future invoked positive emotions, while questions about how to remedy deficits in their emotional and social intelligence behavior with others exaggerated negative emotions. In a variation of that design, with professionals in their midthirties attending a variety of part-time graduate programs, Passarelli (2015) replicated the affective difference Howard found, but also showed that those in the PEA conditions bounced back in terms of physiological measures from initial stress indicators to PNS indicators.

The two fMRI studies examined 30-minute sessions with undergraduates asking about their desired future (i.e., the PEA condition) versus how they were doing in their courses (the NEA condition). In the first study, Jack, et al. (2012) showed that a number of components of the DMN were activated in fMRI screenings of video statements by the coach who conducted their PEA conversation, in contrast to video statements by the coach who conducted their NEA conversations. It revealed that asking about a person's dream or vision stimulated the PEA even three to five days later when going through the scanner. This included a dramatic difference in activation of the lateral visual cortex. It is worth noting that the two coaches were randomly assigned to clients and randomly assigned to whether they were doing the PEA or the NEA condition, and clients were randomly assigned as to whether they received the PEA condition or NEA condition first.

The second study used the same basic design, with the same PEA and NEA conditions and video statements by the coaches, while in the fMRI scanner a few days later (Jack, et al., 2023). Again, the two coaches were randomly assigned to conditions. In other words, the subjects were randomly assigned to one of five conditions: (1) a half an hour NEA oriented coaching session and then the fMRI scan a few days later; or (2) the NEA session and an hour of writing a personal vision and then the fMRI scan a few days later; or (3) the NEA session and one half hour PEA coaching session on the next day, then the fRMI scan a few days later; or (4) the NEA session and two half hour PEA coaching sessions on two more sequential days, then the fRMI scan a few days later; or (5) the NEA session and three half hour PEA coaching session on three more sequential days, then the fRMI scan a few days later (Jack, et al., 2023).

The earlier findings about invoking the PEA versus NEA in terms of neural regions of interest and parts of key neural networks were replicated on the whole (Boyatzis & Jack, 2018; Jack, et al., 2023; Passarelli, et al., 2014). In addition, the vmPFC, which is key to interpersonal relationships, empathy, openness to behavior change, and part of the DMN (Tompson, et al., 2015), was activated with two or three PEA sessions. It was deactivated by one NEA session, and only barely activated by the writing condition or one PEA. The need for "oversampling" the PEA (i.e., having more PEA moments than NEA moments) was supported.

Invoking the PEA has the same effect on leader–follower relationships. In studying 180 leader–follower dyads involving Arab executives, Farraq (2022) found that two sources of PEA arousal helped. He showed that the leader's Ideal Self (personal vision) had a contagious PEA effect on followers' engagement and their perception of the leader's effectiveness. The effects were further strengthened (i.e., mediated) by another source of PEA, the degree of mutually perceived, shared PEA in their relationship (shared vision, compassion, and energy, discussed in detail in Chapter 7) on increased leader effectiveness and both leader and follower engagement.

The degree of perceived PEA in the relationship between a coach and a leader of a major bank showed a direct effect on increasing a leader's career satisfaction and their personal vision (Van Oosten, et al., 2019). Shared vision as perceived by the subordinate in their relationship with their manager had a similar effect on employee engagement (Docherty, 2020). In an interesting twist, Docherty (2020) found this effect regardless of whether the manager was providing feedback that was positive or negative.

Invoking PEA Tipping Points in Teams and Organizations

When interactions with colleagues invoke PEA tipping points through certain qualities in their relationships, there are positive results in various forms of teams. Studying knowledge worker teams in manufacturing and consulting companies, Mahon, Taylor, and Boyatzis (2014) found that the degree of shared vision amplified positive effects of shared emotional intelligence competencies observed in each other (i.e., not self-assessed) on increased engagement. Research engineers showed dramatically increased engagement when they perceived a shared vision (not goals) within their project teams (Boyatzis, et al., 2017). Neff (2015) and Miller (2023) found similar effects on family councils in family businesses. Shared vision enhanced financial performance of the family business over five years (Neff, 2015) and enhanced engagement and development of the next generation leader of the family business (Miller, 2014, 2023).

Inviting a PEA tipping point can occur through three related processes. First, a leader, executive, or key person can repeatedly demonstrate PEA when interacting with others. Over time it may have an effect through modeling, as others begin to adopt the same behavior (Bandura, 1986). At some point, the PEA acts may become norms within the organizational climate and culture (Schneider & Barbara, 2014). A second path to more PEA is through building relationships in coalitions within the team based on PEA experiences like shared vision, compassion, and energy (Boyatzis, et al., 2015). A third path can occur through emotional contagion within organizations or communities (Hazy & Boyatzis, 2015).

A leader modeling PEA was experienced during an observational study of a joint consulting company and US Navy team on board FFGs (Oliver Hazard Perry–class guided missile fast frigate fleet under the command of Rear Admiral Michael Kalleres) when studying command effectiveness (McBer & Company, 1985). I was on one of the teams and observed these effects first-hand.

One of the ships was on a routine arming mission, loading various forms of munitions and returning to their home port. During the return they were testing a relatively new anti-missile defense for the FFGs, the Phalanx. It was a defensive weapon that fired shells faster than anything that had been created up to that point. After a run of the test firing, the Phalanx jammed. The Commanding Officer (CO) immediately got "on the horn" (the ship's broadcast system) and congratulated the team for firing the Phalanx longer than had ever been recorded. Of course, they had to diagnose what caused the jamming and write an extensive situation report on it. Instead of seeing it as just a failure and blaming the firing team, the CO created a PEA moment and dealt with the problem afterward in a timely manner. The morale was in a PEA state, which meant that the officers and crew were open to new ideas—and in this case, figuring out what went wrong with the Phalanx and whether it was a machine or human operator problem, and then fixing it, instead of merely being defensive.

The quality of relationships and interactions with the leader and among the executives has a clear effect on stimulating PEA or NEA tipping points on others and organizational performance. Among executives of high-tech firms, Kendall (2016) showed that the quality of relationships in terms of shared vision, compassion, and energy predicted product and process innovation and relative market presence of these innovations. Among community college presidents, Babu (2016) showed a similar effect on faculty engagement and perception of the president's leadership effectiveness. Among mid-level managers in major Latin American companies, the same dynamic was found: that when relationships with their colleagues were characterized by more shared vision, shared compassion, and shared energy, there was greater engagement and effectiveness (Martinez, et al., 2021).

In professional organizations, the quality of relationships of executives invoked PEA and greater organizational citizenship and engagement for both physician executives (Quinn, 2015) and IT managers (Pittenger, 2015). Clayton (2014) even showed that greater shared vision increased championing behavior during mergers and acquisitions and increased the likelihood of their success, which is quite rare.

A variety of organizational development theories postulated the classic task versus people/process matrix, then appealed and tried to train managers to learn to do both (Blake & Mouton, 1964). Not knowing the antagonistic nature of the PEA and NEA and its underlying oppositional factors of neural networks and hormonal systems that suppress each other, they unintentionally misdirected readers and clients into chasing a somewhat impossible aspiration.

As mentioned earlier, Argyris (1985) and Senge (1990) took a dramatically different approach and encouraged challenging basic assumptions and an orientation toward learning. Both encouraged more openness to new ideas and PEA. They did not fall into the task versus people/process trap. In fact, Argyris (1985) build on his earlier work, showing how important better interpersonal relationships were to new and innovative organizational change. Even Skinner's behavioral reinforcement model focusing on positive reinforcement grew from empirical observations without knowing the underlying biological mechanisms that enabled it to work (Burke & Noumair, 2015).

Many of the organizational-level change theories contended that the process began with dissatisfaction or the realization of a problem, then proceeded to unfreezing via Lewin's classic "unfreeze-change-refreeze" model (Lewin, 1947) and later Schein (2010) and a diagnostic need for change. These initial steps were more likely to activate the NEA, then predispose the next step of feedback to feel like imposition of Ought Self and more NEA (Burke & Noumair, 2015). The various approaches to planned change, from Bennis, et al. (1962), Weisbord (1976), and Lippitt, et al. (1958), made the same mistake. It was not a surprise that a stream of research began to focus on resistance to change as a culprit of inertia. From ICT, the activation of the NEA is what caused the lack of progress or sustainability of change efforts.

The persistent arousal of NEA explains results from a study of 530 corporate restructuring projects (Gilmore, et al., 1997). They found a decrease in commitment to the organization and morale with longer work weeks. But they also found an increase in productivity and quality and perceived competence. None of these effects were tested for durability over long periods of time. Other consequences were a renewed ambivalence to authority, polarized images of the new being good and the old bad, and disappointment and blame as a new norm and what they called behavioral inversion (a reassertion of the hierarchy). What began with the intent of building corporate cultures that were more entrepreneurial, vision-driven, team-based, and adaptive resulted in the conclusion that "unanticipated side effects of culture change can undermine and even defeat the change process" (Gilmore, et al., 1997, p. 174).

The unintended, repeated arousal of the NEA had negative effects. Armenakis and Bedeian (1999) described how initial levels of inertia and stress affected the lack of durability of change efforts. In a review of 79 studies from 1948 to 2007, recipients of the change proejcts showed that negative reactions included increased stress, job insecurity, perceived unfairness, anxiety, and the intention to resist and quit amid efforts to cope. While there were some positive effects, such some increased satisfaction, commitment, and organizational citizenship behavior, these were affected by recipients' greater tolerance for ambiguity, more internal locus of control, and openness to new experiences and conscientiousness.

The consequences of invoking the NEA repeatedly is a narrowing of perspective. The "not invented here" syndrome is one such result of preoccupation with financials, performance measurement, and repeated arousal of the NEA (Antons & Piller, 2015). "That's not the way we do it here" is another variation of this reaction. The result is a narrowing of focus to achieve the specific performance goals or financial metrics. But it also places perceptual filters on what any person can observe or notice in competitors or other stakeholders. In too many cases, the organization develops norms that support and justify such responses and perpetuate cutting the members off from scanning their larger environment for possible adaptations or innovations.

The narrowing of the focus resulting from an NEA arousal could be a wake-up call—a type of shock into awareness that things are not going well as compared to the past or competitors. This provocation of awareness of a need for change can only help in the short term. Once awareness is established that a problem exists, the movement needs to shift into the PEA quickly for context and larger sense of purpose. Otherwise, individuals or collectives respond defensively and cope or CYA behavior with minimizing effort. The result is either a poor resolution or an effort that is not sustainable.

Inviting the PEA in Communities and Collective Action

The role of invoking a PEA tipping point in collective action was nowhere more strongly made then by Reverend Martin Luther King Jr. in his iconic speech at the National Mall when he declared, "I have a dream." The refrain during that speech was electrifying and still resounds decades later. He was describing a nightmarish situation still occurring throughout the United States in unfair and unjust behavior toward African Americans, but he did not dwell on that as the rallying cry for action. His call for nonviolent protests and persistent action was reminiscent of Gandhi's efforts for Indians in South Africa and later in India leading to their independence as a nation. Either one of these inspirational leaders could have quoted from the 10 Commandments or similar moral codes that made clear what a person should *not* do to be a better person. Instead, they invoked what we *could* do. Reverend King was tested, followed, harassed, and challenged. But he held to his principles. For example, he never led a protest at night (Joseph, 2020), as part of not wanting to entice possible nighttime violence.

Instead of surrendering to the tempting emotions of revenge and responding to violence with violence, both Gandhi and Martin Luther King Jr. focused on the higher purpose, core values, and nonviolence. They were persistent, challenging, and provocative, but nonviolent. These were PEA-invoking acts and principles. Contrast this for a moment with the responses invoked from other protest activities in India at the time that resulted in massacres, or jobs lost and fear invoked by Antifa in the US in their pursuit of social justice. Regardless of the outrageous social injustice over decades and even hundreds of years, the effort that invoked NEA in terms of violence, fear, threat, and hatred lacks sustainable effect, and often strengthens the resolve of the opposition instead of furthering sustained, desired change.

Solidarity was an organization and a movement that sustained a positive change in the governance of Poland and the lives of its people. It grew out of a group of unionized workers at the Gdansk Shipyards who, among other things, wanted to create food-buying cooperatives to ensure fresh and sufficient food for their families. The emergent leader, Lech Walesa, kept up pressure on the government but focused on the positive possibilities, invoking a PEA response. Eventually, he became the President of Poland and won a Nobel Prize.

Protests to Riots: Intention versus Consequence

When protests turn to riots, the sad but frequent result is rotating violence and abuse. Protests to confront social injustice, famine, oppression, and racism, or attempts to suppress any group or belief, may be necessary. But when the positive intentions or goals of the protests turn into riots, with burning, looting, beating, raping, and killing, the result is more often than not an unstable change. The events of social contagion in the Jasmine Revolution in Tunisia in 2010, and then Tahir Square in Cairo in 2011, created what was heralded as the Arab Spring. From Egypt to other Middle Eastern and North African countries, people and groups rose up to challenge oppressive regimes and leaders.

In the following decades, many regimes and leaders fell. But they were too often replaced with abusive leaders and groups that created their own form of oppression. When NEA goes wild, it invokes a tipping point into fear, defensiveness, anger, and many acts that betray the need and the desired changes needed.

Intentions do not determine consequences. The enacted process, methods, or behavior often determine consequences. The tipping points of PEA and NEA, when occurring in large human collectives, have a magnetic power. But the magnetic pull might be toward nonsustainable change. That is the difference between invoking PEA repeatedly versus NEA repeatedly. But as history reports, some doses of NEA can awaken a collective or galvanize them into action. The sustainability of the desired change will depend on the timing and dosage of arousing PEA, and not repeatedly depend on an NEA state.

Many community change and development efforts failed to be sustainable or reach their intended objectives because of adversarial (i.e., NEA) assumptions among different groups within the community, boards and staff, and funders and agencies (DeFilippis, 2004). Oddly, the shifts in approach from development to empowerment were observed to often result in further separation (i.e., segregation) and less inclusiveness (Stoecker, 1997).

Not to oversimplify a complex situation, but comparison of the PEA versus NEA efforts in Iceland and the United Kingdom over a number of decades can help to illustrate how mounting PEA creates hope, infuses energy, and spreads excitement about a major societal change, and how the NEA has the opposite effect. Iceland faced escalating dependence on foreign oil and to support some of their industries, like aluminum smelting. At the same time, the UK had a long and rich history as a source of coal and proponent of coal as an energy source. The environmental consequences of the future dependence on fossil fuels were clear to many in both countries.

The government of Iceland developed four working groups of experts and professionals from 2003 to 2012: "Working Group I evaluates what impact proposed power projects will have on nature, landscape, geological formations, vegetative cover, and flora and fauna, as well as cultural heritage and ancient monuments. Working Group II evaluates the impact on tourism, outdoor activities, agriculture, re-vegetation, fishing in rivers and lakes, and hunting. Working Group III evaluates the impact that proposed power projects can have on economic activity, employment, and regional development. Working Group IV identifies potential power projects, both hydro and geothermal, and carries out technical and economic evaluations" (Jóhannesson, 2012, p. 3).

The members of these working groups, and their sponsors, and champions, relied on a shared value of preserving the Icelandic environment and their culture by referring to their proud history, having a sustainable future with hope, and energy independence, building on their desire to continue to be an autonomous country and culture. Being a Scandinavian culture likely helped with the relatively egalitarian values supporting involvement and dialogue among many people. They also worked on possible sources of global distinction and pride using their unique geothermal energy sources of volcanic systems underneath their island, and their desire to become the world's first hydrogen economy. They framed these as opportunities and involved as many people in the discussions as possible. The champions approached their challenge as advocating for these positive outcomes and not compliance (Ministry of Industry and Innovations, Icelandic Master Plan, 2009). The result is a country running on 85% renewable sources of energy.

Meanwhile, across the North Atlantic, the champions and sponsors of similar environmental concerns in the UK took an obligatory approach with the government serving as the regulator (Wood & Dow, 2011). Focusing on the financial aspects of their current use of fossil fuels and the ways to transform to a sustainable energy economy, the advocates emphasized costs and pursued their plans with limited engagement of the many stakeholders (Devine-Wright, 2005). Punishments were established if the targets were not met. The government was regulating the energy transition, whereas in Iceland the government was sponsoring ideas, dialogue, and discovery. The result is that as of 2021, the UK was generating about 40% of its energy from renewable sources, with the rest from fossil fuels.

Change in communities and countries requires social movements, not merely government funding or social policy changes. Social movements occur through emotional contagion that grows into social contagion.

The Spread of PEA and NEA Through Emotional and Social Contagion

As pointed out, PEA and NEA are the tipping points to collective action or inaction (Hazy & Boyatzis, 2015). In our human systems, in addition to direct personal contact, these tipping points work through emotional and social contagion. Emotional contagion can be said to be the arousal of an emotion in one person as a result of the presence of that emotion in another person. It is a type of infection or spread of a state (Elfenbein, 2014). The direct brain-to-brain activation of negative emotion has been shown to be fast (i.e., thousandths of a second) (LeDoux, 2002; Denworth, 2023), but so have the brain-to-brain activation of positive emotions (Lewis, et al., 2000). The observation has been made often that the spread of strong emotions, positive or negative, is pervasive in social settings (Hatfield, et al., 1994). The more recent expression is that something has gone "viral" when the spread is fast and broad through social media.

When people are in a PEA state, they are more receptive to emotional messages and activation of the DMN. This enables broader scanning in environmental and human groups (Falk, et al., 2013). The emotional spread goes both ways in hierarchal relationships. Followers' moods arouse the same moods in a leader (Tee, et al., 2013) in the same way that the moods of patients, students, coaching clients, and children invoke similar moods in the physician or nurse, teacher, coach, or parent. Stress is contagious when observed in friends and others (Li, et al., 2023).

But it also opens people up to being more vulnerable to manipulation, as witnessed in the joining of cults. The socialization of new members moves quickly if the people are perceptually open. A similar process occurs with openness to emotional messages of leaders and the possible use of that condition to recruit people into an emotional or belief-based group (Storr, 1996). On the positive aspect, emotional contagion of the PEA begins new bonding relationships via the PEA into relationships that invoke more hope, gratitude and compassion, mindfulness, and playfulness (Boyatzis & McKee, 2005). The exception to this emotional contagion would be people who are "on the spectrum" (i.e., various degrees and forms of autism) as a result of dysfunctions in their DMN.

Social contagion can be said to be the spread of behavior and emotional reactions to people and events through behavioral mimicry. This can operate with great speed, even with subtle cues that may not be consciously observed or noted by those involved. In the famous epidemiological studies of Fowler and Christakis (2008, 2010) (Christakis & Fowler, 2009), the chain of change was evident. It was shown that when a person knows someone who develops a new habit or changes their mood or behavior, people they know and are in contact with are 15% more likely to change in the same way. People who know or are in contact with the second person but not the first are still 10% likely to change in the same way as the first person. And a third relationship shows a 6% likelihood of change in the same way as the first person without being in contact with the first (Fowler & Christakis, 2008, 2010). All of these changes are statistically significant and notable evidence of three degrees of freedom and influence in social contagion.

Such social contagion begins with observing, witnessing, or noticing the behavior of another person, consciously or unconsciously (Bandura, 1986). The modeling of behavior is at the heart of social learning theory. When the role model is in a position of power or respect, like a leader, the potential infection rate or spreading of the behavior is higher. The role of opinion leaders or persons at nodal points in social networks are the major transmitters of the appeal and emotional arousal that creates an attractor (Hagen, 1962). Such charismatic leaders can move entire communities or countries, creating social movements that may endure for centuries (Hagen, 1962).

This magnetic power of some leaders fascinates scholars and the public alike (Storr, 1996). While some leaders capture the hearts and minds of others for self-centered reasons, some elevate the aspirations and hope of people. Once captured within the pull of such an attractor, the participants will often imbue or attribute the leader with great powers or forgive their foibles or acts that cause them to detest other leaders (Hollander, 1958). Hollander (1958) called this process granting "idiosyncrasy credits" to a leader. Storr (1996) pointed out that manipulative leaders infantilize their followers and arouse primal fears that make some people more dependent on them.

The mechanisms are likely to be internal and social. The internal mechanism likely comes from activation of our mirror neuron network, which is closely related to our motor neuron network (Iacoboni, 2009; Rizzolatti & Sinigaglia, 2008). These networks move us to replicate or mimic the actions of others. The social mechanism emerges from the desire to be included and be viewed as a "good" member of a group. Once a person mirrors another person's actions, a form of bonding occurs.

Emotional and social contagion reinforce each other and may be difficult to separate as to causality and timing. The PEA or NEA, once begun, form a positive feedback loop. The contagion feeds on itself, and the PEA or NEA state is further aroused and continues to be supported if not enhanced. But that is where the similarity ends. When in the PEA state the participants are open to new ideas and people, meanwhile scanning their environment. When in the NEA state, the participants are in varying states of defensiveness and closing themselves to alternatives. Emotional contagion likely determines the velocity of change as well as the speed. These two processes will affect the infectiousness of PEA or NEA states in social settings.

The earlier case discussed of bicycling in communities or countries is an example. The more a person watches others bicycling, the more likely they are to consider or try it. If the cycling is used as a mode of transportation, not just a sport, the practice can spread into many domains of life. The story of how two cities made dramatic reductions in homelessness is another example. Both Houston from 2009 to 2021 and Boston during the COVID pandemic used emotional and social contagion to change the mindset and perspective of entire communities about homelessness.

Mayor Annise Parker of Houston (in office 2010–2016) and her special assistant on homelessness, Mandy Chapman Semple, took a multipronged approach (Alston, 2022; Jolicoeur, 2022; Beekman, 2017; Beretto, 2015). They involved city, county, state and federal agencies, private companies, and philanthropic organizations to come together and pool resources to address homelessness. They used a "housing first" approach. Their decision to begin with the homeless veterans providing an early win and an emotional appeal to the community that had many military installations and groups.

In Boston, Mayor Michelle Wu, during the pandemic, decided to make reducing homelessness a major priority as she took office (Capps, 2022). She immediately approached a wide variety of neighborhood associations and local business associations, as well as nonprofit organizations. By doing so, she invoked many different motives as to why people wanted to reduce homelessness—from compassion to social justice, to fighting drugs and protecting children, and reducing crime to cleaning up neighborhoods. She used emotional contagion as a starting point, and as people began to create alternatives and help families find "a way home," people copied each other.

Swarming Is Social

Emotional and social contagion play a major role in spreading PEA or NEA in human collectives. They work through another concept from complexity theory: swarming (Okubo, 1986; Reynolds, 1987; Kennedy, et al., 2001; Hazy & Boyatzis, 2015). Whether the PEA or NEA is invoked in our collectives, the actual process of change is more likely to be initiated and sustained through swarming than through a process of rational planning.

NEA swarms may become self-reinforcing due to the fear invoked. But because the NEA is involved, it is likely that the NEA swarm will fizzle over time as resources are depleted. In the same way avoidance motivation was shown to be more easily aroused than approach motivation and have a greater intensity (McClelland, 1985), and a prevention self-regulatory focus is more quickly aroused than a promotion focus, NEA swarms will seem faster than PEA swarms. But the PEA swarms appear more durable. Social movements and community change are a form of swarming (Fligstein & McAdam, 2011).

NEA swarms of the past included financial investment bubbles, like the tulip mania in the seventeenth century or beachfront condos in the US and Spain prior to 2008. These swarms began with a false promise of huge gains, like a Ponzi scheme, but reached an upper limit and eventually burst. PEA swarms can be sustained if the leader or nodal person continually re-arouses PEA through reminding people of their shared sense of purpose, core values, core emotions of hope, gratitude and compassion, and mindfulness. This dynamic is mathematically explained in terms of social network or percolation theories.

Organizations devote an amazing amount of time and energy to strategic planning. The process is a rational analysis of the threats and opportunities, obstacles, and resources. But seldom does a strategic plan create a swarm. Borrowing from the fields of ornithology and entomology, Boyatzis and Dalziel (under review) described how three basic principles of swarming can emerge in organizations. The three principles are (1) each participant follows in the direction of a central tendency; (2) each participant travels at roughly the same speed; and (3) each participant avoids collisions (Reynolds, 1987).

Organizations change and show sustained change when a leader seeds a swarm by evoking a PEA through appealing to some value, idea, program, or identity-based brand (Connelly, et al., 2013; Elfenbein, 2014). They pull people to travel in the same direction with the emotional appeal of an idea or possibility. The leader then sets the speed of change through shared excitement and energy. They guide the process of change with a sense of what their organization is capable of within their larger context. Organizations that create new markets and innovate with what are seen as major breakthroughs often appeal to an unmet need in the environment, or a new possibility. The leader avoids collision by managing the dosage of arousal of the PEA and reminders of their purpose and values, and pacing of the activities.

Although needed and useful for resource allocation and planning (and to bankers, equity, and venture capital providers), typical rational strategic planning arouses analytic and abstract processes that pull toward the NEA. This explains why so many strategic plans gather dust and show little energizing, sustainable effect on people in the organization. This lack of effect created an entire consulting industry of plan implementers, or specialists in change management. Companies that developed or worked with a consulting firm to develop a strategic plan often found themselves adrift in knowing how to implement it, and puzzled as to why staff did not show excitement about plan implementation. When a leader or leaders understand these dynamics (whether consciously or intuitively), they seek to combine a rational strategic planning process with the emotional value and appeal of the PEA.

Swarming uses emotional and social contagion to enlist people to join a movement and increase their commitment to it. Regardless of whether the detonating idea or act is PEA or NEA, the sustainability depends on which state becomes the predominant emotional mood. The enrollment and excitement are more likely to follow an exponential curve, which brings us to the next section on distributions and the look of change.

The Look of Change: Normal Is Not Normal

Principle 3: Sustained, desired change in humans and human systems is most often discontinuous and nonlinear.

To grasp the dynamics of change, we must be open to complex system processes that violate many rules we are taught as scholars and professionals. The emergence of the phases and discoveries of ICT during a change process will often appear as discontinuous leaps. Studying change over time leads to three observations. First, sustained, desire change is seldom linear. Second, it does not often follow a "normal" distribution (i.e., Gaussian distribution). Third, sustained, desired change often appears in discontinuous moments of emergence. This section of the chapter is abridged and adapted from Boyatzis & Dhar (2023).

Research is often guided by assumptions about human behavior and change being linear and continuous. Researchers ignore these anomalies or manipulate data to suit the needs of statistical analysis to become Gaussian or normal distributions (Andriani & McKelvey, 2007; 2020; Golembiewski, 1986; Gabaix, 2016; Pek, et al., 2018; O'Boyle Jr. & Aguinis, 2012). In using these statistical unnatural acts, they mask and even hide important properties of the data. For practitioners, these prior assumptions result in inappropriate expectations as to the nature and rhythm of change.

When psychotherapy achieves the desired outcomes, it reveals that "life transition and post-traumatic growth highlight the significance of nonlinear and discontinuous change across areas of psychology" (Hayes, et al., 2007, pg. 715). In subsequent studies and meta-analyses, Hayes and her colleagues (Hayes, et al., 2007) showed that cognitive improvement in response to psychotherapy for depression followed a power curve. Further, documentation of results showed spikes or moments of discontinuous bursts along the power curve. The specific distribution is often called a swallowtail curve.

This observation is not new. In 1892, William James proposed that conscious volition and the exercise of "will" preceded action or behavior. As a result, behavior was purposive. He went on to explain that besides deliberative thought and exercise of will, there were also forms of expression that were impulsive and even explosive. His latter types of will in action were moments of discontinuous emergence. Lindblom (1959) began to create nonlinear theories of performance and change in the organizational sciences. More recently, scholars of complexity theory have offered the same observations and challenged colleagues as to why we perpetuate analytic practices that may hide important revelations and findings (Amis, et al., 2004; O'Boyle & Aguinis, 2012). Further, in the study of mini-computer companies, Romanelli and Tushman (1994) observed that the "large majority of transformations were accomplished by rapid and discontinuous change over the most or all domains of organizational activity" (p. 1141). They added that "small changes in strategies, structures, and power distributions did not accumulate to produce fundamental transformations" (p. 1141).

The persistence of assumptions about rational decision-making being logical consequences of reflection and consideration of alternatives is at the heart of the theory of reasoned action (Fishbein, 1979). As his theory and supporting research shows, a person's intention to act in a certain way appears key to later emergence of that behavior. But it is not sufficient to actually cause that behavior. In addition, the causal path is neither linear nor continuous, so scholars must add more predictor variables.

The most common form of distribution of human change is a power curve, with possible discontinuities. The discontinuities may follow a cusp model, which was first documented in catastrophe theory by Thom (1975) (Zeeman, 1979; Lichtenstein, 2000). Emotional and social contagion of change has been difficult to understand or model, possibly because the underlying dynamics of change are not only nonlinear but require complex mathematics to understand, as predicted in percolation theory (Boardbent & Hammersley, 1957).

Ubiquitous Power Curves

At first scholars were amazed at the regularity of power curves when actually examining histograms and distributions of raw information, instead of questionnaire-based survey results with Likert style response formats. The ubiquity of power curves has been noted in many sciences, from meteorology to geography to population statistics, arrays of wireless networks, terrorist incidents, and cost of wars (Andriani & McKelvey, 2007). Examining human performance and actual behavior or output, O'Boyle and Aguinis (2012) showed power curves evident in distributions from 198 samples including 633,263 researchers, entertainers, politicians, and amateur and professional athletes. They found power curves more descriptive than any other distribution in publications of scholars, Emmy award nominations to performers, elections to the US Congress, and NBA career points scored. A power curve is a nonlinear and non-normal distribution in which the data shows a relatively meaningless mean and a long tail. Mathematically, it is represented by: $y = ax^k + \varepsilon$. It is often described in nontechnical terms as a Pareto curve.

Leadership in small groups or teams often appears as a power curve with a few blips that convert it technically into a "swallowtail distribution" (Guastello, 2007, 2011). Studying 274 distributions of team performance for 200,825 teams, Bradley and Aguinis (2022) found that only 11% could be described as a normal distribution. Of the non-normal distribution of team performance, 73% of them could be described as a power curve or variation of one. In a large study of students who organized themselves into project teams, a description of each team member's demonstration of specific leadership behaviors followed a similar swallowtail pattern. Mallaby (2022) provided numerous examples of dynamic, corporate growth and the role of venture capital and private equity firms to invoke power curve distributions of their clients' performance. Avi Turetsky's (2018) doctoral dissertation showed that the performance of over 5,000 firms who were clients of private equity companies was described by a non-normal distribution that portrayed what he called a double Pareto or double power curve of their internal rate of return (IRR).

Comparable or power curves appear repeatedly when examining strategic decisions and their relationship to actual organizational output in a variety of industries (Andriani & McKelvey, 2007; Gabaix, 2016). Increasing the scope from organizations to industries, it has been shown that domestic deposits of the top 30 US banks and savings and loan companies and financial assets of the top 30 companies, as well as distribution of market values across several industries, followed power curves (Zanini, 2008). Classic studies in complexity scholarship illustrate such distributions with financial crashes and bubbles over hundreds of years (Mandelbrot & Hudson, 2008).

Appreciation of these non-normal distributions could help "researchers to: (1) collect data about actual behavior or change; (2) collect data with periodicities that allow discontinuities to emerge; and (3) use visual and segmented statistical analyses to identify bifurcations or other break points and various distributions that may be embedded within a data set" (Boyatzis & Dhar, 2023, p. 3).

Not only are power curves nonlinear as well as discontinuous, but when we examine human change we see them appear again, repeatedly. No area of individual behavior change has attracted more attention than the challenge of addiction. Recidivism is the result when intended change does not sustain over time. Recidivism from many addictions appears to follow a power curve, as shown in Figure 3.4, which depicts recidivism for smokers, alcoholics, and heroin users (Hunt, et al., 1971). More recent studies focused on smokers attempting to quit also showed power curves (Hughes, et al., 2004), as shown in Figure 3.5. A study of a critical population of 1,689 smoking adolescents aged 11 to 17 showed a power curve in daily cigarette consumption (Byrne, et al., 2001).

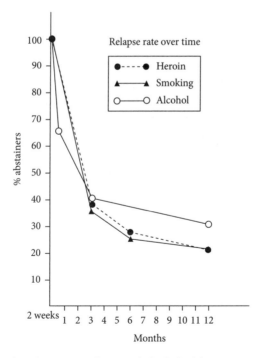

Figure 3.4 Relapse from heroin, smoking, and alcohol addiction
Source: Hunt, et al. (1971, p. 456).

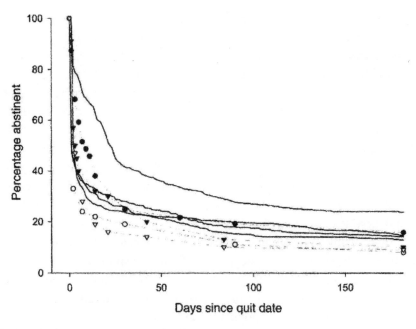

Figure 3.5 Abstinence over time of addicted smokers
Source: Hughes, et al. (2004, p. 33).

Other than being an oddity that should be appreciated by researchers, the ubiquity of power curves and their related nonlinear and discontinuous distributions of human behavior and change, individually or in our collectives, should arouse a curiosity. Why does this happen? And how does that enhance our understanding of sustained, desired change?

Regressive Forces Creating Power Curves and Discontinuities

At least four major forces conspire to create power curves and related non-normal distributions in human systems (Boyatzis & Dhar, 2023). First, when humans act or attempt to change, our actions, feelings, and decisions are connected to each other. Second, humans will seek to defend and protect themselves and their tribes (families, social groups, etc.). Third, we want to be included and typically seek social approval. Fourth, humans will attempt to reduce uncertainty for themselves and others. Without understanding these regressive forces, our insight into how sustained, desired change occurs is reduced to intellectual flailing or attributions to unseen, supernatural forces.

It Is All Connected

An important distinction between power laws and normal distributions are the difference in a central assumption about the relationship of the information being portrayed. Normal distributions assume that events, pieces of information, or data points are independent (Erdi, 2008). Power laws do not assume they are (Andriani & McKelvey, 2007). (A technical feature showing this nonindependence comes from calculations of the exponent of the power law with the Kolmogorov-Smirnov adjustment which is a non-parametric test of the equality of continuous or discontinuous distributions.) When an array of data across levels of human endeavor (individuals, teams, or organizations) appears to follow similar patterns, whether power curves or other distributions, these cross-level observations appear to be "scale-free." That is, they are independent of the level of human endeavor being examined.

This scale-free characteristic suggests something else is affecting the distributional relationships within each level. We contend that each action or thought within a level is dependent on prior ones. This feature is technically called "event dependence." In other words, a person's behavior or feelings are dependent on how they were acting or feeling in the moments, days, or weeks prior to that event.

Consider a person wanting to lose weight. Their battle with sweet foods and drinks will be a function of their prior eating habits and how much of each type of food or beverage is around their home or office. They may crave sweets in a way that is not just a behavioral habit, but could have created nutritional and biological acclimation. The same could be said for a person attempting to reduce their habitual checking of email every hour or less. By continuing that behavior into the evening, their psychological preparation for sleep and rest is likely disturbed. This pattern has been noted with regard to single people wanting to find healthy relationships. Those with a prior pattern of choosing abusive partners are more likely to recreate such dysfunctional relationships rather than the ones they say they wish to have. Sometimes, the exact opposite occurs. Whether in selecting leaders for a team or organization or possible partners in life, the "rebound syndrome" has also been noted, where there is an effort to find someone distinctly different from the prior person. These actions are dependent on previous experiences.

This dependence occurs in relation to physical health as well. If a person contracts a cold, virus, or bacterial infection, their body reacts with inflammation to protect itself from the foreign bodies. Inflammation compromises the immune system, which makes a person more vulnerable to another infection. In any of these situations, prior experiences and actions have a profound effect on the following ones. They are not independent events.

This dependence appears in our social collectives not only with prior behavior, but also with each other. The other people in the team, family, organization, or community become the context for a person's actions. If a member of a project team wishes to focus on the tasks at hand, they are dependent on how much the others in the team are also willing to do that. If it is a Friday in July and other team members are eager to get away to the lake or seashore for the weekend, fostering a focused task orientation will be more difficult. If a person in an organization wants to try a new way to approach clients, but their colleagues like the tried-and-true practices they have used for years, the innovation will face more challenges for adoption. Our behavior, thoughts, and feelings are not only dependent on our own prior ones, but on those of others around us and those with whom we are regularly interacting. They are dependent on the norms and values of the team or organization and the culture. Therefore, power curve and nonlinear distributions are more likely than normal distributions.

Defensive Protection

Humans survive by seeking preservation of life and of the species (Wilson, 2000). This tendency to defensive protection has evolved within our body as the Sympathetic Nervous System or stress response (Sapolsky, 2004). In complexity terms, human behavior is homeostatic with regard to preservation (Casti, 1994; Erdi, 2008). Humans will seek safety and preserve energy and other resources when exposed to a threat. As our societies have evolved, these threats are no longer only physical but also include environmental, social, and spiritual threats. Beyond surviving, when the Parasympathetic Nervous System is activated humans seek thriving or flourishing (Damasio, 2019; Boyatzis, et al., 2021).

Learning a new way of thinking, feeling, or acting and the attempts to change current ways introduces new or different ways to respond. Any such effort invokes self-control and possible failure or threat. These arouse our stress system, the SNS (Segerstrom & Miller, 2004; Dickerson & Kemeny, 2004). Once the SNS is aroused, a person begins to close down to new ideas or changes and we defend ourselves. In a pragmatic sense, thoughts about the costs of switching to a new behavior will likely be perceived as greater than the possible costs of remaining the same.

The defensive response avoids threats or possible threats, which include unusual events, situations, and behavior. Like the rapid activation of avoidance motivation versus the more prolonged activation of approach motivation (McClelland, 1985), a prevention self-regulatory focus is easily aroused, while the promotion self-regulatory focus has a "more distant appeal" (Mogilner, et al., 2008). When this involves social threats, humans seek to avoid or minimize disapproval or expulsion from a social group (Bowlby, 1969; Parsons, 1937; Crowne & Marlowe, 1964). Innovative and different behavior becomes viewed as deviant and is punished or shunned—thereby adding to the restraining forces for change.

Being Included

Humans are social animals; it is a primate tendency to join, belong to, and remain in specific groups (Maslow, 1968; Schutz, 1958; Baumeister & Leary, 1995; Wilson, 2000; Deci & Ryan, 2000). These desires become forces constraining or restraining our innovative or new behavior. They become homeostatic forces. Responding to social values and norms, like humility, can also become a restraining force and limit how different a person is willing to be within a social group or organization. Once set in motion, such restraints extend to interactions among various social groups or organizations fostering competition and aggression evident in "in-group" versus "out-group" dynamics and intergroup conflict (Sherif, et al., 1961).

In Chapter 2, deviations from these forces toward homogeneity and homeostasis were discussed. One example of such moments were discussed as a mid-life or mid-career crisis (Levinson, 1978). In larger social collectives, the growing realization that we have to change and the urgency of such a feeling may erupt like a volcano (Brinton, 1952; Runciman, 1966), resulting in social protests, riots, and even war. But these social movements also seem to involve swarming by a group of people or networks of groups of people, so they are not lone acts. Collectivist cultures emphasize these restraining forces of change or innovation by making them a violation of the social contract, and perceived as a violation of the cultural norms.

The desire to be included and fit within the norms and values of a social identity group, team, organization, community, or country may act to restrain or constrain the variation of behavior, thoughts, or feelings a person may attempt. The tendency to inhibit or restrict change has been called a "negativity bias" (Rozin & Royzman, 2001). When combined with the observation that negative feelings are stronger than positive feelings (Baumeister, et al., 2001), the negativity bias encourages norms of skepticism, hesitation, and negative interpretation about ideas, people, and events in general (Rozin & Royzman, 2001), and greater weight given to negative perceptions (Ito, et al., 1998). Low self-efficacy, whether fostered by religious beliefs that are deterministic or cultural messages passed on from parents, grandparents, and key authority figures, may act as accelerants flaming the fire of the negativity bias. Hanson and Hanson (2018) called this human tendency "Velcro for the negative and Teflon for the positive." The negativity bias also operates asymmetrically regarding the amount of evidence we need to believe a decline or positive change has occurred. We need far more evidence to believe in lasting improvement (O'Brien & Klein, 2017).

When organizations seek consistency of practices, they often claim it is to ensure the quality of services or products. But the largest force promoting such efforts is usually the desire for predictability of performance. This may take the form of valuing performance to predicted budgets and targets, or merely asking people to share the same norms of behavior (Barnard, 1938; Meyer & Zucker, 1989). These forces may help predictability of action assessed against forecasts and budgets, but it also introduces a growing arteriosclerosis of the organization's cardiovascular system. The preoccupation with norming an organization's performance against other organizations or benchmarking is another form of promoting consistency, and could be said to promote a regression to a central condition. All of these factors become restraining forces and result in breakout performance or innovation being rarer and rarer, as exemplified by a power curve rather than a normal distribution. The way we respond to moments of transition or uncertainty reveal this tendency to restrain and restrict.

Reducing Uncertainty

Another force that constrains behavior and contributes to creation of power curves and related discontinuities is the typical human response to uncertainty. During transitions people often feel uncertain and seek to reduce the uncertainty or eliminate it (Ibarra & Petriglieri, 2010, Durrheim & Foster, 1997). As mentioned previously, when the uncertainty invokes fear of the unknown or risk beyond a comfort level, the SNS is aroused and all of the consequences of our stress reaction are engaged. People from cultures with high tolerance of uncertainty are not primed in this manner (Hofstede, 1984), and those seeking novelty amid a transition are not cued for stress (Maddi, 1969). Other than these exceptions, most people seek to reduce risk at such times, thereby imposing limits on their behavior that might be innovative or different from the norm or what is typical.

Leaders in organizations or communities might seek to consolidate their power by limiting options for others. Centralization of authority is typically a restraining force and inhibits or prohibits innovations other than those sponsored by the leader (Storr, 1996). The leader may appeal to primal fears and infantilize their audience, with the result of further imposing limits on their divergent or innovative behavior (Storr, 1996).

Although initiated for ostensible positive reasons, efforts to impose certification requirements for practicing a profession or trade further constrain innovation and variation in practices (Fallows, 1985). What begins in response to a call for quality becomes a vehicle for restricting access for certain populations, similar to the consequences of racial, gender, cultural, or social class prejudices. When norms in an organizational culture emphasize their own distinctive way of doing things and scorn variations, they often suffer "competition neglect," where they are not aware when their market or competitor's shift approaches (Camerer & Lovallo, 1999).

A notable difference is the "heliotropic" effect pursued by proponents of positive psychology (Seligman & Csikszentmihalyi, 2000). Such acts or breakout innovations are relatively infrequent (Cameron, 2008). As a result, they are highly sensitive to initial conditions and likely to skew any resulting behavior of others toward a non-normal distribution, whether a power curve or variation.

When Discontinuities Pop: Tipping Points and Emergence

When an event occurs or observation is made at the long tail of a power curve, it may be misinterpreted as a discontinuous emergence because of its rarity and the perceptual distance from the large cluster of observations near the zero point. Meanwhile, there are times in the change process when discontinuities do occur. Ask anyone who has attempted a diet: some days you lose a pound or two, some days you gain a pound or two, and some days nothing happens. Discontinuities appear and emerge, or disappear and extinguish when a tipping point or trigger point occurs. Knowing which tipping points are potentially involved can help in understanding the change process, but this does not always reveal what is causing it or why it is happening.

The attractors are tipping points interspersed by longer periods of self-organized, homeostatic states (Bak, 1996). Because the complex system is sensitive to initial conditions, the equilibrium of the system can be tipped into what may appear as chaos, but it is more often merely a discontinuous event (Kauffman, 1995). Once one aspect of a tipping point is invoked other factors are invoked as well, creating a cascading effect of changing initial conditions (Dooley, 2004; Marion & Uhl-Bien, 2001).

This is evident in small groups and teams. Gersick (1991) noted that teams develop by passing through moments of "punctuated equilibrium." These are moments within the team's process in which a discontinuous break occurs. Their behavior and norms before and after are noticeably different.

Early efforts to classify different types of organizational change projects resulted in appreciation of the nonlinearity of change (Golembiewski, 1986). Golembiewski (1986) claimed that when the impact of change is assessed using traditional statistical techniques, such as comparison groups, randomization, and measures assessed with test-retest and similar reliability indicators, the result is what he called "alpha" change. Such change assumes linearity because it is part of the statistical descriptive and evaluative methods.

A second form of organizational change occurs when there is "recalibration" along the process affecting intervals of measurement or the measurement used. But "gamma" change appears as a complex system, with specific moments appearing like cusp-like break points on a multidimensional surface. Later, the process of change was shown to often involve nonlinear breaks due to inertia, canceled efforts, deflective problems that emerged and had to be resolved, and the like (Greenwood & Hinings, 1988, 1996).

ICT is a fractal theory of sustained, desired change. It is not merely isomorphic (i.e., similar) at different levels of human collectives. It is quite literally the same. Therefore, moments of emergence emanating following tipping points can occur in teams, organizations, communities, and countries if they are engaged in a process of sustained, desired change. But the restraining and regressive forces that often result in power curves as distributions of actual change data and events occur at each and all of these levels—and they feed the possible change process across levels.

When it works well and follows the ICT process, it feels like magic happens. It seems strange because a sustained, desired change actually occurs.

Concluding Thoughts

The movement toward sustained, desired change, or inhibiting or reversing it, occurs because tipping points are reached that change our state. The change is psychological in how we feel, neurological in the activation of specific neural networks and hormonal arousal. The result is being more open to considering new ideas, learning, and change in the context of a desired future, or being more defensive, focused, and protective of existing conditions. All of this is happening within a person, but also creates psychophysiological states through emotional and social contagion in others. It affects our actions in dyads, teams, organizations, communities, and countries in a similar way. The PEA and NEA states are principles of ICT that move the change process ahead or stall and possibly reverse it. The dynamics of the emergence of these tipping points adds to the likelihood that behavior, change, and learning is better described as a power curve or discontinuous phenomenon than normal distributions. The PEA predominantly addresses the Ideal Self and shared vision. The NEA predominantly addresses the Real Self and shared norms.

4

The Real Self: Who Am I? Who Are We? (Principle 4)

Principle 4: The second phase of ICT is the realization of the Real Self. At the individual level, this is one's strengths and weaknesses relative to their Ideal Self. In human collectives, it is the norms, values, and culture of the specific human system that are strengths or weaknesses relative to a shared vision.

Γνωθει σ'αυτον.

—Thales of Miletus

O, wad some Power the giftie gie us, To see oursels as others see us!
—Robert Burns

The importance of self-awareness in any change effort cannot be overestimated. When we ask the perpetual question *Who am I?*, the answer is likely to be confusing. Besides being a question typically pondered by sophomores in college, the question is often brought on by some existential angst or a tipping point in our lives or work, or acute stress or major tragedies.

It begs the question as to which self is of most interest at that moment. As inscribed in one of the temples at Delphi, the ancient Greeks repeatedly reminded people of the assertion to "Γνωθει σ'αυτον" (i.e., know thyself), which is attributed to Thales of Miletus, one of the Seven Sages of Ancient Greece around 700 BCE (Diogenes Laertius, 1925). (As a side note, it is often misattributed to Socrates, whose public relations people were aggressive.)

We are a combination of our Ideal, Real, and Ought Selves—and there may be multiples of each. So the answer to the question *Who am I?* is a combination of combinations and the next phase of ICT, as shown in Figure 4.1.

No sooner do we compose a response to the question than we are filled with the discrepancies between the various multiple selves (Goleman, 1985).

The Science of Change. Richard E. Boyatzis, Oxford University Press. © Richard E. Boyatzis 2024.
DOI: 10.1093/9780197765142.003.0004

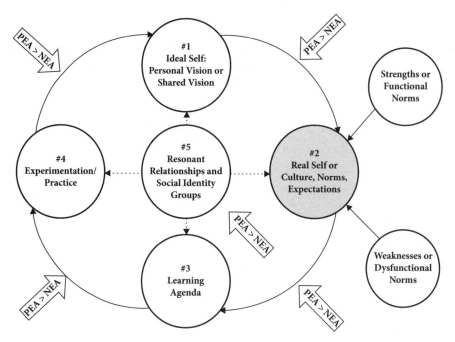

Figure 4.1 The Real Self in the process of Intentional Change Theory
Source: Boyatzis (2008, 2015).

In addition to the issues posed by multiple dreams (Ideal Selves), multiple lived selves (Real Selves), and multiple Ought Selves (multiple social identity groups, cultural and parental expectations), there are the discrepancies between the Ideal and Real Self and between the Ideal and Ought Self, as well as between the Real and Ought Self.

Diogenes and Freud Walk Into a Bar . . .

If the perpetual seeker of a truthful person in ancient Greece, Diogenes, met Sigmund Freud, whose theory of personality included multiple selves (the ego, id, and superego), could they argue to a resolution? In a famous experiment with chronic schizophrenics who each believed they were Jesus Christ, Rokeach (1964) brought three of them into the Ypsilanti State Mental Hospital in Michigan. They were placed in the same ward to see how they would handle each other's claims. Surprisingly, they worked out that each of them was Jesus Christ, but a different aspect or part of him.

Although wondering about yourself and life is likely to have haunted early hominids, the concept of an individual self seems to have gathered momentum around 1,000 CE. It is during this period that a person's separation from their Gods, nature, and other tribe members seems to have begun in earnest. The growth of self-awareness began far earlier, as suggested in cave paintings and early clay representations of others and animals.

Finding the Real Self Is Tougher Than Finding Waldo

Is there a true self? Yes and no. In terms of authenticity and genuineness there is, especially if a person is consistent (i.e., an aspect of being mindful). A person can enact or live a "true" self in that sense. But there is no inner or un-wavering self. The Real Self is dependent on one's past, one's relationships, and context. This is why becoming aware of them is elusive. Our self-awareness falls prey to the Dunning-Kruger effect: "we don't know, what we don't know" (Dunning, 2011)—consciously, that is.

Hostages to the Ought Self

The Ought Self was introduced in Chapter 2. The confusion and distraction from a path of sustained, desired change was the Ought Self and Selves juxta-posed against the Ideal Self. Amid the barrage of well-intended but oppressive Ought Selves provided throughout our childhood, adolescence, and young adulthood, it is not only difficult to establish a dream or vision, but it is also diffi-cult to develop a realistic self-image of how a person acts and appears to others.

When the Ought Self comes from a potent person in our environment, like a loved and respected parent or grandparent, a person may edit or change their dreams and aspirations in wanting to please them, as well as altering their perception of themselves to become more like the person valued by their potent and significant other. In collectivist cultures, this emerges out of re-spect for elders. In any culture, it may also emerge out of fear of disapproval or abuse.

In later life, when seeking to belong to a group, organization, or commu-nity, a person may again alter their perception of themselves to believe they are more like the desired others. The forces propelling such changes may come from socialization practices designed to appeal to inclusion and membership in a special group. They may also come from various forms of brainwashing and manipulation (Schein, et al., 1961; Storr, 1996).

The resulting distortions or changes to a person's image of themselves, when perpetuated over time, become commonplace and accepted as true.

This burrows its way into our personal identity, as discussed in Chapter 2. The emerging perception of one's Real Self will affect choices as to social identity groups, social groups, and work. These changed perceptions, whether consistent or not, whether real or illusory, may affect changes in our core values through changes first on our contingent values. Through many factors, our perception of our Real Self evolves in odd ways.

Forces Distorting Access to the Real Self

At the dawn of psychoanalytic thought, Freud (1894, 1936) postulated that our mind protects itself from unwanted stimuli and possible conclusions by changing how we experience moments and others. These processes were called ego defense mechanisms. These internal processes have dramatic effects on our relationships because they alter how we approach and treat others. Years later, what is often considered the most comprehensive discussion of them was written by his daughter, Anna Freud (1936). As discussed in Chapter 3, aspects of chronic stress and the relatively infrequent moments of renewal contribute to a clouded self-awareness activated by one or more intense ego defense mechanisms (Goleman, 1985; Sommerfeldt, et al., 2019).

The ego defense mechanisms allow or enable social interactions when first meeting another person. They might help a person make sense of their surroundings or events. The ego defense mechanisms change, replace, or avoid undesired emotions and thoughts by hiding them from consciousness to render these undesired thoughts and emotions socially acceptable. Freud's observation was that any of these processes could and most likely would resurface in our consciousness or behavior in disguised or distorted ways. The unwanted eruptions or re-emergence would contribute to psychosomatic illness, emotional and mental distress, or confusing and frightening thoughts. They might appear as the demons of our dreams, becoming nightmares.

Ego defense mechanisms included repression, regression (falling back to safer states and time), projection, reaction formation, sublimation (channeling the libido into socially useful or acceptable ways via emotional self-control), isolation, undoing, introjection, turning against the self, transference, displacement, and variations of these processes. The utility of the nonpathological defenses is vast material for another book, but not this one. For their role in understanding ICT, it helps to examine how ego defense mechanisms alter a person's sense of their Real Self, or our collective's self-perception (i.e., our view of how we and others are acting in our teams, family, organizations, communities, and countries).

Five of these ego defense mechanisms appear to have dramatic effect on a person's awareness of or distortion of their Real Self. They are projection, transference, sublimation, displacement, and reaction formation.

Projection is attributing your feelings as a characteristic of another person or being. It can facilitate a conversation with someone just met by giving each person initial feelings of compatibility or mutual interests. But it can also work the other way. For example, you avoid a colleague at work because you believe them to be a bully. When discussing possible teammates for a project, you share your view of that person and say, "I'd rather not have him on the team. He is a pushy, self-centered bully!" If this person is forthright and says openly when others are not doing their portion of a shared work project, you maybe projecting a characteristic onto him that is rooted in your fears. By projecting your fears or emotions onto others, a person falsely elevates their sense of self-esteem and like a quick coat of paint, hides a patina of rust or mold that covers a surface.

Projection enables racism, sexism, and all prejudicial attributions. In this process, it is often fundamentally a fear of the unknown or someone different. It enables you to hide your feelings and think of yourself as a better person. It allows a person to consider themselves part of an elite, special, or chosen group through the social comparison process, and to avoid an undesirable social identification. Even more extreme, projection may aid a person in exaggerating their membership in a social identity group and antipathy toward another group.

The dynamics of inclusion and belonging in any social identity group can amplify the intensity of feelings with projection. It could lead to acts inconsistent with other parts of a person's behavior, including reducing openness to noticing or understanding others and acknowledging a person's own complicity in a cycle of hate and distrust. It does this by reinforcing current beliefs or attitudes. Changes to a person's Real Self from projection might inhibit consideration of a change by blocking the Ideal Self or vision.

Transference is a process of transferring feelings about one person (or group) to another person (or group) for a reason or via a stimulus that has nothing to do with the other person (or group) or the issues at the time. For example, in meeting with someone, suppose you have a vague feeling that you do not like the person. If you spent more time examining the source of the feeling, you might realize that they remind you of your brother-in-law, and you do not like your brother-in-law. In other words, you do not know why you dislike the person you just met and often follow that vague feeling by seeking to identify things to support that feeling. The classic example of transference is when a patient believes they are falling in love with their psychotherapist when the source of the emerging infatuation is the patient's desire for love and approval from one of their parents.

If you have a positive transference to another person, it could enhance the strength of modeling and the desire to feel or think or act like that person. The opposite could occur with a negative transference. These feelings could affect how you see yourself and possible movement toward your Ideal Self. It might amplify effects of any Ought Self. It could even shift feelings about the source of an Ought Self to others and confuse your Ideal Self or Real Self.

An example is idiosyncrasy credits. Edwin Hollander, a noted psychologist studying leadership, coined the expression "idiosyncrasy credits" in 1958 to refer to allowances you give to someone in forgiving their behavior or statements that you would not bestow on others. At the heart of the reaction that generates an idiosyncrasy credit is a positive liking of the person, most likely because they remind you of someone you liked before. The opposite can happen when they remind you of someone you dislike—you blame or dislike them for things that you tolerate in others.

Reaction formation occurs when a person does the exact opposite of how they are feeling, usually without knowing it. A public statement can push a person to a more extreme and actually antithetical position about someone or something due to reaction formation. For example, you might tease or make fun of someone to whom you are attracted and actually want positive attention from them. Reaction formation could result in a reduction of openness to new ideas or change due to cognitive dissonance reduction. Once you make a public statement or act, you feel an unconscious desire to be consistent with that, so you change your actions or attitudes to fit with the public statement (Festinger, 1957).

Reaction formation could lead to allegiance or membership in a social identity group to which you do not really aspire. In an effort to frame your Real Self as distinctive and different from others, you might take positions opposite to what you feel. A result could be social pressure from others in a social identity group to act in a manner opposite to your values or inconsistent with previous behavior.

Sublimation is swallowing or burying a feeling beneath other feelings to avoid conscious recognition. This could lead a person to underplay a characteristic of themselves to minimize or avoid comparisons with another person viewed more poorly, or something you are ashamed or embarrassed by. For example, if a person feels marginalized, is a member of a visible minority group, or fears being ostracized, they might bury their feelings and adopt characteristics of the majority group or of those central to the group. This might take the form of changing your hair style, clothes, or way of speaking;

racial codeswitching; and other actions in the effort to pass review as if they were actually part of the social group.

Displacement is shifting a feeling that is relevant to a relationship or event to another. A person might say and incorporate into their Real Self-image, "My work is frustrating." What they are really feeling is that their home life is a mess and intolerable. But that realization is too distasteful or invokes a strong feeling of powerlessness, so they displace the feeling onto their work. This could result in many components of a person's Real Self being unrelated to what they are feeling—and thus unrelated to the reality of who they believe themselves to be.

In these ways, any or combinations of ego defense mechanisms can result in distortions or changes to the Real Self. Since these changes do not convey or reflect their true inner feelings, it causes a person to deny changing in desired directions or to attempt changes that are quite different from what would bring them closer to their Ideal Self.

Another powerful force of misleading a person about their Real Self is an underlying desire for approval from certain others (Goleman, 1985). This could be the desire to be included in the "cool group" in high school, or another social identity group that is attractive to others. Teenagers have been observed to do or try actions that they did not really want to do because others from whom they wished approval were acting that way, whether it was smoking a cigarette, drinking alcohol, or trying drugs. Once a person begins to act consistent with the group's norms, they change how they think of themselves. When this process is used to attract and socialize vulnerable or naïve people, it is a form of manipulation and seduction. Once done, the person is too often likely to think of themselves this distorted way. Sedikides (1993) studied the three main reasons people cite for self-evaluation as self-assessment, self-enhancement, and self-verification. The studies showed that among them, the most powerful motivation was self-enhancement. This increases the likelihood of such bias entering the perception and interpretation of any feedback.

Contributors to a Faux Self

The Faux Self is an image of yourself that is false. Any of the ego defense mechanisms can produce or add to a Faux Self. One form of distortion comes from a theater phrase, "believing your reviews." You get described by others in a desired or high-status way, such as you were "magnetic in your performance" or had "great leadership of a project team." If numerous others say it or if it is proclaimed in a public setting, whether in print or social media, you might believe it. Then you begin to act like it's true. The transformation of your Real Self has occurred, and you now think you're magnetic. John Byrne, the editor of *Business Week*, has called this the "CEO disease" (i.e., listening and believing what the sycophants around you keep telling you about how great you are) (Byrne, 1991). You have generalized a reaction to your actions from one moment and one setting to others and to future moments. You have internalized the feedback and now believe it yourself. While it might be true, it might also have been the moment or setting and not be a part of your Real Self that can be carried into the future.

Actors, broadcasters, athletes, politicians, and social influencers receive a lot of feedback about the persona they adopt in public. If that is anywhere from slightly to vastly different from how they feel, they are projecting a false image. Others experience it as real and make the attribution to the person. Fans often confuse actors with the popular characters they portray. To feed their popularity, people in these roles may play into these false perceptions. An inevitable result is confusion about their Real Self.

In nonbroadcast settings, a Faux Self can emerge from confusing a social role a person is enacting with who they are. Sources of drift in one's sense of self and creeping delusion from social identity groups and desire to fit in can result in the same dynamic as believing your reviews. There is a confusion of inner self versus what is shown to others. Following such initial changes and especially early in the process, people might misinterpret cues from others. Lack of concrete or easily observable and verifiable feedback can lead to erroneous images that may occur because others are conflict avoidant, or hiding behind legal requirements that lead people to avoid negative feedback.

A Faux Self can emerge from other characteristics. For example, Taylor and Hood (2011) showed that professional females have a tendency to expect that others (such as a boss, peer, or subordinates) would assess their behavior on desired characteristics in a 360-degree assessment as less than they did. This perpetuates a tendency of female professionals to assess themselves more harshly and critically than others. Meanwhile, professional males tended to overestimate their self-assessment on desired characteristics.

Personality can also contribute to a biased view. Once these perceptions sink into a person's view of themselves, their perceived Real Self becomes a Faux Self—an untrue image of one's self. Bergner, Davda, Culpin, and Rybnicek (2016) showed that more extroverted leaders and those with what they called "intuition preference" were more accurate in their self-assessments as compared to the views of their bosses, peers, and subordinates.

Parts of the Faux Self may come from aspects of yourself to which you are blind. Citing the Dunning-Kruger effect, there is also evidence suggesting that our image of our own body has little relationship to how others see us (Maister, et al., 2021). The same set of studies showed that distortions in one's image of your own face is affected by your values and emotionally toned images of faces of others.

As self-protection, we may develop a Faux Self-image. For example, a person repeatedly selected to enact tough decisions in an organization may begin to see themselves as "the go-to person." But others may see them as an arrogant, overbearing bully who "kisses up and kicks down."

All of these forces encourage more Faux Selves and reinforce distortions of one's self-image that inhibit and more likely prevent any interest in learning or change. Their Real Self blocks any forward movement in an ICT process toward sustained, desired change, even if they have a personal vision and Ideal Self.

Positive Feedback Run Amok

In the 1980s and 1990s, a major movement began in public education to enhance and build each student's self-esteem. It was believed that too many children grew with a poor self-image, and that this squelched their dreams and aspirations for a better future. The theory was that if we bombard a student with positive statements and praise them for every effort, we can help build their positive self-image and increase the likelihood of them becoming satisfied and mature adults who would want to and be able to better themselves. Not all experts agreed, and notably Roy Baumeister, Todd Heatherton, and Diane Tice (1994) contended that we should aim to enhance self-control more than self-esteem.

The experiment with positive self-esteem bombardment went ahead. The result was some progress, but also a generation of people growing up to think they really were elite, special, and should be privileged (Krueger, et al., 2022; Brummelman, 2022; Orth & Robins, 2022). One humorous attempt to capture this was by Garrison Keillor in his famous stories from Lake Wobegon, where "every child is above average." A *Business Week* nationwide survey in 2007 in the US of managers reported that 90% of managers felt they were in the top 10% of performance groupings (Coy, 2007). This effect of lack of accurate awareness was extended to emotional intelligence even despite feedback (Sheldon, et al., 2014). The least skilled among the MBA subjects were the least accurate, even when provided with concrete feedback. They tended to disparage the source and validity of the feedback (Sheldon, et al., 2014).

Positive expectations of others can result in positive change. In the 1970s, a prominent psychologist, Robert Rosenthal, then at Harvard University, conducted a series of experiments on a phenomenon called unconscious expectation effects (Rosenthal & Jacobson, 1968). In one dramatic study, the experimenters gave kindergarten teachers a list of their students in the upcoming class that were thought to be exceptionally smart or gifted. In reality, the list was randomly generated. Nothing else was said during the year. At the end of the year, an analysis of each teacher's descriptions of the student's behavior and potential showed a significant effect of them having been on that original list, which none of the teachers remembered having received.

The adoption of positive expectations of others was called the Pygmalion effect, from the George Bernard Shaw play *Pygmalion* (1912). In the play, Professor Henry Higgins makes a wager that he can transform Eliza Dolittle, a street apple vendor, into a "lady of distinction." Not only does his teaching work, but he falls in love with her, enacting the Greek myth of the sculptor who falls in love with one of his statues. The story has been retold in many forms, such as in the 1983 movie *Trading Places*, with Eddie Murphy and Dan Akroyd.

The expectation effect has been noted and used in experiments to bolster and make a positive change possible. In medicine, the placebo effect occurs when a person is administered a pill that has the illusion of being a potent drug but is in reality a sugar pill or some other formulation of irrelevance to the malady or condition being treated. When the same effects or some of the desired effects are noted as compared to the people taking the real drugs, the result is called a placebo effect. In the first chapter, the story was told of Eysenk's studies (1952) on the effect of psychotherapy on depressive disorders. He found that merely being on the waiting list for a year to get psychotherapy had a similar positive effect on the patients as receiving psychotherapy.

The expectation effect can also result in negative changes in how someone acts and thinks of themselves. Both inflated and deflated self-assessments about task and future performance were associated with the practice of self-handicapping (Kim, et al., 2010). It can be said that cultural stereotypes and many forms of discrimination are expectation effects. All too often people who demonstrate them are unaware, and therefore they are unconscious expectation effects.

The Challenge of Assessment

The challenge of assessment of the Real Self—or in our collectives, the shared Real Self—comes from the possible distortion from all of the factors mentioned above. Self-assessment is too easily a self-fulfilling prophesy. Higgins

(1987) postulated a number of selves worthy of reflection: the Ideal Self (the person we would wish to be), the Real Self (the actual person we currently are), and the Ought Self (the person others wish us to be, the person we should be). Each of these, in Higgins's (1987) model, has an actual and a variation of what we suspect are others' views of us. All of Higgins's the selves were variations of self-assessment. Other conceptualizations of the multiple selves include that of Sedikides and Brewer (2001), who postulated that people formulate three variations of our self-definition: an individual self, a relational self, and a collective self. They are various ways a person can construe who they think they are.

In the 1950s, two psychologists collected data about the false nature of self-assessment. As mentioned earlier, Ed Hollander (1958) documented self-assessment as full of errors when we examine our leadership and own behavior or skills. Chris Argyris (1985) reviewed his claims from decades earlier that we have an espoused self and a self in action. As said previously, in ICT the Real Self or the collective shared Real Self is primarily how others experience or observe us, and a person's assessment of their own behavior is clouded by their Ideal Self and the many Ought Selves impinging upon them, as well as values, social desirability, and ego defense mechanisms.

This framing pushes us into collecting observations from others or direct observation (e.g., live, video, or audio recordings). But even here, we have challenges as to limitations in settings in which specific other people see us in action. There are differences between different people's noticing, perceiving, and labeling of our behavior. The labels attributed are full of the observer's interpretation, which is somewhat based on their prior experiences.

For this approach to the Real Self, the measurement options are direct observation (recorded to determine interrater reliability); video recording of simulations, like group decision-making exercises; audio recordings of events or critical incident interviews; or 360 assessment (i.e., informant assessment). In a 360, the respondents answer survey items with all of the issues of assumed or imputed meaning, and cultural differences in response bias (Batista, et al., 2009). In direct observation or coding of video and audio recordings, a further challenge is the development and use of a clear "codebook," as well as increasing the confidence in the observations or coding (Boyatzis, 1998). The latter can be enhanced by establishing interrater reliability or using multiple coders and seeking consensus on their observations.

A variation on this observation method is to interview others about their views of you or someone else (the focal person). In the late 1970s, colleagues and I began to use an exercise called the Me at My Best. We asked participants in our training programs to interview 10–20 people with whom they live and work. Each of them was asked for an example of a moment or event in which they thought the focal person was at their best. A variation on that emerged in parallel work from colleagues at the University of Michigan in the 1980s called the Reflected Best Self exercise (Roberts, et al., 2005). The result of both of these exercises are stories that the focal person codes, looking for patterns or similarities across situations. Since they are when others were viewing the person at their best, they could be classified as strengths. As with informant observations like 360s, to be of most diagnostic use, these events should be collected from multiple settings with multiple types of people, events, and relationships. It can be suggested that themes or behavior absent from these recollections might be considered weaknesses. The logic of finding something missing is elusive and replete with potential errors, so a leap to that kind of analysis is not recommended.

Motivating and Demotivating Effect of Ideal: Real Self Discrepancies

The earliest research and thinking about ideal and real selves focused on the discrepancies between the two. Higgins (1987) published about a model of discrepancies and elaborated it in his later work. David Kolb and I established the Ideal Self and Real Self as a driving force in self-directed behavior change (Kolb & Boyatzis, 1970a, 1970b). Both of these streams of work were based on a deficiency approach to change. The degree of discrepancy predicted the degree of discomfort (Higgins, 1987). It drew on the level of aspiration and level of activation discussed in Chapter 5 that was thought by Lewin, Dembo, Festinger, and Sears (1944) to affect goals and aims.

In a deficiency model, a gap between something that is (the Real Self) and something desired (the Ideal Self) becomes a reason and motivation to reduce that gap. Although it can be done by changing the Ideal Self, it is far more likely that a person chooses to change their current behavior. Higgins (1987) also introduced the gap between either the Ideal or Real Self and the Ought Self, as discussed in Chapter 2. Again, the Ought Self is an ideal imposed or coming from others.

It has been believed that any discrepancy would create movement to change because it resulted in negative outcomes and mood disorders (Hardin & Lakin, 2009) that people would want to reduce or eliminate. Higgins postulated and reported studies showing that a discrepancy between the Real Self and Ideal Self would predict the absence of positive feelings and outcomes. In an fMRI study, Shi, et al. (2016) cited earlier research that showed greater

Real Ideal discrepancies were associated with negative affect such as shame and embarrassment, and dissatisfaction and disappointment. Meanwhile, the discrepancy of Real and Ought selves would predict negative outcomes and feelings of guilt (Carver, Lawrence, & Scheier, 1999).

Further work clarified and validated that Ideal and Real Self discrepancies predicted a degree of dejection, and Real versus Ought Self discrepancies predicted the degree of agitation (Hardin & Lakin, 2009). The reflections reported from the fMRI study on the discrepancies suggested that it activated parts of the prefrontal cortex, such as the medial prefrontal cortex (mPFC), which is an element of the DMN and is activated when people feel self-conscious and guilty (Ochsner, et al., 2005), as shown in our coaching fMRI studies (Jack, et al., 2013). Moretti and Higgins (1990) showed that only positive self-descriptions emerged from *smaller* Real versus Ideal discrepancies, such as high self-esteem, and only negative self-descriptions emerged from *larger* Real versus Ideal Self discrepancies, such as low self-esteem.

Specifically, the motivating effect on change is often believed to come from increased awareness of the gaps or discrepancies. For example, Schmitt (2020) examined the many potential motivating effects of negative affect and the realization of such discrepancies. As explained earlier, a Real–Ideal Self discrepancy can get the attention of a person or group, but it invokes an NEA state. As such, the durability of this realization as a motivating effect is relatively short-lived. If the negative affect (NEA) lasts longer, it might stimulate other negative feelings, like resentment. Regardless, the sustainability of a change effort is compromised.

This body of work on discrepancies did not address the sustainability of effort and energy needed to pursue the change over time. In yet another twist of the possibilities, Dan Ogilvie (1987) showed that the discrepancies between the Real Self and "undesired selves" was far more predictive of dissatisfaction in life than the Real–Ideal Self gap. Bak (2014) suggested that the "can self" referred to the capabilities and potential a person believed that they had, which is likely part of the Ideal Self. The intensity of the discrepancy was even proposed as incorporating feared selves into the person's Real, Ideal, and Ought Self mixture (Carver, et al., 1999). As a person aged, it was observed that self-discrepancies declined, and that this was positively related to a sense of well-being (Heidrich, 1999).

The deficiency approach may have been further confused by the measurement of these self discrepancies. Higgins's (1987) measure was based on a specific set of adjectives that the respondent was asked to describe their Ideal,

Real, and Ought selves. The Tangney, et al. (1998) measure was also based on an adjective ratings. Hardin and Lakin (2009) attempted to improve on the accuracy of the measurement with their Integrated Self-Discrepancy Index by allowing the respondent to choose those adjectives and attributes most relevant to themselves, and then rate them. With all of the complexity inherent in the Ideal, Real, and Ought selves, it is unlikely that adjective checklists will provide sufficient detail, breadth, and depth to capture the full meaning of a person.

Research on the internal psychophysiological mechanisms driving a desire to change and those affecting the durability or sustainability of such an effort introduced another possibility: that the driver of change and its sustainability may come from the Ideal Self, the power of personal vision and purpose in and of itself, without regard to the Real Self. Some of the neuroscience and hormonal research showing this dynamic was explained in Chapter 3. This was supported in Stanley and Burrow's (2015) study showing that the size of the discrepancy between the Real and Ideal or the Real and Ought self predicted was directly related to a lowered sense of purpose and a poorer body self-image.

In ICT, the NEA state will be activated and reactivated when people focus on discrepancies of any sort. But the PEA state will be activated when people focus on the Ideal Self, their strengths, and their caring relationships, as explained in Chapter 3 (Boyatzis, et al., 2015). It is further postulated that without regularly activating the PEA, the energy needed to sustain a change or learning effort will be foreshortened and exhaust the person (Boyatzis, et al., 2021). Similarly, in our collectives, repeated experiences in the shared PEA will sustain efforts at learning and change. The inevitable venture or slide into the NEA experienced during the change process will be a damper or extinguish any effort at change.

There may be moments of transition or liminality in which awareness of the discrepancies may motivate the beginning of a process of sustained, desired change. For example, at key transitions in life or work, often called mid-life crises, as described in Chapter 2, awareness of a discrepancy may be a wakeup call for the person. But if that increased awareness is not converted into a PEA or sense of purpose and vision, the person will hit the snooze alarm and fall back asleep. The conclusion is that while awareness of a discrepancy or any of the variations of self discrepancies may begin a process of reflection and contemplation of a need for change. But it is the PEA elements of the Ideal Self, caring relationships, and the use of one's strengths that are the driving motivators of sustained, desire change.

In Search of the Real Self

Within the human psyche, what we might call "personality" is a constellation of characteristics. Allport (1937) defined personality as "the dynamic organization within the individual of those psychophysical systems that determine his unique adjustments to this environment" (1937, p. 48). Although there are other definitions and approaches, if we think of this constellation as a set of dispositions of the individual at a point in time, then it opens up the possibility of a multilevel theory. To understand the Real Self, a set of choices have to be made as to which characteristics to examine and use in the construction of the Real Self.

Multiple Levels of Personality

In an early attempt to integrate observations from several fields of research, McClelland (1951) proposed a model or theory of personality with four levels: traits (physical, dispositional affective, and performance), schema (mental models, ideas, and values), needs and motives, and self-schema (a person's perceptions and evaluation of themselves). The next evolution of multilevel models emerged from the perpetual quest to predict who would be effective or successful in life and work—the search for talent.

A group of noted social scientists at the time including David McClelland, Alfred Baldwin, Urie Bronfenbrenner, and Fred Strodbeck (1958) proposed an additional concept: that of a behavioral disposition. Baldwin cited a guiding principle of their shared thoughts that "ability" is a key construct in a theory of behavior (Baldwin, 1958). Furthermore, he clarified that ability reflects a "can-do" capability and should be articulated as a "primary factor" with a link to performance "in a variety of situations" (Baldwin, 1958, pp. 199–201). At that time, roaming around the halls of Harvard was another psychologist, Robert White, who coined the term "competence" as a characteristic of a person that resulted in some form of effective or satisfactory performance in a role in life (1960, 1963).

The concept of ability begins to morph into capability, which became labeled a competency by 1973, and this is distinct from a proficiency, skill, or trait. Interestingly, White (1960) also first used the term "effectance" to describe a person's perception of their causal influence on events—later to become what is known as a sense of efficacy, and later self-efficacy (Bandura, 1981).

Building on this foundation, Boyatzis (1982) introduced a multilevel theory that had behavioral expressions as the most observable level to others,

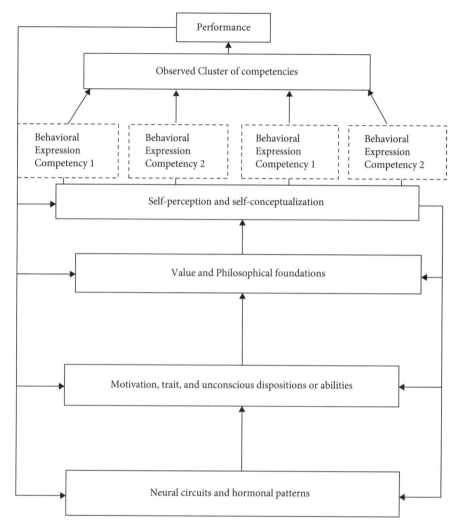

Figure 4.2 A multilevel personality theory
Source: Boyatzis (2018).

as shown in Figure 4.2. The deepest level was unconscious motives and traits (i.e., dispositions to any generalized stimuli). In a later update to this model, Boyatzis (2009, 2018) and Cherniss and Boyatzis (2013) relabeled the deepest, unconscious level as neural networks, hormonal dispositions, and other physiological dispositions. This is the level missing in other well-researched theories of change, from Fredrickson's (2001) to Deci and Ryan's (2000). Fredrickson (2001) postulates the physiological aspects as antecedents or consequences, but stops short of showing the causal interdependence as within the personality structure and process. These neural networks might be DMN or TPN or the others discussed in Chapters 3 and 5. The hormonal systems tend to be the SNS or PNS, as discussed in Chapter 3. Some of these cross-level links have been explored. For example, higher resting levels of testosterone are linked to more power and influence behavior (Schultheiss, 1999; McClelland, et al., 1980). Higher levels of secretion of oxytocin have been linked to more affiliative and social bonding behavior (Taylor, et al., 2000).

At the next level are unconscious motives and traits. These motives are not the conscious response of a person to a question as to why they are doing something. These are unconscious drives. McClelland (1985) and his colleagues studied the Need for Achievement (discussed at length in the next chapter), the Need for Power, and the Need for Affiliation. Their work was built upon Murray's (1938) articulation of 44 such motives or drives. Like their need expectancy theory of motivation, Deci and Ryan (2000) postulated three underlying drives: the desire for autonomy, competence, and belonging. These were both pluralistic theories of motivation, in contrast to particularistic theories, like Skinner's (McClelland, 1985). A third type of motivation theory was developmental, as proposed by Maslow (1943). Various needs were considered more primary than others. The various motives were arrayed in a hierarchy and built upon the previous layers or the satisfaction of the previous needs. From the most basic, they were physiological, safety, belonging, esteem, and self-actualization.

Traits can be classified as affective dispositions (optimism or pessimism), physical (such as walking fast), or performance traits (like efficacy). The most popular typology of traits is the Big Five Theory (McCrae & Costa, 2008). They include five dimensions: neuroticism, openness, extroversion, conscientiousness, and agreeableness. There are other typologies and traits as well. For example, a sense of efficacy can be classified as a trait (Bandura, 1981).

The next level was a subconscious level hypothesized to be just below conscious awareness: values and philosophical orientations. Values can be split into core and contingent values (Rokeach, 1973). Core values are relatively stable over the lifetime. Contingent values are adopted or changed as a result of socialization or social identity groups.

In an attempt to improve the validity of self-perceived values, Boyatzis developed a model of three distinct philosophical orientations with ways of perceiving values and their meaning. They were pragmatic, intellectual (i.e., analytic), and humanistic (Boyatzis, et al., 2000), as discussed briefly in Chapter 2 as part of the Ideal Self.

These previous levels contributed to the development of an image a person had of themselves. At this level, there is interaction with their relational and social environment. The result is a self-image or self-concept, which

Table 4.1 The Emotional and Social Intelligence Competencies

Emotional Intelligence Competencies

<u>Self-awareness cluster</u> concerns knowing one's internal states, preferences, resources, and intuitions. **Emotional self-awareness**: Recognizing one's emotions and their effects

<u>Self-management cluster</u> refers to managing ones' internal states, impulses, and resources:

Emotional self-control: Keeping disruptive emotions and impulses in check

Adaptability: Flexibility in handling change

Achievement orientation: Striving to improve or meeting a standard of excellence

Positive outlook: Seeing the positive aspects of things and the future

Social Intelligence Competencies

<u>Social awareness cluster</u> refers to how people handle relationships and awareness of others' feelings, needs, and concerns

Empathy: Sensing others' feelings and perspectives, and taking an active interest in their concerns

Organizational Awareness: Reading a group's emotional currents and power relationships

<u>Relationship management cluster</u> concerns the skill or adeptness at inducing desirable responses in others

Coach and mentor: Sensing others' development needs and bolstering their abilities

Inspirational leadership: Inspiring and guiding individuals and groups

Influence: Wielding effective tactics for persuasion

Conflict management: Negotiating and resolving disagreements

Teamwork: Working with others toward shared goals; creating group synergy in pursuing collective goals

Cognitive Intelligence Competencies

Systems thinking: Describing multiple causal relationships, like PERT charts; describing multiple chains of if–then causal links

Pattern recognition: Describing themes or patterns in seemingly unrelated information; using metaphors or analogies to interpret patterns observed

Source: Adapted from Boyatzis and Goleman (2007), ESCI, and ESCIU.

incorporates a degrees of self-esteem or comparative evaluation. Each of these levels cause the emergence of certain behavior, behavior patterns, and possibly habits (i.e., competencies). At the level observed by others are the competencies or more typically, the clusters of competencies. The clusters may be theoretically organized, as in the emotional, social, and cognitive intelligence competencies as shown in Table 4.1, or they may appear to others as empirical clusters, which are likely different from the theoretical clusters (Boyatzis, et al., 2000).

This multilevel model provides more specificity and causality within a person than the more traditional knowledge, skills, and attitudes (KSA) model. The KSA models did not specify how and why such personal characteristics may be causally related to each other as well as reinforce each other.

The Behavioral Level of the Real Self Are Competencies

ICT explains and predicts sustained, desired change in any aspect of an individual or people in our collectives. At the individual level, the Real Self in ICT is defined as predominantly the experience and observations others have of a person. For the most comprehensive view, the Real Self should also include aspects of the person that they may choose not to show others in certain settings. When attempting to ascertain who a person is at work, at home, or in leisure settings, the behavioral level of the personality is of central interest to the framing the Real Self. Although we could study any of the other aspects of individual change, from neural plasticity to traits and values, for this reason it seems most appropriate to focus this next section on the behavioral level or competencies. At the collective levels, the Real Self appears as the norms and values (i.e., the culture and climate) of the dyads, teams, organizations, communities, or countries. Before focusing on behavioral competencies, a brief discussion of change in other levels within personality is useful.

Sustained, desired change can occur at levels other than behavioral. For example, neural plasticity has been documented in several forms, from neurogenesis to changing neural pathways. Erikson, et al. (1998) provided early work showing the growth of new neurons in the brain: neurogenesis, emerging from stem cells of an adult in the olfactory lobe or hippocampus. Maguire and colleagues (Maguire, et al., 2000) documented changes in neural pathways by showing changes in neural volume in the upper hippocampus of London taxi drivers after several years of training and experience. Of course, there can be changes at the physiological level that are neither intentional nor desired. Changes in an infant's hormonal systems have appeared as a result of acute stress in the birth mother during pregnancy (Lautarescu, et al., 2019), and heavy alcohol use of the mother resulted in fetal alcohol syndrome or low brain weight at birth (Roszel, 2015). Early trauma and growing in a chaotic, high-stress environment has also been shown to change a growing child's stress levels and decrease the likelihood of physiological resilience (Jaffee et al., 2012; Smith & Pollak, 2020).

Changes in unconscious motives have been tried but not shown to occur (McClelland & Winter, 1969). These and related efforts to provide motivation training have had profound positive effects on behavior and outcomes. For example, Achievement motivation training resulted in the new businesses and new jobs created and taxes paid in multiple studies in India and the US (McClelland & Winter, 1969; Miron & McClelland, 1979). Power motivation training resulted in less recidivism from alcoholism (Cutter, et al., 1977). But there was no evidence that any of the participants changed their dominant, unconscious motives.

Efforts to change one's traits have shown remarkable stability. Studies have shown some change in traits over decades (Heatherton & Weinberger, 1994). Previous studies suggested a lack of malleability of Big Five traits over 70 years (McCrae & Costa, 2008). More recent studies have offered a different picture. For example, in randomized, control group studies of intentional change of Big Five traits, one study showed no effect and another showed positive changes in traits and related behavior 16 weeks later (Hudson & Fraley, 2015). But intentional efforts to change a trait level have not been promising, except possibly in the area of self-efficacy (DeCharms, 1968; Bandura, 1981).

To understand the behavioral level, in 1970, David McClelland at Harvard University proposed to inductively study what enabled people to be effective in various jobs or roles. He called it a "competency study." I was asked to collect and analyze the data for the first study, which was about supervisory chaplains in the US Navy.

After a series of other studies of human service workers (and a few other jobs) in New York City, McClelland published the classic paper "Testing for Competence Rather Than Intelligence" (McClelland, 1973). The work on assessment centers had been growing from the early studies of Doug Bray and colleagues at AT&T, like Bill Byham. The assessment centers used "dimensions" as the characteristics they were coding from participants' behaviors in the simulations and role-plays (Thornton & Byham, 1982). They went on to create a consulting company called Development Dimensions International to expand this work to other organizations. These dimensions were a combination of characteristics of the person, an ability or capability, and characteristics of the job (e.g., specific tasks) to which they were applying or holding.

During 1975, Marvin Dunnette at the University of Minnesota and one of his doctoral students, Robert Silzer, began shifting from coding dimensions in their assessment centers to examining abilities and behavior directly (Silzer, 2023). The consulting company Dunnette founded to conduct this research and examine applications was Personnel Decisions Incorporated, which helped organizations with psychological measurement, and later the research arm Personnel Decisions Research Incorporated. Their key concepts evolved into competencies with that label. Meanwhile, a fifth person added to the McClelland/Boyatzis and Dunnette/Silzer work who was also a key in

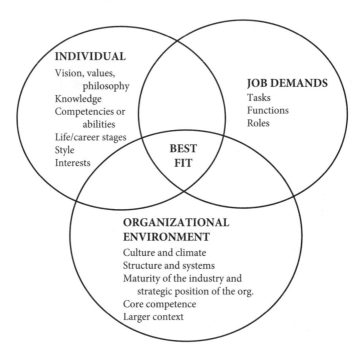

Figure 4.3 Theory of action and job performance. Best fit (maximum performance, stimulation, and commitment) = area of maximum overlap or integration
Source: Boyatzis (1982, 2008).

beginning this competency research, Dr. Patricia McLagan of Minneapolis, was consulting to many organizations.

The proposal was simple: if you wish to discover what enables a person to be effective in a role or job, compare the outstanding (i.e., most effective) performers against average or, if you can find them, poor or inadequate performers (McClelland, 1973). The early efforts used a wide variety of psychological tests to assess various characteristics of how people were thinking and feeling. But those of us doing this work felt that we were ignoring the most obvious observation: the superior performers were doing things differently than others as the theory of performance from Boyatzis (1982), shown in Figure 4.3.

To capture their behavior, as well as thoughts and feelings at the time, a new technique was developed called the Behavioral Event Interview (BEI) (Boyatzis, 1982; Spencer & Spencer, 1993). It began as an evening discussion around my dining room table in 1974. A group of the staff of McBer and Company thought to integrate three methods of data collection: the Thematic Apperception Test (TAT) (Murray, 1938; McClelland, 1985), critical incident interviewing (CII) (Flanagan, 1954), and biographical analysis of biodata (Dailey, 1971).

The idea was to ask people to recall a recent event at work in which they felt effective. The main questions or probes would be adapted from the TAT: What led up to the situation? Who was involved? What did they say or do with whom? What was the result? Additional probes could be asked during the interview especially, such as what someone was thinking or feeling at that moment. The person was then asked about an event in which they felt relatively ineffective. More effective and ineffective incidents were solicited until four to six stories of high salience and relatively recent events were described in detail. The aim was to pull sufficient detail to enable the interviewer to write a script for a video about the event. Interviewers were trained in journalistic approaches rather than traditional therapeutic or psychological ones. The emphasis was on documenting what actually occurred rather than just perceptions on some preconceived model (Boyatzis, 1982; Spencer & Spencer, 1993; McClelland, 1998)

The interviews were recorded and later transcribed. The analysis team would use a compare and contrast analysis going back and forth between the critical incidents from the superior performers versus those from the average performers. A thematic analysis was done and the themes were developed into formal codes and a codebook (Boyatzis, 1998). Because they focused on a set of related behavior (actions) organized around an underlying intent, they were called competencies. Interrater reliability was established to determine confidence in the themes or codes observed (Boyatzis, 1998).

A competency is defined as a capability or ability of a person, not a characteristic of a job, that results in effective performance of a role or job (Boyatzis, 1982; McClelland, 1973). It is a set of related but different behaviors (i.e., a collection of skills), often called alternate manifestations, organized around an underlying construct or intent. This diverges from the earlier KSA models in industrial and organizational psychology. For example, listening and asking questions are skills. Someone may listen or ask questions for different reasons. A person can ask questions and listen to ingratiate themselves or to be seen positively by others. They could ask questions and listen to understand another person. Or they may ask questions and listen to catch the person in a lie or deception. A competency, therefore, is more than a skill or single action. The underlying intent around which the set of skills or behavior are organized is critical to understanding the functions, benefits, and measurement of a competency. Therefore, a competency is a capability and can vary in its expression even from the same person in different situations.

Competencies have been confused with proficiencies, which are often minimal actions needed to perform a task (Bachkirova & Lawton Smith, 2015). The term "competency" does not always translate across cultures. In my work in Italy in the early 1990s, I came to realize that the direct translation of "competency" into "*competenze*" conveyed a different meaning. The more accurate word in Italiano is "*capacitá*." Experiences I had in various parts of England in the 1980s also showed that "capability" was a closer label in the UK for what we meant by competencies.

Another source of confusion is the validation of the competencies or competency model. Organizations and professions often seek valid, easy ways to constitute a competency model by asking a large number of the job or role occupants to describe which competencies they think are needed for effective performance. Sometimes this is done through sophisticated methods like Delphi techniques which are interactive surveys of a panel of experts or those with a lot of experience in a domain to refine a descriptive list. The information collected in this way can be called expert opinion, values, or attitudes about the competencies needed.

A study of the competencies of managers at all levels with samples from 12 large organizations in the public and private sector showed a troubling consequence of expert, opinion, and value-based competency models (Boyatzis, 1982). When managers and executives were asked what competencies were needed for effective performance, they identified a list of characteristics that they might have called competencies. The lists were a confusing mixture of skills, job tasks, style, values, knowledge, and some actual competencies. For example, someone might say that a manager needed to be able to select and hire staff. This is an important task of a manager, but not a personal characteristic. To select staff well, a manager would have to use a number of actual competencies like empathy, organizational awareness, and pattern recognition. When the lists generated from opinion and expert polls were compared against competencies that predicted effectiveness from performance measures, a startling discovery was made (Boyatzis, 1982): about half of the items were accurate and useful, but 25% were irrelevant and 25% were opposite to the competencies that predicted managerial performance.

The use of competency models developed from expert and opinion sources would be a deceptive model against which to help someone develop an image of their Real Self. The organizational applications of training or certifying or hiring people according to these opinion-based lists results in the waste of time and effort. These applications of opinion-based competency models can institutionalize mediocrity in various occupations and limit access of those groups not deemed appropriate at the time (Fallows, 1985). In other arenas, commonly held beliefs about the characteristics that produce performance, even in the face of data refuting those contentions, have resulted in a massive waste of money and sometimes lives (Fallows, 1981).

While the early studies used the BEI interview along with a battery of tests, the tests soon were dropped because of the richness of the observations from the interviews. After conducting several hundred of these inductive competency models, similarities were appearing. For example, every study of mid-level managers or executives included influencing others, emotional self-control, adaptability, and empathy as characteristics of the outstanding performers and were not consistently present, if at all, in the average or poor performers (Boyatzis, 1982).

This resulted in the ability to develop a generic competency model. Boyatzis (1982) was an empirical reanalysis of raw data to yield a generic competency model for managers, from supervisors to executives and leaders. Conceptual synthesis was done to describe generic competency models for human services and resource jobs, sales jobs, and technical jobs (Spencer & Spencer, 1993). These were later further synthesized into a generic competency model for professionals and managers (Goleman, 1998).

The competencies appeared to form a number of clusters. The observation was that seldom in real life or at work does a person use or demonstrate only one competency at a time. Empirical clusters were discovered as a result of factor analysis, discriminant function analysis, or other multivariate statistical analyses. In Boyatzis (1982), five clusters were reported in analysis of coded, qualitative themes from behavioral event interviews. They were the goal and action management cluster, the leadership cluster, the human resource management cluster, the directing subordinates cluster, and the focus on others cluster (Boyatzis, 1982). Spencer and Spencer (1993), in their synthesis of various performance-based models, revealed six clusters: achievement and action, helping and human service, impact and influence, and managerial, cognitive, and personal effectiveness. Goleman (1998) proposed four clusters that later emerged as emotional and social intelligence competencies as self-awareness, self-management, social awareness, and relationship management (Boyatzis & Goleman, 2007), as shown in Table 4.1. The cognitive or analytic reasoning competencies formed a fifth cluster (Boyatzis & Goleman, 2007).

From hundreds of competency studies on dozens of jobs in the public, private, and nonprofit sectors from over 120 countries, the various performance validated behavioral indicators were used to create a multi-rater questionnaire (a 360-degree assessment) that would be easier to administer and less costly for assessing the most vital competencies. Based on an earlier form called the Self-Assessment and External Assessment Questionnaire, developed in 1991, Boyatzis and Goleman (1996, 1999, 2007) developed and refined two 360s. One was called the Emotional and Social Competency Inventory (ESCI) and the other was called the ESCIU (for the university version), which included a cluster of cognitive and analytic competencies, notably systems thinking and pattern recognition, also shown in Table 4.1.

In contrast to other efforts to assess emotional intelligence at the trait (Petrides & Furnham, 2001) or performance trait (Mayer, Salovey & Caruso, 2000) or self-image level (Bar-On, 1997), the ESCI and ESCIU provided assessment at the behavior level as observed by others (Cherniss, 2010). A series of studies over 25 years established the reliability and validity of these competencies as to psychometric standards and against performance in many jobs (Boyatzis, Gaskin & Wei, 2015; Boyatzis, 2018). Access to the ESCI for research or to the ESCI or ESCIU for development are explained in the appendix.

The Boyatzis and Goleman multi-rater assessment was built on a circumplex model: each competency is theoretically linked to certain others. For example, the demonstration of the empathy competency would often require or be shown with demonstration of the emotional self-awareness competency. Psychometrically, these two competencies would both be expected to be enacted in real-life situations in the same events at closely related moments than, say, empathy would be with other competencies like influence or adaptability.

One result of this circumplex model is that empirically, the competencies do not always operate as separate characteristics. As a result, empirically derived clusters may or may not be the same as the theoretical clusters. Boyatzis, Goleman, and Rhee (2000) examined clusters from numerous separate competency studies and found this to be the case. In the earlier Boyatzis (1982) study of competency models of managers from 12 large organizations, the theoretical clusters were entrepreneurship, interpersonal, intellectual reasoning, and social emotional maturity. Using a multivariate analysis, the empirical clusters were goal and action management, leadership, human resource management, directing subordinates, and focusing on others clusters (Boyatzis, 1982).

Another example comes from a competency study of senior bank executives, in which Van Oosten, McBride, and Taylor (2019) found that the competencies formed two clusters. One they called emotional acumen, which consisted of competencies like emotional self-awareness, empathy, emotional self-control, and teamwork. The other cluster they called change leader, which consists of competencies like achievement orientation, change catalyst, and inspirational leadership. The emotional acumen cluster predicted career satisfaction and engagement of the bank executives. Meanwhile, the change leader cluster predicted perceived leadership effectiveness, but was negatively predictive of career satisfaction and engagement.

Regardless of whether the clusters are theoretically or empirically determined, the observed behavior by others at work or at home that constitute the Real Self will not be about single competencies, but clusters of them. The sources of the multi-rater assessments or observations may influence the clusters as well. Battista-Foguet and colleagues (2014) showed that certain competencies were more likely to be observed by work colleagues. The observations from personal relationships or friends and family members may be different. A manager or boss is more likely to observe a person networking or making presentations than subordinates, who are more likely to observe a person demonstrating teamwork or influence competencies. In a classic paper reviewing a series of studies, which continued to be reaffirmed by later research, Lewin and Zwany (1976) found that peers were the most consistently valid observers of a person's performance than bosses or subordinates. Because of this phenomena, it is likely that people from different vantage points will notice different aspects of a person's behavioral repertoire.

If the Real Self is constructed from observations of others, it is therefore important to collect observations from many different people who are in as many different roles vis-à-vis the focal person as possible. As mentioned earlier, the Me at My Best exercise asks a person to interview 10 to 25 people with whom they interact in work, home, and social settings. In this exercise, the patterns reveal a person's strengths in multiple relationships and settings.

In 1998, David McClelland proposed that tipping points of the competencies were important to understand. A certain frequency in the use of a competency could tip a person from average performance into effective, superior, or outstanding. In an empirical test of that idea on senior partners in a Big Five accounting firm, Boyatzis (2006a) empirically observed tipping points for each competency. The financial contribution (i.e., operating profit) from the accounts of each senior partner over seven quarters showed that those partners demonstrating competencies above the tipping point contributed significantly more operating profit than those senior partners below the tipping point. When the analysis was conducted at the cluster level, two additional observations were made. First, it did not have to be the same competencies from within a cluster shown above the tipping point to move a senior partner into outstanding financial performance. Second, the most effective senior partners demonstrated some competencies above the tipping point from each of the clusters. The clusters in this model were labeled emotional intelligence (self-management and self-regulation), social intelligence, and cognitive intelligence.

Strengths and Weaknesses: Our Personal Balance Sheet

Our Real Self when compared to our Ideal Self yields a set of judgments. When they are consistent, it can be called a strength. When they are divergent, it can be called a weakness. The odd twist is that we do not always wish to use our strengths. We may have behavioral habits and competencies that others consider strengths but that we do not see as part of our Ideal Self, and we may not wish to focus on them in the future. For example, if a person sees themselves as an individual contributor—what Ed Schein called a career anchor as individual contributor—they may not want a leadership or management position even if they were effective in them previously (Schein & Van Maanen, 2013). For others, a promotion to a leadership position is sought after and a key part of their Ideal Self. But for a person with an individual contributor career anchor, management and leadership is a chore or obligation. It becomes another Ought Self. So not all strengths of a person in others' views are consistent with their current Ideal Self.

Similarly, behavioral capabilities or competencies that are shown less frequently than needed in a person's Ideal Self are not always weaknesses. A person may have a low tolerance for administrative details, for example. Such attention to detail is a competency needed in some jobs, like accounting or research, but can be delegated to others when in management or leadership roles. A tendency to not use attention to detail may therefore not be a weakness that needs development or attention.

But when the comparison is made between a person's Ideal Self and the Real Self, the gaps or discrepancies may be parts of their behavioral repertoire that need work. In this way, they may be a weakness for the person.

When placed on a summary sheet, a person's strengths and weaknesses form a type of personal balance sheet. These are personal or human assets that can be used to generate current performance in the analogous way an organization's balance sheet summarizes assets and liabilities that can be used for performance.

Although originally intended to compensate for the problem and deficiency approach predominant in our families and work norms, strength-based approaches to development might communicate misinformation and misdirection. A preoccupation with weakness or failings is not only a quicksand of NEA, but precludes valuing and using strengths. At the same time, various aspects of the positive psychology movement and self-esteem programs in schools may start with laudable intent, but have often deteriorated to deflections and disinformation, and contributed to inflated or incorrect self-images.

When the strengths are PEA arousing actions, like behavior that invoke hope, compassion, mindfulness, and playfulness, the contagion spreads to others. The theory of positive psychology is that strengths beget strengths, or at least encourage others to show and use their strengths. While widely supported in research, an alternative can also occur. When frequently used NEA behaviors, like pride, arrogance, being evaluative, excluding others, and narcissism, the contagion would work the same way and encourage or stimulate more of the same negative behavior in others.

It can also be observed that any competency or behavior when used repeatedly can become a weakness. Overusing a strength may invoke feelings of inadequacy in others; when someone shows energy levels that are perceived as over the top compared to their peers, for example, some describe it as "drinking from a fire hose." This does not raise the level of shared energy, but may in fact curtail others, their engagement, or organizational citizenship.

Changing the Real Self

At the individual level, sustained, desired change of the Real Self, how one acts and is experienced by others, begins with changes in a person's behavior and habits. Either preceded by behavior change or following it, changes in how a person actually views themselves is part of a process of sustained, desired change.

Competencies Can Be Developed

The genesis of the concept of a competency was something that produced effective performance, citizenship, and well-being. It described how a person acted. The roots of thought and emotional processes and cognitive, affective, and physiological processes would be part of such changes and either be preceded by or followed by self-awareness of the changes. In 1974, a group of us were asked by several US federal authorities in higher education (including the National Institutes of Education and the Fund for the Improvement of Post Secondary Education) to help colleges and universities seeking to assess the changes or outcomes occurring with their students during their journey through their academic programs.

The impetus for outcome assessment was twofold. First, there was a national priority to aid the development of what were called at the time "nontraditional" students. These were collegiate students beginning their studies after

21 years of age, women, and members of visible minority groups. Second, given our emerging research on competencies that predicted effectiveness in a wide variety of jobs, roles, and careers, there was a priority to develop the "whole person": that is, it was thought that attending college should develop knowledge and abilities that are needed in work and life. A result of the whole person movement in education included what we call today emotional, social, and cognitive competencies, as well as knowledge and values.

The essence of outcome assessment was answering the simple question, "What are our students learning?" How were the students different at graduation than they were at entry? Were these the capabilities and knowledge (i.e., declarative, procedural, and metacognitive knowledge, which included technical skills) needed for effectiveness in life and work?

Few schools were engaged in such assessment at the time. A notable exception was Alverno College in Milwaukee (Mentkowski & Associates, 2000). When the administration of President George H. Bush insisted that accreditation associations would have to require outcome assessment if they were to be eligible for federal funding in 1989, the process entered the hallowed halls of every college and university. A few years later, similar requirements would be made of colleges and universities throughout the European Union through the Bologna Accords in 1999.

In 1979, Jerry Zoffer, a visionary dean of the Katz School of Management at the University of Pittsburgh, was chair of the American Association of Collegiate Schools of Business (the accrediting body for management schools first in the US and then elsewhere) Accreditation Research Committee. They were searching for more empirical and relevant ways to accredit management schools than the traditional counting of books in their library or the number of PhDs on the faculty. They initiated a series of research outcome studies of MBA programs. Given our research on competencies since 1970 and David McClelland's influential 1973 paper in the *American Psychologist*, McBer and Company was asked to propose a set of studies. Because of the work I was doing in preparing what became my 1982 research book on competencies of managers, I led the McBer team.

The good news was that we found that above-average MBA programs had a significant value added in that their graduates showed more of certain competencies than the entering students. Cross-sectional research designs were used to get results in a timely manner. It was also found that the set of competencies on which value added was shown were different for different programs. The bad news was that the number of competencies on which there was significant value added was greater than the impact of four-year undergraduate programs, but much less than what would have been expected given the time and money spent on the MBA programs. Within 12 years, vision- and mission-based accreditation became the basis for evaluating MBA programs for accreditation.

In 1979, seeing the emerging research and track record at training and development from McBer and Company, the American Management Associations (AMA) asked us to develop a competency-based MBA program to prepare learners for actual management and leadership jobs. It was a Sisyphean effort against the current norms and practices. An innovative former dean of the Management School at Ohio State University, Harry Evarts, was asked to lead this effort for the AMA. A program was developed, and eventually received degree granting authority from one or two states. But changes in management at the AMA resulted in dropping the priority of the program and funding, and over a few years, the program fizzled.

When I joined the full-time faculty at the Weatherhead School of Management (WSOM) at Case Western Reserve University in the spring of 1987, Dean Scott Cowen, John Aram, and the chair of the Organizational Behavior Department, David Kolb, asked me to begin an outcome assessment process. They wanted it to further focus and enhance efforts they already had underway to transform the MBA into a relevant and useful degree graduating students with the knowledge and competencies ready to lead and manage effectively.

As a result of a few years of baseline, cross-sectional, and one longitudinal outcome study, the faculty rose in consensus and decided to dramatically change the MBA program to build needed competencies and add value orientations to the knowledge and technical skills they were already imparting.

A new MBA program was launched in 1990. One of the design principles was ICT. Every MBA received a semester-long course designed with ICT and focusing on competency development. During the first third of the course, the students created a personal vision (Ideal Self). They discussed it with a coach, a faculty member, and with peers. In the second third of the course, they received feedback on professional coding of competencies from audio-recording of critical incidents at work, video-recordings of group simulations, and a 360. Then they identified strengths to use in pursuit of their vision and several weaknesses to develop prior to graduation.

Early longitudinal studies showed a dramatic increase in competency development in the one- and two-year MBA programs (Boyatzis, et al., 2002; Boyatzis, et al., 1995) for the students entering at about 27–28 years old, with typically five years of prior work experience. The program and outcome assessment continued from the baseline studies in 1987–1990 to 2014, and the results continued to be impressive (Boyatzis & Cavanagh, 2018).

A comparative graph is shown in Figure 4.4 of the impact of this program on the emotional and social intelligence (ESI) competencies as discussed earlier in this chapter. When compared with published studies of outcome assessments of above-average MBA programs and leadership training in government and industry (Cherniss & Adler, 2000), the WSOM MBA design improved these competencies in our students and did so dramatically better than other above-average MBA programs and leadership training in government and industry. In longitudinal studies following several cohorts for two to three years after they graduated, the improvements in ESI competencies as viewed by others maintained at about 50% improvement from their initial levels when entering the MBA (Wheeler, 2008). Comparable efforts with students in the Professional Fellows Program, who were mostly in their mid- to late forties, showed similar results (Ballou, et al., 1999).

The results of 39 longitudinal studies, including one following people five to 19 years after graduation, showed that with an appropriate design, the Real Self could change in sustained, desired ways. One study showed that the same course delivered at Escola Superior d'Administració i Direcció d'Empreses (known worldwide as ESADE) in Barcelona was able to document significant increases in an MBA's clarity, specificity, and comprehensiveness of their vision (Mosteo, et al., 2016).

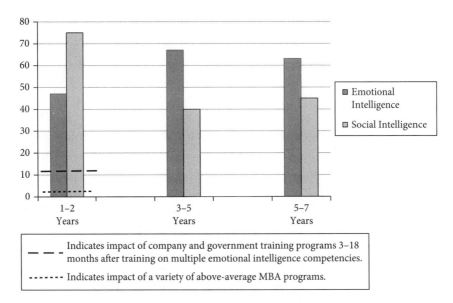

Figure 4.4 Percentage improvement of Emotional and Social Intelligence Competencies of different groups of MBA graduates taking the Intentional Change Course for 1990 to 2000

Source: Adapted from Goleman, et al. (2002), and appeared in Boyatzis (2008).

The Shared Real Self at Other Levels

Principle 8: As a fractal theory, ICT describes sustained, desired change at all levels of human endeavor from individual to dyads, teams, organizations, communities, countries, and global processes.

Team Shared Real Self (Norms) and Possible Conflict

The shared Real Self (shared norms and values) in teams can propel them to excellence or slow them down, or push them in the opposite direction to their shared vision (shared Ideal Self), as shown in Figure 4.5. Druskat and Kayes (2000) conceived an ingenious field study. They studied the norms (i.e., rules of behavior) and Real Self of 26 MBA teams of five to eight members in the first semester of their program. In the second semester, when continuing to work together on projects in other courses, each team was evaluated in terms of their performance (such as grades on a team project and faculty subjective assessment of the quality of their work) and the team members' description of their degree of learning. Team learning was defined and measured as continuously seeking feedback, sharing knowledge with each other, and focusing on solving problems.

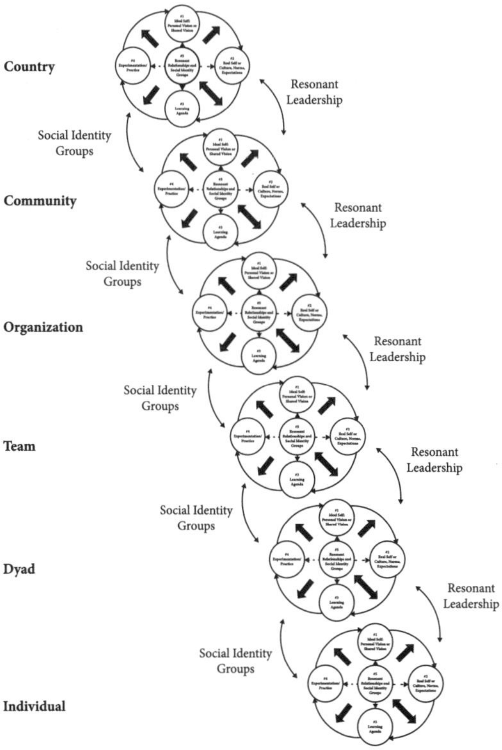

The norms that predicted performance distinctively were proactivity in problem solving, and negatively (inversely) confronting team members who break their team norms. That is, performance was better when team members avoided confrontations. Meanwhile,

Figure 4.5 The multilevel fractals of Intentional Change Theory
Source: Boyatzis (2008, 2015).

norms that predicted team learning were proactive problem solving, inter-personal understanding (i.e., using empathy with each other), and inversely creating clarity about work procedures. In other words, except for problem solving, the norms that produced the most learning were somewhat opposite to the norms that produced the best performance.

In most settings, teams are formed to produce a product or service, as well as innovate or improve something. They are also expected to learn for the sake of future adaptation and innovation. And yet this study suggests that aspects of team norms may polarize the outcomes and be self-defeating. In this way, the shared Real Self in teams can help or hinder the purpose to which the team aspires.

For example, the Adventure Consultants, in preparation for their ascent of Mount Everest (explained in more detail in the next chapter), ignored the need for team shared behavior. They did not spend time training as a team, instead relying on their individual training as mountaineers. They did not develop any shared norms to handle conflicting advice from base camp about weather conditions. It resulted in only a few reaching the summit and several dying on the return down the mountain. The theme of prior training norms in teams is reiterated in the Deep Cavers example reviewed in previous chapters as well.

In another arena of physical danger, wild-fire forest fighting, work is done in teams. Each team is headed by an incident commander. In a study of outstanding level 1 incident commanders of the US Forest Service versus their less effective counterparts, critical incidents from work revealed that even during the down times between fires, the better incident commanders prepared training materials and contacted and performed some training exercises with possible future team members (Boyatzis, et al., 2017). This was particularly impressive because there was a high probably that incident commanders would be part of in future teams, not necessarily the people they were training.

Team development was at the heart of several processes attempting to im-prove quality of services and products. These efforts were called quality circles, self-managing work teams (Druskat & Wheeler, 2003), lean manufacturing processes, and Agile (Burke & Noumair, 2015).

Norms and Culture as Shared Real Self in Organizations

The shared Real Self of organizations, also evident in their norms and values, can account for dramatic differences in later performance or even survival. At a time when Blockbuster was building new outlets in shopping malls around the US, Netflix developed a mail order system for delivering DVDs to people's homes. When the founders of Netflix offered to sell to Blockbuster, their owners refused, saying that they were in a different business. They had brick-and-mortar buildings to allow customers to come in and physically browse the stacks to find a VHS or DVD to view, and their staff were trained to help customers find something of interest. Netflix did not have that norm of personal conversation. Of course, some 20 years later, Netflix is the model of streaming videos and so successful that they finance their own movies and series. Meanwhile, younger readers may not know what Blockbuster was, because the company no longer exists. Their organizational Real Self was part of a previous retail model and way of accessing videos—and sticking to this model held them back from sustained, desired change.

Culture change became a major theme in organizations since the 1980s. Some approaches sought changes in practices and procedures through work simplification or business process re-engineering (Hammer & Champy, 1993), or changing the degree of differentiation and integration in the structure (Lawrence & Lorsch, 1967). As with the team-level change seeking quality improvements, the flaw in these efforts was often an assumption that everyone involved shared the same vision and were committed to changing their current behavior (shared Real Self) to suit the new practices. Culture change often sought a change in the organizational climate (i.e., what it was like to actually work at the company) (Litwin & Stringer 1967). Like the efforts at improving performance management (Likert, 1968), *if* the change process involved building a shared vision and *if* there was a consensus as to the data fed back to people about their current, shared Real Self, then changes were possible, like with the Burke-Litwin model (1992).

But all too often the change effort focused on a larger concept, changing the existing organizational culture (Burke & Noumair, 2015; Burke & Litwin, 1992; Weisbord, 1976; Beckhard & Harris, 1987). Unfortunately, an organization's history of attempting change, and their relative success or failure, influenced the likelihood of any new changes occurring (Armenakis & Bedeian, 1999). When a discrepancy approach (Real vs. Ideal culture) was taken, the NEA and Ought Self were aroused, confusing the effort.

Many organizations determined that culture was too enduring to be able to change. In one pharmaceutical company with which colleagues and I worked, we found current practices and norms that would dramatically help reduce the time to develop and get new drugs approved. One of those norms or practices was to use the Federal Drug Administration (FDA) as a source of consultative advice before submitting the voluminous forms and studies for approval. Sadly, the current organizational culture had a lingering belief in the FDA as an adversary, stemming from conflicts the top executives had with federal authorities many decades earlier, and had trouble using this action to improve their drug development process. The Community Pulls Together or Apart: The Community Shared Real Self Community-level change in the Real Self of its constituent members (their behavior change) or the overall shared Real Self in terms of norms and values is not subtle. Sometimes, to overcome cognitive dissonance reduction or expectation effects, assessment of the change at the individual member level is elusive. In the MBA program of WSOM, we had an excellent setting to observe such changes over a 25-year period.

One community within which these changes are occurring are the multiple cohorts attending the program. Changes in the program and school are organizational levels. For them, the larger university and surrounding national and global issues are the larger environment. The political and social environment is a larger community of employers of the graduates, alumni, clients, donors, staff, and administrators.

As described earlier, the desired changes were implemented in 1990 for the full-time and part-time MBAs (other graduate programs followed). Entering MBAs were assessed on a variety of behavioral measures and assessed again a month before graduation up until 2014, when the formal outcome assessment of MBAs ceased. The full data sets can be seen in Boyatzis and Cavanagh (2018), with detailed baseline data in Boyatzis, Stubbs and Taylor (2002). Due to a few computer crashes and mishandling of the graduating data, two years were lost in the late 1990s. The full 25-year history and trends were recorded in parts in several publications (Passarelli, et al., 2018; Boyatzis, et al., 2013). To ensure comparable data sources (i.e., the same tests and measures), a subset of 2001 to 2012 were examined in detail in Passarelli, Boyatzis, and Wei (2018) and are portrayed in two graphs in Figure 4.6. One graph is the change in self-assessment of the MBAs on the emotional, social, and cognitive intelligence competencies. The second graph is the change in behavioral assessment collected from observers and informants (a 360), which is claimed to be the Real Self in ICT. The person's own self-assessment is their mental model and image of their abilities and behavior, but often flawed, for reasons discussed earlier.

Change in Competencies as Rated by Self

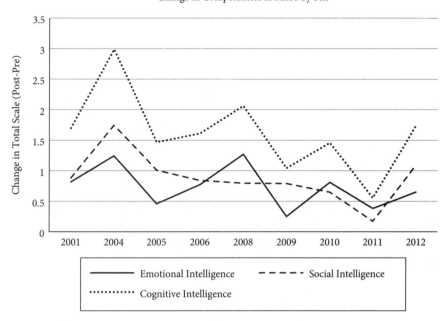

Change in Competencies as Rated by Others

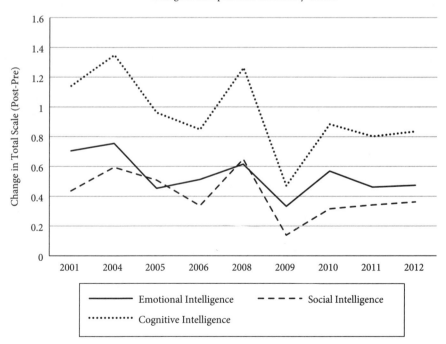

Figure 4.6 Entering to graduating changes in EI, SI, and CI Competencies, 2001 to 2012

Source: Adapted from Passarelli, et al. (2017) and Boyatzis, et al. (2012.)

This analysis allows interpretation at the community level of the shared Real Self and how it affected individual student change. Statistical analyses on which the graphs are based showed significant improvement on most of the competencies in many of the cohorts (Boyatzis & Cavanagh, 2018). Cognitive competencies improved the most every cohort. This is to be expected, since an MBA program is predominantly focused on analytic processes with a heavy emphasis on quantitative subjects like accounting, finance, economics, and operations. To further support the concerns about self-assessment, it is worth noting that in every cohort there is a difference in perception of improvement of emotional intelligence (EI) competencies versus social intelligence (SI) competencies. Self-assessment shows more improvement in SI competencies in four cohorts, while others saw EI competencies with greater improvement than SI competencies in six cohorts.

This may be because self-perceptions are delusional; or, it may be because MBAs believe that they have made more progress in their social talent than others observe. Meanwhile, others see improvement in both, but greater improvement in the EI competencies.

A program dynamic noted in this data is a "sawtooth effect." This means that often one cohort of MBAs will show the opposite effect of improvement than the previous or following cohort. This effect has been noted in many programs and may be the result of the "star effect" and limited programmatic resources. The star effect refers to members of one cohort who are seen as distinctive stars in their performance, community involvement, and job performance, and it is difficult for the following cohort to live up to that standard. In part, resources are not independent. For example, various clubs that participate in community volunteer programs, case competitions, and internal committees would have leadership changes and programmatic efforts that span multiple years and therefore affect the availability of posts and programs to two consecutive cohorts.

Another organizational- and community-level factor is institutional leadership. Large drops in competency improvement (Real Self) of MBAs, sometimes to nonsignificant changes, were seen in 2005, 2006, 2009, and 2011 and were in part due to leadership changes. Between 1998 and 2007, the school had four sitting deans and four interim deans, while the university during this period had four provosts and four interim provosts, and four presidents and four interim presidents. Such leadership turmoil affects the rest of the system. Regardless of written vision statements, each dean, provost, and president has their own version of a desired vision. They have their own values and leadership style. This degree of uncertainty in leadership and possible direction created an NEA climate. When people are uncertain beyond a reasonable comfort level dictated by norms of their culture, defensive postures are adapted to protect from unwanted possibilities.

The mere fact of the rapid changes revealed conflicts at the board, administration, donor, and prospective employer levels. Two of the sitting deans serving from 2003 to 2006 did not like or value behavioral aspects of an MBA and felt that the only true subject should be finance. Such views were expressed and evident to students, faculty, staff, alumni, donors, employers, and others, which created a critical, NEA tone about the school and a key aspect of its distinctiveness.

The social fabric, motivation, organizational citizenship (e.g., doing more than your job), and engagement were thus at relative lows. It is not surprising that students did not increase their emotional, social, and cognitive intelligence as much during the last few years of this reign of confusion in 2005 and 2006. For example, a climate survey of faculty views conducted in 2007 showed that faculty felt that their satisfaction with their academic community, quality of colleagueship, and school leadership were at all-time lows. The good news was that with a faculty-driven dean selection process in 2007, there was a rebound in these perceptions in the faculty climate survey of 2008.

The dramatic drops in improvement of the Real Self of MBAs in 2009 and again in 2011 seemed to be driven by even larger environmental issues. A global recession and financial crisis that began in 2008 and spread rapidly in 2009 severely limited jobs, raising NEA fears about the future and employment possibilities. Investment banks previously considered "too big to fail" went under. There were runs on bank deposits in many countries. People were losing their homes as the mortgage and liquidity crisis gained momentum. US unemployment rose to 10% in 2009, and other countries were far worse. Employment of the MBAs from this program—which typically at three months following graduation was in the 90th percentile—was at 53% in 2009 and 71% in 2010. As anxiety spread among students and the staff who were trying to help with placement, many diverted any discretionary time to basic skills and subjects, believing that stronger financial skills and knowledge would be more fundamental than leadership or management competencies.

Many forces were occurring in the program, school, university, and wider environment during these years. The norms and values (e.g., climate and culture) of the MBA community changed. The ups and downs of positive, desired improvement on the competencies that would predict their success and effectiveness in leadership and management jobs varied.

Some of these same larger environmental factors drove other aspects of community change. Crime increased as uncertainty and fear increased. A reaction formation (one of the ego defense mechanisms) in response to the drop in certainty and fear of loss of jobs, homes, and standard of living resulted in a dramatic increase in communities and countries claiming more exceptionalism. Openness to new ideas decreased, while the blockades caused by the parochialism of "not invented here" increased. These community, country, and global forces during that time all contributed to the organizational and community shared Real Self in terms of norms that restrained and inhibited the possibility of adaptation and sustained, desired change.

Concluding Thoughts

The Real Self is a constellation of the ways we think about ourselves, but most importantly in the context of ICT, it is the way others experience us. In our collectives, it is our norms. Many forces conspire to deceive or deflect a person or group from achieving accurate observations. Some of those forces are self-protective, like ego defensive mechanisms. Others are imposed self-deceptions arising from social desirability, fears, and NEA experiences. Our behavior as experienced by others, which we call competencies, enable us to develop relationships and perform effectively, engage with our work, be a better family member and citizen, and innovate. Competencies can be developed, but they also have a direct effect on how a person or group might continue their pursuit of sustained, desired change. We need the Ideal Self or personal vision as a motivating force. But without the grounding in comparisons to how we act, individually or collectively, the focus of desired change can be elusive or deceptive and waste energy and precious moments of readiness to change. The Ideal and Real Self lead to preparing for new experiences and actions or norms—the actual learning and change in how we act.

With a motivating Ideal Self or shared vision in our collectives, articulation of the real or shared Real Self focuses those involved on how we act as experienced by others. PEA tipping points interrupt the visits of the NEA to enable participants to move ahead. In the context of the Ideal Self or shared vision, the norms and culture of our collectives and the Real Self of individuals create an instantaneous set of comparisons. These comparisons may add to the energy and commitment to change but they may also confuse and deflect it, thereby inhibiting or diminishing the durability of any change effort. The motivating effect of the Ideal Self or shared vision, and to the extent that a PEA tipping point occurs or is invoked at this moment, will determine the likelihood of ICT continuing. The next phase of ICT is to convert these discoveries into an agenda and plan for future action.

5

A Path to My/Our Dreams: Joyful Planning and Preparation (Principle 5)

Principle 5: The third phase of ICT is articulation of a learning agenda and plan to use one's strengths to move closer to the Ideal Self, while possibly working on developing one to two weaknesses. Collectively, it is a shared learning agenda and plan. For best progress and sustainable effort, the weaknesses chosen should be closest to the tipping point of becoming strengths.

Fortune favors the prepared mind.

—Louis Pasteur

There is an idiom in the US that says "getting there should be half the fun." Sadly, with regard to learning and growth, that is seldom true. The saying was popularized by the travel industry decades ago, but between COVID-19, security checks, and delays, it is not that true for geographic travel today either. No parent has driven their children on a family trip and not heard the frustrated voices asking from the back seat, "Are we there yet?" The challenge of making the process and experience of learning and change joyful and exciting begins in the planning stage, when a person or collective formulates where they wish to go and how they wish to get there.

Planning purposive action as an individual or collective is the next phase of sustained, desired change according to ICT, as shown in Figure 5.1. The organization of effort becomes a learning agenda. Articulating specifics of what might be tried becomes a learning plan. For the individual, this is where the vague desire or intent is turned into action, or at least the intent to act. In organizations, a strategic plan is often created to perform this function. But the insistence that change and learning is facilitated by the creation of specific, time-phased goals forces a person—and possibly our teams and organizations—into premature focus and limits exploration of our options or desires. Our studies suggest that while creating and articulating a vision or dream facilitates the sustainability

The Science of Change. Richard E. Boyatzis, Oxford University Press. © Richard E. Boyatzis 2024.
DOI: 10.1093/9780197765142.003.0005

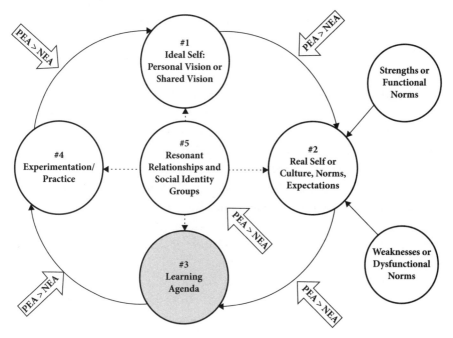

Figure 5.1 The learning agenda in the process of Intentional Change Theory
Source: Boyatzis (2008, 2015).

of a change process, beginning change and learning efforts with specific goals may inhibit progress and certainly the sustainability of the effort. Some of the ideas and observations in this chapter update and expand upon those that were first articulated in Boyatzis and Howard (2013).

A learning agenda can be the articulation of an overall plan of action. It is often phrased in terms of desired activities and possible outcomes. These may be expressed in a variety of forms, from vague to specific or from impressions to observable results. A learning plan, on the other hand, outlines specifics actions to be taken, often in sequence or at specific times. A learning plan may also include anticipation of obstacles, identification of resources to overcome these obstacles, and observable benchmarks of progress or outcomes.

Goal setting and planning are a functional activity in most aspects of life and work. For an individual, they are the intended path to one's Ideal Self, personal vision, and dreams. A learning agenda and plan are a thoughtful guide. In our collectives, they are in part an expression of the desires of those in power (such as top management, parents). In part, they are organizing principles to coalesce and focus collective effort.

To be overly simplistic, goal setting and planning are useful. The research on goal setting has been reviewed and summarized by Edwin Locke and Gary

Latham (1990, 2002, 2013) and integrated into their goal setting theory. Their earlier work concluded that specific and challenging goals were more effective than easy goals, telling someone to "do your best," or no goals at all (Locke, et al., 1981).

In a critique of goal setting, Ordonez, Schweitzer, Galinsky, and Bazerman (2009) described possible undesirable side effects, including being too specific, being too narrow, having too many, making them too challenging, and being unrealistic about the time needed to complete them, as well as increasing risky behavior and promoting unethical behavior. In the same issue of the journal as this critique, Locke and Latham (2009) refuted most of their claims as poor scholarship and not addressing the vast body of research available. Not wanting to make similar mistakes, but allowing for Ordonez, et al.'s (2009) points as possible, in this chapter goal setting is not challenged— but a more nuanced perspective is raised.

Planning helps us to prepare for our path to our vision. It requires mental and emotional preparation for what needs to be done, and for anticipating things that might get in the way. For example, walking through the woods creates a path that others can see and follow. Planning is a form of behavioral preparation that creates a new neural pathway that we later use when we actually practice new thoughts, feelings, or behavior (Kreiman, et al., 2000; Edelman, 1987; Carter, et al., 2000; Bennett-Goleman, 2001). Part of planning might even be contingency planning and require some activities from Phase 4, which is experimentation and practice to determine the full elements of a plan.

Over the decades, efforts to understand or use goal setting have resulted in qualifications and conditions as to its utility and effectiveness. In this chapter, a wide variety of streams of research will be discussed to help understand when, how, and with whom goal setting and planning can be useful in the quest for sustained, desired change.

Focusing Attention and Effort: Putting on Blinders

The intent of goal setting is to focus one's attention and effort. Specific goals help to allocate resources and energy to any effort, including learning and change. As such, the cognitive functioning needed activates the Task Positive Network (TPN) within the NEA to focus, reduce options, and pursue the desired state or outcome (Jack, et al., 2013). It helps to reduce distractions. But if the function of goal setting for human change (individually or in groups) is to reduce options and remind us to focus, it may also reduce the ability to be open to new ideas and scanning the environment (human and otherwise), and thus curtail ongoing adaptation and adjustments during a learning or change process.

Setting a specific goal can help us get to a place we wish to go, but it might also inhibit important learning and change. Obsessive passion that suppresses awareness and consideration of alternative goals is a process called "goal-shielding," which was detailed in a series of five experiments (Belanger, et al., 2013). For example, Kayes (2006) described the ordeal of Adventure Consultants in attempting to reach the summit of Mount Everest. Their desire to reach the summit resulted in members of the climbing team ignoring emerging weather conditions, as described in Chapter 2. They had been told not to attempt the summit after 11 a.m., in order to avoid bad weather and allow time to safely return to base camp. More influential members of the expedition were so focused on the goal of reaching the summit that they systematically denied each of the possible objections. Five of the eight clients on the trip did not reach the summit, and two clients and two guides died along the way back to base camp. Although Kayes does not invoke the PEA/NEA argument in his analysis, he does make the point that when commitment to a goal or set of goals becomes exceedingly important, it involves a blindness to other possibilities, and the ignoring of potential threats. The danger is the cognitive and perceptual limits, which are a consequence of arousing the NEA.

A goal-setting process may shift a person away from the excitement and motivation found in their vision. It may convert a person's commitment into a fixation. Excitement turns into compulsion, and single-minded stubbornness replaces reasoned thought. This process has been called "escalation commitment" or "commitment bias" (Brockner, 1992).

Understanding the mechanism through which the undesirable effects of specific goals affect sustained change will help understand when, how, and for whom specific goal setting is useful and when it gets in the way of progress. When a specific goal is set, both the TPN (Elton & Gao, 2015) and another "instrumental" network is co-activated (Seeley, et al., 2007). The activation of the TPN suppresses the Default Mode Network (DMN). Since the DMN is engaged when we think of our vision and purpose, the focusing effect of a specific goal can suppress the ability of people involved to remember their purpose during the activity and to consider new information along their way to the goal.

As described earlier, specific goal setting and pursuit seems to activate the NEA more than the PEA states. In a study of coaching to one's vision (PEA) or coaching to one's current problems (NEA) with mid-career dental professionals, Anita Howard (2015) found that positive affect rose for those in the PEA and negative affect rose for those in the NEA types of coaching. But both groups had a rapid escalation in negative affect when asked to discuss what they should do about their reflections. In other words, when asked about their plans, they all felt more negative. In a variation of this study, Angela Passarelli (2015) engaged mid-career professionals and found a similar overall effect occurring with people in PEA and NEA coaching sessions.

Another important neural network is engaged during goal setting and the pursuit of specific goals: the frontoparietal control network (FPCN) (Mareck & Dosenbach, 2018). It appears to be activated when a person engages in "instrumental thinking and actions." If a person's thoughts or actions are focused on a goal or end point, they can be said to be instrumental toward achieving that specific goal or target. This network supports many forms of goal-directed thought (Spreng, et al., 2010).

The FPCN can be co-activated with components of either the TPN or DMN, but with a different twist. The authors explained that autobiographical planning with future visualization activates the DMN. This was similar to our own fMRI studies showing substantial components of the DMN activated when creating and discussing one's dreams and vision (Jack, et al., 2013; Jack, et al., 2023). Meanwhile, when engaged in visuospatial planning, which is more specific goal and task-oriented, the TPN is activated (Spreng, et al., 2010).

Appreciating and using the focusing aspect of setting specific goals may help people desiring specific performance or performance improvement to engage themselves. Because the focused goal setting co-activates the TPN along with the FCPN, we can also expect some suppression of the DMN (Anticevic, et al., 2012) (such as openness to new ideas and others). This may lead to a tendency for people in such moments to assume that others need the focusing power of specific goals and therefore impose the process on them, which is a form of projection. Features and functions relevant to goal setting and focused attention attributed to the TPN are often aggregated from several independent networks that have since been identified and studied, like the dorsal attention network (Menon & D'Esposito, 2022).

There appears to be a dramatic difference in the sustainability of efforts in pursuit of a desired change that emerges from one's Ideal Self instead of a possible Ought Self. Obligatory change is likely short-lived precisely because it requires more effort. When pursuing a change that someone else has suggested or demanded or even just hinted at, self-control is enlisted repeatedly to maintain the effort (Converse, et al., 2019). While others setting goals for a person might logically seem to be an imposition, management and people in organizations assume that organizationally relevant goals cascading down to those for whom they apply is typical behavior. But as another source of Ought Self or imposed goals, goals set by an organization stimulate more anxiety, defensiveness, and ultimately lower performance (Welsh, et al., 2019). Passarelli (2014, 2015) found that after a PEA session, the mid-career subjects viewed the goals they set as less difficult and were more willing to strive toward them than goals set after an NEA-coaching session.

Engaging self-control helps by reminding someone of why they are doing the new activity, but also may also invoke guilt, and therefore the NEA. Depending on the frequency and duration of such feelings, the effort becomes more and more emotionally laborious. When the nature of the goal pursuit has shifted from "want to" to "have to" or "should do," the shift has been linked to a sense of exploitation versus exploration activities (Inzlicht, et al., 2014). The description of these different experiences appears to be a shift from PEA to NEA states.

The framing of the desired intent may be key to how self-control is engaged. Impulse control may require more effort. Reframing the goal to something desired rather than something to be avoided may change the nature of self-control needed (Ludwig, et al., 2020). The positive goal to be approached is more likely to revitalize the desire and purpose of the change rather than the need to control one's typical impulses or acts (Roney, et al., 1995).

Specific goals can cause a person to focus on the wrong things. Pursuit of changes or behavior appropriate to what others want you to do enlists one of many possible Ought Selves as discussed in an earlier chapter. The Ought Self not only invokes the NEA and further inhibits sustained effort, but it also moves the person away from their own or autonomously-directed desires. When this occurs, the goal pursuit as well as goal attainment becomes a part of extrinsic motivation that chases out intrinsic drive (Deci & Ryan, 2000). Tory Higgins (2006, 2015) has said that "When a goal becomes an obligation, it moves the person to prevention."

Consistent with the stress literature (Dickerson & Kemeny, 2004), the more pressure a person experiences to work toward a goal, the more self-control is required and the more stressful it becomes. At these moments, the person begins to close themselves off to sustaining any change effort (Holding, et al., 2021). The more self-control is exercised, the more stress is aroused, with its deleterious consequences (Baumeister, et al., 1994).

A meta-analysis of interventions into physical health (e.g., smoking reduction, dieting, and exercise) showed that the number of different goals has a curvilinear relationship to goal progress, with a moderate number of goals being most effective (Wilson, et al., 2015). Their analysis showed that when goals are clustered around a single theme or domain, like lowering one's blood pressure, it is better for progress. More goals add to the amount of self-control a person must exert, which decreases the sustainability of any change effort. They also found, as ICT predicts, that motivation to change was crucial. If the desire to change was given to them by others, like healthcare providers, and is not a part of their personal dream or vision, more self-control was needed and less progress was made.

The use of self-control in these settings has been referred to as ego deple-tion events that drain a person's energy reserves (Baumeister, et al., 1998; Baumeister, 2003). In contrast, a desired change rooted in one's Ideal Self and vision, such as the novelty of a learning goal, can periodically activate the PEA and replenish internal energy or resources—like refueling your car's gas tank or recharging a battery. Invoking or priming the Ideal Self has been shown to enhance motivational strength during goal pursuit (Spiegel, et al., 2004; Passarelli, 2014), while invoking the Real Self has been shown to assist adapt-ive responses to experiences and events that require us to prove or protect ourselves (French, 2001).

Ubiquitous SMART Goals and Need for Achievement

Work organizations and schools socialize people into believing that we need SMART goals (specific, measurable, achievable, relevant, and time-phased) to be motivated, efficient, and effective. Rebellion against such practices came as a rude awakening to many in management. When the United Auto Workers held a strike at the Chevrolet Vega plant in Lordstown, Ohio in 1972, one of the abuses cited was the specific production goals set by management and posted in large signs along the production line (Jaffe, 2019).

Many sources were likely contributors to the evolution of goal setting and its desired characteristics. In the practice sphere, George Odiorne's "manage-ment by objectives" (i.e., managing others and collective effort by focusing ac-tivities of specified targets or aims) is often cited as a key source (Locke, et al., 1981). One source was the work of David McClelland and his colleagues on an unconscious motive called the Need for Achievement (abbreviated as N-Ach) (McClelland, et al., 1953).

It began as a search for how sleep deprivation would affect sailors on ex-tended watch and tours of duty in submarines. The researchers discovered that their unconscious fantasies, as assessed through responses to projective tests and specifically a variation of the Thematic Apperception Test (TAT), did not show fantasies of food acquisition or sleep deprivation, but instrumental activity.

Using Henry Murray's (1938) compendium of possible unconscious motives, these researchers began a series of laboratory experiments to pinpoint the structure and functioning of these fantasies. After repeated studies, they found that individuals who performed best on individual tasks, such as a ring toss game, had dominant imagery in their fantasized projections on TATs about doing better and how to do better. They developed a code for the overall imagery of what they later called N-Ach. Then, they were able to further document specific elements in the structured thought of people following such arousal experiments. When people had responses to TATs with this imagery and more of the structural elements of this imagery, they sought out and did better on numerous types of individual performance tasks.

People with higher scores of N-Ach tended to prefer working in sales, because their personal results were evident and measurable (McClelland, 1961). They preferred starting and owning their own businesses, because they could attribute the results to their own actions. They preferred reading detective stories and biographies. They preferred individual sports, like golf or bowling, and avoided team sports and recreational activities.

The indicators of N-Ach imagery were thoughts of doing better than they had previously, long-term personal career planning, and moderate risk activities (i.e., neither long shots nor sure things, but as likely to succeed as to fail). The components of such stories included what were called subcategories of N-Ach: specification of the desire for and anticipation of success, specification of fear and anticipation of failure, personal obstacles, obstacles in the wider world, instrumental actions, and getting help from others (Atkinson, 1958).

McClelland, his colleagues, and his students began to explore more implications of these thought patterns in life outside of the laboratory (McClelland, 1961, 1985). They found that cultures with more of this imagery and structured thought in primary school readers had significantly more successful entrepreneurial activity about 25 years later. Historically, this was even validated in coding religious hymns, popular ballads, and sea stories for this imagery and predicting coal imports to London between 1400 and 1830. Coal imports into coal producing regions were believed to be a strong indicator of vibrant economic activity, so strong that they needed more coal as energy sources than they could produce. Similar studies were done with historical documents like images in pottery and literature in many countries from Ancient Greece (N-Ach peaked about 700 BCE and again in the Athens trading area about 450 BCE) to Medieval Spain (N-ach peaked about 1550) (McClelland, 1961, 1985).

But it was the individual success in specifying targets or goals of desired results that garnered attention in psychology and organizations. The logic was simple: If people who had these N-Ach thought patterns were distinctively successful at entrepreneurship and business, including sales, why not teach people to think this way and improve their performance?

Projects were begun in various countries including India, Tunisia, Iran, Poland, and the US to stimulate entrepreneurial activity—quite literally, to create more small businesses that would create more jobs, pay more taxes, and grow. Training programs showed dramatic improvements in these business indicators (McClelland & Winter, 1969; Miron & McClelland, 1979).

Business leaders thought they had found the recipe for success: teach people how to think with N-Ach. Individuals with relatively high N-Ach regularly set goals in their lives. They did it for work and tasks; they did it by determining the quickest way to drive from home to work; they did it when planning vacations. They identified and articulated goals that were specific behaviors and easily measured (observable to someone else), moderate risk (would fail as often as succeed), and time-phased.

To connect this line of reasoning with the previous section, activated unconscious goals were found to hijack executive functions pertaining to any other pursuit and block their functioning in these other domains (Marien, et al., 2012). Also, higher levels of N-Ach, as measured through a self-report scale, were shown to negatively associate with the activation of several elements of the DMN, namely the medial prefrontal cortex (mPFC) and orbitofrontal cortex (OFC) (Ming, et al., 2015). Even when examining two forms of N-Ach—both the positive hope of success and the negative fear of failure—both showed the same pattern of neural activation in a large sample of undergraduates. There were some differences between these two types of N-Ach and neural activation. The authors concluded that the hope of success would have a stronger and positive differential effect on reward-seeking and intrinsic motivation than fear of failure.

In 1967, David Kolb and I analyzed data from a set of studies of the degree to which the Massachusetts Institute of Technology's version of MBAs achieved their personal behavior change goals (Kolb & Boyatzis, 1970a, 1970b). The studies showed that setting clear, observable goals predicted more successful behavior change.

This line of research either helped to create or at least added to the rise of what was later called SMART goals. Like most panaceas, it was years later that the limits of such thinking were uncovered. In a 20-year longitudinal study, McClelland and I showed that N-Ach was a kiss of death for managers' performance at middle and above levels of management (McClelland & Boyatzis, 1982).

People with relatively high N-Ach will be drawn to and motivated by specific goals. It is one of the dispositional characteristics that differentiates how individuals respond to specific goals or objectives. A confusion often occurs because the value connotation of Need for Achievement suggests people with this disposition want to succeed, are ambitious, or have a sense of purpose with their work (i.e., appear driven). The specific unconscious motive, N-Ach, is not all of those things. It is a measurement orientation and focus on one's own progress. It is a perpetual internal competition. Again, people who enjoy sales or starting a small business often have higher N-Ach than most others. For them, specific, measurable goals will be a motivating force. For others, it does not have the same effect.

In summary, a person's sense of purpose, vision, and dreams (their Ideal Self) appears to have a positive motivating effect on the pursuit of change and the sustainability of such efforts. Specific, measurable goals only appear to have a comparable motivating effect for people with an unconscious motive called N-Ach. The motivating effect of goals may also be dependent on how a person approaches and frames their intention.

Learning Versus Performance Goal Orientation

Another individual disposition that can affect the degree to which a specific, measurable goal is motivating has been studied by industrial organizational psychologists since the 1990s. A performance goal orientation with an emphasis on specific targets has been shown to invoke avoidance goal orientation and lower performance (VandeWalle, et al., 1999). Meanwhile, a learning goal orientation, which is about novelty, experimentation, and learning, has been shown to enhance performance (VandeWalle, et al., 1999). Learning goals for a department were shown to result in higher performance than performance-oriented or "do your best" goals (Porter & Latham, 2013). This could be a result of arousing the NEA, with a performance, versus PEA, with a learning goal orientation.

A performance-oriented goal might be "to lose 25 pounds to fit into my bathing suit by July 1." In the same situation, a learning goal orientation might result in a differently framed intent, such as "I would like to feel better and enjoy beach activities this summer." The former often leads people to join health clubs after making a New Year's Eve resolution in performance-oriented goal terms. Typically, the activity loses appeal and visiting the health club becomes less frequent by February.

These studies and streams of research have shown repeatedly that performance-oriented goals were less effective than learning-oriented goals for sales, and almost everything else (Beaubien & Payne, 1999; Brett & VandeWalle, 1999; Chen, et al., 2000). Performance-oriented goals forced people into needing to "prove" that they could make the goals—a defensive, NEA state. Learning-oriented goals are often experimental, novelty-driven, aspirational, and fuzzier.

The possibility of context being a factor was a conclusion from a comprehensive study showing that a performance goal orientation and specific goals enhanced performance when the tasks were routinized, but did not improve performance when learning or adaptation was needed (Seijts, et al., 2004; Seijts & Latham, 2005). For example, tracking students in a statistics course over a semester revealed that time pressure invoked a performance goal orientation and lower performance (Beck & Schmidt, 2013). Another study showed that MBA interns demonstrated greater performance and learning when the intern had a learning goal orientation and the supervisor did as well, as contrasted to interns or their supervisors with a proving or performance goal orientation (Beenen, 2014).

Reactions to feedback on tasks is another area in which goal orientation affects performance. People assigned a learning goal showed less tension and performed better than those assigned a performance goal when receiving negative feedback (Cianci, et al., 2010). In a study of managers' reactions to feedback assessed periodically five times a day for three weeks revealed that managers with a disposition to use performance goal orientation responded with stronger negative and weaker positive emotions to task importance and feedback than those with low performance goal orientation (Fisher, et al., 2013). In this study, they found that conscientiousness amplified the negative reactions and resulted in even lower performance for those assigned a performance goal.

Examining the context in which each type of goal is effective suggests that performance-oriented goals may help when people have the needed skills and experience for tasks, even complex tasks (Seijts & Latham, 2005). But the earlier study showed that when tasks required learning and adaptive behavior—less certainty or more novelty—a learning goal orientation worked better (Seijts, et al., 2004). Another way this variation was approached was to classify goals as either performance, learning, or behavioral (Latham & Seijts, 2016).

When the desired change in behavior occurs in an interpersonal context, the persistence of effort and conscious commitment to the new behavior may require less specific goal expression. Leonard (2008) showed that MBA students showed significantly more frequent behavior related to competencies that were intentionally targeted in learning goals written two years earlier, than with other competencies on which they were assessed. All of the competencies were related to managerial effectiveness, even those not targeted in their own learning plans. Similar results were found in an executive development leadership program (Johnson, et al., 2012). A surprising finding in the Leonard (2008) work was that significant improvement on those learning goal competencies occurred and persisted whether they remembered the specific goals two years later or not. Similarly, van Hooft and Noordzij (2009) found that pursuit of learning goals enhanced the outcomes of unemployed job seekers engaged in a job search process. Their use of learning-oriented goals led to more search intentions, behavior, and higher re-employment possibilities.

The defensive nature of the arousal (i.e., transforming into avoidance or proving orientation) with a performance goal orientation is comparable to Tory Higgins's prevention self-regulated focus (1997; Brockner & Higgins, 2001). In a prevention orientation, a person is preoccupied with preventing something undesired from occurring. It has all of the psychophysiological characteristics of the NEA state. Higgins (1997) also postulates that a promotion self-regulated focus has an opposite effect, in which a person is excited about something new, adaptation, and growth—a PEA state.

Another parallel is in Carol Dweck's growth versus fixed mindset (2006). A fixed mindset has imposed limits on the perceived context and likely outcomes. It is an NEA state. Meanwhile, a growth mindset enables a person to be open to new ideas, scanning the environment, and considering possibilities. It is a PEA state.

In summary, when the challenge is not routine nor task-defined, learning-oriented goals help sustained, desired change more than performance-oriented specific goals. A growth mindset or promotion oriented self-regulatory focus helps a person continue to be open during the learning and change process. Meanwhile, a fixed mindset or prevention self-regulatory focus, like specific goals, invokes NEA and diminishes a person's perceptual, cognitive, and emotional openness and sustainability of the effort.

A Different Approach to Planning

Michael McCaskey published a landmark article in the *Academy of Management Journal* in 1974 titled "A Contingency Approach to Planning: Planning with Goals and Planning without Goals" (McCaskey, 1974, 1977). This predated the performance and learning goal orientation, with a twist. In this paper, McCaskey labeled the alternative to specific, measurable goals as "domain and direction planning." It appeared more like vision and purpose than goals, as most of us understood them at the time.

Years later, Anthony Grant developed a concept that seems remarkably similar called "strategic purpose" as the main focus of effective coaching (Cavanagh & Grant, 2018). In one conversation, Grant said that it was the same as what we called vision (personal communication, 2016).

In an effort to be more comprehensive but also to expand on McCaskey's distinction, Annie McKee studied a full range of planning styles (McKee, 1991). She found that following full-time MBAs six months after graduation revealed that about 25% showed a propensity for objective-oriented goals, about 25% showed a propensity for domain and direction goals, about 25% showed a propensity for task-oriented goals, and about 25% were existential (McKee, et al., 2008).

In summary, people with a planning style favoring specific, measurable goals (probably those high in N-Ach, as previously explained) will naturally gravitate toward framing any planning process in that manner. But for most people, that is not their predilection.

Goal Intention

The desire and intent to act on a goal has been examined as a causal factor in goal-setting processes that result in change (Nowack, 2017). The two important concepts from the research that consistently emerge are goal commitment and goal intention, which has also been described as goal striving. Goal intentions and striving appear to facilitate conversion into persistent action when accompanied by a detailed plan of action, including contingencies or "if-then" plans (Gollwitzer & Sheeran, 2006). Despite many published studies, Webb and Sheeran (2006) challenged the common wisdom with a meta-analysis to examine the causal impact of goal intentions. Forty-seven studies with randomized controls revealed that "medium-to-large change in intention engenders a small-to-medium change in behavior. Thus, intention has a significant impact on behavior, but the size of the effect is considerably smaller than correlation tests have shown" (p. 260).

The specific types of actions that would increase the likelihood of goal attainment would include those that suit a person's preferred learning style (Kolb, 1984, 2014). Kolb's experiential learning theory (ELT) explains that although learning is more successful and retained when the entire learning process is engaged, people have preferences for what types of actions are motivating and exciting. Some people may prefer immersing themselves in an experience, while others may prefer reflecting on events and feelings. Others may prefer to build or understand a model or concept that explains events, while others may prefer to try actions and see how they work. People might also have preferences that are combinations of these four basic styles of learning.

Creating a learning plan to pursue one's learning agenda and goals can help or hinder the process depending on the types of activities selected. If the action fits within a person's learning style preference, it is inherently more comfortable and easier. When it suits a different learning preference the person has to work harder, possibly enlist more self-control, and introduces more NEA into the process. The sustainability of change efforts and goal pursuit may become limited when this extra effort needs to be engaged. More challenging learning may also require more effort when people put themselves into leaning modes that are not of their preference, but may be useful in the overall process of change. These excursions into the NEA do not inhibit sustained, desired change as long as the vision and purpose of the effort is repeated and the person receives periodic doses of PEA along the way.

Kolb (2014) also explained the discovery of adaptive learning styles. That is, some people may be able to use a style that although not preferred, is accessible in their behavioral repertoire. Keeping motivated while enacting the learning plan is helped by integrating self-awareness of one's planning style and learning style (this will be examined in greater detail in the next chapter). Ways to access the Learning Style Inventory for research are documented in the appendix.

Commitment to a goal is another strong predictor of actual performance (Klein, et al., 1999) beyond goal intention and striving. But as discussed previously, strong goal commitment can backfire and inhibit performance and successful change if it decreases the ability to scan the environment and adapt.

Building Sustainability of Effort Into a Plan

Creating a plan that will increase the likelihood of the sustained effort required to achieve the learning or change should not invoke NEA, stress, or the need to prove you can meet the goals. As mentioned, the number of goals set in a plan will also have a curvilinear or some non-normal effect on effort (Wilson, et al., 2015), with the moderate number of goals set as the most effective. Too many goals will diffuse effort or call for repeated maximum effort, which invokes NEA and exhausts a person. On the other hand, too few goals may not result in much change, and the person may slow progress or effort and not achieve the desired end state or goals.

Another factor affecting the likely sustainability of effort is the distance between the current state and the ideal state or goal. Scholars have claimed that the discrepancy between one's Ideal Self and Real Self, which can be translated into the size of the goal effort required, is a major motivating factor in change (Higgins, 1987), and was discussed in Chapter 4. Without a perception of the feasibility of the goal being achieved, the effort is doomed to be lost in the waves of exhaustion or loss of hope (Wilson, et al., 2015). In the Need for Achievement research, this was found to be one of the components of achievement-motivated thought. It was called the expectation of goal attainment (Atkinson, 1958).

The concept of tipping points from complexity theory helps to provide one possible solution. The tipping point is the moment in which the desired new behavior, thoughts, or feelings are enacted, or the goal achieved. Articulating a goal closer to the tipping point is more likely to allow for periodic PEA moments along the way. Milkman (2021) described the process, based on a series of studies, that small doses and "a spoonful of sugar" can make the change process fun and feasible.

Seeing signs of progress and the likelihood of success inspire hope and the PEA. Passarelli (2014, 2015) found that after a vision-based PEA coaching session, mid-career participants reported more positive affect, greater goal striving and joy, and greater willingness to devote overall effort to the goals than when they participated in an NEA coaching session focusing on their problems and challenges. The Ideal Self and vision recharges or renews a person's internal resources and can boost the change effort to continue. In contrast, seeing the remaining distance to the goal may easily invoke a sense of futility or loss of hope and the NEA. At that point, the engine driving or sustaining the change effort loses steam and energy.

The common practice and motto of Alcoholics Anonymous has been "one day at a time." Other efforts at behavior change and trying to break undesired habits have adopted this idea as well. It reduces the time span of the effort needed to something perceived as manageable. Compared to "I will never drink again," it is actually more hopeful. It brings the new behavior closer to a tipping point.

One of my colleagues, Dr. Steve Kelner, used this idea as he described how his wife, a mystery novel writer, was able to keep making progress on her writing. The desire to write 2,000 words a day was daunting at times due to life events. Once she reduced her target to 600 words a day, four times a week, she was able to get into a rhythm and was eventually able to build up to 1,000 words a day.

Shared Planning with Others

Principle 8: As a fractal theory, ICT describes sustained, desired change at all levels of human endeavor from individual to dyads, teams, organizations, communities, countries, and global processes.

The third phase of ICT in our collectives requires discussing possibilities and coming to consensus on the best choices regarding steps to take, anticipated obstacles, timing, and allocation of resources, as shown in Figure 5.2. The details of how to best develop an agenda and plan in teams, organizations, communities, and countries is the same as the process used for individuals, with all of the caveats discussed in this chapter. The challenge raised with ICT is how to make sure the desired end state is the vision, not merely a goal, and how to make the journey and process more joyful, exciting, and introduce episodic experiences of PEA.

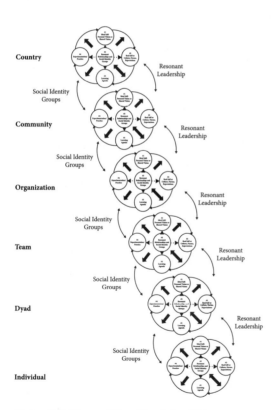

Besides the different goal orientations and planning styles described earlier in this chapter, goals manifest themselves in teams and larger collectives. Fisher (2014) shows empirically that teams can engage in task planning and process planning. Task planning predicts the degree of coordination while controlling for team processes. Team process planning predicts more interpersonal relationships and processes while controlling for the opposite. In ICT terms, the team task planning co-activates the TPN and FCPN, which results in arousing the NEA, while the team process planning co-activates the DMN and FCPN, which will likely result in arousing the PEA.

Figure 5.2 The multilevel fractals within Intentional Change Theory
Source: Boyatzis (2008, 2015).

Both are needed for a team or organization to move toward their vision and better performance, but since they rely on somewhat antagonistic internal processes, the best recipe is being able to move back and forth and consider both types of planning.

Deep-Caving and Going Deeper Into the Earth: Shared Planning in Teams

In our collectives, training for contingencies is a form of planning. In military applications, it is often referred to as training "muscle memory" so that when a contingency occurs, the person does not have to engage in a slow, deliberative conscious process of analyzing the situation and options. Instead, they react—but the reaction is one that has been anticipated, and the person has been trained to respond in a preferred manner.

An excellent example is the experience of two bold, deep-caving teams seeking to set the world record in exploring the deepest caves on Earth. Deep-caving is a cross between spelunking (the exploration of caves) and speleology (the science of caves). It invokes the imagery of Jules Verne's *Journey to the Center of the Earth*. Think of going into a perpetually dark, freezing small space with poisonous gas, spiders and snakes, and a lot of waterfalls and rivers, while carrying everything you need on your back for several weeks in the darkness.

Bill Stone led one team, called the Cheve Team, on many explorations in Oaxaca, Mexico over decades, especially between 1994 and 2004. Stone saw himself as an explorer (Stone & Hunter, 2004; Vetter, 2004). As a PhD, he loved the science, but saw himself as an engineer. Caving captured his fascination with being a pioneer and explorer. It also provided an opportunity for him to invent new devices and technologies. His style was pragmatic, driven to win the competition to discover the deepest place on Earth (Tabor, 2010).

With an uncompromising leadership style, his expeditions met with success at times, but also resulted in a number of accidents and at least one death. He selected mostly experienced cavers. When they practiced it was with new technology, such as the rebreather he invented. They did not practice as a team: "Stone led by challenging people because that was what best motivated him" (Tabor, 2010, p. 158). One of his critics called him "obsessive" (Vetter, 2004). Stone was at times impatient and exuded a profound sense of urgency. He was also disinterested in team sports (Tabor, 2010).

In contrast, Alexander Klimchouk led the Krubera Team on multiple expeditions during these decades as well, seeking the same goal of the record descent, but his quest was in Abkhazia, Georgia. On October 18, 2004, his team reached 6,825 feet below sea level in the deepest cave to date (Kimchouk, 2005; Meek, 2004), and then later members of his team, Yury Kasjan and Samokhin, pushed to new depths of 7,072 and 7,188 feet respectively. Every member of the team reached the final chamber in 2004, and all returned safe. These teams held the world's record as of early 2024, until a Russian team reached 69 feet deeper in 2018 in the Veryovkna cave.

Alexander Klimchouk saw himself as a scientist and team builder. He believed deep-caving was a multigenerational project that required enlisting and training waves of cavers and leaders. He rotated leadership and practiced on various expeditions as a team. Off-season, the team would go caving with existing members and new members to practice techniques and working with each other. As reported by Tabor (2010, p. 327), "One happy result of Alexander Klimchouk's organizational skills was that his expeditions ran like Swiss watches. Another was his ability to mount multiple expeditions in a single year." Klimchouk even encouraged them to write and publish academic papers between expeditions to remind them of the bigger picture.

Both Stone and Klimchouk are competitive, expert cavers and scientists with PhDs. While one saw himself as a pioneer, the other saw himself as steward to future generations and a scientist. Stone focused on leadership, whereas Klimchouk focused on teamwork. Preparation and careful planning was key to Klimchouk, who "preferred to work with caves rather than 'attack'; he believed, as well, that happy, comfortable cavers could explore more effectively than those strung out by Spartan conditions . . . In addition to staples like rice and pasta, [they] stocked up on comfort foods: candy, cookies, cakes, sausages, cheese . . . pate, nishtyak . . . spirits and foods for appropriate celebrations along the ascent" (Tabor, 2010, p, 330). In the three weeks of preparation in the Krubera caves and camps for the descent, they even took time to wire telephone lines to the deepest camps. Stone and his teams emphasized reducing weight to extreme degrees, like removing the cardboard insert from rolls of toilet paper, and stocking freeze-dried meals.

The unexpected is bound to occur on explorations under harsh and threatening conditions. Klimchouck prepared his team for contingencies by training, rotating roles, and analyzing what they were doing in a scholarly way.

This was similar to what the most effective incident commanders of the US Forest Fire Fighting Service did. In between fires, when there was a little down time, the most effective incident commanders would call for practice sessions with various teams (Boyatzis, et al., 2017). It was not a practice used by their less effective counterparts. These specialist fire-fighting teams and "hot shots" were on call all year and fighting many fires in various parts of the United States.

While the fire, winds, and unpredictability of events made fighting these wildfires dangerous and deadly, it was often the organizational complexities that added fuel to the fires. Imagine landing your specialist team and immediately having to coordinate with state and local fire-fighting teams, law enforcement at local, county, and state levels, mayors and town councils, resident or ranch and farmer associations, environmental groups, and occasionally residents who did not recognize the authority of the US federal government and warned teams off with their rifles. The research study showed that not only did the most effective incident commanders demonstrate more emotional and social intelligence behavior during these events, as mentioned in Chapter 4, but they had to do it with both intact teams and new members. The use of time between fires to train for eventualities was an effective use of a limited resource—time—in preparing for the next crisis.

The challenge is how to make the activities serving this phase of ICT sustainable, not just a tedious task that invokes the NEA and further inhibits change. Even if you achieve a shared vision in a team, not everyone will have the same view of goals or the best tactics to be used to get there. A fascinating study of this challenge of asymmetric goals in teams revealed that a learning goal orientation (as described earlier in this chapter) and high team identification (i.e., a social identity with the team, as described in Chapter 2 and explored in depth in Chapter 8) resulted in the most effectiveness of the teams. It was bursts of PEA in what is too often an entirely NEA experience: task planning.

These examples and research suggest that using interpersonal practice as preparation (such as contingency planning) and addressing goals that are both task and team processes (a relationship focus) helped create an exciting and sustainable agenda and plan for change. Besides emphasizing these dual agendas in planning and preparation, Hackman and Wageman (2005) also emphasized the timing of interventions or activities as key to helping or coaching a team to change.

Shared Planning in Organizations

The leadership of organizations need planning for determining resources and allocation. They also need it to help anticipate obstacles and adjust plans before being hit with surprises, whether from competitors, market changes, new technology, or human resource challenges. Every theory and model of organizational change and development includes a stage of planning for specific next steps (Burke & Noumair, 2015). As said, at the individual level, planning and preparation is useful, and it does this by focusing attention. That is an analytic process and requires engaging the TPN, which brings with it a certain degree of NEA. If an organizational unit (whether a plant, division, or retail outlet) engages in planning without some periodic PEA episodes, people lose their excitement, interest, and eventually their engagement. It ceases to be a viable, operational plan.

Although counterintuitive for people involved in strategic planning, the real energy to sustain efforts to move toward the shared vision comes from swarming. As discussed in Chapter 3, swarming uses emotional contagion to infect others with enthusiasm, hope, and PEA. Emotional engagement and the possibility of positive swarming around an idea, a program, or a value only can become PEA for others if contagion is possible, which requires presence and often dialogue or some form of participation. It requires the inclusion of others. In a meta-analysis of organizational development projects, Oreg, et al. (2011) reported that "the degree to which change recipients were involved in planning and implementing the change ... creates a sense of agency, contribution and control over the change" (p. 491).

Preparing a Community for Change: Shared Planning

Homelessness is a complex mix of major tragedies: it is a human, social justice, mental health, drug addiction, and economic challenge. With the COVID pandemic stimulating the fear of being in shelters for the homeless and immigrants, the seriousness of the problems in most cities of the world escalated rapidly. Boston was able to reduce homelessness by more than 24% during COVID with an ingenious plan. First, Mayor Michelle Wu organized a city-wide Commission and enlisted help from police, social service agencies (such as food banks), local businesses and their associations (Newmarket Business Association), and a variety of nonprofits (Capps, 2022). Second, they decided to focus on family homelessness and take a "housing first" strategy (Jolicoeur, 2022; Alston, 2022). The latter meant that the focus of the efforts would be to move families from tents to temporary "threshold" housing and then to permanent housing.

Meanwhile, Washington, DC also was able to reduce homelessness during this period, but it still sustained nine times the per capita homeless as compared to Boston. The dilemma might have been because the growing frustration with the visible homelessness was widespread, and there was urgency to do something (Swenson, et al., 2022). The strategy in DC began with sweeps and clearing encampments before adequate facilities were erected to provide housing (Bronitsky & Donachie, 2022).

Tackling the same complex challenge, two other communities also had dramatically different results. Houston focused on creating permanent housing, with Mayor Annise Parker organizing many local groups, but she also had the insight that veterans who were homeless felt like a dual tragedy and that the city was letting them down after they had served their country (Beekman, 2017). She led the city in creating the "100 veterans in houses in 100 days" campaign (Beretto, 2015). It helped to enlist many groups that might not have become active to combat homelessness in general, but for veterans they would.

Once accomplished, they then leveraged that win into a major program called The Way Home (Beekman, 2017), with more than 100 partner organizations. It helped to have a unique champion on the staff, Mandy Chapman Semple, who was empathic and charismatic without alienating the other groups the effort needed (Keomoungkhoun, 2021). In this situation, the specific goals of 100 veterans in 100 days was useful because many alternatives had been examined, and focusing on this specific target helped at this stage in their desired change. From 2009 to 2021, Houston decreased the homeless by 60%. The last few years were during the COVID pandemic, with wave after wave of undocumented immigrants arriving during that same time as well.

Analogous to the DC experience, during the same period San Diego attempted to eliminate homelessness through a series of what appeared to be disjointed efforts, such as providing outdoor toilets on city streets, programs to eliminate drug and alcohol dependency, creating temporary safe camps, and weekly sweeps by the police (Jensen, et al., 2020). The result was that the homeless population became even more alienated and distrustful, and from 2009 to 2021, San Diego's homelessness rose by 3%. Observers claimed that there was not a lack of vision or desire, but a lack of a strategic plan and coordinated leadership (Halverstadt, 2021).

These examples help to illustrate that a compelling and shared vision alone does not result in sustained, desired change; good intentions do not ensure good results. Stoecker (1997) commented that community development efforts empowered community development corporations to take over and manage housing to make it quickly available. But it turned out that the very agencies intended to be the change agents and catalysts became landlords, which embedded a degree of structural antagonism. For success with the highly complex issue of homelessness, planning was needed to avoid challenges and creating new problems. Planning was needed among large groups of people from different parts of the community. It took special leadership to bring them together and remind everyone of the vision while taking steps to address the challenge.

Concluding Thoughts

Goal-based coaching seems to help its utility, but the duration of the sustainable effort is always a challenge. While change researchers have long understood that intentional change is a conscious process that occurs over time, research on Intentional Change Theory has helped identify when in a change process, context, and specific people for whom goal setting can be most helpful in the process of change.

For most people, setting specific goals will not help early in a change or learning effort. It can prematurely limit options and exhaust the internal energy needed to continue, and it can be stressful. But if the early process has a context of the person's dream or vision, and periodic revisiting and talking about the vision that occurs during the process, a person may be able to use the renewal of PEA moments to sustain the needed effort. Later in the change process and when the person has sufficient moments of PEA built into their thoughts and discussions with others, specific goals can help focus attention toward the new thoughts, feelings, or behavior and toward achieving the desired change.

People in helping roles can benefit from understanding this sequence and dosage concept. Sometimes a coach, parent, physician, nurse, or teacher needs to provoke the NEA. In moments of denial, the other person may need a wake-up call. Sometimes a person being helped is fearful and cannot see a desired future. They feel stuck. For example, when coaching someone who appears to be creating an escape fantasy, looking for relief or a break from current tension, they may identify a desired future that seems inappropriate or suboptimal to the coach or helper. Some suggestions that might otherwise invoke the NEA might arouse a sense of efficacy by breaking the fear.

In summary, specific and measurable goals can be useful in sustained, desired change. But they are NEA and instrumental, and in that sense typically will not provide the motivating effect of renewal and the PEA over time. Specific goals will help intentional change at the point in the change process when the person (or group) can venture into the NEA occasionally to focus and reduce behavioral options and get things done. It is most likely of benefit later in the ICT process. But it would only work if the person had their vision to rejuvenate their PEA and sustainable effort, was consciously aware of strengths they could use, and had access to caring relationships to help them forward. The most effective use of a learning agenda and learning plan may be found in the dosage, timing, and sequencing of the intention.

6

Exploring Possibilities: Experimenting and Practice to Mastery (Principle 6)

Principle 6: The fourth phase of ICT is the sequence of repeated experimentation with new feelings, thoughts, attitudes, or behavior, and then moving into repeated practice to the point of mastery (beyond the point of comfort).

What you can do, or dream you can, begin it, boldness has genius, power, and magic in it.

—**Goethe, translated by John Anster, 1835**

Once a person or collective has a vision and an assessment of their typical actions, culture, and norms, and has established a learning agenda (and possibly a plan), they are ready to begin the next iterative aspect of change or learning. This phase of ICT is the exploration or experimentation with the new thoughts, feelings, behavior, mindset, or norms, as highlighted in Figure 6.1. Some are selected as most efficacious (i.e., most likely to get closer to the vision or shared vision) and feasible (easier to implement and practice). The person or collective at that point begins the more repetitive (and sometimes tedious) process of practice, practice, and more practice. The challenge is to practice to the point of mastery. The difference of practicing to the point of comfort versus mastery is the difference between a musician of practicing a new piece to the point of comfort (such as being ready to play for the next lesson with their teacher) versus practicing to mastery (automaticity or unconsciously driven behavior, and ready to perform in front of a large audience).

Experimentation: Trying It On for Size

The basic experience of the experimentation aspect of this phase is for the person or group to determine how the new thoughts, feelings, behavior,

The Science of Change. Richard E. Boyatzis, Oxford University Press. © Richard E. Boyatzis 2024.
DOI: 10.1093/9780197765142.003.0006

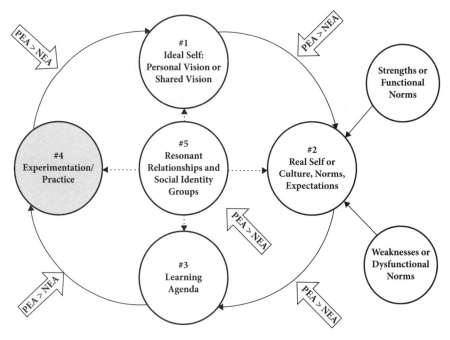

Figure 6.1 Experimentation and practice in the process of Intentional Change Theory
Source: Boyatzis (2008, 2015).

mindset, or norms feel. They explore how it fits into the rhythm and structure of their current life and work. It is labeled experimentation because at this point the specific change can be called a "provisional self" (Ibarra, 1999).

In a PEA Mode

Trying new ways of thinking, feeling, or acting requires effort. It requires exercising self-control and focusing on the change target. Given the earlier explanation of such conscious, intentional effort discussed in Chapter 3, this is stressful and depletes internal resources (Inzlicht, et al., 2013). Conscious experimentation is one of the experiences of ICT in which the NEA is a useful and inherent part of the process. Conscious experimentation is effortful. Arousing the NEA may be important at this phase in the process of change, but the key is the degree of arousal and dosage. Even if the experimentation uses an existing strength applied in new domains of life or work, it requires intentional effort.

To increase the likelihood of sustaining or continuing the learning or change, the experimentation aspect of this phase requires periodic excursions into the PEA to replenish and revitalize the energy needed. Without such moments, the motivation wanes and the effort atrophies.

There are several ways to introduce periodic moments of PEA into the process. In addition to reminding those involved in the vision and purpose of the effort, another technique is to reduce the stress invoked and possibly reframe the experience into play through experimenting in safe settings. The story of EMBA student Juan Trebino was told in our 2008 book (Boyatzis & McKee, pp. 196–198). He was a marketing executive at a major oil and gas company. He and his wife's dream was to return to their native Venezuela when the political and economic conditions returned to a semblance of reason. But they wanted to remain in the US for the time being, and to ensure that their two children would have access to great education and healthcare.

As part of a course based on ICT, Juan developed his vision, discussed it with his wife and a coach, and shared it with the faculty teaching the course (Boyatzis & McKee, 2005). Besides the family and lifestyle aspects of his vision, he aspired to be a top executive in a major oil and gas company. When the next phase of the course occurred with 360 feedback, Juan was surprised to learn that his subordinates did not see him as using the coaching and mentoring competency, even in the context of him consistently demonstrating most of the other emotional and social intelligence competencies assessed. This was a surprising observation to both his faculty member and to Juan. In class and during social moments, his classmates enjoyed being with Juan. He was charming and had a sense of humor (Boyatzis & McKee, 2005).

In trying to understand this apparent gap, Juan explained that although he was now in marketing, his training and early jobs had been as an engineer (Boyatzis & McKee, 2005). He admitted that when subordinates approached him with an issue, he saw them as "problem-bearing platforms." He knew that his vision would be accessible if he used his strengths, but he had to work on this one weakness. In discussing possible ways to try being more of a coach, his wife suggested he volunteer to coach for his 11-year-old son's soccer team. This was a safer setting than trying out these new behaviors and mindset at work. Juan also admitted that with his son in his peripheral vision during practice or games, he was more likely to focus on his son's and teammate's feelings and enjoying the game rather than merely winning.

About eight years later, an audience member in a lecture the faculty member was giving at another university suggested that Juan had succeeded in mastering the coaching and mentoring competency (Boyatzis & McKee, 2005). He had coached his son's soccer team that late spring and summer, working with his son and teammates, and had a great time. He focused their practice sessions on basic skills but did it knowing that being that age, they would enjoy it more as a game. He tried to emphasize what they did correctly and only occasionally pointed out something they did wrong or could do differently. They enjoyed going for pizza after games. They even enjoyed practice sessions. Juan didn't even remember how the team did in their competitions. Throughout the summer he was experimenting with new ways to coach others, and when he found something that seemed to work, he would put it to work during their practice sessions and games.

The following year, Juan changed companies to take a position with a major international consulting firm specializing in oil and gas clients. Because of his background and language skills, he was put in charge of the Sao Paolo office. By this time he was continuing to use (and practice) coaching his subordinates, not just pushing for maximum performance. Within several years, he had over 20 consultants who saw him as their mentor when the company norm was may be two or three for a partner at his career stage (Boyatzis & McKee, 2005). One of his subordinates said that Juan was seen as the most desirable mentor of all partners in Latin America. Juan had used the safe setting of his son's soccer team to develop and refine a competency that was key to executive leadership.

From the self-regulatory focus field, a technique for PEA activation during experimentation or practice is to refocus on a promotion mindset (Higgins, 1997). A promotion focus is linked to PEA experiences (Jack, et al., 2023), and a prevention focus is linked to NEA experiences. In a study of informal field-based learning as an alternative to training to improve performance at work, a promotion self-regulatory focus had a dramatic positive effect (Wolfson, et al., 2018). The underlying mechanism was explained by Lin and Johnson (2015) as the opposite of an ego depletion effect of prohibitive voice (such as a prevention focus) in two multiwave field studies in organizations. Encouragement of a promotive voice decreases ego depletion, while a prohibitive voice increases ego depletion. Juan was able to create a focus on development of himself and others. He had found a fun and family-centered approach to developing a weakness, and it enabled him to work on his work–life balance and have regular doses of being in the PEA while doing the hard work of trying a new competency.

Visualizing as Experimentation

Another approach to invoking the PEA while experimenting is visualizing or using visual imagery to try a new approach or set of actions. Visual imagery has been shown repeatedly to be a powerful training and preparation tool for golf putting (Smith & Holmes, 2004) and for Olympic athletes. Laura Wilkinson had broken her foot while preparing for her diving event at the Sydney Olympics. She described in detail how her coach made her sit on the side of the pool while recovering from the broken foot and practice visualizing each dive for hours a day (Loehr & Schwartz, 2001). She won a gold medal. Ole Bjoerndalen won five gold medals in the biathalon in the Salt Lake City Olympics with positive imagery and thinking (Le Duff, 2002). He practiced visualizing a ski run, the rapid stop, preparing his rifle, aiming and firing. He visualized a perfect 10 for each shot. Sylvie Bernier told a similar story of weeks of visualization as well as actual diving practice to master her dives (Bernier, 2010). She talked about visualizing climbing the stairs of the platform and approaching the end of the diving board. She imagined her lift-off, sailing down toward the water, performing the various twists and rotations, and her perfect entry into the pool. Her visual practice began to surpass her hours of actual diving about six weeks before her event—and she won Canada's first gold medal in diving in the 1984 Olympics.

It works in music as well. Meister, et al. (2004) documented how visualizing a performance for classical pianists actually created new neural pathways that were then used when the musician actual played the piece. The same neural cells were fired when playing as when imagining playing (Kreiman, et al., 2000). Other research supports the conclusion that strengthening neural pathways does occur through practice and visualization (Bennett-Goleman, 2001; Davidson, et al., 2000; Knowlton, et al., 1996; Natraj & Ganguly, 2018).

Using Your Preferred Learning Modes

Another technique for engaging the PEA periodically during the effort of experimentation is to engage in activities that are consistent with your preferred learning style. David Kolb developed experiential learning theory (ELT) in 1969 and continued to refine it (Kolb, 1984, 2014). To enable research as well as help learners in their adventures, he developed the Learning Style Inventory to assess preferred learning styles. Later, he also developed the Adaptive Style Inventory to explore which styles a person can use easily if needed by the demands of a situation.

In the first 30+ years of research, ELT predicted that a person would prefer to take in new sensations and perceptions from their environment in four modes (Kolb, 1984). The four modes were the result of two dialectical dimensions: concrete experience to abstract conceptualization (apprehending to comprehending), and active experimentation to reflective observation (extension to intension). These two dimensions yielded four modes: accommodative learning style (concrete and active), divergent (concrete and reflective), assimilative (abstract and reflective), and convergent (active and abstract). In more recent years, Kolb has expanded the modes to nine possible variations: reflective (including concrete and abstract), abstract (including reflective and active), active experimental (including abstract and concrete), concrete (including active and reflective); and balanced, which includes all four of the earlier modes (Kolb, 1984). Thousands of research studies are reviewed in his 1984 book and updated in his 2014 book.

The research has shown that when people were engaged in learning something using a preferred learning style or mode, they felt more engaged and less tense (Kolb, 2014). The preferred learning style or mode was part of their Real Self. Other learning styles or modes might be used or were accessible, but using them felt obligatory and more like an Ought Self, with the associated NEA reactions. This was even evident when learning styles of faculty were assessed. It was found that students did better in courses taught by faculty with the same preferred learning styles they had. It was observed that faculty tended to design their courses and the experiences and assignments to be consistent with how they thought they learned (i.e., to use their own preferred learning style) (Kolb, 2014).

Kolb's ELT clearly and emphatically makes the point that learning involves the entire cycle. It is a process of moving through each of these modes around the ELT cycle with increasing integration among the observations, perceptions, and felt experience. ELT also explains why some topics and settings provide learning within a particular style or mode. For example, it is difficult to learn about advanced calculus, manipulation of imaginary numbers, and set theory without being predominantly in the abstract mode. So although it feels easier and more comfortable working within a person's preferred learning style or mode, they need to utilize the entire cycle and may be in situations demanding the predominant use of a style or mode that is not preferred. When a person experiments using activities with their preferred learning style or mode, it feels more accessible, comfortable, and somewhat more PEA. This also implies that within teams, organizations, communities, and countries, experimentation will most likely require activities that engage people in the entire learning cycle and all learning modes, given diversity of learning preferences across any large population. It increases the likelihood of engaging people with some moments of PEA by using the diversity of learning preferences in these larger human groups.

Another technique to allow and encourage experimentation is the use of temporary work assignments, task forces, and sabbaticals to allow for volunteer or charitable organizational work. For example, if a person wants to develop their ability to involve all members of a team but is reluctant to try new behavior at work, they might volunteer to chair a task force for a nonprofit. During the task force meetings, the person would consciously (i.e., intentionally) experiment with asking each team member what they thought. They might do this once per person for each meeting. Afterward, they might ask specific people for their views when they see nonverbal expressions suggesting that they disagree with the turn of the team discussion. In each situation, a person can feel safer to experiment with new feelings, thoughts, behavior, and mindset without worrying about long-term consequences on their compensation or career.

Role-playing is a technique that allows people to explore new ways of interacting with others while minimizing the consequences (Bandura, 1977). For example, when trying to develop the ability to have difficult conversations, a person might pretend to be the manager facing a subordinate who made a major mistake and caused a key customer to leave. Such role-plays are often more effective if there are observers to help process and interpret what is said, and body language, or video recordings that a person can review afterward. If doing something different might be more effective, the person could do another role-play experimenting with the new behavior. Using social learning theory (Bandura, 1977), Latham and Saari (1979) showed how powerful role-playing can be used to initiate a behavioral modeling change.

Practice to Mastery, Not Just Comfort

Reinforcing a strength requires practice. Developing a weakness that is close to the tipping point requires practice. Practice requires effort and self-control. Without moments of PEA to revitalize an effort and remind those involved of the big picture (i.e., purpose and shared vision), the sustainability of any practice is doomed. When that occurs, we either forego some practice sessions or cut back on the effort.

Think about the challenges of learning a new language. It requires memorization, but also context for retention. Immersion techniques like repetition seem to help. In the early stages, remembering vocabulary is a major hurdle. Later, as the vocabulary is consciously accessible, memorizing verbs and tenses, sentence structure, and sensitivity to context (such as when to use which expression) feel like mountains to climb. Reading and comprehension seem easier than listening to a conversation. Listening and understanding seem easier than speaking. To be effective when using a new language with its native speakers, you need the full range of memory and skills of expression beyond the rudimentary robotic repeating of phrases. Once accessed, reinforcement is important because without use, the comfort fades and memories become elusive as you ponder how to use the future subjunctive tense.

The level of aspiration to which most sustained, desired change efforts are aimed is not mere comfort with the new thoughts, feelings, mindset, or behavior, but sufficient mastery so that it becomes an unconsciously usable habit. Professional musicians practice way beyond a point of comfort to the point of mastery, to the point where sheet music is not needed and they can attend to the other musicians and conductor with whom they are performing. A common aphorism and statement from parents to their children is "practice makes perfect," or the refinement to "perfect practice makes perfect." This begs the question of how much practice is needed and what kind, and it gives rise to a stream of research on deliberate practice (Ericsson, et al., 1993).

The 10,000 Hours of Practice Myth or the Real Work

The rule of thumb often quoted about how much practice is needed is that it takes 10,000 hours to master something. It was popularized by Malcolm Gladwell (2008), who devoted an entire chapter to it in one of his books. The main citation comes from a landmark set of studies by Ericsson, Krampe, and Tesch-Romer (1993) on deliberate practice. Their definition of deliberate practice is what ICT describes. Practice was focused toward a vision, purpose, and outstanding performance. This is a case where going back to the original research is helpful to see what was actually found and to clarify the meaning before generalizing to other settings or not.

Ericsson and his colleagues (1993) studied the development of virtuoso musicians, first violinists and then pianists, in noted symphonic orchestras. They monitored people and compared those considered expert. Expert status was attributed when the person had won numerous international competitions and was seen as a distinctive expert by well-respected classical music faculty, as compared to peers who were merely considered "good." All were esteemed symphonic musicians. In the second study of pianists, the experts were compared to amateurs who were not symphonic musicians. These musicians were asked to reflect on when they began practicing their instrument, and how many hours they had played or practiced every week and every year since they began playing.

They found that the experts had spent typically 10 years learning, practicing, and performing (around 7,606 hours for the violinists and about 10,000 hours for the pianists). But further comparison of recollection versus weekly logs suggested at least a 10% or more perceived escalation in the degree of effort spent as compared to actual logs. No one is sure how accurate their recall of their childhood and teenage years was.

The major conclusion from their research was that deliberate practice is needed for greatness in classical music—as well as for chess masters, in fields like mathematics and physics, and for Olympic-level athletes. All were distinctively elite performers in rarified endeavors. To reach their level of expertise or mastery at an elite level, they practiced about three hours a day, or 20 hours a week, for 10 years. They slept as much if not slightly more than their less effective peers, but they spent significantly less time pursuing leisure activities.

It was also observed that the effort "is not inherently enjoyable" (Ericsson, et al., 1993, p. 368). In ICT language, such persistent practice is often NEA. To sustain the effort and dedication, ICT predicts that regular and periodic excursions into PEA would be required. As said previously, the use of self-control itself is NEA and depleting of energy (Muraven & Baumeister, 2000). In their studies, they concluded, "the level of practice an individual can sustain for long periods of time is limited by the individual's ability to recover and thereby maintain a steady state from day to day" (Ericsson, et al., 1993, p. 370). Recovery in their terms is renewal or PEA.

Several other relevant observations were made in their studies. One is that the relationship between deliberate practice and actual performance was graphed as a power law, as suggested by the discussion of human performance and human behavior change in Chapter 3. That means that a person might practice for an extended period of time without noticing discernable improvement in their skill or performance. But at the next practice session, a dramatic jump might be noticed in their ability. The relationship between practicing and noticeable improvement is hardly ever linear.

The small sample sizes, potential errors in recollection of childhood experiences, and elite nature of the experts reduce the direct generalization of their findings, but does not threaten the power of their overall message. It is clear that deliberate practice is needed, and a lot of deliberate practice is needed to achieve mastery in anything.

Christine Dreyfus (2008) studied branch chiefs at NASA. They were all scientists and advanced engineers with PhDs who had devoted their professional lives to their work. She documented that those considered to be outstanding branch chiefs in performance had demonstrated high frequencies of using teamwork and empathy as competencies. She asked a subset of the outstanding performers who demonstrated current use of these competencies on each of several measures to recall when they had first experimented with each competency. They typically went back to moments in their childhood or early teens. When she asked when they first recalled using the competency regularly, they thought of moments and experiences in high school or graduate school. For example, most recalled using the teamwork competency in music bands. They then recalled experiences when they refined the competency and their degree of "successful use" (what we might call mastery), which tended to be interests outside of work during their early years as bench scientists doing predominantly solo research studies at NASA. Many cited volunteer work with groups like the Boy Scouts or the Four H Club.

A meta-analysis of deliberate practice studies in sports (Macnamara, et al., 2016) showed a large amount of variability in the amount of deliberate practice over the years. They cited other factors as significant contributors, such as genetically influenced factors in a particular physical domain, amount of competition experience, confidence, the person's degree of performance anxiety or aversion to negative outcomes, sensitivity to rewards, as well as the ability to control one's attention. Perceptual and psychomotor speed were also thought to contribute to elite performance. The genetic dispositional factors were reiterated in the meta-analysis from a slightly earlier study of twins and music ability claiming that inherited genetic factors accounted for 40% to 70% of the performance distinctions (Mosing, et al., 2014). In less rarified roles and occupations, the genetic factors will likely account for a lower percentage of performance distinctions.

How Long Should I/We Practice?

The answer to this question is: as long as it takes to perform the new thoughts, feelings, behavior, or mindset smoothly, well, effortlessly, and eventually unconsciously (i.e., not consciously thinking about it). In our collectives, practice as long as it takes for the new thoughts, feelings, behavior, or mindset to become a team or organizational norm. As explained above, the 10-year idea is to become a virtuoso performer. Most people seek sustained, desired change that is effective in their role or vision and to fulfill their sense of purpose. The deliberate practice research establishes that it takes time and perseverance.

To explore how long it would take to change habits, Lally and colleagues (2010) asked 96 volunteers to choose a behavior change goal, such as eating less, changing their drinking style, or exercising more. They were to choose something that they would work on each day within their current normal life routine. They recorded their behavior in this regard daily. The question was how long it would take them to get to a state of automaticity, in which the new behavior became a consistent habit (unconscious behavior). For the 62 individuals who continued with their effort, they achieved a degree of automaticity in 18 to 254 days.

A number of activities can be viewed as necessary and sufficient to help the desired changes become sustainable. First, practice in multiple settings. The new thoughts, feelings, behavior, or mindset need stimulus generalization and to be invoked in a wide variety of settings to be accessible. Jane Wheeler's research (2008) showed that when adults practiced the competencies to be developed from their learning plan at work, they improved. But when they practiced those competencies at work and at home, they improved significantly more. And when they practiced the desired competencies at work, at home, and at leisure or in other social settings, they improved the most. Practicing in multiple settings allows more frequent opportunities to practice and expands the variety of perceptual cues calling for the new activity.

Second, practice consistently over time, with perseverance. Lewis, Amini and Lannon (2000) commented on learning new skills and abilities: "The neocortex rapidly masters didactic information, but the limbic brain takes mountains of repetition. No one expects to pay the flute in six lessons or to become fluent in Italian in 10. But while most can omit a Ravel [symphony] or a part of Dante['s Trilogy] from their lives without sacrificing happiness the same cannot be said of emotional and relational knowledge. Their acquisition requires an investment of time at which our culture balks" (p. 189).

Rhythm and Dosage of Practice

The length of time needed for ample practice will of course vary by the nature of the affirmation (reinforcing existing desired characteristics) or change desired. Reducing the aspirations from virtuoso performances with musical instruments, international competitions, or chess tournaments, most desired changes are likely to be in how a person feels, thinks, and acts or their mindset (their overall approach and framing). For example, generating a significant increase in the empathetic behavior of physicians toward their patients was affected by three one-hour videos, discussions, and practice (Riess, 2018). When the desired changes were behavioral demonstration of desired competencies for management and leadership among MBA students ages 25–35 in both full-time and part-time programs, significant improvements were observed by others through 360 assessments, coding of video simulations, and coding of audio critical incident events from work within a year to two years (Boyatzis & Cavanagh, 2018), as reviewed in Chapter 4.

As discussed in previous sections, repetition is key to moving toward mastery and building the new neural pathways (Lewis, Amini, & Lannon, 2000). The best rhythm would depend on the person (e.g., vision, intensity of desire to change), the topic of the change (feelings, behavior, mindset), and factors in the person's life and work (opportunity and time for practice moments). Lewis, Amini and Lannon (2000) claimed, "When a limbic connection has established a neural pattern, it takes a limbic connection to revise it" (p. 177).

As in the deliberate practice research, resting periods are considered crucial to development of new or enhanced capability. An impressive study of waking resting periods was conducted to test development of a motor skill using magnetoencephalography (MEG) neuroimaging (Buch, et al., 2021). They were testing specific hippocampal sensory motor learning. They found that skill learning was 20 times faster with waking rest periods interspersed among the practice sessions than with longer practice periods—what they termed a "spacing effect."

Convenience and dosage considerations suggest that more frequent, briefer efforts at practice are more useful. Research on micro-interventions and the use of micro-breaks at work support this (Davidson, et al., 2003). This is similar to the reported findings of Boyatzis, Goleman, Dhar and Osiri (2021) on the benefits of more and briefer doses of renewal to ameliorate the ravages of stress, as discussed in Chapter 3. Four 15-minute experiences of renewal spread out throughout a day are more beneficial than spending one hour at any point in the day in renewal. This was a pronounced positive effect when the type of renewal activities or experiences were varied.

Stealth Learning and Multitasking

One of the many challenges of practicing is finding the time and energy to do it. Besides the many PEA-evocative ways to make the process more engaging and motivating, another is the idea of stealth learning—finding settings to practice in that are fun. They may be settings in which you are involved for another reason but that also provide an opportunity to practice or learn. Just like the Juan Trebino example of using his son's soccer team as a way to practice coaching others, there are a wide variety of volunteer activities that would serve multiple purposes. Doing it will help others (and be a PEA in and of itself), but it can also provide an opportunity to practice new thoughts, feelings, behavior, or mindset of interest.

The same can be said for multitasking. Say a person wishes to practice doing fun things with their family and is seeking a better work–life balance.

The person also enjoys being outdoors and exercising. Taking their family on a canoeing or kayaking trip could work on all three desired activities. The expanded benefits to PEA through renewal is added to the setting generalization of the new practiced activity, as described previously in Jane Wheeler's (2008) research. Practicing new things at work, home, and during leisure time increased the degree of improvement.

Exploring possibilities (i.e., experimenting) is helped by "play" (Mainemelis, 2010; Mainemelis & Ronson, 2006) or identity play (Ibarra & Petriglieri, 2010). The nature of such play is to suspend constraints of current organizational norms or Ought Selves imposed. It gives a person permission to explore and experiment with new thoughts, feelings, or actions. Encouraging a person to be playful can become a norm in organizations that support innovation. Sometimes this is referred to as creating space for play, innovation, or mind-wandering, which is a feature of activating the DMN (Smallwood & Schooler, 2014).

Nudges versus Nagging

The durability of the changes may require booster experiences, or reminders or nudges to refresh the person's repertoire, as predicted in social learning theory (Bandura, 1977). Like immunizing a person from a virus or flu, periodic deliberate practice acts as a booster or reinforcement. In Kegan and Lahey's (2009) Immunity to Change Theory (ITC), they discuss the importance of becoming aware of the obstacles, both self-imposed and in the environment, to continuing a learning or change process. They further show how anticipation of such obstacles enables a person to prepare for possible scenarios in advance, including options to address or avoid the presenting issues. This in turn serves to mitigate potential damage.

Nudges are gentle reminders (Thaler & Sunstein, 2008). Leaving an apple in front of a person is a nudge, for example, while prohibiting eating of junk food is not. The latter transgresses into the domain of nagging, which is often a persistent reminder with pejorative feedback and the emotionally toned statement that the target should feel guilt. Nagging invokes an NEA on the intended target. Nudges, if constructed properly, offer a reminder without emotionally laden overtones. The person is in control of noticing and deciding how to act next. Research does not consistently endorse the power of nudges, but its potential function as a reminder with minimal if any NEA is appealing.

A mobile phone application based on the Boyatzis, Smith and Van Oosten 2019 book *Helping People Change* was designed with daily reminder nudges.

But just as when frequent texts from a restaurant reminding you of your reservation goes from helpful to annoying, nudges can unintentionally slide into nagging.

Nagging may not come from others. In his desire to enhance his moral reasoning and behavior, Benjamin Franklin developed an elaborate scheme to monitor his progress on 11 of 13 important virtues with daily record-keeping in the eighteenth century. He wanted to develop habits of using and showing these virtues beyond his existing behavioral repertoire. Although he professed to have made progress on many of the virtues, his progress was not consistent across all of them. In particular, the pursuit of "order" (i.e., keeping things in their place and having appropriate time spent on them) had the opposite effect: "[It] cost me so much painful attention, and my faults in it vexed me so much, and I made so little progress in amendment, and had such frequent relapses, that I was almost ready to give up the attempt, and content myself with a faulty character in that respect" (Franklin, [1784] 2004, p. 58). In this case, the nudges or reminders had become NEA and led him to consider giving up.

In teams and organizations, the frequency of practice may not be measured in sequential time. Practice may be the number of meetings or events in which people are together and can practice a new norm. The same could be said of practicing a new norm in an organization.

Habit Formation

The mastery of a desired change is forming a new habit. The study of habit formation has identified six critical factors in the development and retention of habits (Harvey, et al., 2021): "Habits are independent of goals; habits are cued by specific contexts; habits are learned via repetition; habits are automatic; reinforcement promotes habits; and habits take time to develop" (Harvey, et al., 2021, p. 3). Further analysis of these studies features three characteristics: "Habits do not depend on goals . . . habit memory has rapid activation of specific responses and resistances to change" (Harvey, et al., 3021, p. 1). The authors emphasize that habit responses "are activated regardless of goals" (Harvey, et al., 2021, p. 1), which is relevant in light of the discussion of goals in Chapter 5.

The downside is that once formed, habits are difficult to break. The most profound evidence for this comes out of the addiction field, as shown in power curve figures in Chapter 3. Substance abuse is often a combination of physiological patterns that become associated closely with behavioral patterns. Many frequent smokers talk about the difficulty in not having a cig-arette while relaxing with a cup of coffee. But the emotional memories, stim-ulated by olfactory sensations and memories of the nicotine high, include the activation of parts of the nucleus accumbens and amygdala, which create a PEA moment (Breiter,, et al., 1997). The process of changing such habits requires changing behavior and reframing the emotional cues to powerful memories.

Cognitive reframing is the construction of a new way to think or feel about an event, experience, or relationship. It had roots in systematic desensitiza-tion, but became more potent and sophisticated with the development of cog-nitive behavior therapy (CBT) (Barkham, et al., 2021). The reframing involves many neural networks and the links to other physiological and psychological adaptations (Huepe & Salas, 2013). The more holistically embedded a habit becomes for a person, the stronger the likelihood of activating the habit, and the more difficult it would be to break.

Role of Feedback

Feedback on progress may serve multiple purposes. First, it informs the person how they are doing in their effort to develop. Second, it reminds the person and possibly others in their social system to attend to the aspiration or desired change. Monitoring progress on goal attainment dramatically affects the success of a change effort (Harkin, et al., 2016). The feedback serves as a reminder and possible source of encouragement.

On the whole, if feedback is to help facilitate change, research does not show that it is as useful as typical practices in organizations or family life would sug-gest. Most people receive unsolicited feedback. Whether positive, negative, or some combination of the two, feedback provided the way most people ex-perience it puts a person on the defensive (NEA) and reduces the likelihood of it helping in sustained, desired change. Professional women and people of color receive less feedback than their counterparts (Ely, et al., 2011; O'Neil, et al., 2015), and professional women do not even receive executive coaching as often as their male counterparts (Laff, 2007; O'Neil, et al., 2015).

These observations often bring incredulous reactions from people who think of those they are trying to help change. The challenge is whether those people did change. Except for people high in the McClelland (1985) motive Need for Achievement (see Chapter 5 for a discussion of this motive), most other people do not find feedback helpful or useful—and that assumes they are listening to it and not sticking their fingers in their ears.

While possibly well intended, Chapter 3 described how when managers, executives, therapists, clerics, physicians, nurses, and parents provide feedback to someone, it is more often than not a process of coaching for compliance. This invokes the NEA in the recipient, and actually closes them down to sustainable change.

When people are experimenting or practicing a change, they may want feedback on their progress or to adjust the nature of their practice. In such situations, the receipt of the feedback is more likely to be a PEA experience.

Role of Training

Research on the outcome from training programs is disappointing, if not embarrassing. Long noted as the "honeymoon effect," participants in organizational training programs are eager to try to practice new skills within days or a week or so of leaving the training. But the new skill often atrophies within three weeks to three months (Campbell, et al., 1970). Except for oral presentation skills and technical skills, like welding, training has been found to be grossly inadequate in helping people develop emotional, social, and cognitive intelligence competencies, as explained in Chapter 4.

It is not that formal training programs are useless and merely guilt reduction for executives. Training can be a powerful technique to stimulate awareness and the possible need for change. In that sense, if done well, training can be a wake-up call and motivate participants to seek a sustained, desired change effort.

As mentioned earlier, role-plays are potent sources of deliberate practice and learning (Bandura, 1977). A meta-analysis of 354 HIV prevention interventions showed that behavioral skills training, as well as behavioral skills argument and attitudinal arguments, were the most powerful in changing HIV prevention practices (Albarracin, et al., 2005). They were active, involved emotional practice focused on the participant's intention. Meanwhile, they found that interventions attempting to induce fear or the negative consequences of not practicing HIV prevention were the least effective.

ICT predicts that if a training program adopts the person's own Ideal Self, sense of purpose, and personal vision as the context of the training, feedback and practice would then have the most sustainable impact on change. Given the need for continuous practice, training programs that involve skill and competency practice as well as action learning assignments as practice would be most effective.

Booster shots, as discussed previously, are also needed. But so too are specific transfer mechanisms to help training program participants consider and practice the transfer of the new learning in various settings, events, and with other people with whom they interact at work or home.

Other Development Activities Organizations Can Use

Besides coaching, training, and feedback on performance and career development, and peer coaching in groups, organizations can offer other activities that are experienced as developmental by employees (Dhar, 2022a). In his thesis, Dhar (2022a) reported survey results from a wide variety of organizations showing that these other activities might include social and networking activities at work or at industry conferences. Organizations can provide partial or full tuition reimbursement in degree programs, and they can also organize short-term projects or task forces outside of a person's job to provide opportunities to experiment and practice new leadership or team collaboration behaviors. In addition to coaching, an organization can create programs or encourage employees to seek out mentors and role models who are outstanding performers or examples of career advancement from which they can learn. Organizations can sponsor and encourage employees to participate in corporate social responsibility projects, nonprofits, or other projects with a social impact, such as bringing healthcare to a rural community. They can also provide voluntary or sabbatical breaks for employees who have been with the organization for a number of years.

The Promise of Peer Coaching in Groups

The formation of peer coaching groups that continue to meet after training can be one of the most effective outcomes. Coaching is emerging as a quite popular form of development in organizations and for individuals wanting to change. It is personalized and more acceptable than training programs in hierarchal cultures. The early results and outcomes from randomly assigned control group studies are promising (Boyatzis, et al., 2022; DeHaan, et al., 2019). But coaching is highly labor-intensive, and as a result costly. So far, it has been predominantly offered as one-to-one coaching.

The promise and possibilities of peer coaching are substantial, and provides credibility to the client and benefits of status equalization. It is also highly sensitive to the dispositions, competencies, and idiosyncracies of the participants (Parker, et al., 2008; Parker, et al, 2014; Parker, et al., 2015; Holbeche, 1996).

Peer coaching in groups can bring the developmental aspects of coaching to millions of people who work in organizations, but not close enough to the top levels to warrant one-to-one coaching. It could also provide development for those who do not work in organizations that provide developmental resources. Peer coaching in groups has three major benefits in addition to the benefits of one-to-one coaching: it creates an egalitarian context to explore development; it can be offered at low or no cost to organizations or the participants; and it can incorporate diversity of thought, experiences, and approach above and beyond one-to-one peer coaching. The biggest challenge is to provide enough guidance or training so that group discussions don't devolve into complaint sessions.

Early studies by Volkova-Feddeck and Terekhin suggest a sequence in peer coaching groups that develop over time (Volkova-Feddeck, 2022; Terehkin, 2024). They focused on helping participants with a specific problem or task. If the relationships and quality of discussion evolves, then the group becomes a type of support group, helping participants with personal as well as professional development. The third stage of evolution is that the peer coaching group becomes a reference group (Merton, 1968) or social identity group (Tajfel, 1974; Ashforth & Maehl, 1989). This is similar to the team development process that has already been described by various small-group researchers who examined and studied leaderless groups, self-managing or self-designing groups, and quality circles, like Bennis and Shepard (1956), Bales (1970), and Druskat and Wolff (2000).

The effectiveness of the support and help participants can provide each other is to a large extent dependent on whether they use coaching with compassion (i.e., coaching to the PEA). This process maximizes the perceived benefits of participating, and helps each participant feel maximum engagement in the process and motivation to continue learning and changing, as well as helping others learn and change.

Peer coaching in groups has a long and rich history. Archeological evidence at various ancient sites, like in front of the library at Ephesus, reveals that the "seminar" was a structure for a group of men (in those days) to sit and discuss whatever learned topics they chose. This approach to learning probably began with the most simple process of sitting around a fire (once fire was intentionally used) by hunting and gathering societies. Telling stories was and still is a primary form of participants helping each other.

Thousands of years later, Alcoholics Anonymous capitalized on this design with their meetings of peers and creating both group support and the one-to-one sponsor. The use of this approach spread to help to other forms of addiction, from heroin addiction to families of alcoholics and drug addicts, to those seeking to lose weight.

Few graduates of doctoral programs, including in medicine and law, graduate without participating in study groups. Professionals and managers have also created study groups, often called juntas or reading groups, outside of work. The same process is used widely in professional groups, like the Young Presidents' Organization (Terehkin, 2024). Terehkin (2024) showed that compared to administrative groups, peer coaching groups created more individual development, greater sense of belonging, and more team emotional intelligence norms. Many work organizations, both private and government, use employee resource groups, study teams, and peer coaching to provide the developmental benefits of peer coaching in groups without using that as a formal title. It is a form of development everyone can access, Higgins and Kram (2001) and is referred to as developmental networks or groups.

Similar processes have also been used to socialize people into group identities for specialized groups, from basic training in the military to cults and sects. Some of the same processes were used in collectivist cultures to further enhance conformity, like training the cadres in Mao's Red Army.

Experimentation and Practice at Other Levels

Principle 8: As a fractal theory, ICT describes sustained, desired change at all levels of human endeavor from individual to dyads, teams, organizations, communities, countries, and global processes.

Experimentation and Practice in Teams

Experimentation and practice at other levels is a powerful predictor of the longevity of music groups (as shown in Figure 6.2) as to whether they experiment with alternatives to their existing music or genre. U2 and Bono have reinvented themselves and try something new repeatedly (Braunstein, 2022), as have Green Day and Metallica. They have all extended their live performances and recording for decades (as compared to the Police, Oasis, or the Sex Pistols). In the case of U2, they used setbacks to go on retreats, explore their roots, and

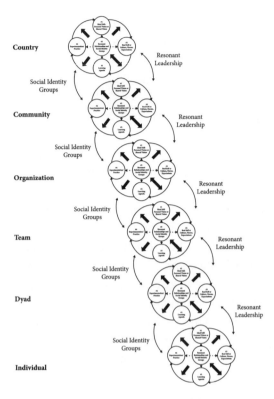

Figure 6.2 The multilevel fractals within Intentional Change Theory
Source: Boyatzis (2008, 2015).

discover new musical possibilities, truly using an experimentation phase of their evolution. In the eight-hour *Get Back* series of the Beatles developing and rehearsing for their last album, they were shown opening their studio sessions playing rock and roll oldies from the 1950s as a warm-up. Both during and between their sessions, they were continually working on ideas and practicing, trying new things.

The Krubera team of deep-cavers rotated leadership and spent time training before diving into the deepest and most hazardous cave systems on earth (Kimchouk, 2005; Meek, 2004), as described in Chapter 5. Meanwhile, competitive teams like the Cheve Team had talented individuals, but decided on a limited vision ("achieve the greatest depth on record at all costs"); had a single, individualistic leader; and did not train for many weeks. The result was a negative set of team norms that interfered with their ability to make crucial decisions while in the dark, cold, and wet depths of a cave system.

The heavy use of practice as a team was used by Eric Weihenmayer in preparing for their ascent of Mount Everest, as described in Chapter 2 (Weihenmayer, 2001). The most effective incident commanders of the wild-fire forest-fighting teams used down time for more training and practicing various eventualities, as described in Chapter 4.

Organizational Experimentation: Amazon versus Sears

Without specific organizational norms encouraging experimentation and practice, organizations tend to drive people to performance the same way they have in the past, including treating customers the same way for years and even decades. Loehr and Schwartz (2000) made the observation that professional athletes spend a huge amount of time practicing to perform for short, episodic durations. Meanwhile, executives typically spend no time practicing and all of the time performing.

Amazon is a leading company with norms of experimenting at new levels (Stone, 2013; Neate, 2014), from selling books online to music and then numerous other products—and then Alexa, buying Whole Foods, creating Prime delivery, launching a video streaming service, and using drone delivery. Jeff Bezos sees himself as a pioneer and encourages his organization to use small teams to try new things. When they find something that works, they practice it and continuously improve it. In contrast, the first corporation in the US in the mail order business— Sears Roebuck, founded in 1892—eventually went bankrupt, and was purchased and dismantled (Howard, 2017). It did not adapt, and successive leaders failed to see the need for innovation beyond physical retail outlets and establishing their own product brands.

Experimentation and Practice in Communities

At the community level, encouraging experimentation with new ways of behaving was a brilliant insight of Akhter Hameed Khan in the mid-1950s (Boyatzis & Khawaja, 2014). Khan approached the government for funds to create an academy in the capital, Comilla, in one of what was then East Pakistan's (now Bangladesh's) poorest state. He approached villages that were suffering where people were losing land, livestock, and did not have sufficient food for their families. He met with all of the adults in a village, which was a new behavior in the hierarchal, male-dominated, highly traditional Muslim communities.

He offered to train someone from the village in better crop-raising practices, and to bring rural electrification, clean irrigation water, and better seeds to the village. The villagers had to agree to try a range of new norms, one of which was sending a volunteer to the academy one day a week. The academy provided the bus to pick them up and bring them home. Another new norm was that all of the villagers, including women, would meet as a collective weekly, and elect a chair and a scribe to keep notes, as well as someone to keep their accounts. The person receiving the training would bring back the techniques and knowledge and teach it to the others.

Within a year, food production was increasing. Soon the villagers saved enough money and created cooperatives with other villages and bought tractors, irrigation pumps, and other equipment. Within a few years, their food production tripled. The villagers had healthier water and sanitation. All of this was happening in a region with the largest pogrom in the history of the world in progress about 600 miles to the east in China, where over 30 million people died, mostly of starvation (Becker, 1997).

Khan's approach was to offer help but do so firmly, and require that the villagers develop a shared purpose (i.e., vision) and create new norms that included trying and experimenting with new behavior. They then continued refining and practicing the new ways of farming and working together.

Khan repeated his success at community development over 30 years later in downtrodden and deprived refugee neighborhoods of Karachi. He used the same approach in different neighborhoods. Again, within short periods of time, the health and safety from microbial infections and crime experienced by residents improved dramatically. With both projects, Khan inspired Mohamoud Yunnus to establish the practice of micro-finance to help people create new lives for themselves and their children in the poverty areas of Bangladesh.

Beyond individuals using experimentation and practice to change thoughts, feelings, behavior, and mindset, people in teams, organizations, and communities can also experiment and practice new norms in how to act. In our collectives, it is clear that people need better relationships to support, motivate, and help change occur. This brings us to the next phase of ICT, creating and maintaining resonant relationships.

Concluding Thoughts

Sustained, desired change requires periods of experimenting with possible new thoughts, feelings, or behavior. To continue the process, extended periods of practice are needed. These must continue until the desired changes have sunk in and become part of the person's repertoire—practicing to the point of mastery. In our collectives, practice is needed until the desired changes have become new norms and practices in the team, organization, community, or country. Visualizing or mental visioning helps as a low-risk form of experimenting.

To sustain the effort of deliberate practice over time, the person or group must adjust the rhythm and dosage of practice. Stealth learning—multitasking by practicing while doing something else—can make practice more enjoyable. Various activities can be developmental and encouraged by organizations, which might include coaching, mentoring, and training. These will usually require feedback along the way and periodic nudges or reminders on the path to creating new habits or norms.

Experimentation and practice create the setting for another iteration of ICT by feeding into an evolving Ideal Self or shared vision. Of course, affecting this and every other phase in the process of ICT are the quality of relationships with people with whom a person is interacting regularly. In ICT, these are called resonant relationships.

7

Resonant Relationships Are the Context for Change (Principle 7)

Principle 7: The fifth phase of ICT is the establishment and maintenance of resonant relationships.

No man is an island, Entire of itself; Every man is a piece of the continent, A part of the main.

—**John Donne**

Change happens in context. In earlier chapters, each of the phases of ICT was discussed (the Ideal Self, Real Self, learning agenda, experimentation, and practice) as the context and process of sustained, desired change. In our collectives, it is the shared vision, norms of the culture, shared agenda, and common experiences with experimentation and practice. The fifth phase of ICT, resonant relationships, is different from the others in that it permeates and modifies experiences in each of the other phases along the entire process of sustained, desired change, as highlighted in Figure 7.1.

Our key relationships are with the people with whom we interact or depend on most frequently, as well as those with whom we feel the closest. Our relationships are both antecedents and consequences of changes in the way we think, feel, and act. But not all relationships and types of relationships have the same effects on sustained, desired change.

Relationships as the Context for Life

Relationships are the context for our lives and work because humans are social animals. Although there are trait differences in the degree to which various people enjoy interacting with others, everyone needs to interact, to laugh or solve problems, to come up with ideas, and to feel safe.

The Science of Change. Richard E. Boyatzis, Oxford University Press. © Richard E. Boyatzis 2024.
DOI: 10.1093/9780197765142.003.0007

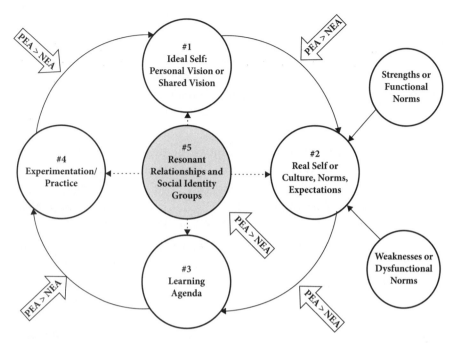

Figure 7.1 Resonant relationships in the process of Intentional Change Theory
Source: Boyatzis (2008, 2015).

Safety in and through our relationships is traced to hunting and gathering societies and hypothesized to predate Homo sapiens and frame our need to belong to and with others (Baumeister & Leary, 1995). Attachment theory explains that people seek proximity for protection or support (Bowlby, 1969/ 1982; Mikulincer & Shaver, 2007). From this perspective, maintaining our relationships appears to be a function of managing proximity (physical and emotional closeness), as well as frequency of contact.

The need to belong and feel a part of relationships is strongly evident in today's post-COVID world. Social isolation of the first few years of the pandemic seems to have resulted in many people continuing to live more isolated lives. This exacerbated a growing trend noted in a survey of 10,400 people by Cigna Corporation in January 2020 (Feintzeig, 2020) that "more than 80% of employed members of Generation Z—many of whom are just entering the workforce—and 69% of employed millennials are lonely."

The perceived substitution of Facebook friends and social media contacts for actual interaction proves to be illusory. In studying young adults, it was shown that more frequent use of Facebook predicted less satisfaction with their lives and their moment-to-moment feelings (i.e., sense of well-being). Interacting with others face to face did not reveal either of these patterns (Kross, et al.,

2013). The growing tendency for people to feel alone was documented prior to the COVID era in numerous studies and books (Putnam, 2000). In 1973, in a lecture I gave on radio and assorted historical associations, I attributed the destruction of intimacy in America to the growing popularity of television and the frequent use of box games, like Monopoly, as a vehicle for interaction that bypassed or limited human interaction. And that was before the internet, smart phones, streaming, and social media.

The need to belong is part of every motivation theory, from Maslow's hierarchy of needs (1943) to Deci and Ryan's Self-Determination Theory (2000). A human's Need for Affiliation was postulated by the McClelland-Atkinson expectancy value theory of motivation (discussed in Chapter 5 about Need for Achievement) that emerged from Murray's (1938) earlier work. When this stream of research was initially developed in the 1950s, the Need for Affiliation was seen as deficiency need that had to be satisfied (McClelland, 1985). Some people had more of it than others. Even Maslow (1943) saw relationships as a middle level of motivational need and viewed it as something to be satisfied or sated in order to move ahead.

In my PhD thesis (Boyatzis, 1972), I observed that this view of affiliation was based on a history of seeing love and intimacy as insecurities from Freud onward. I proposed a new theory that offered two forms of unconscious drives toward intimate and close relationships: rejection anxiety and affiliative interest. The major difference was whether the unconscious thought patterns were filled with anxiety-related themes, like the need for proof of another person's feelings toward you based on the amount of time spent with them and how often they told you they loved or cared for you. Prior studies developed the thematic codes for assessing the presence and intensity of the anxiety-filled need for affiliation on the basis of aroused rejection concerns and feelings of how others were judging a person or how much they liked the person.

The alternative was a nonanxious drive in which the intent was caring and loving relationships, like the harmony Martin Buber (1937) described in "I-Thou" relationships. This was evident in the sustaining the feelings of being in the relationship without frequent contact. It was even proposed that the transformation of rejection anxiety to affiliative interest could be a development progression, according to the type of relationship. A person might make the shift to affiliative interest with friends, which would precede the shift with an intimate, loved person, which would precede that with one's parents, which would precede that with one's children. The relationships with parents and one's own children are deeply embedded in biological and intricate emotional ties that are predominantly unconscious. The psychoanalytic theory explaining this is too expansive to discuss in this book. Making a change in the emotional tone and degree of anxiety associated with parental relationships requires changing many layers of associations, networks and feelings, and, therefore, is much more resistant to change than relationships with friends and an intimate partner.

In the following several decades, McAdams and Constantian (1983), Kelner (1990), and Weinberger and Smith (2011) expanded on this difference and enhanced the understanding of the nonanxious forms of affiliation and intimacy. This perspective followed the often referenced approach-avoidance dichotomy of drives. Attachment theory clarified that the process was complicated by the nature of a person's approach or avoidance behavior regarding others (Bowlby 1969/1982; Ainsworth & Bowlby, 1991). Further, it was proposed that among adults, mental representations of partners who might provide care and protection were experienced as a form of symbolic proximity leading to attachment. A person's attachments became their secure foundation for other relationships in life and work.

How Relationships Create Context

Relationships early in life have a profound effect on a person's feelings and behavior later in life, in part because that is how our brains are constructed and networked (Lieberman, 2013). Close and caring family relationships can "ameliorate the impact that adversity has on life span physical health" (Chen, et al., 2017, p. 555). In a series of papers in a special issue of the *American Psychologist* in 2017, the benefits of positive family relationships were shown to affect a person's health beyond their early years into adulthood (Chen, et al., 2017). It was believed that better family relationships could help reduce inflammation from stressors earlier in life, which would then influence biological systems and alter how a person reacts to stressors later in life, and also help by strengthening their immune system.

As described in Chapter 3, engaging the PEA, and in particular the PNS, stimulates the secretion of oxytocin, which has been shown to not only induce a renewal state but to "increase overall effectiveness of synaptic connections and bring about enduring change," including neuroplasticity (Doidge, 2007, p. 118). Oxytocin was even called a neuropeptide for affiliation (Insel, 1992). It helped people form relationships and increase their level of trust with specific others (Kosfeld, et al., 2005). As explained in Chapter 3, arousal of the PEA also activates the DMN, the Empathic Network (Jack, et al., 2013; Jack, 2024; Mars, et al., 2012). Activation of a specific element of the DMN, the ventromedial prefrontal cortex (vmPFC), is key to social tendencies, social interaction, and activation of the PNS (Eisenberger & Cole, 2012). This is the neural network that is at the center of a person's openness to or vulnerability to emotional contagion.

Oxytocin appears to prepare the brain for new learning by extinguishing of avoidance behavior and memories associated with it (Kosfeld, et al., 2005). It was proposed that oxytocin "melts" existing neural connections and makes room for new ones, which is a form of neural plasticity. Specifically, the Brain Derived Neurotropic Factor (BNDF) helps learning in the hippocampus and minimizes memory deterioration within days after dosage (Doidge, 2007). Along with Nerve Growth Factor (NGF), it "exercise[s] induced improvement that has been directly associated with neurogenesis, an increase in activity-dependent synaptic plasticity and altered gene expression, with many of these improvements observed in the hippocampus" (Hennigan, et al., 2007, p. 425).

Close relationships create a context for change by providing refreshers and reminders of the intent or desire to change, and possibly reigniting our interest and passion for change. Conversations with others help us interpret feedback from our surroundings, as well as provide support and encouragement for change.

When we have ties to others who are socially integrated into our lives and work, and especially those with strong ties, these relationships promote a happier and longer life (Inagaki & Orehek, 2017). The benefits go both ways. In the same reciprocity described by Boyatzis, et al. (2006) when describing the benefits to leaders if they coach others with compassion, both those perceiving and those providing the social support experience the psychophysiological benefits (Inagaki & Orehek, 2017). A brilliant neuroimaging study showed that by focusing on helping and caring for others, a person transcended their natural self-centeredness (Kang, et al., 2018). With a study of 220 somewhat sedentary adults, appeals (i.e., priming) of both affirmation and compassion for others resulted in activation of the vmPFC, which in turn led to greater physical exercise during a month following the arousal. This effect was reiterated in repeated studies by Adam Grant (2007, 2012; Grant & Gino, 2010) showing the power of prosocial motivation as both leading to and resulting from acts of gratitude and compassion.

The term "working alliance" has been used for many years to describe functional relationships (Graßmann, et al., 2020). The working alliance is characterized by a mutuality of goals, the tasks to reach them, and bonds of trust, respect, and liking. Research in psychotherapy found that the degree of synchrony between the therapist and patient was evident in multiple physiological measures and psychological perceptions (Marci, et al., 2007; Riess, 2018). When the therapeutic sessions were described by the patient or observers as "better" sessions, the patient and therapist had a high degree of concordance among these many measures and their real-time variations during therapy sessions. Brain-to-brain synchrony has gained an increasing body of research evidence, especially from animal studies (Kingsbury, et al., 2019; Denworth, 2023).

Graßmann et al. (2020) focused their working alliance research on coaching relationships. Their meta-analysis showed that the better the working alliance, the greater the desired outcomes were from the coaching, and inversely related to negative coaching outcomes. An interesting finding of their meta-analysis was that the "matching hypothesis" of helping relationships was not supported. The matching hypothesis claims that a helper (such as a coach) should look like and have similar experiences as the client in terms of race, gender, age, or ethnicity (Graßmann & Schermuly, 2020). They also found that matching personality traits and similarity was not related to effectiveness of the working alliance, but behavioral similarity was (using similar competencies as described in Chapter 4). This was further supported in a study of 74 coach–client pairs participating in a leadership program at a major US military academy (Boyce, et al., 2010). They tested randomly assigned dyads versus those with a systematic matching. Looking the same (what they called commonality) did not affect the significance of the outcomes. The quality of the relationships established did, as did some degree of complementarity of learning styles and relevant job credibility.

Throughout the change process, a person's resonant relationships enable each phase to develop and emerge. For example, discussing one's Ideal Self and personal vision with a trusted person can invoke PEA tipping points and thereby facilitate movement to the next phase of change (Jack, et al., 2013, 2023). Conversely, if the conversation is dissonant (NEA), a tipping point may provoke a regression to the previous phase and essentially slow down or stop the change and learning.

Major progress on theorizing the nature of relationships that help functioning and change was developed by Dutton (2003) and Dutton et al (2010) with a concept called high quality connections (HQCs). The characteristics of resonant relationships just described appear to spark these connections in the moment. They become a foundation or basis for future actions.

The quality of relationships is key to organizational-level change, as first proposed by Argyris (1985) in his work in the 1950s and 1960s. But it was also viewed as key in Tichy's (1983) theory of change. Most organizational development theories mention or discuss norms that facilitate change as resulting from better quality relationships (Burke & Noumair 2015) and a basic orientation toward people (McGregor, 1960).

As discussed in the following sections of this chapter, the qualities of relationships that are experienced as resonant are a degree of shared hope through vision, caring through compassion, centeredness through mindfulness, joy through playfulness, and energy through resonance in degree of activation (Boyatzis & McKee, 2005; Boyatzis & Rochford, 2020).

These relationships enable a person to understand and validate a phase of ICT within which they find themselves. The interaction provides support and reality testing. The conversation provides the psychological safety and trust a person needs while exploring and progressing in search of sustained, desired change.

One of the features of such conversations is deep listening. Besides hearing what the other person is saying, deep listening helps the person undertaking change or learning feel as if they are being heard. It involves attentiveness and nonverbal cues to the person's presence. The interaction may involve questions, but they are questions that help the person be open to change and learning, not closed. They are invoking more PEA than NEA.

Qualities of Resonant Relationships

High-quality relationships are beneficial not only for their instrumental value as the context for nurturing sustained, desired change, but they are beneficial in and of themselves. The benefits include greater psychological well-being (Reis & Gable, 2002), better physical health (Berscheid, 1999; Uchino, et al., 1996), better job performance (Gittell, et al., 2010), more learning (Carmeli, et al., 2009), coordination (Gittel, 2003), and error detection (Weick & Roberts, 1993). It is precisely these benefits of high-quality relationships that make them a powerful transformer of individual and dyadic characteristics into much a larger, shared impact on people. This section is updated and adapted from two earlier papers, Boyatzis (2018) and Boyatzis and Rochford (2020).

To those of us doing organizational change work in the 1960s and 1970s, it was clear that regardless of an executive's or leader's characteristics and behavior, some organizations flourished and others atrophied. Sometimes this occurred with the same person in a key position in different organizations or at different times. The organizations developed cultures that had long-lasting effects on the people within them and for their clients and suppliers. The same dynamics were observed in families and communities.

Building on the work of Freed Bales and Talcott Parsons (1955) with families of alcoholics, my own experiences with alcoholic patients highlighted the importance of the qualities of the families from which they came and into which they would attempt to return once sober. Again, some thrived and some languished into relapses. In the context of the work reviewed earlier in this chapter on motivation, relationships that fostered harmony, well-being, and hope seemed to do better in helping people adapt to change.

Thanks to a sabbatical at London Business School in 2006, the search for the specific qualities of relationships that nurtured growth, development, and sustained, desired change came into focus. In social psychology, in studies of couples, families, and teams, values and caring (i.e., prosocial) behavior were key to a desired future. In management studies, the only streams of research were leader–member exchange (LMX) (Graen & Uhl-Bien, 1995) and high-quality connections (HQCs) (Dutton, 2003). LMX helped us to understand what was transferred between a person and their boss, manager, or leader (Graen & Uhl-Bien, 1995). Later variations of the concept included the exchange of emotions with leader-member social exchange (LMSX). But it did not capture a full range of emotions in such relationships, or whether or not they were helping.

At the same time, no one had attempted to measure HQCs. HQCs at work were focused on momentary and temporary aspects of the relationships (Heaphy & Dutton, 2008). High-quality relationships appear to have a high degree of relational coordination (Carmeli & Gittell, 2009). Both studies characterized this as shared goals, shared knowledge, and mutual respect. This left an open question about measuring aspects of the quality of relationships that helped performance, leadership, engagement, and other desired outcomes (i.e., the qualities of relationships that nurtured or helped change). In subsequent years, more leadership research has examined the relationships between the leader and follower in terms of how they affect each other (Riggio, et al., 2008; Tee, et al., 2013), which will be examined in the next chapter as resonant leadership relationships.

Resonance or Being In Sync with Others

As a result of the emotional contagion discussed in Chapter 3, people will pick up emotions from others (Hatfield, et al., 1994; Hazy & Boyatzis, 2015; Boyatzis, et al., 2015; Elfenbein, 2014), which is enhanced by social mimicry (Boyatzis, et al., 2015; Fowler & Christakis, 2008). When people feel a dependence or interdependence on one another, many will likely tune in to others' feelings at least unconsciously. As Lewis, Amini, and Lannon (2000) suggested from their neurological studies, when people feel in sync or in a form of harmony with each other, they are both better at infecting others with their emotions and picking up on those felt by others. It is a quality captured by Martin Buber's I-Thou relationships (Buber, 1937). Resonant relationships can be one-to-one or in small groups, like developmental networks (Higgins & Kram, 2001), a board of directors (Boyatzis & McKee, 2005), or peer coaching groups.

If relationships can foster contagion, the specific qualities of relationships that are likely to help people be open to or sustain efforts at learning and change will be those that engage the PEA state or a tipping into the PEA. From medical and psychological research into the PEA and those that stimulate renewal, three shared emotions were of the most interest: hope, compassion, and positive affect (Boyatzis, et al., 2006; Janig & Habler, 1999). The first effort at measurement was the PNEA Survey (Boyatzis, 2018) assessing the degree of shared vision, shared compassion, and shared positive mood. After a few dozen studies examined the impact and mediating or moderating effects of these qualities of relationships, another effort was made to refine the variables and measure. The focus became the degree of shared vision, compassion, and energy (Boyatzis & Rochford, 2020). The resulting instrument was called the Relational Climate Scale (RCS), and is presented in the appendix (Boyatzis & Rochford, 2020). It is a validated and reliable measure of this approach to quality of relationships among dyads, teams, organizations and communities. Such relationships fostered greater psychological safety. Like trust, psychological safety is an experience or feeling that extensive research literature has linked to a wide range of desirable outcomes.

Shared Vision

As we said in Boyatzis and Rochford (2020), "shared vision is defined as the extent to which members of an organization (or team or dyad) share a common mental image of a desirable future that provides a basis for action" (adapted from Pearce & Ensley, 2004, pp. 260–261). As discussed in Chapter 2, this can take the form of shared ideals, values, identity, and purpose.

With a shared sense of purpose or vision in the relationship, people are quite literally moving in sync with each other toward the same ends in terms of purpose rather than merely goals. By having a common vision or purpose, people can act independently within their own situation but still move together (Kantabutra & Avery, 2010). It can help minimize a preoccupation with tasks and instrumental behavior, or act solely in service of short-term goals. A shared vision may seem fuzzy in comparison to thinking about specific goals (Carton, et al., 2014; Griffin, et al., 2010; Waldman, et al., 2014). There is not something necessarily explicitly exchanged among the people in these relationships, but something to which they all share a commitment at both rational and emotional levels.

Therefore, having a higher degree of shared vision means that those in the relationship are more resonant with each other in terms of a sense of belonging, social identity, and values (Kahn, 2007). They can also signal that the relationship has moved beyond belonging (Baumeister & Leary, 1995) to deeper and more sustainable relationships. In four longitudinal studies, including three observational studies, Prinzing et al. (2023) followed people for five weeks to 18 months. They found that positive resonance in their interactions characterized by mutual care and social synchrony resulted in an increased sense of meaning in life. Even attachment theory contended that shared vision has a power for deeper emotional and more positive relationships (Bowlby, [1969] 1982).

The earlier PNEA Survey or the refined RCS were used in over four dozen studies to reveal the impact of shared vision in a wide variety of settings. Shared vision was shown to predict leadership effectiveness in next-generation leaders in family businesses (Miller, 2023). With 100 next-generation leaders, shared vision, shared compassion, and shared positive mood were all crucial components of the quality of relationships in determining the family business climate, which in turn predicted engagement of the leaders (Miller, 2023). But among the scales, it was shared vision that was most powerful in predicting leadership effectiveness and engagement (Miller, 2023). The effect of shared vision partially mediated the impact of emotional and social intelligence competencies on leadership effectiveness or engagement, as reviewed in Chapter 4.

Also, in family businesses, Neff (2015) showed that among 110 family business executives, shared vision was the highest loading factor in creating an effective family business culture, which in turn predicted financial performance of the firm and financial performance as compared to competitors. Overbeke et al. (2015) showed that among 50 pairs of fathers and daughters in family businesses, the daughter's succession to the head of the family business was a function of shared vision with the founder, typically her father, which mediated the effect of sexism in the family and enhanced the daughter's self-efficacy.

One form of professional services is private equity. Examining the effect of relationships on 306 private equity partners in mergers and acquisitions

(M&A), Clayton (2014) showed that shared vision was one of two variables predicting championing behaviors that have been shown to predict effectiveness of M&A. Shared vision was the strongest predictor of the other variable, autonomous motivation. In the related world of investment management, Lord (2015) analyzed how open-mindedness of 168 university endowment officers affected their learning capacity. She found that shared vision moderated this relationship.

In the domain of research and advanced professional roles, Mahon et al. (2014) showed that in knowledge worker teams from consulting and manufacturing research and development, shared vision significantly predicted engagement and positively moderated the relationship of emotional and social intelligence of team members (as seen by others, not self-assessed) in predicting engagement. Among 795 IT managers and professionals, Pittenger (2015) showed that shared vision mediated the effect of emotional and social intelligence on engagement. In a comparably designed study, Quinn (2015) reported that among 677 physician leaders, shared vision mediated the effect of emotional and social intelligence on organizational citizenship behavior.

Even in the hallowed halls of academia, the quality of relationships matters. Among 218 community college presidents, Babu (2016) showed that the degree of shared vision they experienced in their management teams predicted their personal engagement. It was also found to mediate the impact of emotional and social competencies as seen by subordinates on the engagement of the presidents. In another study of 414 community college faculty, Babu (2016) showed that shared vision predicted both emotional and cognitive engagement. Professors who inspired their students at a large Mexican university had a perceived shared vision with their students that resulted in the students feeling more engaged in their studies (Juarez-Barco & Ehasz, 2023).

Khawaja (2010) showed similar results in doctor–patient settings. Doctors who created a shared vision and shared positive mood with their patients among 375 Type II diabetics were shown to fully or partially mediate all other features of the doctor–patient relationship in predicting increased treatment adherence. Even the doctors' perception of their relationship with the patients in these terms predicted treatment adherence, as reported by the patient's caregiver.

Shared vision in relationships at the organizational level also predict commitment. Straub (2015) found that 412 US Army acquisition managers showed that shared vision and shared compassion were predictive of engagement. A dark side of shared vision was found to be a narrowing of focus on an organization's bottom line, which elicited unethical actions (Resick, et al.,

2023). In the Resick et al. (2023) study, their finding did not seem like the effect of shared vision that invokes hope, but rather of imposing a more NEA agenda of task-oriented, financial performance.

When relationships experience a shared or common vision, people feel a part of the same effort. They share a sense of purpose. Their activities and work feel more meaningful. The bond and purpose invoke hope of a better future. This creates more PEA moments in their interactions and facilitates sustained, desired change.

Shared Compassion

Another quality of relationships that invokes the PEA is gratitude, which is stimulated by the act and experience of compassion with others. This approach uses the Boyatzis, Smith, and Beveridge's (2012) definition of compassion as "an interpersonal process that involves noticing another person as being in need, empathizing with him or her, and acting to enhance his or her well-being in response to that need" (p. 154–155). It is different from a Western or Buddhist view of compassion as feeling for someone in pain or suffering (Goleman, 2003). Grant and Gino (2010) showed that invoking gratitude predicted increased prosocial behavior.

This approach substitutes a more encompassing definition with hedonic as well as eudemonic feeling for others. It is caring for others in need and for others who wish to grow, learn, and change (Goleman, 2003; Boyatzis, et al., 2012). The source is Confucian philosophy, often interpreted by Mencius (Chan, 2002) as well as Aristotle. It still incorporates elements of compassion often cited in research: noticing or attending to another's need, other-regard feelings such as empathic concern, and acting to ease the suffering or enhance well-being of others (Dutton, et al., 2006; Kanov, et al., 2004; Boyatzis, et al., 2012). Attachment theory contended that shared compassion and caring created greater security and sense of safety in relationships (Bowlby, [1969] 1982).

In a marvelous series of longitudinal, observational studies, people who felt appreciated by their romantic partners and appreciated their partners in turn felt gratitude (Gordon, et al., 2012). They were more likely to remain in the relationship. It was the gratitude exchange, or mutuality, that resulted in observers seeing both people as responsive and committed to each other.

In a broader context, compassion has been claimed to be a driver of initiation, maintenance, and regulation of people in relationships that are not family connections (Algoe, et al., 2013; Gintis, 2000; Nesse, 1990). It appears to stimulate feelings of prosocial behavior, altruism, and a desire to collaborate with others (Gintis, 2003; Grant, 2007, 2012). In this way, it provides a different value and meaning in relationships than shared vision or purpose (Dutton, et al., 2014; Frost 2003; Frost, et al., 2000) and strengthens the bonds among the people involved (Dutton, et al., 2002). A qualitative study of executives from seven small to mid-sized companies revealed that shared compassion was predictive of positive social and behavioral outcomes as well as financial performance (Leah, 2023).

It is the mutual caring and trust that provides the emotional glue within dyadic or team relationships. In the Pittenger (2015) study, shared compassion among IT managers and professionals predicted two of the engagement scales. Physician executives showed a strong link between role endorsement as a leader and shared compassion and organizational citizenship task behavior (Quinn, 2015). Although shared vision and positive mood in the relationship with their doctor mediated its effect on treatment adherence, shared compassion also showed a significant effect on treatment adherence for Type II diabetics (Khawaja, 2010). Although less potent than shared vision, shared compassion did predict engagement for community college presidents (Babu, 2016) and for US Army procurement managers (Straub, 2015).

Compassion is experienced when people feel gratitude, are cared for by others, and care for others themselves. Positive affect, as well as hope and compassion, are associated with arousal of the PNS and therefore the PEA.

Shared Energy

A quality not directly emerging from PEA or PNS activation is a degree of shared activation or energy. In physics, resonance is two or more objects vibrating at the same frequency. So it is with people. The degree of shared energy in a relationship is probably a more direct measure of the emotional contagion discussed in Chapter 3 and being in tune with each other than any other quality of resonant relationships. In Ryan and Frederick's (1997) work on subjective vitality as a comparable quality, they defined it as "a specific psychological experience of possessing enthusiasm and spirit" (p. 530). Quinn and Dutton (2005) expanded on this study to define shared energy as "the extent to which relationships in an organization are a source of energy in that they result in feelings of positive arousal, aliveness, and eagerness to act" (Boyatzis & Rochford, 2020). Of all of the characteristics of resonant relationships, the sharing of energy is perhaps most directly associated with direct brain-to-brain communications, as discussed previously in the context of emotional contagion. Besides the limbic resonance discussed in Lewis et al. (2000), there is a growing neuroscience literature on synchrony between brains (Marci, et al., 2007; Dumas, et al., 2010).

Shared energy in relationships was shown to predict job performance, especially when mediated by engagement (Owens, et al., 2016) and increased feelings of bonding and organizational citizenship within organizations (Carmeli, et al., 2009). Owens et al. (2016) went further to explain that the absence of shared energy led to burnout or disengagement, spread through social contagion, and was likely to affect recruitment, retention, and performance. A comprehensive review of energy in relationships reveals that it appears to be closely related to perceived social support and the quality of the leader–follower relationships (Baker, 2019).

In more personal experiences, think of a couple that does not have shared energy. One is eager to go out on a particular evening and have an exciting adventure, while the other may be longing for a quite evening at home. The central issue is the degree of activation desired by each person in the relationship, which is also a function of how much they activate or arouse each other's energy.

Overall Quality of Resonant Relationships: When All Three Function Together

Some research does not differentiate the impact of each of these three qualities of resonant relationships. Such studies have used and reported the results with the RCS as a total score.

All three of the original scales (shared vision, shared compassion, and shared positive mood) were used as a total indicator of quality of relationships in four studies. For 239 mid-level managers in Latin American companies, Martinez et al. (2021) showed that the composite quality of resonant relationships score predicted psychological well-being and engagement, but not effectiveness as measured by the Reputational Effectiveness Survey (Tsui & Ashford, 1994). As a meditator of the manager's personal Ideal Self (personal vision), the composite did predict engagement with full mediation, and psychological well-being with partial mediation.

This composite of quality of resonant relationships was shown to predict all five forms of corporate social responsibility (CSR) in a sample of 149 managers (Thornton, 2015). Perhaps more importantly, the quality of relationships affected efficacy and conscientiousness in their impact on corporate social responsibility in either a full or partial mediation in predicting CSR. Among 222 Indian manager–subordinate dyads in service companies, Pardasani (2016) found that this quality of resonant relationships composite predicted resonant leadership and resilience. A subset of five items from the shared compassion and shared positive mood scales, in concert with another set of items from a different instrument, moderated the impact of emotional and social intelligence competencies of 85 bank executives on engagement, career satisfaction, and personal vision (Van Oosten, et al., 2019).

Meanwhile, another two studies tested all three scales of the RCS as a measure of quality of resonant relationships. Kendall (2016) showed with executives from high-tech companies that behavioral, emotional, and social intelligence competencies (not self-assessed), as discussed in Chapter 4, was significantly predictive of quality of resonant relationships and that it predicted product innovation, perceived improved competitive performance in innovation with other companies, and perceived relative market share of change. This was found for both exploitative and explorative innovations.

Resonant relationships were also important in a study of senior executives and their subordinates (Warr, 2023). Professional development mindset was predictive of quality of resonant relationships with each other, as were several EI competencies of the executives as seen by the subordinates. Both resonant relationships and EI predicted engagement of the subordinates and their perception of the executive's leadership effectiveness. Again, as in almost every study reviewed, the qualities of the resonant relationships either mediated or partially mediated these effects. Their resonant relationships were the context that led to effectiveness, engagement, citizenship, and innovation.

Resonant Relationships in Each Phase of ICT

The mechanisms through which resonant relationships facilitate sustained, desired change, in addition to emotional contagion discussed in Chapter 3, vary by phase of ICT. They enhance or create the atmosphere for initiation or maintenance of the Ideal Self, or in our collectives, a shared vision. It enables those close to us to encourage us to dream, or remind us of the dreams we've forgotten or relegated to a low priority and awareness than current Real Self issues.

Our resonant relationships can facilitate awareness of our Real Self, or norms in our collectives. People with whom we have resonant relationships can notice and endorse our strengths. They are in a position to observe and identify weaknesses that are close to the tipping point, and we are ready to listen. People in resonant relationships can reality-test candidates for change in a learning agenda or plan, helping us consider whether they are too distant to be a helpful target of change.

People in resonant relationships can help us prepare for experimenting and practicing a new thought, feeling, behavior, or mindset individually or in our collectives, and to develop a learning agenda or plan. They can help us consider potential obstacles as well as identify resources to overcome them. They can remind us to practice our intended change.

Such relationships can help sustained, desired change in the experimentation and practice phase by providing feedback on progress toward our vision or learning goals. Because they have shared compassion, they are more likely to allow each other to nudge them in a PEA manner and not have it feel like nagging (NEA). Those in resonant relationships can become a cheering squad, champions, or sponsors of change.

As people within our perceptual sphere, they can be models for the feelings, thoughts, behavior, or mindset to which we aspire. But the modeling has to be experienced as helpful toward our existing vision and within a tipping point of feasible change. Eisenberg et al. (2013) showed how modeling new behavior can backfire. They studied young adults who wished to lose weight by dieting and found that when exposed to others dieting (i.e., social comparison), for some individuals, especially females, the effect of the model was the opposite, almost like a reaction formation. It resulted in them binge-eating. Clearly, the observation and social comparison was an NEA experience and led to dysfunctional or defensive actions.

As described above, resonant relationships can help initiate or invoke a PEA state from each of the phases of ICT. The same acts or moments could turn into initiating an NEA state when taken to excess or when they invoke social comparison or evaluation. This will be discussed at length in Chapter 8.

Resonant Relationships at Other Levels

Principle 8: As a fractal theory, ICT describes sustained, desired change at all levels of human endeavor from individual to dyads, teams, organizations, communities, countries, and global processes.

Within the many forms of dyads in a person's life (e.g., subordinates, boss, partner, children, parents, friends), sharing compassion and caring invokes a developmental mindset. Coaching others can be described as a role but also as a process used by anyone in dyadic relationships. In organizations, Bell and Goldsmith (2013) advocated for managers adopting coaching practices as part of their role and responsibilities to develop everyone who reported to them.

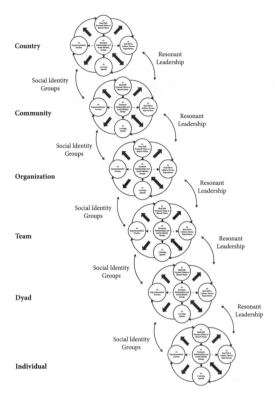

Figure 7.2 The multilevel fractals within Intentional Change Theory

Source: Boyatzis (2008, 2015).

Mentoring is a developmental relationship in which there is a shared vision and hopefully, a shared compassion (Ragins & Kram, 2007; Kram & Hall, 1989). Socioemotional or relational mentoring appears to be the same as coaching (Ragins & Kram, 2007). As described in the previous chapter about peer coaching in groups, mentoring and coaching can be parts of "developmental networks" for a person (e.g., a group of people devoted to their development and growth) (Kram, et al., 2011).

In previous chapters, a number of examples of ICT at various levels have been described, as highlighted in Figure 7.2. The many months of training for each deep-cave exploration was being planned by the Krubera Team, who trained not just for the technical aspects of each exploration but also worked on the quality of their relationships. The same was observed in the Erik Weihenmayer Everest expedition. They did not train for months and years just because Erik was blind, but also to build a secure foundation of their relationships.

Whether in deep caves or at the heights of Mount Everest, moments of danger can happen without warning. Communications have to be clear and fast. Resonant relationships enable the people in these teams to be ready to listen to each other. They have a common purpose and vision, which often means shared values. They can communicate via these values.

At the community level, the benefit of resonant relationships is never clearer than during a disaster. A positive story of people and groups coming together, forming resonant relationships and saving lives is found in the Chilean Mine Disaster of 2010. A copper mine in the Atacama Desert had a major cave-in. Tons of rock crashed into the entrance and trapped 33 miners 2,000 feet underground. They were buried for 69 days, but all came out alive.

No successful rescue had ever been attempted at this depth before. The company that owned the mine was Compania Minera San Esteban Primera. Another company involved in the rescue was CODELCO, Chile's largest government-owned mining company, which also included the mining company BHP Escondida. And there was also the government of Chile. The President of Chile, Sebastian Pinera, and their Mine Minister, Laurence Golborne, were immediately and directly involved when they arrived on-site. Meanwhile, CODLECO offered their senior mining engineer, Andre Sougarret; a psychologist, Rene Aguilar; a senior geologist, Jose Toro; and 320 other people, as well as food, provisions, and equipment, to help the rescue effort. The first thing observers noted was that every person who arrived and had relevant expertise was participating in discussions (Sanfuentes, et al., 2021). Everyone quickly settled on a shared vision: rescue the miners as soon as possible.

They formed two drilling teams with three parallel plans to drill a ventilation shaft and then a new escape shaft. The escape shaft failed, but fortunately a third shaft was being drilled. They had formed a life support team, an extraction team, and developed 10 options.

Meanwhile, a young engineer from NASA proposed the idea of using an escape pod that NASA had designed for a quite different setting. Drilling manager Walter Veliz from BHP Escondida, mining manager Marcos Bermudez, and Nicholas Cruz, who was a geologist, joined as team leaders. Even the Chilean Navy got involved. The people in charge, mostly Andre Sougarret, put a priority on creating living space on site for the families of the trapped miners. They kept the press away from the families. They felt compassion for the trapped miners and their families, as well as for everyone who arrived at the scene to help.

Each of the many different leaders adopted a consultative style, gathered people for discussions, divided the work, and went into action (Useem, et al., 2011). They encouraged open communication among all levels, and vowed to keep all communication honest and flowing. Their sense of urgency revealed the degree of shared energy. The quality of their resonant relationships meant they could safely assume they had a common purpose. They could focus on solutions to complex problems without competitive vying for supremacy of their ideas.

Meanwhile, the 33 miners knew they initially had provisions for only 48 hours. They formed a micro-society: the foreman organized them, they agreed on the rationing of supplies, they talked with their families daily through the ventilation shaft, listened to each other and the experts, and intentionally worked on keeping morale high. They were using their resonant relationships with each other to survive.

With these many different organizations represented, different fields of expertise, and different cultural backgrounds, it could have spelled a disaster and cost the miners their lives. But the opposite happened. People worked together, forming resonant relationships with a shared vision, shared compassion, and a high level of shared energy. Each of the many leaders, with dramatically different status, adopted a resonant leadership style that will be discussed further in Chapter 8. The people in these resonant relationships cared about each other. That bred a mutual respect and was contagious in building new relationships with those arriving on the scene.

All of the miners were rescued. It worked so well that a Harvard Business School case was created about this mine rescue.

Sadly, there are many stories of the opposite happening and costing lives. One such event was the explosion and sinking of Deepwater Horizon and the largest man-made oil spill in history, in 2010. A problem was noticed in pieces of rubber floating to the surface around the rig, and the chief engineer reported it to the rig manager and asked the manager to stop the drilling and send divers down to examine what was wrong. The rig manager and other members of the management team resisted, but finally gave in and called their base in Houston for a corporate recommendation. The Houston management discussed it and called London to BP's headquarters for guidance (National Commission, 2011). By the time the meetings were held and phone calls made, Deepwater Horizon blew up, killing 11 of their crew and unleashing more oil into the Gulf of Mexico than had been anticipated and causing environmental damage to wildlife and property (Michel, et al., 2013).

In dramatic contrast to the Chilean events, there seemed to be little if any shared vision in this case. The chief engineer had his sense of purpose, and the rig manager had his. The Transocean and Haliburton executives had their vision, and the BP executives and managers had a different one. There was little caring or listening to each other, thus there was no shared compassion, and there was uneven energy across the individuals and groups. In the midst of the crisis, the CEO of BP was caught on television saying, "I want my life back!" The lack of resonant relationships and lack of resonant leadership created a context for little agreement or action toward sustained, desired change. In the same way resonant relationships worked to spread positive emotional contagion in the Chilean mine disaster, dissonant relationships spread a defensiveness among the relationships involved in Deepwater Horizon.

Another contrast at the community level is the experience during and after three massive hurricanes in the US: Katrina (2005), Ike (2008), and Sandy (2012). Each was a powerful hurricane that caused enormous damage, estimated at $100 billion from Katrina, $30 billion from Ike, and $65 billion from Sandy. But the death toll was a different story: Hurricane Katrina resulted in 1,392 deaths, while there were 57 deaths during Hurricane Ike, and 117 for Hurricane Sandy. The greatest cause of the damage from Katina was that some of the levees surrounding New Orleans failed—but the lack of resonant or courteous relationships among key figures in the Katrina disaster amplified everything and made matters worse (Cowen & Seifter, 2014).

Mayor Ray Nagin, Governor Kathleen Blanco, the FEMA Director Michael Brown, and President George W. Bush did not agree and were disconnected. The governor refused to mobilize the National Guard and put them under federal authority. The mayor failed to mobilize thousands of buses sitting in parking lots that were eventually flooded, but had earlier been at his disposal to evacuate citizens. The city did not use their emergency alert system, nor their emergency plans sitting on desks in heavy binders.

An example of the chaos was in a speech given by the New Orleans Police Superintendent, Eddie Compass, at a national conference of the Royal Canadian Mounted Police (RCMP) a few years later in Vancouver. I was there giving a keynote later in the day. As he told episode after episode of not knowing where his own relatives were, as well as many of his officers, and running into what felt like impossible situations repeatedly, his refrain was "We are only human." I asked a variety of senior RCMP superintendents afterward what was missing. They said that getting the families of every police and fireperson on buses and to safety days before the hurricane hit landfall would have freed the first responders to do their jobs. Clearly, the way that the response to Hurricane Katrina was a confusing mess that cost lives and prolonged damage to property and infrastructure. The lack of functional relationships added to the confusion and their inability to engage in sustained, desired change. Defensiveness and dissonant relationships were the norm.

Hindsight no doubt helped mayors, governors, and FEMA deal with the future major hurricanes. FEMA changed directors and put specialists in disaster relief and logistics in charge. They reframed their mission as helping before, during, and after disasters. Mayors and governors worked with each other and the White House differently. Governors Chris Christie and Andrew Cuomo, as well as President Obama, worked together and by the time Hurricane Sandy hit in 2012, had formed resonant relationships to mitigate the effects of the disaster.

Mobilizing Grandmothers: Friendship Benches

When most people think about resonant relationships, especially in an exercise I have often done for years about Who Helped You the Most in Your Life, people often think of grandparents. In particular, many people hold a reverence for their grandmothers. A psychiatrist in Zimbabwe, Dr. Dixon Chibanda, tapped into these relationships and memories of them in an ingenious program to reduce depression and other forms of mental illness (Chibanda,, et al., 2016). It is called "friendship benches," from the label printed in large letters that were placed on the wooden park benches. They began building park benches and placing them outside of clinics, and later added them to other meeting places in villages. They trained grandmothers in basic counseling skills using cognitive behavior therapy as a foundation.

The grandmothers devised a process of six 45-minute sessions with a prospective client—for free. The results have been impressive in randomized control group trials (Chibanda, et al., 2016). It has spread widely in Zimbabwe and to other countries like Malawi and Zanzibar, and even New York City, to over a thousand grandmothers and tens of thousands of clients.

The friendship benches are reminiscent of an experiment conducted in the 1960s to reduce the number of chronic schizophrenics in locked wards of the Topeka State Hospital, a mental health facility. They noticed that the people to whom the patients talked the most were the orderlies, not the physicians or nurses. Orderlies were trained in basic interpersonal skills: listening and asking open questions. They were taught to build a caring—that is, resonant— relationship with the patients. Over the one-year pilot and four-year experiment of the Ward H program, a dramatic increase in discharges into half-way homes, nursing homes, full release occurred among patients who many thought would never leave the locked wards and move on in life (Colarelli & Siegel, 1966).

The behavior of most of the patients on Ward H became healthy and functional during the four years of the experiment. There was a 365% increase in off-grounds passes granted, an 850% increase in patients getting jobs and individual assignments, and a reduction in readmission rates from the entire hospital's previous average of 37% down to 5%. Of the patients in the Ward H program, 92% were discharged to independent living or nursing homes. This was in contrast to the entire hospital's discharge rate of around 50% during the same period (Colarelli & Siegel, 1966). At the time, critics complained that they were teaching orderlies social skills inspired by good bartenders. But regardless of the inspiration, it worked: better relationships, more resonant ones, helped people overcome a wide range of mental health disorders and dysfunctional behavior.

Concluding Thoughts

Relationships are the context for sustained, desired change. They enable iterations of PEA tipping points and cycling through the phases of ICT. The qualities of resonant relationships—notably shared vision, compassion, and energy—enable individuals or our social collectives to pursue desired change. Two key aspects of any complexity-based theory like ICT is that there is multilevelness and a way to communicate information and emotions across levels. It is a fractal theory. In each chapter, as each phase was discussed, there has been an attempt to show how that phase works at all of the levels, from individual change to dyads, teams, organizations, communities, and countries. In the next chapter, the two components of ICT that move information and emotions across levels, namely resonant leadership relationships and social identity groups, will be discussed.

8
Leading Change at Multiple Levels (Principles 8, 9, and 10)

Principle 8: As a fractal theory, ICT describes sustained, desired change at all levels of human endeavor from individual to dyads, teams, organizations, communities, countries, and global processes.

Principle 9: Resonant leadership relationships facilitate moving information and emotions within and across levels of human systems facilitating sustained, desired change.

Principle 10: Social identity groups facilitate the enduring quality of sustained, desired change by helping or hindering progress toward one's Ideal Self (vision) or a group's shared vision, and moving information and emotions within and across levels of human systems to facilitate sustained, desired change.

As introduced in Chapter 1, sustained, desired change for humans is a complex system. At every level of human change efforts, whether individual, dyads, teams, organizations, communities, or countries, sustained, desired change will follow the phases of ICT. The process uses PEA tipping points to advance or NEA tipping points to inhibit along what is likely to be a nonlinear, discontinuous process. A review of the research and dramatic examples of ICT have been illustrated in the previous chapters.

A complex system has a number of requirements (Erdi, 2008; Casti, 1994). It is often nonlinear (as described in Chapter 3), and has moments where some phenomenon emerge. In the case of sustained, desired change, and specifically ICT, moments of emergence are either a time when a new awareness dawns or bursts into a person's consciousness. These moments of emergence will feel like epiphanies or discoveries, and have discontinuous distributions (discussed in Chapter 3). This discontinuous and nonlinear distribution will also apply to the temporal dynamic of ICT. That is, the phases and tipping

The Science of Change. Richard E. Boyatzis, Oxford University Press. © Richard E. Boyatzis 2024.
DOI: 10.1093/9780197765142.003.0008

points will causally move a person or human collective to sustained, desired change, but with different periodicity.

Another property of a complex system is a recursive process. ICT is described as an iterative process in the search for sustainable change, and a complex system also has sensitivity to initial conditions. This is why early adopters or initiators of change events often have more potency and leverage than later participants, such as in igniting a swarm or going viral in the age of social media. In ICT, the PEA and NEA tipping points are examples of initial conditions that can facilitate forward growth, learning, and change or inhibit progress, as explained in Chapter 3.

A complex system also has a property called scale dependence. Scale dependence means that the system has multiple levels observed in a hierarchy. Miller (1978, 1995) proposed that human systems have many levels, from cells and organs to groups, organizations, communities, and society. He then attempted to show the multilevel interactions.

A multilevel system implies a hierarchy of some sort (Rousseau, 1985). In human systems the hierarchy is often assumed to be size, such as Miller's (1978, 1995) multiple human system from the cellular to global. Each level should be distinct to be considered an independent level, but that does not imply that the levels do not affect or more accurately *cannot* affect each other (i.e., scale dependence). Multilevelness is not just a function of aggregation or disaggregation (Rousseau, 1985); each level can function on its own. This quality of ICT can be complicated by confusing different units of analysis and measurement (Klein, et al., 1994).

Klein, Dansereau and Hall (1994) described the three criteria for multilevelness as homogeneity, independence, and heterogeneity. Each level within ICT functions as a change process unto itself, satisfying their requirement for homogeneity, and each level of the process of change within ICT can function independently without the other levels, which satisfies their criteria of independence. But this should not be confused with the possibility that events within a level may trigger or affect events or processes in another level. The criteria of heterogeneity is also present in each of the levels within ICT in that the degree of change occurring in one level may be different from the degree of change even on the same issue at other levels.

As a complex system, ICT proposes that at various levels the process appears the same. It is beyond isomorphic or similar, and is actually a fractal (i.e., the same), as shown in Figure 8.1. In a complex system, a process is described and predicted at one level, and is purported to be the same at each other level (Henderson & Boje, 2016). This supports ICT as a fractal theory. Among humans, the levels ICT addresses are individuals, dyads, teams,

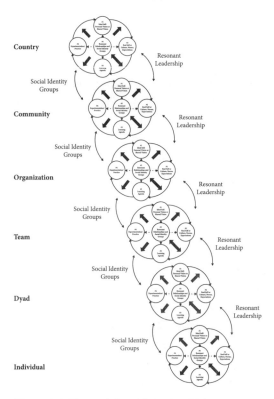

Figure 8.1 The multilevel fractals within Intentional Change Theory
Source: Boyatzis, (2008, 2015).

organizations, communities, countries, and global processes. The examples of cases and research cited in Chapters 2 through 7 were offered to support the multilevelness of ICT up to the country level.

For example, in the Chilean mine disaster example, individuals were engaged in a process of changing their approaches and ideas as to how to save the miners. Teams working on various options identified and studied different shaft concepts, and engaged in a change process. At the same time, each of the organizations present at the mine site were engaged in a change process. Meanwhile, different members of the larger community—the families of the trapped miners, managers and experts from the mining companies, the Chilean government, and external concerned groups like NASA—were also exploring different ways to help each other, maximize resources, and keep hope alive. They were engaged in a change process at the community level. The vision or mission was the same at each of these levels: save the trapped miners. The norms of interaction were the same at each level in terms of listening to each other, being open to considering all ideas, and providing emotional support and hope. Even the attention and prayers of the people of Chile and through the media and those of people throughout the world were focused on saving the miners.

A complex system will not only have multiple levels that are fractals of each other (like various possible focal planes in observing the same phenomenon), but also contain factors that move information across levels. In human systems, a key aspect of information is emotional. In ICT, it is proposed that two factors move information and emotions across levels: resonant leadership and social identity groups (SIGs). These are the vehicles of contagion or cross-level interaction.

Cross-level communication is a transfer or transmission of information and emotion (Baer, et al., 1987). Miller's (1978, 1995) proposal is that cross-level communications can be in the form of matter, energy, or information. In ICT, being in a PEA state makes the boundaries more permeable. Like sensitizing neural synapses, this may mean that being in the PEA at one level means the person or people are more open to sensing, noticing, or tuning in to the offered transmissions from other levels. As a cynical view, this also means they may be more susceptible to being influenced by such transmissions.

Consistent and multiple transmissions or multiple vehicles of transmission will increase the likelihood that the information or emotion crosses the boundaries. It is also likely to minimize signal deterioration and the possible contamination of signal noise (Miller, 1978, 1995).

Transmissions can go in both directions across levels (Yammarino & Gooty, 2019). The potency of the transmission or strength of the infectiousness is likely to be affected by the vehicle of transmission or the levels that appear more powerful in a social status sense. A parent making a plea to the family at dinner to quiet down is more likely to have an effect than if one of the children sitting around the dinner table makes the same appeal.

One of the ways either resonant leaders or social identity groups (SIGs) effect cross-level transmissions are through the PEA and NEA tipping points. Invoking or stimulating a PEA moment in others may enable movement toward a shared vision and sustained, desired change. In an analogous way, stimulating an NEA moment will likely invoke defensiveness or fear. Once begun and as a result of homeostasis, there will be a lack of change or exploration of change. Yammarino and Gooty (2019) raised the question as to whether these cross-level effects are moderating or mediating change at other levels. The research reviewed in Chapter 7 on the effect of shared vision, compassion, and energy within resonant relationships suggests that both types of effects are possible. Another way to examine this possible difference is to ask whether the cross-level transmission will cause a change in the other level or will have a catalytic effect on such a change occurring.

This has to be more than the ecological fallacy (Robinson, 1950) that occurs when attributions of dynamics at one level are made because the entities are constituents of another level. The impact factor of a particular journal when applied to a faculty member or paper is a typical ecological fallacy in faculty promotion committees and reviews, for example, when the error in assessing the quality of a faculty member's research is made by imputing the rank or impact factor of the journal in which it appears (Ramani, et al., 2022).

Resonant Leadership

For sustained, desired change, resonant leaders are needed at multiple levels. They not only provide leadership within a level, such as within the organization or community, but they also transmit information and emotions across levels. Resonant leadership occurs when a leader and those around them have a resonant relationship, as explained in detail in Chapter 7. The leader and others (sometimes called followers regardless of the formal role relationship), would experience the relationship and their interactions in a similar manner. As described previously, they would describe the experience as one of shared vision (with hope), shared compassion (with gratitude and caring), and shared energy (with activation).

Resonant leaders and their relationships with others at various levels is an efficacious vehicle for cross-level transmission. As explained in Chapter 7, resonant relationships are characterized by parties vibrating at the same frequency and being in tune with each other. Lewis, Amini, and Lannon (2000) referred to this as "limbic resonance" or "neural synchrony" (Marci, et al., 2007; Kingsbury, et al., 2019; Denworth, 2023). People transmit or activate neural networks in others within their sphere of influence. This may be people within visual contact or people within emotional contagion range, which can be worldwide with the help of social and visual media. Those in such relationships—such as leader–follower, manager–subordinate, physician or nurse–patient, teacher–student, or parent–child—would have the degree of resonance in their relationship as the basis for the likelihood of tuning into the frequency of the leader (i.e., the person transmitting).

A brilliant analysis by two prominent leadership and emotions scholars, Neal Ashakanasy and Ronald Humphrey, described a multilevel theory of leadership that explains processes of emotional transmission across levels (Ashkanasy & Humphrey, 2014). They contend that the demands and opportunities of such cross-level transmission carries a burden, which they called emotional labor to the leader, and to a lesser extent to the followers or recipients at the various levels.

Americans of a certain age cannot hear the phrase "I have a dream" without visualizing the Reverend Martin Luther King Jr. standing on a podium at the National Mall in 1963 and feeling the passion and hope of his call. Other speeches by leaders that resonate with many others have had a similar effect. There's the famous phrase "You cannot shake hands with a clenched fist," from Indira Gandhi, the first female prime minister of India. Or President John F. Kennedy's explanation for why we were going to the moon in 1962, which has intellectual and emotional appeal: "We choose to go to the moon in this decade and do the other things not because they are easy, but because they are hard." Shakespeare's *Henry V* speech to the troops preparing for battle at Agincourt has a similar stirring of emotions across levels (individuals, platoons, and entire companies of soldiers): "From this day to the ending of the world, But we in it shall be remember'd; We few, we happy few, we band of brothers." Another example of an oft-quoted phrase that invokes strong emotions is from Malala Yousafzai, a Pakistani who later won a Nobel Prize. On her 16th birthday, she was asked to give a speech at the United Nations on July 12, 2013. In it, she said, "I raise up my voice—not so I can shout but so that those without a voice can be heard . . . We cannot succeed when half of us are held back."

Leaders often have power and social status to be more infectious and spread contagion faster than others. Resonant leaders can spread the transmission of emotions and information across levels to individuals, teams, organizations, communities, and entire countries. Such transmissions across levels are more difficult with larger numbers of people and greater distances, whether geographic, psychological, or temporal distances. An important research question is whether such cross-level effects are proportionate or discontinuous, or distributed like a power curve dependent on some other factor, such as the intensity of the relationship.

A moving and amazing example of resonant leadership inspiring people at multiple levels is the story of Nomusa Zikhali, who became the founding principal of the Nkomo Primary School and expanded it despite a lack of resources, as told in our 2005 book (Boyatzis & McKee, 2005, pp. 147–151). When Zikhali was asked to start a new elementary school in 1998 approximately midway among three Zulu villages in Kwazulu Natal, the government gave her a plot of land with four trees and assigned 60 children to her as the one teacher. They told her that the trees were her classrooms Cross & Simpson, 2019). She quickly enlisted a volunteer from the community to help, and then expanded the volunteers to include the parents of each of the children who would be attending. Watching the children was amazing as they sat on mats under the shade of the tree that was their class. They leaned in and were eager to learn. It was a refreshing image compared to the reluctance too many children have about school in other parts of the world.

By 2022, Nkomo Primary School had over 1,000 children attending, 19 concrete classrooms, and two concrete resource rooms with computers, 24 teachers, and eight staff. They even have a special AIDS orphan program that places them in homes with families (Cross & Simpson, 2019; And Beyond, n.d.). The Republic of South Africa assigns and hires a teacher for each classroom made of concrete. Knowing this, Zikhali made it a personal mission to raise donations to build concrete classrooms (Boyatzis & McKee, 2005).

Little did the government know that they had hired a resonant leader with imagination, unending energy, and an infectious smile. Zikhali first enlisted the parents of the children to help clear away brush and any plants that might be harmful to the students, and erect a temporary fence to keep animals outside the school grounds. She enlisted the help of the management of a local game reserve, Phinda, to put her school on the community tours they offered to clients in the afternoon between safari game rides (Boyatzis & McKee, 2005). Guests came and were emotionally struck by her enthusiasm and the cheerfulness of the children, and as a result many donated and kept donating for years. She also wrote to the leaders of companies in South Africa (in her region and beyond) and asked for any resources they could spare (Cross & Simpson, 2019). Some sent money. One company sent a truckload of desks and chairs they were discarding. One company sent a truckload of copier paper they could no longer use.

Each year, Zikhali assembled all of the children's parents who would be attending the school for a daylong session before classes began (Boyatzis & McKee, 2005). They spent the first segment of their meeting discussing and arriving at a shared vision. The author and his wife read the butcher block pages of the vision that hung on the walls of the first concrete classroom. It was a vision, a dream with a deep sense of purpose, to help the children learn and create a new future for themselves, their families, and their communities. This was created anew each year by those present.

Then, Zikhali explained what they would be doing in each class. In the early years it was just three grades, and as the school and staff grew, all grades were staffed. Each class, and each week of classes, had a plan (Boyatzis & McKee, 2005). The teacher would enlist specific parents to help as teacher's aides. Each student's growth and learning became a mission for all three of the villages.

Zikhali used her instincts to design experiential learning and engage the children physically and emotionally, not just their analytic brains. Being Zulu and knowing Zulu customs, she began each day with the children and staff singing and dancing. She used another Zulu norm of shared responsibility: the children helped clean windows when they could reach them, and picked up any litter in the classrooms or school yard (Cross & Simpson, 2019). They were keepers of the Nkomo Primary School. Zikhali is a playful person with a huge smile and generous sense of humor. But when she gave a student "the look," they ran and did their chore (Boyatzis & McKee, 2005).

She used her personal style and knowledge of Zulu customs to create a school that inspired curiosity and eagerness to learn in each of the students (Boyatzis & McKee, 2005). She worked to make sure each of their parents understood and were emotionally committed to the vision and plan. The activities and her style reached across individual, dyadic, team (i.e., family), and community (tribal and village) levels. But she didn't stop there. She used aspects of creating what could be called PEA trigger experiences every day to create a shared sense of the Nkomo Primary School to transmit emotions and energy, along with hope and caring, to everyone in the school as an organization. It was intentionally extended to the families and elders of the three Zulu villages so that the community could be a part of the vision and achievements. Through her example and accomplishments, nongovernmental organizations spread the word throughout other parts of South Africa and to other adjacent countries. Zikhali was and is a resonant leader who worked many levels of sustained, desired change at the same time.

Leadership Magic

The potency of a shared sense of purpose extends beyond professional service firms, and nonprofits, all the way into management and leadership in many forms of organizations. With a similar effect noted in Chapter 7 within resonant relationships, resonant leadership relationships have a substantial effect on engagement and various motivational factors. Hartz (2014) showed that among 79 manager–subordinate in dyads that shared vision predicted shared positive mood, this predicted management effectiveness through in-role behavior and engagement. Straub (2015) studied 412 procurement managers in the Department of Defense and found that shared vision predicted engagement.

Leaders can have a motivating effect on those around them through sharing a compelling vision. "In the presence of a strong vision, adaptivity increased for individuals high in openness to work role breadth self-efficacy" (Griffin, et al., 2010, p. 180). Their results supported the idea that helping subordinates invoke a PEA state and be more open to new ideas would help them be more susceptible to stimulating adaptation, proactivity, self-efficacy, and innovation. In a study of manager–subordinate dyads in manufacturing companies, Docherty (2020) found that the degree of shared vision, compassion, and energy, along with role clarity, predicted engagement of subordinates, with shared vision having the strongest impact. Feedback, either positive or negative, did not have an impact on engagement.

The source of the emotional transmission can come from various levels, emphasizing that the direction of transmission can work either top-down or bottom-up. Grant and Hofman (2011) found that the transmission of ideological or inspirational messages was even stronger when the source was the beneficiary or followers than the leader themselves, especially for what they labeled as prosocial messages.

A leader with a personal vision would be expected to have a stronger cross-level impact on others around them. Farraq (2022) showed this effect with a 180 leader–follower Arab and Egyptian dyads. The leader's Ideal Self (personal vision) predicted the perceived effectiveness of the leader. In studying executives at purpose-driven companies, Berg (2016) found that the personal Ideal Self (vision and purpose) predicts better performance, engagement, and life satisfaction. Being in a company with a higher purpose in their rhetoric and cultural norms predicted higher performance and commitment. Those executives related to their corporate purpose through an instrumental task orientation or a meaning or transformational orientation.

Shared vision was the strongest predictor or engagement and commitment. Berg (2016) also suggested that without a personal vision, the executives had a more difficult time relating and being excited by a corporate vision and purpose. The disposition to focus on shared vision and a social mission is typical of many Indian CEOs, along with an "aggressive investment" in development of their people (Capelli, et al., 2010), with a distinctive positive effect being witness to cross-level stimulation of meaning.

The field of followership studies has focused on the leader–follower relationships more than other forms of leadership research (Riggio, et al., 2008). Lord (2008) pointed out that leaders function through their followers; they are dependent on the people around them. In many organizations, a high-level leader might have six layers of managers below them, each dependent on the next layer to motivate, engage, and inspire others to do the work. Those leaders who create and maintain resonant relationships may invoke the benefits of the motivation to explore sustained, desired change. Those who mistake their role as managing a strategic plan or budget, or who focus on narrowly envisioned financial metrics in their personal dashboard, lose a relationship with the others around them, which results in loss of engagement and motivation of those people and often the people below them in the hierarchy.

A study of the multilevel effect of resonant leaders in the information technology industry in India found that the more the leader acted with emotional intelligence and with a resonant leadership style (shared vision, compassion, and energy), the greater the engagement of the people in the next levels, either directly or indirectly. They showed that these leaders raised a psychological sense of empowerment, which in turn escalated people's engagement in their work (Pardasani, 2016). Shared vision was again shown to be a significant predictor of small business growth among 298 African American entrepreneurs (Conley, 2018). The entrepreneurial perseverance had an effect on business growth and was mediated by the degree of shared vision they had created.

As mentioned previously, resonant relationships and cross-level transmission of information and emotions appear to be a two-way process. In one study, it was shown that followers often generalize to leaders they admire and with whom they have a resonant type relationship by attributing to them other desirable characteristics that might not even be directly observed (Hogg, 2008). In a direct link to the other characteristic that transmits information and emotional across levels, SIGs Hogg (2008) showed that the greater the follower's centrality to the SIG and the stronger their identification with the SIG, the more perceived legitimacy (i.e., power) is granted to the leader.

Multiple Levels of Resonant Leadership Are Needed

To ensure maximum transfer of emotions and relevant information across levels, a system needs multiple levels of resonant leaders. This increases the likelihood that all levels are moving toward a shared vision and enact shared norms (their collective ideal and real selves). In professional sports teams, the team captain (the real one, not merely the official role) is an emotional glue that moves emotions and information between the team level and the individual players. A resonant head coach moves information and emotion across organization to team levels. Meanwhile, a resonant general manager or owner moves information and emotion across the organization and community levels. In professional sports, the community level focuses particularly on the fans and press (any form of news media).

During the early 2000s, the World Association Futbol team FC Barca had more than a decade of consistently winning almost every tournament in which they were eligible to play. Their major competitor, Real Madrid, despite having spent much more money on their players, did not have an illustrious record during those years. Barca had a team captain who was resonant, and Pepe Guardiola as an amazing head coach. As a teenager, he was raised in the famous school of Barca, La Masia. It was here that Guardiola learned Futbol skills, Catalan culture, building moral character, and teamwork. When asked to be the head coach, the chairman of the club willingly took a back seat to Guardiola in the press and allowed the other levels of resonant leaders to flourish (Burns, 2012). The 1986 Super Bowl winning Chicago Bears had Walter Payton as an emotional glue, Michael Ditka as a resonant head coach, and Michael McCaskey as a resonant general manager (Pierson, 2008).

Another example occurring a few continents away from these teams was the string of championships of the Kolkata Knight Riders (KKR), a famous Indian cricket team. During a two-year span, they surprised and awed fans throughout the world with the longest winning streak of any Indian team and were the champions of the Indian Premier League in 2012 and 2014.

Cricket is the second most popular sport internationally. In India, it has the popularity of all US and European sports combined. The KKR had an ownership group of famous Bollywood Indian actors and their spouses. One of the owners, Shahrukh Khan, was called the world's biggest movie star by the *Los Angeles Times* in 2011. Their coach at the time was Trevor Bayliss, and the team captain was Gautam Gambhir, who was the emotional glue for the team. The team had a strong vision connected to the community. The well-known owners worked hard at deferring attention to the team, the coach, and the team captain. Gambhir was a charismatic and resonant player, captain, and team representative. The three levels continued to inspire hope and pride within the team, the KKR organization, their immediate Kolkata community, and India as a whole (Gambhir, 2023).

A similar pattern has been seen in the potency of leaders who use emotional and social intelligence (ESI) competencies in education. A series of studies from five different countries have shown that when teachers use more ESI, the students do better (they graduate, have less truancy and absenteeism, and get better grades and performance better on standardized tests) (Mahoney, et al., 2021). When principals or head teachers use more ESI, the teachers do better with high climate scores and fewer union actions (Williams, 2008; Schultz, 2005). When the superintendent of a school system uses more ESI, the principals or head teachers do better (Fulcher-Gutierrez, 2017).

Separate studies also suggest the same pattern in companies, especially in sales organizations. When sales managers use more ESI, the salespeople perform better and have more engagement (Spencer & Spencer, 1993). When sales executives use more ESI, the sales managers do better (Massa, et al.,

2009). As said previously, resonant leaders are only one of the vehicles that transmit or transfer information and emotions across levels for sustained, desired change, and social identity groups are another.

It should be noted that dissonant leadership relationships have a potent negative contagion and move NEA across levels. In studying 530 corporate efforts at restructuring, it was noted that "unanticipated side effects of culture change can undermine and even defeat the change process" (Gilmore, et al., 1997, p. 174). When the change program was imposed and became another layer of Ought Self, or when the leadership were dissonant in style and relationships, it provoked additional ambivalence to authority, an increase in messages with polarizing images of others and various topics. It also spread disappointment and blame throughout the organization and reasserted the importance of the hierarchy. Dissonant relationships seem more frequent at times and have potent and sadly enduring inhibitory effects of sustained, desired change.

Social Identity Groups

Two components of the Ideal Self are personal identity and social identity groups. Personal identities are those aspects of who you believe yourself to be and the application of your values in terms of social roles, like being a parent. Social identity groups are those groups of people from whom you draw part of your identity and how you would describe yourself, such as being an FC Barca fan. Social identity groups can be aspirational or membership organizations. For example, a person may identify themselves as an alumna of a particular university, a fan of a particular sports team, or as a member of or aspirant to a professional specialty (e.g., social psychologist, oncological surgeon, intellectual property attorney, tax accountant). Other often cited SIGs include specific faiths; communities built around a church, temple or mosque; a particular ethnicity; a gang; or combinations of these distinctions.

An early appearance of the concept was by sociologist Robert Merton, which he called reference groups in the 1940s (Merton, 1968). They became the intellectual domain of social psychology as scientists attempted to discern intergroup behavior (Kelman, 1961; Tajfel, 1974; Ashforth & Mael, 1989). In the past, some social scientists referred to them as one's tribes or what anthropologists called subcultures.

Belonging or wanting to belong to a social identity group involves a social comparison and evaluation process. A person compares themselves to others with the same or similar interests, values, or some characteristic of salience to them, and identifies with this group. At the same time, the social comparison process helps the person differentiate themself from other groups. The comparison process describes "an in-group and an out-group" (Tajfel, 1974, 1982). The SIG becomes a frame of reference (Merton, 1968) for the person to locate themselves among others and within society. It will affect how they view, feel about, and interact with other SIGs (their intergroup relationships). A person may have multiple SIGs.

Social identification with a SIG creates a perception of oneness with that group. It often involves some form of categorization of people as to distinctiveness, implying a different degree of prestige (Ashforth & Mael, 1989). The identification can be actual (such as formal membership) or symbolic. A person can feel various degrees of centrality to the SIG (the inverse of degree of marginality experienced). A particular SIG can be of varying degrees of importance or salience within the individual's value system, operating philosophy (see Chapter 2), or social status. This valence can be expressed as positive (a group a person wants to be a part of or associated with) or negative (a group a person wishes to be distant and different from). Our ego defense mechanisms will attempt to protect us by attributing "bad" or negative characteristics onto others not in their SIG, a form of outsourcing emotions.

A person's SIGs create a sense of social place and order within their environment (Ashforth & Mael, 1989). A SIG will lead a person to act in a certain way (congruent with the SIGs beliefs or norms) and join in certain activities. In response, the person may receive support and confirmation of stereotypes of their SIG members and outsiders, which reinforces the antecedents of their identification with the SIG (Ashforth & Mael, 1989). A person's various SIGs can reinforce and aggregate around some themes, values, or issues, such as attending an elite university, playing polo, being part of an elite special operations military unit, or being a member of a golf club. But a person's various SIGs can also pose a conflict, confusing the person with their behavioral choices as well as confusing others as to how to classify them.

An example of the power of SIGs can be found in the development of perhaps the longest-standing effective multinational treaty, the Antarctica Treaty, which was signed by 12 nations in 1959 with expanded signatories since then to 45 countries, consisting of 80% of the world's population. Meanwhile, many attempts to achieve a multinational, shared vision or agreement on some goals of various climate international conclaves have not made much progress, like the Kyoto Treaty, Paris Accords, or the Rio de Janeiro Convention.

In discussing the atmosphere, conversations, and people at the Antarctic Treaty meetings, it was observed by a person present that most of the people sitting around that table were scientists. They related to each other and used a common language of science, even if they were from different scientific fields.

They agreed to the following principles for the treaty: it would be for peaceful purposes only; military activities would be banned; it would promote freedom of scientific investigation; scientific plans, staff, and information would be exchanged; it would include the Cape Roberts Geological Drilling Project; political claims would be frozen; nuclear explosions and waste would be banned; stations, ships, and aircraft would be open for inspection; and all claims to territorial sovereignty would be set aside. The framers of the Antarctic Treaty had a clear SIG to which most of them belonged and it helped them talk, argue, and agree. It enabled them to communicate across multiple levels. In contrast, most of the national representatives sitting at tables as part of the efforts to achieve any of the treaties on climate were lawyers and people selected to specifically represent their country's interests. They lacked the common values and language of the scientist's SIG, and acted as protective representatives and often contentious negotiating among disparate groups. It was a different interpersonal dynamic that the Antarctica Treaty experience.

SIGs may be part of a person's Ideal Self or their Ought Self. If part of an Ought Self, it comes with relatively more NEA arousal or some limits on the PEA felt when interacting with the group. The internal conflict between one's Ideal Self and Ought Self would manifest itself in an uneasy feeling about SIGs that are identified with each. In a series of studies of Asian Americans, it was found that when people experience a conflict with aspects of their social identity or SIGs, they shorten their time horizon and planning efforts. It is a defensive move to increase certainty, but it also erodes confidence in their Ideal Self or shared identity (Yu & Zhang, 2022).

A SIG can be formed for support and evolve to become a potent source of identity. Twelve female partners of Coopers & Lybrand (C&L) decided to create a source of personal and professional support (Himelstein & Forest, 1997). They were among about 200 female partners within C&L's approximately 8,000 partners worldwide at that time. They began meeting once a month for a long dinner. As the years moved on and some were transferred to other cities or left C&L, most of them would fly into San Francisco for their monthly meetings. They had created a SIG within the SIG of partners that was more intense and felt to be important to their well-being and success (personal communication, 1996).

Another example of how a SIG can be a source of support even when in contrast to prominent cultural norms was Suad Dukhaykh's dissertation (2019). She examined factors helping and hindering Saudi Arabian women entering what were considered nontraditional professional roles within Saudi culture, such as professors and physicians. She found that the women preferred to return to Saudi Arabia to live after undergraduate or graduate schooling in other counties because of the strong SIG as a Saudi and the closeness to their extended families. Some Saudi women experienced strong support from their immediate family to pursue being an advanced professional. When this coincided with an Ideal Self as a professional and a shared vision within their family, the women experienced high career satisfaction and commitment. The familial SIG support was statistically inversely related to the potency experienced from other prominent social barriers in the culture surrounding them.

Changing SIGs would be an integral part of a developing or emerging new Ideal Self, or in human collectives, a shared vision. The tension experienced between the aspirations to the new SIG and the feelings of loyalty or obligations of membership to the old SIG create a regressive force, inhibiting a change. Having multiple SIGs can result in exhaustion from switching efforts (Van de Brake, et al., 2023).

Changing SIGs: Belonging or Always an Outsider

SIGs can help or hinder a person's movement along the phases of intentional change in two major ways. The first way is that a new SIG might be a key element in a person's emerging Ideal Self, or personal vision. As described in Chapter 2, changes may be needed in a person's SIGs to help them move closer to their vision. Similarly, within our collectives, team or organizational change might involve a person seeing themselves as part of a different SIG. In strategic terms, organizations attempt to change their brand and reputation by pursuing a new SIG vigorously through marketing campaigns.

How central a person is or believes themselves to be within an SIG, as well as how salient the SIG is to the person, both factor into the strength of the ties. This strength will determine the degree to which the SIG could help or hold a person back from a sustained, desired change.

SIGs may become social support groups. A person's personal board of directors might be a collection of individuals helping a specific person, or they may form as a SIG and have an impact on all participants. Lisa Fischer and Darlene Love were backup singers in many major rock and roll hits and groups but they were never known as stars in their own right, as marvelously described in the Oscar winning documentary *20 Feet From Stardom* (Neville, 2013). They were the background sound that often enabled a recording to become a major hit with distinctive verbal effects, phrases, and emotion (Barnes, 2013). At the time, Fischer and Love enjoyed being off center stage and did it amazingly well. Their SIG was being a background singer. Each eventually recorded solo songs and albums, and decades later toured nationally within the US. By this time in their lives, their prominent social identity groups had changed. They were each no longer a backup singer.

All of these forces contribute to a person feeling marginal or central in a group, or rejected or accepted, or belonging or expelled. Social media appears to have accentuated the degree to which people feel isolated. The COVID-19 pandemic also exaggerated social isolation with lockdowns, working from home, and other social distancing. Without the episodic and informal hallway chats, tea and coffee room encounters, and lunch or drinks after work, people report feeling more and more disengaged from their organizations. As the shared sense of identity increases, members of a SIG can and often do provide social support and can ameliorate some of the effects of stress (Haslam & Reicher, 2006).

Another powerful example of changing SIGs is found in the movie *Miracle* (O'Connor, 2004) about ice hockey in the 1980 Olympics. The Russian team was heavily favored to win the Gold Medal. In the directorial chat on the DVD of the movie, the coach of the US men's hockey team, Herb Brooks, explains a set of scenes in the movie. During early and extensive basic skill practice drills long into the night and past the player's sense of their own fatigue, Coach Brooks would ask two or three of the players to introduce themselves to the rest of the team. During the first few rounds of introductions, the players gave their name and then would add "I play for . . . ," naming the college or university they attended and for whom they played. Coach Brooks kept them going on this cycle until one of the players said his name, and then added, "I play for Team USA!" At that point, Coach Brooks knew he could let them go for the night. The US team, with relatively little time to practice as compared to many of the other teams competing, won with a team approach to playing that surprised most viewers. They had become an important SIG to each other.

SIGs can also be a source of differentiation, discord, and discomfort. Exclusion and feeling marginal occurs when a person receives verbal and nonverbal signals that a SIG in their work or community does not see them as a member. When such actions become norms of organizations, communities, or countries, forms of systemic prejudice permeate life in these social systems. Efforts to ameliorate or rectify the social injustice when the SIG is defined around race, gender, ethnicity, social class, or faith are crucial to reformulating the SIG to be more inclusive and to be shared among a wider proportion of the people in the social collective.

While initial efforts to change the SIGs may require some NEA moments, if continued as NEA moments they can also backfire. Workplace norms of being "politically correct" may have positive intentions of including people, but when they are imposed with an NEA approach, the people involved and exposed are often "depleted," which results in anger and withdrawal (Koopman, et al., 2022) and might generalize to the person's emotional state at home. It can manifest itself as deviance and unethical behavior at work, reduced offers to help others, and reduced engagement (Koopman, et al., 2022). The challenge to the people wanting to change the systems and norms is to develop shared vision, norms, and values and engage more PEA moments along the path to sustained, desired change of inclusive collectives and new SIGs.

Creating New SIGs to Cross-Levels

In addition to providing a social context for a person's Ideal Self or shared vision, a second function of SIGs during the process of change is that they transmit and transform information from others and the larger external world in the social component of your identity. At all levels other than individual, developing and using an intentional social identity and affiliation has the benefit of branding. Beyond the reputational effect, it reinforces each member's identification with the team, organization, community, or country. The National Park Service has used it to appeal to sports and nature enthusiasts, as well as to families, to create a broad appeal to multiple possible SIGs (Burns, 2009; Rettie, 1995). This is reminiscent of how the Dutch built their bicycling culture, as discussed in Chapter 2. On the other hand, the lack of coherent SIGs and SIGs that are possibly too narrowly defined has haunted the Bureau of Indian Affairs throughout its existence (Prucha, 1986). Companies like Netflix defined their audience and themselves as bringing entertainment to everyone, while Blockbuster defined themselves as strictly a brick-and-mortar place for shoppers of entertainment. The former was an innovator and is thriving, and the latter is bankrupt (Harress, 2013). In the nonprofit arena, the YMCA grew in members and impact for decades while similar organizations, like Hull House, failed to create and maintain an identity (Hopkins, 1951).

SIGs also help to create rituals, which are symbolic actions with emotional meaning (Armenakis & Bedeian, 1999). When the rituals are practiced often, they become shared habits or norms and drift into unconscious enactment. An example is the use of the Serenity Prayer for members of Alcoholics Anonymous, a key practice in the AA meetings. Members of this SIG are encouraged to say it often. Even a word or phrase shared among members in settings other than meetings can signal or trigger a host of emotional messages supportive of the shared effort to maintain sobriety. An fMRI study of members of AA praying showed that the powerful emotions invoked with the prayer occurred even when a person was alone (Galanter, et al., 2016).

Activation of the ventromedial prefrontal cortex (vmPFC) appears key to considering behavior change (Tompson, et al., 2015). This works through using cultural or personally tailored messages, like using a SIG's language and symbols to raise the consideration or support in continuing a change effort. By using such language and symbols, it also enables cross-level communication of the encouragement about change and transcends individual or collective levels. Ten years after the break-up of the Beatles, for example, John Lennon explained that his identification was as an activist, musician, and partner with Yoko Ono. The Beatles had been an important SIG of his past, but that was no longer true (Sheff, 1981).

Socialization into being an academic is an exhausting and multiyear process. Two former professors who left academia to continue their work in public policy in nonprofit organizations, foundations, and advocacy organizations (Wanchisen & Schweingruber, 2023) talked about the feeling of expulsion from their prior SIG during academic conferences: "The feeling of being an outsider quickly emerged, and only grew over time. It was often difficult to find relevant sessions to attend. Few if any people suggested going for a drink . . . The mere mention of nonacademic work often brought blank states and an almost palpable lack of interest. Some even asked, 'Didn't you get tenure?' mystified that we had left academia" (p. 510). They were able to find a new home with colleagues and friends—a new SIG that helped them on their path to their emergent vision.

A SIG communication from a member or central person (i.e., some form of leader) could ignite or invoke emotions through the expression of the shared vision, purpose, and meaning, like the Martin Luther King Jr. speech referred to earlier. Once a SIG creates the vision as a central theme it encourages members to develop a common language, which at times can verge on jargon or code. Nelson Mandela used music and performed a style of dancing called the "Madiba Jive" that became a symbol of his leadership and a free South Africa.

Working with resonant relationships within a SIG, shared compassion can also be invoked and become an emotional glue for the organization as well as the larger systems of which it is a part. Think of the use of symbols, heroes, and iconic images, like the photo or statue of Marines raising the US flag on Iwo Jima in 1945. The members of a SIG can become ambassadors for a cause (shared vision) and bring the emotions and message to other communities, organizations, families, and countries, like the cadres in Mao's People's Army going to villages throughout China waving their Little Red Books as a symbol of the new China.

Other symbols can communicate SIG membership and meaning to others, such as wearing merit badges for Scouts, or medals for military personnel (Walker, 2010). Technology can also move emotions across levels. Librarians who embraced digital technology, for example, came to see themselves with a new and updated social identity (Nelson & Irwin, 2014).

In the 1990s and early 2000s, Apple and Sony competed in some of the same markets. While SONY emphasized the technical elegance and long-term durability of their products, Apple developed their products and image to be fun and "cool," thereby capturing the larger market of consumers who were young and eager to embrace technology, but did not see themselves as "techies." They appealed to new and existing customers through reactions to their products and the mere images of their products (Champniss, et al., 2015).

While early in their corporate life cycle, Amazon's mission was to sell books online and make books available worldwide to many who could not otherwise have access to bookstores. On the other hand, Borders created bookstores where people could browse. As noted earlier, a similar difference is evident with the brand definition and sense of shared vision of Netflix versus Blockbuster.

Whether through brands or the development of SIGs, companies that foster social identification of their people with the firm have several desired effects. They have a significant increase in the feeling of personal control of their people, which significantly predicts social identification effects in many arenas from political to academic, and community to national groups (Greenaway, et al., 2015). A stronger personal identification with an organization results in greater performance (Meleady & Crisp, 2017). In their study, Meleady and Crisp (2017) even found that imagining positive experiences and contact with an effective (i.e., resonant) leader of their organization also resulted in escalation of organizational identification. As stated earlier, when members enter a PEA state, as evident in strong positive emotions and a significant reduction in biomarkers of stress, they are more open to organizational identification and feeling a part of a SIG, and in terms of hearing the other emotional and informational messages being transmitted (Wegge, et al., 2012).

Sustained, desired learning is advanced when ICT operates across levels. Creation of new SIGs helps. Working with a team in 2013, I launched one of the first Massive Open Online Courses (MOOCs) on Coursera for Case Western Reserve University, called Inspiring Leadership Through Emotional Intelligence (modeled after a course we had been delivering in person). It was modeled after a face to face course was required in most of our master's programs in the School of Management, as well as offered to companies through executive education. The MOOC course was asynchronous with 24 modules, each involving a 10-minute video. Most modules had reflective and interpersonal exercises along with readings.

The first run of the course attracted about 110,000 learners, and subsequent cycles attracted similar numbers. To invoke aspects of ICT we required participation in the online discussion groups, hoping for some increased form of interpersonal interaction. The shock came from the spontaneously formed study groups. Groups of learners would appeal to each other in the discussions and form separate groups. There were groups of introverts, military veterans, city-based groups, and ethnicity-based groups from all around the world. Learners formed groups within the course but also used Google Friends, Facebook, and other social media. They did not care that those interactions didn't count toward a certificate or successful completion of the course. They wanted to learn and talk with others about their insights, fears, hopes, criticisms, and progress. Six months later, I learned that five such spontaneous study groups had formed with administrative staff from various parts of my own university. All of these are examples of people forming SIGs for the purpose of helping each other learn. These study groups enabled people to exchange feelings and insights, use emotional contagion to promote more learning, and to interpret course-related experiences.

Creation of a new SIG may foster movement toward a vision for individuals, but it may also need to transmit the vision and hope across groups of people, creating new communities. An example is the PhD Project, first created in 1994 by the Graduate Management Admissions Council and the accounting firm KPMG. The first step was to inspire more African Americans to enter and graduate from PhD programs. Instead of traveling around the country or world and berating schools for their lack of diversity (NEA), these two organizations decided to create a positive force for change (PEA) and thus created a new SIG. Since its creation it has enabled and promoted a huge increase in African American professors in management and business schools—from 294 in 1994 to 1,764 at the time of this writing. It worked because it was carried out in a positive way.

The project also created an annual conference appealing widely to master's programs, MBA programs, and business professionals in the African American community interested in the possibility of a research, scholarly, and academic career. A close colleague and friend, Melvin Smith, benefited from the experience and is still involved over 30 years later. He learned about it from network advertising in *Black Enterprise*, the magazine most widely read by African American professionals at the time. He remembers the advertisement that caught his attention: "You can be a VP today or a PhD forever!" As for so many others, it reminded him about the ephemeral nature of promotions in the corporate world. One of his undergraduate classmates had joined the PhD Project, and encouraged Melvin to join too.

The two-day conference was about how to get into a PhD program, from the vision level to the pragmatics. It helped Melvin get into the PhD program at the University of Pittsburgh, after which he joined the faculty at Case Western Reserve University. Both schools had an unusually high number of African Americans in their PhD programs (at CWRU for the Organizational Behavior program in particular). Continued involvement in the PhD Project helped with support, solace, guidance, and motivation at those existentially chal-lenging moments in anyone's academic career. For Melvin, as for so many, the PhD Project created an immediate network from universities throughout the US. The network quickly became more than a support group: it became a SIG.

The conference used techniques to highlight and honor progress that members had made each year. They had rituals at the major banquet, such as the Capping Ceremony for individuals who completed their program that year. They had sessions with past graduate students, who provided newer members with hope. The emotional transfer was across individuals to small groups with specialized interests, to a community of scholars and aspirants. They stayed in touch with each other throughout the year. Over time various splinter groups formed, such as the Management Doctoral Students' Association for those in organizational behavior, management, human resources, and strategy, and for the alumni, the Management Faculty of Color Association. They remained active in the larger PhD Project while also expanding upon it with other SIGs.

The success of the PhD Project is evident: it has helped foster a major sus-tained, desired change in the recruitment, socialization, development, and identification of legions of African Americans, and now includes graduate students from other underrepresented groups. The creation of a set of re-lated SIGs within and across multiple levels is what made it successful. The impact has been so profound on the higher education system and commu-nity of African American professionals that Smith created a new leadership program called the Executive Leadership Experience for African American Professionals at CWRU. The five-month program involves personal coaching and many of the techniques in SIG development from the PhD Project, in-cluding a WhatsApp Group for alumni active in fostering continued profes-sional and personal development. The same strategy of creating new SIGs has been a key element in the pedagogy of a leadership development program for women professionals in STEM careers (Van Oosten, et al., 2017).

The Other Side of Demagogues and SIGS: Elitism versus Inclusiveness

These two vehicles for transmission of information and emotions across levels can work against sustained, desired change. Leaders who feel resonant to a small group of insiders but detest or reject outsiders are demagogues. As mentioned earlier, such leaders are often exceedingly narcissistic and charismatic, but play to Storr's (1996) terms of "the child in each of us" in terms of searching for simplicity and certainty. In the process, people in other levels of collectives around them are seduced into a narrative of how their group is "correct" while the outsiders are misguided, stupid, or evil.

Demagogues use the easy arousal of fears to create false enemies, target individuals or groups, and dehumanize them (French & Jack, 2014; Jack, et al., 2013). In other words, they use all of the tools of SIGs to strengthen their internal camaraderie, but focus their shared compassion to only those selected. Their shared vision is limited to those inside the elite group, not those they would refer to as the heathens outside of their group.

The symbols, rituals, and norms of strong SIGs enable the fast transmission of information and emotions across levels as well as across different groups. In a sense, they enable faster socialization. A sad example of this is the rapid spread of the control of the Taliban in Afghanistan after the withdrawal of the US forces in 2021 (Gill, 2021). The speed of their takeover of the country and its vast and varied tribal regions surprised many international observers, but it shouldn't have. The Taliban were a long-standing SIG with rituals, symbols, and practices that were already well-established.

While this is evidence of using cross-level vehicles to invoke emotions and transmit information, values, and mindset, at some point, the NEA nature of the message will lead to exhaustion. The negative affect and SIG affiliation can last decades and hurt or inflict severe damage on millions of people. Age-old feuds among communities or extended families share this dynamic, as do communities or tribes fighting with each other over territorial disputes or access to resources.

Concluding Thoughts

Cross-level forces can be regressive. They can cause or maintain relationships to be dissonant, which activates NEA and inhibits change. A shared negative vision can also be contagious. Narrowly defining the relevant groups is often a signal of exclusiveness, elitism, and separatism. In these situations, at some point the NEA invoked about others will infect the relationships inside the supposed elite group as well. In the same way that social identity signaling enables people to use impression management in organizations and professions to communicate to others their desire to belong to a particular SIG, it also enables demagogues and negative SIGs to signal who is in and who is out.

Resonant leadership—especially at multiple levels within social systems—and SIGs can propel and enhance sustained, desired change. They can invoke the PEA and transmit it as a tipping point for change and learning across levels, from individuals to countries to global processes. To help sustained, desired change and move people and their collectives closer to a shared vision with norms of hope, compassion, energy, and positive affect, the resonant leaders and SIGs must be inclusive and adaptive.

9

What Next? The Call to Study Change

If you are reading this book you are likely involved in creating, promoting, or leading change and learning. Even if you do not think about it with your students, colleagues, clients, patients, subordinates, or family members, you are integrally involved in change efforts. This book should sensitize you to this aspect of your work or life.

The purpose of research on change is to understand sustained, desired change and discard the false beliefs of prior eras, and correct earlier interpretations that came from prior research. Change will happen. Efforts at change will be thwarted. Reactions to change will often be regressive.

The vision of this book is that research on sustained, desired change will help us all— recipients, change agents, or people in change roles—to develop processes that can help unleash more people's dreams and collective possibilities. In this way, research can launch possibilities of a better, more innovative, compassionate, and just life, institutions, and society. This is where the critical role of science and inquiry steps into the picture.

If you are an advanced professional but not currently involved in research, this book should help you be a better consumer of research on change. It should help you be skeptical of slick claims and marketing fads. The ideas and critiques in each chapter are designed to equip you with a lens of the possible, while adding the rigor of knowing what to look for when reading research on change and learning.

Beliefs about change may drive research, but they need to be tested, refined, and adjusted. Development of theory begins a process of discovery and raises questions. Testing its elements and principles and predicted causality with empirical research should tease out even more questions.

In the domain of change, practitioners often respond to needs and innovate faster than researchers can. The felt needs of individuals to battle addiction, become more effective, or innovate tug at our curiosity and compassion— so we experiment with new approaches to action. The intent is to help. The consequences or outcomes are not always what we had intended. At the team, organization, community, and country levels, practitioners may provoke and invoke the attention of researchers with their change efforts. They may create

The Science of Change. Richard E. Boyatzis, Oxford University Press. © Richard E. Boyatzis 2024.
DOI: 10.1093/9780197765142.003.0009

innovative approaches and theories or models of change that can be sustained. But it rests on empirical research, whether qualitative or quantitative, as a way to move science ahead, increase our understanding, and reduce our vulnerability to distortion and manipulation.

As any researcher and scholar knows, it is not an easy path. In this chapter, some of the ideas, issues, and questions will be raised that may spark curiosity in current and future scholars of change.

Research Questions and Needs

Hopefully, scholars of change will have their own questions and puzzles emerging from reading this book. Graduate students may have an intellectual theme that overlaps with one of the many topics and dynamics described in these chapters. Some graduate students are searching for a research question, and the following ideas are offered for them as things to consider about studying and helping understand sustained, desired change.

Longitudinal Studies and Distributions

We cannot study change without longitudinal studies. Although scholars can start with cross-sectional data, to obtain further insight they must go to longitudinal designs, such as the Harvard Study of Adult Development (Waldinger & Schulz, 2023) or the Framingham Study (Christakis & Fowler, 2009). The Harvard Study began in 1938 seeking to study what helped people thrive or fail. They began with 268 Harvard sophomores and 456 inner-city Boston boys. They collected comprehensive interviews with subjects and their parents, and in-depth medical exams with blood samples, followed by EKG, EEG, and fMRI in later years. Longitudinal studies are much better than retrospective studies, which ask people to reflect on episodes of their past, which presents the challenge of accuracy of memory. Selective filters of current needs for social approval, changing social values, and hot-button issues may also distort what is recalled and how it is portrayed. Today, many prominent journals do not accept pre- and post-measures as sufficient sampling even for longitudinal studies.

The speed and velocity of change as well as the periodicity of change efforts and events are relatively unexplored topics. The period in which the subjects—whether individuals or collectives—are studied in research on change must be sufficiently long to compensate for exhaustion effects and the honeymoon effect. The discussion and research cited in this book on sustained, desired change begs the question of how long any observed change lasts. This of course leads to another set of questions about what processes might assist in extending the durability of the desired change.

Speed, velocity, and periodicity will affect the distributions of actual change outcomes, as explored briefly in Chapter 3. The outcomes will most likely not be linear or continuous. The convenience of using recall assessed through surveys provides data with normal distributions, but is it real or an artifact of recall, and of a constrained response set? Visual examination of actual outcomes would require creative portrayal of the data, whether through scatterplots, histograms, or an elaborate three-dimensional array created on a computer.

Retrospective reconstruction of past events, emotions, and perceptions often violates the irreversibility of time with individuals and collectives. We often reinterpret the past in terms of current perceptions and changing vision, values, and views. Our recall of the mediating and often moderating impact of our close relationships on any aspect of change will be altered by the changing nature of current relationships and social identity groups. All of this emphasizes the need for longitudinal studies.

Calculating Change and Dependent Variables

Deciding on the dependent variable and how to measure the degree of change are not easy problems to resolve in change studies. First, the change being studied should have a clear outcome, such as weight loss, winning games, selling albums, developing new products, or creating a successful "housing first" program for the homeless. Depending on the level of change being studied, settling on the appropriate outcome or dependent variable requires creativity. Unobtrusive measures or archival data offer valuable possibilities. When appropriate, physiological measures can be considered direct outcomes, such as assessing stress through skin conductance.

Second, if the outcome is not readily available or too difficult to assess— such as trying to determine a manager or leader's effectiveness when they are not the branch manager, plant manager, or CEO—means that a mediator variable must be used. If the mediator has a strong track record of validation studies showing the impact on the desired outcome variables, then it can be used. For example, for managers or professionals without a measurable output like sales, the choice could be a 360 degree assessment of their perceived effectiveness such as the Reputational Effectiveness Survey (Tsui & Ashford,

1994). Another alternative in this situation would be to use a mediator such as the degree of engagement felt by the manager's direct subordinates or other people in the organization. Moderators are not sufficiently causal to the outcome to be useful as a proxy-dependent variable.

Third, when studying change at collective levels such as team, organization, or community, a direct causal link must be established to avoid contamination of extraneous variables. For example, if one is studying change in manufacturing plants and have chosen sick days as an inverse indicator of organizational commitment or engagement, care must be taken in the sampling to ensure that the physical location of the plants vary by region. Selecting all plants in the Southern US, for example, might show fewer sick days because the climate is warmer, making employees less prone to influenza and other cold-weather ailments.

Fourth, to study sustained, desired change, the longitudinal time periods between measurement points should be sufficient enough to avoid short-term effects.

Once the variables are identified and causality is shown to be possible based on prior research, the next challenge is how to calculate the degree of change. A time series analysis of longitudinal effects could be helpful, as discussed in Chapter 4 regarding the organizational-level impact on improvement of emotional and social intelligence competencies of MBA students.

Statistical methods of analysis should ideally take into account multiple measures of the dependent variable and not be limited by assumptions of "normal" distributions and continuous variables, as raised in Chapter 3. Repeated measures used in analysis of variance (ANOVA) tests or t-tests (i.e., tests of differences between samples) are simple routines to use, but they address multiple measures. Unfortunately they assume normal distributions, unless using variations of routines that are designed for ordinal data. Nonparametric tests of significance are claimed to provide this adjustment.

Calculating change scores may seem a logical step, such as using a Time 2–Time 1 score. But because this does not adjust for initial levels, some prefer to adjust for it with a (Time 2–Time 1)/Time 1 as a percentage change score. Negative change scores of either type have to be considered before examining significance or robustness of observations.

Multiple Source versus Single Source Data

Longitudinal studies with multiple assessment points are best to study change because they allow for noticing discontinuities, bifurcations, and power curves. Too often, the use of single source and single time data is convenient in terms of speed, but it distorts or creates false discoveries. When studying human change, we need creative use of multiple sources of information and multiple time points of assessment. While consensual validation (i.e., validation from multiple sources) does not ensure truth, it can increase confidence and reduce contamination from the single source's views, mood, values, and mindset.

Similarly, at the team, organization, community, and country levels, single collective studies are limiting. To study one organization brings its history, culture, and biases into every aspect of the data collected as forces affecting what the researcher might find, but this can also reduce generalizability. To collect data from multiple collectives either requires using archival information or committing to larger research teams that can collect data from many more units of analysis. This may also mean that the data collection periods need to be much longer.

As mentioned in Chapter 1, a limitation of this book is that it does not do justice to the scholarship on organizational, community, or country-level change. That may occur with future editions, but more likely it will come from other scholars taking on the challenge of testing the adequacy of ICT processes and principles in explaining and predicting sustained, desired change at those levels.

Better Dependent Variables, Sample Sizes, and Sensitivity to Dynamics

Change studies at collective levels are usually presented as case studies, or with multiple examples. In many of the chapters I used extreme comparative case examples to illustrate a contrast of when sustained, desired change at that level worked and when it did not. While narrative research appears appropriate to this challenge, at some point scholars should also look for patterns through multiple cases, meta-analyses, or large sample sizes. In David McClelland's studies of the impact of unconscious motives on behavior, he and his colleagues went beyond experiments and personality studies to examine cultural-level presence of the motivation themes and related it to community, tribal, and country-level outcomes. For example, he showed that indicators of economic activity could be related to a causal sequence from a high level of presence of Need for Achievement imagery in children's readers (McClelland, 1961). He also showed that Need for Power imagery from popular literature appeared causally related to national statistics on blood pressure, cardiac events, and health (McClelland, 1975, 1985).

Once large sample sizes of collectives are examined, the dynamics of change can be examined with more precision. Looking for tipping points is needed as well, to avoid glossing over important observations (a possible result of data smoothing) or finding the moments of nonlinearity and bifurcation. The discovery of *relative* deprivation (and not deprivation itself) as the detonating point of revolutions would not have been possible without such careful examination of timing, causal possibilities, and unforeseen factors across many units of analysis (Brinton, 1952; Runciman, 1966).

Difficulty Getting Subjects

There are many reasons why change is not studied as often as it should be. First, it takes a long time, and that challenges any doctoral student wanting to complete their studies and move on with their career. For junior faculty it prolongs the number of years to publication, which makes amassing compelling evidence for a tenure or promotion decision difficult.

Second, during transitions people are uncertain, stressed, and often scared. They may not want to consciously admit to themselves what they are thinking or feeling, let alone express it to others in surveys and interviews. If they are not sure or comfortable that the change effort has reached a stable or desired end point (or plateau), they may be reluctant to jinx or contaminate the desired outcome by judging it too soon. It is natural that people may feel vulnerable and defensive during transitions and therefore reluctant to participate in research on the changes they are attempting or experiencing.

In our collectives, to acquire sufficient variance the researcher may have to not only study teams, organizations, communities, or countries that are successful, but also those not doing well or not developing on a path to sustained, desired change. The people in the latter groups may feel angry or defensive, and the distrust of their leadership may be transferred to the researchers.

In one study, we were able to build a research sample of merely 5% of the eligible population (Boyatzis, et al., 2017). The company was doing well and better than their competitors, and their products were highly regarded. The division being studied was respected inside of the organization and in the industry. Several of the possible subjects who happened to be alumni of my university called me in response to the request for participation in the study.

They shared privately the fears of manipulation that were causing them and others to not participate. It was not clear whether this fear and suspicion was produced by a widespread climate problem in the organization or by a specific set of dissonant managers who made people in their reporting lines feel defensive, but the result was a small sample size when all prior indications suggested that a sufficient sample size would be easy to obtain.

When the leadership of an organization, community, or country is dissonant, clueless, or encourages demagogues, they are less likely to support or champion a change study. Others around them tune in to their negative bias, and the emotional contagion dooms the samples size of the study.

All of these factors were examined in a thoughtful discussion of why more coaches and their clients do not volunteer to participate in coaching research (Hinn & Kotte, 2021). In addition to all of the issues mentioned above, sometimes people don't want to know if they are really changing. If the process feels good, why get on the scale and check your weight?

Research Questions Specific to ICT

Within each chapter are hundreds of possible research questions begging to be asked. Many are at the individual level of change, but even more are at the collective levels. An exponentially greater number of research questions are possible as to the mechanisms that move information and emotions across levels. Aspects of resonant leadership and social identity groups need to be studied as to how they affect sustained, desired change within and across levels. Perhaps the scholarly challenge is to create mathematical models with advanced calculus, set theory, and systems dynamics simulations of change, like we attempted to begin in Hazy and Boyatzis (2015). To provoke some curiosity in researchers, the following sections will present multiple series of questions. These questions are certainly not exhaustive, but they are offered in the spirit of sparking synaptic leaps, posing puzzles, and stimulating intrigue.

In Pursuit of the Ideal Self

How does the Ideal Self change? How often and when should people and groups revisit their vision? How can trauma and other challenges to dreaming be overcome?

In establishing a shared vision in teams, organizations, communities, or countries, what are methods for inclusion of all people involved? When a vision is shared, among whom is it shared? How can leaders or change agents and people at nodal points in the social networks invite others to share a vision without adding another layer of Ought Self, the resulting NEA, and being a bully?

How can a vision or shared vision be revisited to stimulate a PEA moment during a change process? What are the techniques for reminders and refreshers about the shared vision to periodically activate PEA?

In Pursuit of PEA versus NEA Tipping Points

How often and how intensely do we need a PEA tipping point to occur to continue the ICT process? In other words, what is the dosage of renewal needed for individuals and for collective levels?

Under what conditions can NEA events be converted to PEA events, or vice versa?

If NEA is the default to maximize survival, would predispositions toward optimism, efficacy, hope, and other positive traits, states, and emotions affect the intensity or frequency of NEA needed?

Are there other neural networks besides the DMN, TPN, FCPN, and the Enteric Nervous System that create tipping points and should be included in a model of PEA and NEA experiences?

In Pursuit of the Real Self

How can we increase self-awareness, somatic awareness, and sensitivity as to how others experience us? What is an optimum balance of strengths and weaknesses?

How far from a tipping point into effective use does a weakness have to be to enable the change to help us move closer to a vision or shared vision, as opposed to being demotivating?

How can you make feedback on performance, behavior, and change more PEA? What are the doses of NEA feedback that do not deflate and deflect the change process?

At collective levels, how, when, and among whom is it feasible to develop an existing weakness into a strength? That is, how much of the experience can be NEA and still achieve sustained, desired change? How can we distinguish strengths from weaknesses within our team, organization, and community norms? Will weaknesses be experienced or evaluated differently by different groups within the collective?

How can we encourage and encompass diversity of thoughts, feelings, values, and mindset without violating limits of credible conformity (such as forcing conformity and becoming another layer of Ought Self and source of NEA)?

How do you work with many cultural and subcultural norms that are different within collectives? How do you promote inclusive acceptance while pursuing a shared vision, effective performance, and innovation, and maintain cultural compatibility?

In Pursuit of a Learning Agenda

How does a person find the space and time to pursue a change and move closer to one's vision? How does a person reassess and set priorities and find joy in the process?

In our collectives, how do groups and communities agree on priorities without regressing into contentious, compromising approaches and negotiating as representatives of groups instead of sharing common pursuit of overall vision, values, and goals?

How do individuals use their learning style preferences to manage their motivation to continue on a change process? How do people compensate for situations demanding learning styles that are not within their personal preferences, especially in shared pursuits in collectives?

In Pursuit of Experimentation and Practice

How much experimentation and practice is needed or optimal for sustained, desired change? Do different settings, relationships, and context affect the amount of experimentation and practice needed?

When are nudges and reminders helpful, versus nagging and regressive?

How do we create and sustain social identity groups to support the change process along the way?

Are there forms of visualizing or imagining that are cognitive and emotional experimentation and practice?

In Pursuit of Resonance and Resonant Leadership Relationships

How do the quality of relationships moderate and mediate relationships between independent and dependent variables or outcomes?

What are the key qualities of relationships that matter most to sustained, desired change?

With whom are the leaders resonant? How many of the various constituent groups should be "inside" the resonance versus being excluded or not feeling included?

How do you cultivate a network of coaches, trusted advisers, and resonant relationships to help you as you develop?

How do these and other aspects of relationships change over time and events? Which of these changes help or hinder sustained, desired change?

When and how do resonant leaders lose being in tune with others? What factors or forces convert otherwise resonant or resonantly possible relationships into dissonant relationships?

How and when do you initiate actions to change someone who is a dissonant leader? When and how do resonant leaders begin to believe their reviews and evolve into demagogues?

How do resonant leaders promote cross-level transmission of emotions and information?

In Pursuit of Social Identity Groups That Promote and Sustain Change

How do we use emotional and social contagion to get closer to a shared vision while incorporating differences? How do we sequence change processes? How do we manage the best balance between PEA and NEA experiences to keep the momentum toward sustained, desired change going?

Are the cross-level resonant leaders and social identity groups effects proportionate or discontinuous, or distributed like a power curve dependent on some other factor, such as intensity of the relationship?

How might faith and membership in religious organizations or communities help a person renew their Ideal Self? How might interactions and prayer foster more PEA in a typical day or during difficult moments in life?

How do you create new social identity groups that foster and support ongoing change without becoming elitist and recreating the same forces that made people feel marginalized before?

How do social identity groups of previously marginalized people within a system find a new identity without being exclusionary and creating an NEA backlash from others? Is that even possible?

A Review of Key Observations and Examples

Of all the alternatives considered for how to end this book, it seemed that a summary or reminder of the various ideas and examples addressed in the chapters might help. Following is a list of some of the key topics discussed by each of the 10 ICT principles and the examples and case studies used.

1. The first phase of ICT is the driver of sustained, desired change—the Ideal Self, or personal vision and at the collective levels, a shared vision.
   - The articulation of a compelling and holistic Ideal Self or personal vision is a major motivating force of sustained, desired change and learning.
   - In our collectives, this constitutes a shared vision when it reflects a consensus or majority of the people in various collectives.
   - One's Ideal Self morphs over one's life and career eras, as a result of salient experiences and socialization.
   - The nemesis of the Ideal Self is the Ought Self, or the many Ought Selves imposed on us from others.

Examples: family businesses, leader–follower (manager–subordinate dyads), the Beatles versus the Rolling Stones, Adventure Consultants attempt at Everest versus the Weihenmayer expedition, mergers and acquisitions, Netflix versus Blockbuster, Summa Health System's vision, the Cleveland Orchestra, the YMCA, bike-sharing programs in cities, bicycling as country-level norms, distinctive leaders like Martin Luther King Jr. and Nelson Mandela.

2. Being in the PEA allows a person or human system to be open to new ideas, other people, emotions, and scanning their environment. It is a tipping point into the next phase of Intentional Change Theory. The psychophysiological states called the Positive Emotional Attractor (PEA) and Negative Emotional Attractor (NEA) have three axes: Parasympathetic (PNS) versus Sympathetic Nervous System (SNS) arousal, neural activation of the Default Mode Network (DMN) versus Task Positive Networks (TPN), and positive versus negative affect.

- The movement toward or inhibiting sustained, desired change occurs when a tipping point is reached.
- The PEA is energizing and restorative.
- The NEA acts as a brake, slowing or stopping awareness, and is draining and deflating.
- More renewal (i.e., PEA) is needed each day and week to ameliorate the dysfunctional effects of chronic stress (i.e., NEA).
- The NEA may be a wake-up call, but it needs to shift into the PEA quickly to facilitate sustained, desired change.
- Unless the PEA is reinforced over time, a deterioration will cause a tipping point into the NEA state.
- Emotional and social contagion via swarming play a major role in spreading PEA or NEA in social movements and human collectives.

Examples: coaching to the PEA (i.e., coaching with compassion versus coaching for compliance), physician patient dyads, US Navy innovation and on-board climate, distinctive leaders (like Martin Luther King Jr., Mahatma Gandhi, and Lech Walesa), transitioning to renewable energy in Iceland versus the UK, reducing homelessness in Houston and Boston.

3. Sustained, desired change in humans and human systems is most often discontinuous and nonlinear.
   - The dynamics of the emergence of the tipping points add to the likelihood that behavior, change, and learning is better described as a power curve or discontinuous phenomenon than "normal" distributions.
   - Power curves are ubiquitous among humans because our actions, attempts to change, feelings, and decisions are connected to each other. Humans will seek to defend and protect themselves and their tribes, strive to be included and seek social approval, and attempt to reduce uncertainty for ourselves and others.

Examples: addiction recidivism, fMRI studies of coaching, protests turned into riots, the Arab Spring, rent-a-bike programs in cities, and national norms of bicycling.

4. The second phase of ICT is realization of the Real Self. At the individual level, this is one's strengths and weaknesses relative to their Ideal Self. In human collectives, it is the norms, values, and culture of the specific human system that are strengths or weaknesses relative to their shared vision.

- Self-protective forces such as ego defensive mechanisms, social desirability, fears, and NEA experiences mask our self-awareness and create a Faux Self.
- Focusing on Real–Ideal Self discrepancies uses a deficiency approach to reduce this gap. It invokes an NEA state, and the motivating effect is relatively short-lived.
- Competencies are the behavioral and observable aspects of a person and can be developed.
- Our relative strengths and weaknesses emerge as a personal balance sheet. A preoccupation with weakness or failings is a quicksand of NEA.

Examples: Adventure Consultants and the Weihenmayer Everest attempts, deep-cavers, incident commanders of US wildfire fighting teams, Netflix versus Blockbuster, competency change at the organizational and community levels.

5. The third phase of ICT is articulation of a learning agenda and plan to use one's strengths to move closer to the Ideal Self, while possibly working on developing one to two weaknesses. Collectively, it is a shared learning agenda and plan. For best progress and sustainable effort, the weaknesses chosen should be closest to the tipping point into becoming strengths.
   - In ICT, a learning agenda is a joyful exploration of possibilities.
   - Specific and measurable goals are NEA and instrumental, in that they typically will not provide the motivating effect of renewal.
   - Planning helps us to prepare for our path to our vision.
   - When the TPN is activated along with the FPCN, we can expect suppression of the DMN.
   - The Ought Self not only invokes the NEA and further inhibits sustained effort, but it also moves the person away from their own desires.
   - When the nature of the goal pursuit has shifted from "want to" to "have to" or "should do" (i.e., obligatory change), the increased use of self-control needed is an ego depletion that drains a person's energy, leaving them feeling deflated.

Examples: deep-cavers, US wild forest fire fighting incident commanders, reducing homelessness (e.g., Boston and Houston versus DC and San Diego).

6. The fourth phase of ICT is the sequence of repeated experimentation with new feelings, thoughts, attitudes, or behavior and then moving into repeated practice to the point of mastery (beyond the point of comfort).
   - To increase the sustainability of learning or change, experimentation requires periodic excursions into the PEA to replenish and revitalize the energy needed.
   - Reinforcing a strength requires practice.
   - To achieve mastery with the change, deliberate practice is needed, interspersed with moments of PEA to revitalize the effort.
   - Successful practice is often experienced as a power law.
   - Rhythm, dosage, feedback, training, stealth learning, and multi-tasking can help, but not in the way they are typically offered.
   - The promise of peer coaching in groups is a way to further development of change.

Examples: Juan Trebino, extended success of musical groups (U2, Green Day, Rolling Stones and Metallica versus the Police, Oasis, and the Sex Pistols), deep-cavers, the Weihenmayer expedition, Amazon versus Sears, Khan's work in Comilla and Karachi.

7. The fifth phase of ICT is the establishment and maintenance of resonant relationships.
   - Relationships are the agar agar in the petri dish of life. They are the context for sustained, desired change.
   - Resonant relationships have three qualities. Through shared vision, we experience hope. Through shared compassion, we experience caring and gratitude. Through shared energy, we activate and vibrate to the same frequency as others. Through shared mindfulness, we achieve a degree of centeredness, and joy through playfulness.
   - By having a shared vision, people can act independently within their own situation but still move together.

Examples: the Wiehenmayer expedition, the Chilean mine disaster, Deepwater Horizon, hurricanes (Katrina, Ike, and Sandy), friendship benches, the Ward H program.

8. As a fractal theory, ICT describes sustained, desired change at all levels of human endeavor from individual to dyads, teams, organizations, communities, countries, and at the global level.

- A complex system has scale dependence (i.e., the system has multiple levels observed in a hierarchy).
- A complex system also has sensitivity to initial conditions of PEA and NEA tipping points.
- Each level within ICT functions as a change process unto itself.
- There is the possibility that events within a level may trigger or affect events or processes in another level.

Examples: the Chilean mine disaster, distinctive leaders (Martin Luther King Jr., Indira Gandhi, Nelson Mandela, and John F. Kennedy), Nomusa Zikhali and the Nkomo Primary School, FC Barca, the Kolkata Knight Riders, Antarctic Treaty versus other climate treaties, female partners at Coopers & Lybrand, backup singers, professional women in Saudi Arabia, the US Olympic ice hockey team, the National Park Service, Amazon versus Sears, Netflix versus Blockbuster, MOOCs, YMCA, Alcoholics Anonymous, and the PhD Project.

9. Resonant leadership relationships facilitate moving information and emotions within and across levels of human systems facilitating sustained, desired change.
    - Resonant leadership relationships are characterized by multiple parties vibrating at the same frequency, being in tune with each other, and being in synchrony.
    - Maximum transfer of emotions and information across levels requires multiple levels of resonant leaders.
    - When leaders feel resonant to a small group of insiders but detest or reject outsiders, they are demagogues. Demagogues use the easy arousal of fear to create false enemies.

10. Social identity groups facilitate the enduring quality of sustained, desired change by helping or hindering progress toward one's Ideal Self (vision) or a group's shared vision, and move information and emotions within and across levels of human systems to facilitate sustained, desired change.
    - Social identity groups (SIGs) are groups of people from whom you draw part of your identity—how you would describe yourself and your brand.
    - Changing SIGs may create tension between the new SIG and feelings of loyalty or obligations to the old SIG.

- SIGs transmit information across levels by creating rituals, which are symbolic actions with emotional meaning that invoke emotions through the expression of a shared vision or creation of a common language (such as jargon or code).
- The members of a SIG can become ambassadors for a cause or shared vision and bring the emotions and message to other communities, organizations, families, and countries.

Concluding Thoughts

The mystery and awe of discovery about change can help drive the pursuit of truth, justice, beauty, and a better society—and can also open us to new puzzles, to explore "where no one has gone before" to find the magnificence of sustained, desired change.

For all that we humans are doing to damage our environment and each other, we also have a distinctive ability to innovate, adapt, and care. Discovery can drive innovation. Research can drive discovery. Iterations of the cycle of puzzles to discovery to research to innovation have often served us well as a civilization. These iterations have helped create better lives for many people and our institutions and have not fallen prey to the subjugation of others. As you consider your research on change:

> Be Inspired
> Be Curious
> Be Careful (rigorous) and
> Be Compassionate!

Resources for Research on ICT Process and Principles

The following tests and measures are available for free use in research unless otherwise noted, with the proviso of maintaining the copyright to that respective test or measure and citing the relevant published validation studies.

Ideal Self Test

The Ideal Self Test is used for assessing the clarity and comprehensiveness of the Ideal Self or personal vision. © Richard Boyatzis, Kathleen Buse, and Scott Taylor (2010). Fee use is permitted.

Describe, in as much detail as possible, your dreams of your ideal life for 10 to 15 years from now. The following categories may help stimulate your reflection.

- Your passion, calling, and sense of purpose_____

  _____

  _____

  _____

- Your legacy_____

  _____

  _____

  _____

- Your values and philosophy_____

  _____

  _____

  _____

- Your dreams, fantasies, and aspirations_____

  _____

  _____

  _____

- How you feel about your future possibilities _____

  _____

  _____

  _____

- Other components or elements of your dream_____

  _____

  _____

  _____

Answer the questions below by circling the response to the right that best describes your response to the question as it concerns your image of your ideal life described in the previous sections.

Strongly Disagree 1	Disagree 2	Somewhat Disagree 3	Neither Agree nor Disagree 4	Somewhat Agree 5	Agree 6	Strongly Agree 7

1. I feel inspired by my vision of the future. 1 2 3 4 5 6 7

2. My vision reflects many possibilities 1 2 3 4 5 6 7

3. My vision includes fun activities. 1 2 3 4 5 6 7

4. My vision includes my work in terms of my jobs and career. 1 2 3 4 5 6 7

5. My vision includes my family relationships. 1 2 3 4 5 6 7

6. I am excited about my vision. 1 2 3 4 5 6 7

7. My vision includes leisurely activities. 1 2 3 4 5 6 7

8. I feel hopeful about my vision. 1 2 3 4 5 6 7

9. My vision includes my physical health. 1 2 3 4 5 6 7

10. My vision includes my values and philosophy. 1 2 3 4 5 6 7

11. I feel optimistic about my vision. 1 2 3 4 5 6 7

12. My vision includes my contributions to others and the community. 1 2 3 4 5 6 7

13. My vision includes relative priorities of things important to me. 1 2 3 4 5 6 7

14. My vision includes my intimate/love relationships. 1 2 3 4 5 6 7

15. My vision includes my spiritual health. 1 2 3 4 5 6 7

16. I have a clear vision of my desired future. 1 2 3 4 5 6 7

17. My vision includes my desired legacy in life. 1 2 3 4 5 6 7

18. My vision of the future reflects the things most important to me. 1 2 3 4 5 6 7

19. My passion, calling, and sense of purpose are clear to me. 1 2 3 4 5 6 7

20. I see many possibilities in my future. 1 2 3 4 5 6 7

Scoring and Interpretation

There are two options.

1) Add all responses into one overall scale score. OR
2) Add the responses in each of the categories below (with the numbers representing the questions in each category) as subscale scores.

Hope	1, 2, 4, 6, 8, 11, 16, 20
Sense of Purpose	13, 17, 18, 19
Holistic Vision	5, 9, 14, 15
Deeper Meaning	10, 12
Fun	3, 7

Philosophical Orientation Questionnaire

The Philosophical Orientation Questionnaire is used for assessing a person's philosophical disposition which determines how they assess the meaning of specific values. © Richard E. Boyatzis, 1992.

Answer the following questions by indicating your current preference in terms of ranking the choices for each item. The option ranked "1" should be your first choice; the option ranked "2" should be your second choice; and the option ranked "3" should be your last choice. Although it is sometimes difficult to determine a preference, please indicate your ranking in terms of the order that best reflects your preferences. Some of the choices have multiple parts, separated by "OR." For each such item, select the most important part (the segment separated by an OR you most like), underline it, and assign the rank for that item (the rank reflecting your preference for the part underlined while disregarding other parts of the item).

1. I think of my value, or worth, in terms of:

   (a) My relationships (e.g., family, friends)
   (b) My ideas OR ability to invent new concepts OR
       ability to analyze things
   (c) My financial net worth OR income

2. I feel most proud of organizations to which I belong when they:

   (a) Have created new products or services
   (b) Create financial worth for individuals (regardless of the
       people being employees, investors, or partners) OR create jobs
   (c) Have helped people live easier and healthier lives

3. When someone asks me to commit to spending time on a project, I ask myself:

   (a) What can I learn from doing it?
   (b) Will it help someone, or is someone counting on me to do it?
   (c) Is it worth it to me?

4. Sometimes I will do something for no other reason than because:

   (a) I want to figure out why something works the way it does
   (b) It has to be done in order to do something else
       OR get something I want
   (c) It will allow me to be with a person I care about OR
       it would please someone I care about

5. The way I can best contribute to others' lives is to:

   (a) Help them find jobs OR develop financial security and independence
   (b) Help them develop principles with which to guide their lives
   (c) Help them build relationships with others or me
       OR help them feel better about themselves

6. I get most done when I am with someone I would describe as:

   (a) Pragmatic
   (b) Caring
   (c) Analytic

7. I consider my contribution to society in terms of:

   (a) Ideas, concepts, or products
   (b) Money
   (c) People and relationships

8. I define myself in terms of:

   (a) What I accomplish OR what I do (my activity or behavior)
   (b) My thoughts, values, and ideas
   (c) The people with whom I have relationships

9. I would describe myself as:

   (a) Analytic
   (b) Caring
   (c) Pragmatic

10. I consider the most important stakeholders of the organization for whom I work to be:

    (a) The field or industry of which we are a part
    (b) Employees
    (c) Shareholders and investors OR customers and clients

11. When I read or listen to the news, I often think about:

    (a) Whether it gives me an idea as to how to make money OR seize an opportunity
    (b) The statement it makes about the nature of our society
    (c) The people in the stories (i.e., those affected by the events)

12. I believe many of society's problems could be resolved if more people were:

    (a) Pragmatic
    (b) Analytic
    (c) Caring

13. When I have free time, I prefer to:

    (a) Do things that need to be done (e.g., chores duties)
    (b) Figure out things OR think about what, why, and how things work
        and are the way they are
    (c) Spend time talking or doing things with specific other people

14. The following are good principles to live by:

    (a) Don't put off until tomorrow what you can do today.
    (b) Do unto others as you would have others do unto you.
    (c) To contemplate the meaning of life and events is an important activity.

15. I have the most fun, stimulation, or excitement when I am with someone who I describe as:

    (a) Pragmatic
    (b) Caring
    (c) Analytic

16. I feel that an organization should contribute to society by:

    (a) Providing a place for people to realize their dreams, develop, and contribute
    (b) Creating ideas, products, or services
    (c) Creating increased net worth (helping individuals build their net worth) OR creating jobs

17. People have spent a full life if they have:

    (a) Cared for others and built relationships
    (b) Made a million OR achieved financial security OR created jobs
    (c) Developed ideas, products, or methods

18. Individuals should:

    (a) Identify their goals and then work toward them, making sacrifices when necessary for
        their long-term goals
    (b) Seek fulfillment through their relationships
    (c) Understand themselves and why they do things

19. I will feel successful if in 10 years I have:

    (a) Written articles or books OR taught people ideas, concepts OR invented new concepts, ideas, and products OR have figured a number of things out

    (b) Known many people well OR a number of meaningful relationships

    (c) A greater net worth than I do now OR financial security and freedom

20. My time is well spent in an activity if:

    (a) I make friends OR meet interesting people

    (b) I get interesting ideas OR observations from it

    (c) I can make money from the activity

Scoring, Profiling, and Interpretation Guide

To calculate your scores on the Philosophical Orientation Questionnaire, copy the number you placed next to each item in the questionnaire (item 1 (a) is the first item, item 6 (c) is the last item on the first page) to the right of that item on the chart below. Add all of the items in each column for a column subtotal. Then, subtract the subtotal of each column from 60 to obtain a score for Pragmatic Value, Intellectual Value, and Human Value. The adjustment to the rankings makes it easier to understand.

Item	Pragmatic Value	Intellectual Value	Human Value
1	1.c _____	1.b _____	1.a _____
2	2.b _____	2.a _____	2.c _____
3	3.c _____	3.a _____	3.b _____
4	4.b _____	4.a _____	4.c _____
5	5.a _____	5.b _____	5.c _____
6	6.a _____	6.c _____	6.b _____
7	7.b _____	7.a _____	7.c _____
8	8.a _____	8.b _____	8.c _____
9	9.c _____	9.a _____	9.b _____
10	10.c _____	10.a _____	10.b _____
11	11.a _____	11.b _____	11.c _____
12	12.a _____	12.b _____	12.c _____
13	13.a _____	13.b _____	13.c _____
14	14.a _____	14.c _____	14.b _____
15	15.a _____	15.c _____	15.b _____
16	16.c _____	16.b _____	16.a _____
17	17.b _____	17.c _____	17.a _____
18	18.a _____	18.c _____	18.b _____
19	19.c _____	19.a _____	19.b _____
20	20.c _____	20.b _____	20.a _____
Add the scores			
Subtract from 60 for your TOTAL			

Pecentile	Pragmatic OP 30+	Intellectual OP 32+	Human OP 38+___
100%	**98**___ **96**___ **94**___ **92**___	29___ 28___ 26___ 24___	31___ 30___ 28___ 27___	37___ 35 ___ 34 ___ 33 ___
90%	___ ___	23___ 22___ 21___ 20___	26 ___ 25___ 24 ___	32 ___ 31 ___
80%	___ ___ ___	20___ 19___ 18_	23___ 22___	30___ 29
70%	___ ___ ___	17___	21___	28___ 27
60%	___	16 ___ 15_	20___	26___
50%	___ ___ _18	14 ___ **13**	19 ___	25 ___ 24___
40%	___ ___ ___ ___	12 ___	17 ___ 16_	23 ___ 22___
30%	___ ___ ___	11 ___	15 ___ 14_	21 ___ 20 ___
20%	___ ___ ___ ___	10 9 ___ 8	13 ___ 12_	19 ___ 18 ___ 17___ 16___
10%	___ ___ ___ ___	7 ___ 6 ___ 5 ___	11 ___ 10 ___ 9 ___ 8 ___	15 ___ 14 ___ 12 ___
0%			

My Values Exercise

The objective of this exercise is to help you clarify your values, or beliefs at this time. Since our values and beliefs change from time to time, after reflection or certain events it is useful to review and consider our values and beliefs. This exercise was adapted by me in 1991 from numerous instruments used to assess one's values based on the ideas of M. Rokeach, described in *The Nature of Human Values* (New York: Free Press, 1973).

Attached is a list of 49 values, beliefs, or personal characteristics for your consideration. The following steps should help you identify which are most important to you as guiding principles in your life. You might find it useful to determine degrees of importance by considering whether you would be upset or elated if your present state or condition in life regarding a particular value would be significantly reduced or increased. You might find it helpful to consider two values at a time, asking yourself about the relative importance of one over the other.

Whatever technique or method you use:

1) Please **identify the 15 or so values that are most important to you,** and mark them with an asterisk or circle them.
2) From this list of 15 or so, **identify the 10 that are the most important to you** and write them on the lines on the following page.
3) From this list of 10, **identify the five that are the most important to you.**
4) **Rank each of the five** from "1" being the most important value to you to "5" being the least important of these five important values.

If you would find it helpful, you may want to rank the next five values (the remaining five from the list generated in step 2).

List of Values, Beliefs, or Desirable Personal Characteristics

ACHIEVEMENT	(a sense of accomplishment, success, or contribution)
AMBITIOUS	(aspiring to promotion or progress within career)
ADVENTURE	(new and challenging experiences)
AFFECTION	(love, caring)
BEAUTY	(aesthetics in nature, art, or life)
BROAD MINDED	(open-minded)
CHEERFUL	(joyful)
CLEAN	(tidy, sanitary)
COMPETENT	(capable, effective)
COMPETITIVENESS	(winning, taking risks)
COMFORTABLE LIFE	(prosperous or easy life)
COOPERATION	(working well with others, teamwork)
COURAGEOUS	(standing up for beliefs)
CREATIVITY	(being imaginative, innovative)
DISCIPLINED	(self-controlled, restrained)
ECONOMIC SECURITY	(steady, adequate income)
EQUALITY	(egalitarianism in life, equal opportunity for all)
EXCITING LIFE	(a stimulating or challenging life)
FAME	(being famous, well known)
FAMILY HAPPINESS	(nuclear or extended family that is happy)
FAMILY SECURITY	(nuclear or extended family that is safe)
FORGIVING	(willing to forget a judgment of others)
FREEDOM	(independence, autonomy, free choice, self-reliant)
FRIENDSHIP	(close relationships, companionship)
HAPPINESS	(contentedness)
HEALTH	(being physically and mentally well)
HELPFULNESS	(assisting others, improving society)
INNER HARMONY	(being at peace with yourself)
INTEGRITY	(honesty, sincerity, genuineness)
INVOLVEMENT	(participating with others, belonging)
INTELLECTUAL	(conceptual, abstract, or symbolic)
LOGICAL	(rational)
LOVING	(affectionate, tender)
LOYALTY	(duty, respectfulness, obedience)
MATURE LOVE	(sexual and spiritual intimacy)
NATIONAL SECURITY	(protection from attack)
ORDER	(tranquility, stability, conformity)
PEACE	(a world at peace, without war or conflict)
PERSONAL DEVELOPMENT	(personal growth)
PLEASURE	(fun, laughs, an enjoyable, leisurely lifestyle)
POLITE	(courteous, well-mannered)
POWER	(control, authority, influence over others)
RECOGNITION	(social recognition, respect from others, status)
RELIGION	(strong religious beliefs)
RESPONSIBLE	(dependable, reliable)
SALVATION	(eternal peace)
SELF-RESPECT	(self-esteem, pride, sense of personal identity)
WEALTH	(making money, getting rich)
WISDOM	(understanding life, discovering knowledge)

My 10 Most Important Values:

_____

_____

_____

_____

_____

_____

_____

_____

_____

_____

My Five Most Important Values:

Most Important Value Rank #1 _____

Next Most Important Value Rank #2 _____

Next Most Important Value Rank #3 _____

Next Most Important Value Rank #4 _____

Next Most Important Value Rank #5 _____

Projection to _____ [pick a year about 10–15 years in the future]

Project yourself into the future: it is today in the year 2xyz. When answering, develop the image of what you most hope and dream your life and work will be on that day.

In 2xyz, I am _____ years old.

If I am working, my work is best described as _____.

In that context, my major work responsibilities are _____
_____.

The people I will see or talk to today include _____
_____.

The people who I live and socialize with are _____
_____.

My most important possessions are _____
_____.

If someone were describing me to a friend today, they would say that I am _____
_____.

When I have some free time, I spend it _____
_____.

My leisure or fun activities in a typical week include _____
_____.

At least once a year, I try to _____
_____.

Taking a Fantasy Job

This is an opportunity to imagine yourself doing the kind of work or jobs that you sometimes fantasize, or wonder, "What would it be like if I were doing X?"

Imagine the following three events have occurred:

1) You enter a new machine called a Neurophysiological Remaker. A few minutes inside of the machine, which uses genetic re-engineering and noninvasive neural implants, gives you the body, knowledge, and capability to do any job—and do it well.

2) You are given the financial resources or certifications (such as licenses) based on your new capability to do any job well.

3) For one year, you are free of all personal, social, and financial responsibilities in your current or desired life.

List five to 10 jobs that you would love to do or try. Consider a wide variety of jobs including those in other countries, jobs in sports, music, medicine, politics, agriculture, religion, and so on. Consider jobs you have heard about or seen in the movies or on television.

1. _____

2. _____

3. _____

4. _____

5. _____

6. _____

7. _____

8. _____

9. _____

10. _____

Choose the three to five of the jobs in your list that most interest you or seem the most exciting or rewarding. Describe each of them below, including what you will enjoy or look forward to most about each job.

1. _____

_____

_____

_____

2. _____

_____

_____

_____

3. _____

_____

_____

_____

4. _____

_____

_____

_____

5. _____

_____

_____

_____

Sometimes a person describes a fantasy job as one they really want to do. Other times, the job represents some interesting or exciting activities or conditions. In other words, sometimes, it isn't the job that is the fantasy, but some aspect of it or condition under which the job is done. As you read your descriptions of the three to five jobs you would most like to do or try, do you notice themes or patterns? How are these different jobs similar? Are there activities (such as being outside) that are part of each? Are there conditions of the work (such as working with a team) that are part of each? Are there consequences (such as being famous) that are a part of each? List those themes or patterns below.

Subjective Liminality Scale

The Subjective Liminality Scale assesses the degree to which a person feels they are in a liminal state (i.e., in-between states and changing) (Dhar and Boyatzis, 2023).

On a scale of 1 to 6, indicate your agreement with the following statements (1 = strongly disagree, 6 = strongly agree)

"Lately, at work [or about your professional life in general], I am feeling . . ."

1. more restless than usual about who and what I am
2. more dissatisfied than usual about who and what I am
3. as if I am no longer contented about who and what I am
4. like I don't know who I am anymore
5. at a loss to describe myself to others
6. at a loss to identify the most important aspects about myself
7. uncomfortable identifying myself with any one specific group
8. difficulty belonging to one group or another
9. somewhat disconnected with the groups that matter

Measurement Key:

Dimension 1 (Anxiety): Items 1–3

Dimension 2 (Ambiguity): Items 4–6

Dimension 3 (Reduced Group Identification): Items 7–9

Personal Sustainability Index (PSI)

The Personal Sustainability Index is used for assessing the degree of and variety of renewal versus stress experiences a person is having during a typical week (Boyatzis, et al., 2021). © Richard Boyatzis and Daniel Goleman (2016).

Reflecting on *last week* (refer to your calendar or planner if it helps), indicate how many times you had the experience or did the activity listed below in the left-hand column. Write the number in the right-hand column. If last week was not typical or out of the ordinary for you, consider using the prior week for your reflection. If you leave a box blank, it will be assumed that means you did not experience or do that activity that day.

Activity	Number of times
Waking up: Did I think of what I had to do, a problem, something troubling orworrying me?	
Difficulty getting myself or my family ready for the day	
Traffic or delays in getting to or returning from work	
Someone at work frustrated me or caused a problem	
Someone at home frustrated me or caused a problem	
Pressure about a report, task, project, performance goal, or deadline	
My cell phone dropped an important call	
Was angry at a specific person	
Had an argument with my spouse or partner	
Someone cut me off in traffic	
My computer or the internet was slow	
Someone yelled at me	
I was late for a meeting, appointment, or meal	
Ate a meal with family that was tense	
Had an auto accident	
Felt ill	
Worried about something important to me that would not turn out well	
Others in power were observing or evaluating me	
STRESS ACTIVITY: sum all of the numbers listed in the boxes for each column	
STRESS VARIETY: sum of the number of different activities or experiences for theweek (1 for each activity or experience regardless of the number of times it occurred)	

Activity	Number of times
A loving moment with your spouse, partner, or significant other	
Having fun with your spouse, partner, or significant other	
Coaching or mentoring someone (formally or informally)	
Helping a friend or colleague with a compassionate approach (as opposed to trying to "fix" them)	
Thinking about your values or purpose	
Talking with others about your shared values or purpose	
Meditated	
Practice yoga, tai chi, or the like	
Prayed	
Physical exercise	
Played with a pet (dog, cat, horse, monkey)	
Walked or exercised a pet	
Volunteered or provided care for someone in need	
Ate a meal with family that was pleasant or fun	
Walked in nature	
Laughed with others	
Played with a small child	
RENEWAL ACTIVITY: sum all of the numbers listed in the boxes for each column	
RENEWAL VARIETY: sum of the number of different activities or experiences for the week (1 for each activity or experience regardless of the number of times it occurred)	

Interpreting My PSI Scores

You have calculated two scores of possible relevance.

Intensity of Sustainability Score = Renewal Activity–Stress Activity = ____ - ____ = ____

Variety of Sustainability = Renewal Variety–Stress Variety = ____ - ____ = ____

Your Intensity Score shows how many renewal activities you do in a week minus the number of stressful events or activities. More renewal than stress will indicate greater sense of well-being, less anxiety and depressing thoughts, less damages from chronic stress, and more energy.

Your Variety Score shows how many different types of renewal activities you do in a week minus the number of different stressful activities you experience. The more variety of renewal activities, the better. It allows a person a wider menu from which to choose which renewal activity will work best in a given moment or day, and variety, which helps alleviate boredom. Even doing something you love and enjoy can become stressful if done too often or so repetitively that it becomes routine.

PSI: Intensity of Sustainability Score

To determine how your score compares to a sample of 1,716 other professionals and executives, find your number below and circle the corresponding percentile. These percentile norms are based on a sample of professionals and managers from various English-speaking countries. The overall statistics are mean = 22; median = 14; standard deviation = 45; skew = 1.3; kurtosis = 13.9; range = -424 to 334).

PSI: Intensity Score	Percentile	PSI: Intensity Score	Percentile
-27 or less	5%ile	15–18	55%ile
-26 to -16	10%ile	19–22	60%ile
-15 to -10	15%ile	23–26	65%ile
-9 to -6	20%ile	27–31	70%ile
-5 to -1	25%ile	32–37	75%ile
0 to 2	30%ile	38–43	80%ile
3–5	35%ile	44–52	85%ile
6–8	40%ile	53–66	90%ile
9–11	45%ile	67+	95%ile
12–14	50%ile		

PSI: Variety of Sustainability Score

To determine how your score compares to a sample of 1,716 other professionals and executives, find your number below and circle the corresponding percentile. These percentile norms are based on a sample of professionals and managers from various English-speaking countries. The overall statistics are mean = .35; median = 0; standard deviation = 4; skew = .30; kurtosis = .09; range = -11 to 13).

PSI: VARIETY Score	Percentile	PSI: Variety Score	Percentile
-5 or less	5%ile	1	55%ile
-4	10%ile	1	60%ile
-3	15%ile	2	65%ile
-3	20%ile	2	70%ile
-2	25%ile	3	75%ile
-2	30%ile	3	80%ile
-2 to -1	35%ile	4	85%ile
-1	40%ile	5	90%ile
0	45%ile	6+	95%ile
0	50%ile		

Emotional and Social Competency Inventory (ESCI)

The ESCI and ESCIU (the university version) are designed to assess a person's demonstration of the behavior patterns of emotional and social intelligence competencies (Boyatzis and Goleman, 1996, 2000, 2007) (Boyatzis, 2018).

There is a provision in the distribution license for Korn Ferry that graduate students and faculty doing approved research are permitted to use the test for free. For research approval, please contact the Korn Ferry Support Team directly; they have all of the forms, procedures, and training to set people up on the platform and answer questions. The email address is support2@kornferry.com. Due to the low price of the ESCI-U, there is no such free use in research provision for that test.

Kolb Learning Style Inventory

The Kolb Learning Experiential Learning Profile is used for assessing learning style preferences, adaptability (Kolb, 1984, 2014).

Go to the website of Experience Based Leaning Systems to learn how to access the Kolb Experiential Learning Profile (KELP): KELP Assessment (learningfromexperience.com).

Relational Climate Survey

The Relational Climate Survey can be used for assessing the quality of relationships in terms of degree of shared vision, compassion and energy with dyadic, team, organizational and community levels (Boyatzis and Rochford, 2020). © Richard E. Boyatzis and Kylie Rochford (2020).

Definition of relational climate: a relatively stable collective structure that represents the socioemotional atmosphere that is created and maintained as people interact in a dyadic relationship, team, or organization.

Construct definitions:

Shared vision: The extent to which members of an organization share a common mental image of a desirable future state that provides a basis for action.

Compassion: The extent to which members of an organization notice another person as being in need, empathize with him or her, and act to enhance his or her well-being in response to that need.

Relational Energy: The extent to which relationships in the organization are a source of energy in that they result in feelings of positive arousal, aliveness, and eagerness to act.

Items:

Measured on a 7-point Likert scale ranging from "strongly disagree" to "strongly agree."

Notes:

1. Although initial findings look promising, the team and dyad (e.g., coaching and mentoring, doctor–patient) versions of this scale are yet to be fully validated. They earlier scales in the PNEA Survey were validated at these levels. The organization version has been fully validated.
2. If you use this scale at the individual level (i.e., you are not testing for agreement between members), then you should refer to it as "perceived relational climate," "perceived shared vision," "perceived compassion," and "perceived relational energy" and adjust the construct definitions accordingly.
3. Item order should be randomized.

Relational Climate Survey (for an organization)

Instructions to participants:
The following questionnaire is concerned with how you view the climate in your organization, and in particular, how people in your organization interact with each other. Please circle the response that best indicates the extent to which you agree or disagree with the statements below.

	Strongly disagree	Disagree	Somewhat disagree	Neither agree nor disagree	Somewhat agree	Agree	Strongly agree
1. My organization's daily work aligns with our vision.	1	2	3	4	5	6	7
2. My organization's purpose is clear.	1	2	3	4	5	6	7
3. Members of my organization have a shared purpose.	1	2	3	4	5	6	7
4. My organization's actions are guided by a shared vision.	1	2	3	4	5	6	7
5. Members of my organization have similar visions of the organization's future.	1	2	3	4	5	6	7
6. Members of my organization are empathetic toward each other.	1	2	3	4	5	6	7
7. People in my organization notice when others are in need.	1	2	3	4	5	6	7
8. Members of my organization care about each other's well-being.	1	2	3	4	5	6	7
9. When someone in my organization is in need, my organization takes action to assist them.	1	2	3	4	5	6	7
10. The relationships in my organization are a source of energy.	1	2	3	4	5	6	7
11. The atmosphere in my organization is vibrant.	1	2	3	4	5	6	7
12. Interactions in my organization are lively.	1	2	3	4	5	6	7

For the researcher, the main noun of each item can be changed to a dyad, team, organization, or community.

Construct	Item
Shared Vision	My organization's daily work aligns with our vision.
Shared Vision	My organization's purpose is clear.
Shared Vision	Members of my organization have a shared purpose.
Shared Vision	My organization's actions are guided by a shared vision.
Shared Vision	Members of my organization have similar visions of the organization's future.
Compassion	Members of my organization are empathetic toward each other.
Compassion	People in my organization notice when others are in need.
Compassion	Members of my organization care about each other's well-being.
Compassion	When someone in my organization is in need, my organization takes action to assist them.
Relational Energy	The relationships in my organization are a source of energy.
Relational Energy	The atmosphere in my organization is vibrant.
Relational Energy	Interactions in my organization are lively.

References

Ackerman, N. W. (1959). Transference and countertransference. *Psychoanalysis & the Psychoanalytic Review, 46*(3), 17–28.

Addis, D. R., Pan, L., Vu, M. A., Laiser, N., & Schacter, D. L. (2009). Constructive episodic simulation of the future and the past: Distinct subsystems of a core brain network mediate imagining and remembering. *Neuropsychologia, 47*(11), 2222–2238.

Addis, D. R., Wong, A. T., & Schacter, D. L. (2007). Remembering the past and imagining the future: Common and distinct neural substrates during event construction and elaboration. *Neuropsychologia, 45*(7), 1363–1377.

Aiken, J. R., Hanges, P. J., & Chen, T. (2019). The means are the end: Complexity science in organizational research. In S. E. Humphrey & J. M. LeBreton (eds.), *The handbook of multilevel theory, measurement, and analysis* (pp. 115–140). American Psychological Association.

Ainsworth, M. S., & Bowlby, J. (1991). An ethological approach to personality development. *American Psychologist, 46*(4), 333–341.

Ajzen, I. (1991). The theory of planned behavior. *Organizational Behavior and Human Decision Processes, 50*, 179–211.

Akrivou, K. (2005). Deconstructing efficacy, optimism and hope: A study. Unpublished paper. Case Western Reserve University.

Akrivou, K., Boyatzis, R. E., and McLeod, P. L. (2006). The evolving group: Towards a prescriptive theory of intentional group development. *Journal of Management Development, 25*(7), 689–709.

Albarracín, D., Gillette, J. C., Earl, A. N., Glasman, L. R., Durantini, M.R., & Ho, M. H. (2005). A test of major assumptions about behavior change: a comprehensive look at the effects of passive and active HIV-prevention interventions since the beginning of the epidemic. *Psychological Bulletin, 131*(6), 856–897.

Algoe, S. B., Fredrickson, B. L., & Gable, S. L. (2013). The social functions of the emotion of gratitude via expression. *Emotion, 13*, 605–609.

Alinsky, S. D. (1971). *Rules for radicals: A pragmatic primer for realistic radicals.* Vintage.

Allport, G. (1937). *Personality: A psychological interpretation.* Holt, Rinehart & Winston.

Alston, P. (2022, September 13). For people leaving Mass. and Cass, a community waits inside the cottages at Shattuck. GBH News. https://www.wgbh.org/news/local-news/2022/09/13/for-people-leaving-mass-and-cass-a-community-waits-inside-the-cottages-at-shattuck.

American Express, Kantar Futures (2017). *Redefining the C-suite: Business the millennial way.* https://www.americanexpress.com/content/dam/amex/uk/staticassets/pdf/AmexBusinesstheMillennialWay.pdf?ref=wrkfrce.com

Amis, J., Slack, T., & Hiunings, C. R. (2004). The pace, sequence, and linearity of radical change. *Academy of Management Journal, 47*(1), 15–39.

And Beyond (n.d.). Mama Zikhali: A mother to all. https:www.andbeyond.com/impact/impact-stories/mama-zikhali-a-mother-to-all/.

Anderson, C. S., & Zaballeo, A. G. (2015). Organization development and change models. In W. J. Rothwell, C. S. Anderson, C. M. Corn, C. Haynes, C. H. Park, & A. G. Zaballero (eds.), *Organization development fundamentals: Managing strategic change* (pp. 13–42). ATD Press.

Anderson, P. (1999). Perspective: Complexity theory and organization science. *Organization science, 10*(3), 216–232.

Andrews-Hanna, J. R., Reidler, J. S., Sepulcre, J., Poulin, R., & Buckner, R. L. (2010). Functional-anatomic fractionation of the brain's default network. *Neuron, 65*(4), 550–562.

Andriani, P., & McKelvey, B. (2007). Beyond Gaussian averages: Redirecting international business and management research toward extreme events and power laws. *Journal of International Business Studies, 38*, 1–19. https://doi.org/10.1057/palgrave.jibs.8400324.

Andriani, P., & McKelvey, B. (2020). From Gaussian to Paretian thinking: Cause and implications of power laws in organizations. *Organization Science, 20*(6), 1053–1071.

Anticevic, A., Cole, M. W., Murray, J. D., Corlett, P. R., Wang, X. J., & Krystal, J. H. (2012). The role of default network deactivation in cognition and disease. *Trends in Cognitive Sciences, 16*(12), 584–592. https://doi.org/10.1016/j.tics.2012.10.008.

Antons, D. & Piller, F. T. (2015). Opening the black box of "not invented here": Attitudes, decision biases, and behavioral consequences. *Academy of Management Executive, 29*, 193–217.

Argyris, C. (1985). *Strategy, change, and defensive routines.* Pitman.

Armenakis, A. A., & Bedeian, A. G. (1999). Organizational change: A review of theory and research in the 1990s. *Journal of Management, 25*(3), 293–315.

Armenakis, A., Harris, S., & Feild, H. (1999). Paradigms in organizational change: Change agent and change target perspectives. In R. Golembiewski (ed.), *Handbook of organizational behavior* (pp. 97–128). Marcel Dekker.

Ashforth, B. E., & Mael, F. (1989). Social identity theory and the organization. *Academy of Management Review, 14*, 20–39.

Ashkanasy, N. M., & Humphrey, R. H. (2014). Leadership and emotion: A multilevel perspective. In D. V. Day (ed.), *The Oxford handbook of leadership and organizations* (pp. 783–804). Oxford University Press.

Ashkanasy, N. M., & Paulsen, N. (2013). The influence of follower mood on leader mood and task performance: An affective, follower-centric perspective of leadership. *Leadership Quarterly, 24*(4), 496–515.

Astin, A. W. (1993). *What matters in college? Four critical years.* Jossey-Bass.

Atkinson, J. W. (ed.). (1958). *Motivation in fantasy, action, and society.* Van Nostrand.

Babu, M. (2016). *Characteristics of effective leadership of community college presidents.* Unpublished doctoral dissertation, Case Western Reserve University.

Baburoglu, Oguz N. & Garr, M. A. (1993). Search conference methodology for practitioners. In M. R. Weisbord (ed.), *Discovering Common Ground* (pp. 73–82). Berrett-Koehler Publishers, Inc.

Bachkirova, T., & Lawton Smith, C. (2015). From competencies to capabilities in the assessment and accreditation of coaches. *International* Journal of Evidence Based Coaching and Mentoring, *13*(2), 123–140.

Baer, E., Hiltner, A., & Keith, H. D. (1987). Hierarchical structure in polymeric Materials. *Science, 235*(4792), 1015–1022.

Bak, P. (1996). Complexity and criticality. In *How nature works* (pp. 1–32). Copernicus.

Bak, W. (2014). Self-standards and self-discrepancies: A structural model of self-knowledge. *Current Psychology, 33*(2), 155–173.

Baker, N. (2019). The combined effect of leader–member exchange and leader optimism on follower job outcomes, *Business and Management Studies, 7*(5), 2525–2555

Bales, R. F. (1970). *Personality and interpersonal behavior.* Holt, Rinehart and Winston.

Baldwin, A. L. (1958). The role of an ability construct in a theory of behavior. In D. C. McClelland, A. L. Baldwin, U. Bronfenbrenner, & F. L. Strodtbeck (1958). *Talent and society: New perspectives in the identification of talent.* Van Nostrand.

Ballou, R., Bowers, D., Boyatzis, R. E., and Kolb, D. A. (1999). Fellowship in lifelong learning: An executive development program for advanced professionals. *Journal of Management Education, 23*(4), 338–354.

Bamboo.com (2023, November 28). *The great gloom: In 2023, employees are unhappier than ever. Why?* Report of global survey. *The Great Gloom: In 2023, Employees Are Unhappier Than Ever. Why?* (bamboohr.com).

Bandura, A. (1977). *Social learning theory.* Prentice Hall.

Bandura, A. (1981). Self-referent thought: A developmental analysis of self-efficacy. In J. H. Flavell & L. Ross (eds.), *Social cognitive development: Frontiers and possible futures* (pp. 200–239). Cambridge University Press.

Bandura, A., & National Inst. of Mental Health. (1986). *Social foundations of thought and action: A social cognitive theory.* Prentice-Hall, Inc.

Bar-Anan, Y., Wilson, T. D., & Gilbert, D. T. (2009). The feeling of uncertainty intensifies affective reactions. *Emotion, 9*(1), 123–127.

Barkham, M., Lutz, W., & Castonguay, L. G. (2021). *Handbook of psychotherapy and behavior change, 50th anniversary edition.* Wiley.

Barnard, C. I. (1938). *The functions of the executive.* Harvard University Press.

Barnes, B. (2013, June 6). The voice behind Mick (and others). *New York Times.*

Barnes, C. M., Wagner, D. T., Schabram, K., & Boncoeur, D. (2023). Human sustainability and work: A meta-synthesis and new theoretical framework. *Journal of Management, 49*(6), 1965–1996.

Bar-On, R. (1997). *Bar-On emotional quotient inventory: Technical manual.* Multi-Health Systems.

Barrett, F. J., & Cooperrider, D. L. (1990). Generative metaphor intervention: A new approach for working systems divided by conflict and caught in defensive perception. *Journal of Applied Behavioral Science, 26,* 219–239.

Barsade, S. G., & Gibson, D. E. (2007). Why does affect matter in organizations? *Academy of Management Perspectives, 21,* 36–59.

Batista-Foguet, J. M., Revilla, M., Saris, W., Boyatzis, R. E., & Serlavós, R. (2014). Reassessing the effect of survey characteristics on common method bias in emotional and social intelligence competencies assessment. *Structural Equation Modeling: A Multidisciplinary Journal, 21,* 596–607.

Batista-Foguet, J. M., Saris, W. E., Boyatzis, R., Guillén, L., & Serlavós, R. (2009). Effect of response scale on assessment of emotional intelligence competencies. *Personality and Individual Differences, 46* (5–6), 875–880.

Baum, J. R., Locke, E. A., & Kirkpatrick, S. A. (1998). A longitudinal study of the relation of vision and vision communication in venture growth in entrepreneurial firms. *Journal of Applied Psychology, 83*(1), 43–54.

Baumeister, R. (2003). Ego depletion and self-regulation failure: A resource model of self-control. *Alcoholism: Clinical and Experimental Research, 27*(2), 281–284.

Baumeister, R. F. (2023). Pragmatic prospection, the matrix of maybe, uncertainty, and human agency. *Possibility Studies & Society, 1*(4), 404–413. https://doi.org/10.1177/2753869923 1178180

Baumeister, R. F., Bratslavsky, E., Finkenauer, C., & Vohs, K. D. (2001). Bad is stronger than good. *Review of General Psychology, 5,* 323–370.

Baumeister, R., Bratslavsky, E., Muraven, M., & Tice, D. (1998). Ego depletion: Is the active self a limited resource?. *Journal of Personality and Social Psychology, 74,* 1252–1265. doi: 10.1037/0022-3514.74.5.1252.

Baumeister, R., Heatherton, T., & Tice, D. (1994). *Losing control: How and why people fail at self-regulation.* Academic Press.

Baumeister, R. F. & Leary, M. R. (1995). The need to belong: Desire for interpersonal attachments as a fundamental human motivation. *Psychological Bulletin, 117*(3), 497–529.

Beaubien, J. M., & Payne, S. C. (1999). *Individual goal orientation as a predictor of job and academic performance: A meta-analytic review and integration.* Paper presented at the meeting of the Society for Industrial and Organizational Psychology, Atlanta, April.

Beck, J. W., & Schmidt, A. M. (2013). State level goal orientation as predictors of the relationship between time pressure and performance: A longitudinal study. *Journal of Applied Psychology, 98*(2), 354–363.

Becker, Jasper (1997). *Hungry ghosts: Mao's secret famine.* Free Press.

Beckhard, R., & Harris, R. T. (1987). *Organization transitions: Managing complex change, 2nd edition.* Addison Wesley.

Beekman, D. (2017, October 12). Houston's solution to the homeless crisis: Housing—and lots of it. *Seattle Times.* https://www.seattletimes.com/seattle-news/homeless/houstons-solution-to-the-homeless-crisis-housing-and-lots-of-it/.

Beenen, G. (2014). The effects of goal orientations and supervisor concerns on MBA intern learning and performance. *Academy of Management Learning & Education, 13*(1), 82–101.

Beer, M., & Nohria N. (2000). Cracking the code of change. *Harvard Business Review, 78*(3), 133–141.

Beissner, F., Meissner, K., Bär, K. J., & Napadow, V. (2013).The autonomic brain: An activation likelihood estimation meta-analysis for central processing of autonomic function. *Journal of Neuroscience, 33*(25), 10503–10511.

Belanger, J. J., Lafreniere, M. A., Vallerand, R. J., & Kruglanski, A. W. (2013). When passion makes the heart grow colder: The role of passion in alternative goal suppression. *Journal of Personality and Social Psychology, 104*(1), 126–147.

Bell, C. R., & Goldsmith, M. (2013). *Managers as mentors: Building partnerships for learning.* Berrett-Koehler.

Bennett-Goleman, T. (2001). *Emotional alchemy: How the mind can heal the heart.* Harmony Books.

Bennis, W., Benne, K., & Chin, R. (1962). *The planning of change.* Holt, Rinehart & Wonston.

Bennis, W. G., & Shepard, H. A. (1956). A theory of group development. *Human Relations, 9,* 415–437.

Beretto, H. (2015, September 1). The way home. *Downtown Houston.* https://www.downtownhouston.org/news/article/way-home/.Berg, J. L. (2015). The impact of symbiotic visions on performance and a sense of personal accomplishment: Increasing engagement and motivation through vision alignment. *Frontiers in Psychology, 5,* 1335. doi: 10.3389/fpsyg.2014.01335.

Berg, J. L. (2016). *Purpose matters at a personal and corporate level.* Unpublished doctoral dissertation, Case Western Reserve University.

Bergner, S., Davda, A., Culpin, V., & Rybnicek, R. (2016). Who overrates, who underrates? Personality and its link to self–other agreement of leadership effectiveness. *Journal of Leadership & Organizational Studies, 23*(3), 335–354.

Bernier, S. (2010). Personal communication. Winnipeg, Canada.

Bernstien, W. M., & Burke, W. W. (1989). Modeling organizational meaning systems. In R. W. Woodman & W. A. Pasmore (eds.), *Research in organizational change and development* (pp. 117–159). JAI Press.

Berscheid, E. 1999. The greening of relationship science. *American Psychologist, 54*(4), 260–266.

Berry, J. W., & Worthington Jr., E. L. (2001). Forgivingness, relationship quality, stress while imagining relationship events, and physical and mental health. *Journal of Counseling Psychology, 48*(4), 447–455. https://doi.org/10.1037/0022-0167.48.4.447

Bethune, S. & Brownawell, A. (2010). *APA: Americans report willpower and stress as key obstacles to meeting health related outcomes.* American Psychological Association.

Bijlani, R. L., Vempati, R. P., Yadav, R. K., Ray, R. B., Gupta, V., Sharma, R., . . . & Mahapatra, S. C. (2005). A brief but comprehensive lifestyle education program based on yoga reduces risk factors for cardiovascular disease and diabetes mellitus. *Journal of Alternative & Complementary Medicine, 11*(2), 267–274.

Black, Robert. (2022). *Machiavelli: From radical to reactionary.* Reaktion Books.

Blake, R. R., & Mouton, J. S. (1964). *The managerial grid.* Gulf.

Blumenthal, J. A., Sherwood, A., Babyak, M. A., Watkins, L. L., Waugh, R., Georgiades, A., Bacon, S. L., Hayano, J., Coleman, R. E. & Hinderliter, A. (2005). Effects of exercise and stress management training on markers of cardiovascular risk in patients with ischemic heart disease: A randomized controlled trial. *JAMA, 293*(13), 1626–1634.

Blustein, D. L. (2008). The role of work in psychological health and well-being: a conceptual, historical, and public policy perspective. *American Psychologist, 63*(4), 228–240. doi: 10.1037/0003-066X.63.4.228. PMID: 18473608.

Boldero, J., & Francis, J. (1999). Ideals, oughts, and self-regulation: Are there qualitatively distinct self-guides? *Asian Journal of Social Psychology, 2,* 343–355.

Bolger, N., DeLongis, A., Kessler, R. C., & Schilling, E. A. (1989). Effects of daily stress on negative mood. *Journal of Personality and Social Psychology, 57*(5), 808–818.

Bower, J. (1977). Effective public management. *Harvard Business Review, 55*(2), 131–140.

Bower, G. H., & Forgas, J. P. (2001). Mood and social memory. In J. P. Forgas (ed.), *The handbook of affect and social cognition* (pp. 95–120). Lawrence Erlbaum.

Bowlby, J. ([1969] 1982). *Attachment and loss: Volume 1 attachment, 2nd edition.* Basic Books.

Bowles, S., Cunningham, C. J. L., De La Rosa, G. M., & Picano, J. (2007). Coaching leaders in middle and executive management: goals, performance, buy-in. *Leadership and Organizational Development Journal, 28*(5), 388–408.

Boyatzis, R. E. (1972). *A two-factor theory of affiliation motivation.* Unpublished doctoral dissertation, Harvard University.

Boyatzis, R. E. (1982). *The competent manager: A model for effective performance.* Wiley.

Boyatzis, R. E. (1998). *Transforming qualitative information: Thematic analysis and code development.* Sage.

Boyatzis, R. E. (2006a). Using tipping points of emotional intelligence and cognitive competencies to predict financial performance of leaders. *Psicothema, 18,* 124–131.

Boyatzis, R. E. (2006b). Intentional change theory from a complexity perspective. *Journal of Management Development, 25*(7), 607–623.

Boyatzis, R. E. (2008). Leadership development from a complexity perspective. *Consulting Psychology Journal: Practice and Research, 60*(4), 298–313.

Boyatzis, R. E. (2009). A behavioral approach to emotional Intelligence. *Journal of Management Development, 28,* 749–770.

Boyatzis, R. E. (2018). The behavioral level of emotional intelligence and its measurement. *Frontiers in Psychology, 9.* doi.org/10.3389/fpsyg.2018.01438

Boyatzis R. E. (2020). Personal communication of Katherine (Katie) Grace Siwy to the author in July and September.

Boyatzis, R. E., & Akrivou, K. (2006). The Ideal Self as a driver of change. *Journal of Management Development, 25*(7), 624–642.

Boyatzis, R. E., Buse, K., & Taylor, S. N. (2014). *The Ideal Self test.* Case Western University. Reproduced in the Appendix.

Boyatzis, R. E., & Cavanagh, K. V. (2018). Leading change: Developing emotional, social, and cognitive competencies in managers during an MBA program. In K. Keefer, J. Parker, & D. Saklofske (eds.), *Emotional intelligence in education* (pp. 403–426). Springer.

Boyatzis, R. E., Cowen, S. S., and Kolb, D. A. (1995). *Innovation in professional education: Steps on a journey from teaching to learning.* Jossey-Bass.

Boyatzis, R. E., & Dalziel, M. (in review). *Swarming as a model for strategic change: Why university presidents and deans should not depend on conventional strategic planning.* Unpublished paper, Case Western Reserve University

Boyatzis, R., & Dhar, U. (2021). Dynamics of the Ideal Self. *Journal of Management Development, 41*(1), 1–9.

Boyatzis, R. E., & Dhar, U. (2023). When normal is not normal: A theory of the non-linear and discontinuous process of desired change and its managerial implications. *The Journal of Applied Behavioral Science, 59*(3), 364–390. https://doi.org/10.1177/00218863231153218.

Boyatzis, R. E., Frick, C. & Van Oosten, E. (2003). Developing leaders throughout an entire organization by developing emotional intelligence competencies. In L. A. Berger and D. R. Berger (eds.), *The talent management handbook: Creating organizational excellence by identifying, developing, and positioning high-potential talent*. McGraw Hill.

Boyatzis, R. E., Gaskin, J., & Wei, H. (2015). Emotional and social intelligence and behavior. In D. Princiotta, S. Goldstein, and J. Naglieri (eds.), *Handbook of intelligence: Evolutionary, theory, historical perspective, and current concepts* (pp. 243–262). Spring Press.

Boyatzis, R. E., & Goleman, D. (1996, 1999). *Emotional competency inventory*. The Hay Group.

Boyatzis, R. E., & Goleman, D. (2007). *Emotional and social competency inventory*. The Hay Group (now Korn/Ferry Hay Group).

Boyatzis, R. E., Goleman, D., Dhar, U., & Osiri, J. K. (2021). Thrive and survive: Assessing personal sustainability. *Consulting Psychology Journal. 73*(1). 27–50.

Boyatzis, R. E., Goleman, D., & Rhee, K. (2000). Clustering competence in emotional intelligence: Insights from the Emotional Competence Inventory (ECI)s. In R. Bar-On and J. D. A. Parker (eds.), *Handbook of emotional intelligence* (pp. 343–362). Jossey-Bass.

Boyatzis, R. E., & Howard, A. (2013). When goal setting helps and hinders sustained, desired change. In S. David, D. Clutterbuck & D. Megginson (eds.). *Goal setting and goal management in coaching and mentoring* (pp. 211–228). Routledge.

Boyatzis, R. E., Hullinger, A., Ehasz, S. F., Harvey, J., Tassarotti, S., Galloti, A., & Pinafore, F. (2022). The grand challenge for research on the future of coaching. *Journal of Applied Behavioral Science, 58*(2). doi: 10.1177/00218863221079937.

Boyatzis, R. E., & Jack, A. (2018). The neuroscience of coaching. *Consulting Psychology Journal, 70*(1), 11–27.

Boyatzis, R. E., & Khawaja, M. (2014), How Dr. Akhtar Hameed Khan led a change process that started a movement. *Journal of Applied Behavioral Science. 50*(3), 284–306.

Boyatzis, R. E., & Kolb, D. A. (1999). Performance, learning, and development as modes of growth and adaptation throughout our lives and careers. In M. Peiperl, M. B. Arthur, R. Coffee, and T. Morris (eds.), *Career frontiers: New conceptions of working lives* (pp. 76–98). Oxford University Press.

Boyatzis, R., & McKee, A. (2005). *Resonant leadership: Renewing yourself and connecting with others through mindfulness, hope, and compassion*. Harvard Business School Press.

Boyatzis, R. E., Murphy, A. J., & Wheeler, J. V. (2000). Philosophy as a missing link between values and behavior. *Psychological Reports, 86*(1), 47–64.

Boyatzis, R. E., Passarelli, A. M., Koenig, K., Lowe, M., Mathew, B., Stoller, J. K., & Phillips, M. (2012). Examination of the neural substrates activated in memories of experiences with resonant and dissonant leaders. *Leadership Quarterly, 23*(2), 259–272.

Boyatzis, R. E., Passarelli, A. & Wei, H. (2013). Developing emotional, social and cognitive competencies in MBA programs: A twenty-five year perspective. In R. Riggio and S. Tan (eds.), *Building interpersonal skills in management programs* (pp. 311–330). Routledge.

Boyatzis, R. E., & Rochford, K. (2020). Relational climate in the workplace: Dimensions, measurement, and validation. *Frontiers in Psychology, 11*. 10.3389/fpsyg.2020.00085. 11.

Boyatzis, R. E., Rochford, K. & Cavanagh, K. (2017). The role of emotional and social intelligence competencies in engineer's effectiveness and engagement. *Career Development International, 22*(1), 70–86.

Boyatzis, R. E., Rochford, K. & Jack, A. (2014). Antagonistic neural networks underlying differentiated leadership roles. *Frontiers in Human Neuroscience, 8*, 1–15.

Boyatzis, R. E., Rochford, K., & Taylor, S. N. (2015). The role of the positive emotional attractor in vision and shared vision: toward effective leadership, relationships, and engagement. *Frontiers in Psychology, 6*. http://dx.doi.org/10.3389/fpsyg.2015.00670.

Boyatzis, R. E., Smith, M. & Beveridge, A. (2012). Coaching with compassion: Inspiring health, well-being and development in organizations. *Journal of Applied Behavioral Science, 49*(2), 153–178.

Boyatzis, R. E., Smith, M. L., & Blaize, N. (2006). Developing sustainable leaders through coaching and compassion. *Academy of Management Learning & Education, 5*(1), 8–24.

Boyatzis, R. E., Smith, M. L., & Van Oosten, E. (2019). *Helping people change: Coaching With compassion for lifelong learning and growth.* Harvard Business Review Press.

Boyatzis, R. E., Stubbs, E. C., & Taylor, S. N. (2002). Learning cognitive and emotional intelligence competencies through graduate management education. *Academy of Management Journal on Learning and Education, 1*(2), 150–162.

Boyatzis, R. E., Thiel, K., Rochford, K. & Black, A. (2017). Emotional and social intelligence competencies of incident team commanders fighting wildfires. *Journal of Applied Behavioral Science, 53*(4), 498–516.

Boyce, L. A., Jackson, R. J., & Neal, L. J. (2010). Building successful leadership coaching relationships: Examining impact of matching criteria in a leadership coaching program. *Journal of Management Development, 29*(10), 914–931.

Bradford, D. L., & Burke, W. W. (2005). *Reinventing organization development: New approaches to change in organizations.* John Wiley & Sons.

Bradley, K. J., & Aguinis, H. (2022). Team performance: Nature and antecedents of nonnormal distributions. *Organization Science, 34*(3), 1266–1286.

Brann, N. L. (1981). Abbott Trithemius (1462–1516): The renaissance of monastic humanism. Brill.

Bratman, G. N., Daily, G. C., Levy, B. J., & Gross, J. J. (2015). The benefits of nature experience: Improved affect and cognition. *Landscape and Urban Planning, 138*, 41–50.

Braunstein, A. (2022, June 13). U2 Band history: The story of the biggest band from Ireland. *Rock Era Insider.* https://rockerainsider.com/bands/u2-band-history/

Breiter, H. C., Gollub, R. L., Weisskoff, R. M., Kennedy, D. N., Makris, N., Berke, J. D., Goodman, J. M., Kantor, H. L., Gastfriend, Riorden, J. P., Mathew, R. T., Rosen, B. R., & Hyman, S. E. (1997). Acute effects of cocaine on human brain activity and emotion. *Neuron. 19*(3), 591–611.

Brett, J. F., & VandeWalle, D. (1999). Goal orientation and goal content as predictors of performance in a training program. *Journal of Applied Psychology, 84*(6), 863–887.

Brinton, C. (1952). *Anatomy of a revolution, 2nd edition.* Vintage Books.

Broadbent, S., & Hammersley, J. (1957). Percolation processes I. Crystals and mazes. *Mathematical Proceedings of the Cambridge Philosophical Society, 53*(3), 629– 641.

Brockner, J. (1992). The escalation of commitment to a failing course of action: Toward theoretical progress. *Academy of Management Review, 17*(1), 39–61.

Brockner, J., & Higgins, E. T. (2001). Regulatory focus theory: Implications for the study of emotions at work. *Annual Review of Psychology, 86*(1), 35–66.

Bronitsky, J., & Donachie, R. (2022, June 6). DC Mayors new homelessness policy bot inhumane and political. *Newsweek.* https://www.newsweek.com/dc-mayors-new-homelessness-policy-both-inhumane-political-opinion-1712867.

Brosschot, J. F., Van Dijk, E., & Thayer, J. F. (2007). Daily worry is related to low heart rate variability during waking and the subsequent nocturnal sleep period. *International journal of psychophysiology, 63*(1), 39–47.

Brown, P., Chaskin, R., Hamilton, R., & Richman, H. (2003). *Toward greater effectiveness in community change: Challenges and responses for philanthropy.* Chicago: Chapin Hall Center for Children at University of Chicago.

Brummelman, E. (2022). How to raise children's self-esteem? Comment on Orth and Robins. *American Psychologist, 77*(1), 20–22.

Buber, M. (1937). *I and thou.* Transl. by R. G. Smith. T. and T. Clark.

Buch, E. R., Claudino, L., Quentin, R., Bönstrup, M., & Cohen, L. G. (20210. Consolidation of human skill linked to waking hippocampo-neocortical replay. *Cell Reports, 35*(10), 109193. doi: 10.1016/j.celrep.2021.109193.

Buckingham, M. (1999). *First break all the rules*. Gallup Press.

Buckner, R. L., Andrews-Hanna, J. R., & Schacter, D. L. (2008). The brain's default network. *Annals of the New York Academy of Sciences, 1124*(1), 1–38.

Buckner, R. L., & Carroll, D. C. (2007). Self-projection and the brain. *Trends in Cognitive Science, 11*(2), 49–57.

Bulley, A., & Schacter, D. L. (2020). Deliberating trade-offs with the future. *Nature Human Behavior,* 4(3), 238–247.

Burke, M. J., & Day, R. R. (1986). A cumulative study of the effectiveness of managerial training. *Journal of Applied Psychology, 71*(2), 232–245.

Burke, P. J. (2006). Identity change. *Social psychology quarterly,* 69(1), 81–96.

Burke, W. W. (2014). Organizational change. In N. B. Schneider & K. M. Barbara (eds.), *The Oxford handbook of organizational climate culture* (pp. 457–483). Oxford University Press.

Burke, W. W., & Litwin, G. (1992). A causal model of organizational performance and change. *Journal of Management, 18*, 532–545.

Burke, W., & Noumair, D. A. (2015). *Organization development: A process of learning and changing, 3rd edition*. Pearson Education.

Burns, J. (2012). *La Roja: How soccer conquered Spain and how Spanish Soccer conquered the world*. Nation Books.

Burns, K. (2009). *The National Parks: America's Best Idea*. Public Broadcasting Service.

Buse, K. R., & Bilimoria, D. (2014). Personal vision: enhancing work engagement and the retention of women in the engineering profession. *Frontiers in Psychology, 5*, 1400. doi: 10.3389/fpsyg.2014.01400

Byrne, D. G., Mazanov, J., & Gregson, R. A. M. (2001). A cusp catastrophe analysis of changes to adolescent smoking behavior in response to smoking prevention programs. *Nonlinear Dynamics, Psychology, and Life Sciences, 5*(2), 115–137.

Byrne, J. (1991, April 1). CEO disease/ *Business Week*, pp. 52–59.

Cacioppo, J. T., & Berntsen, G. G. (1994). Relationship between attitudes and evaluative space: A critical review, with emphasis on the separability of positive and negative substrates. *Psychological Bulletin, 115*(3), 401–423.

Camerer, C., & Lovallo, D. (1999). Overconfidence and excess entry: An experimental approach. *American Economic Review, 89*(1), 306–318.

Cameron, K. S. (2008). Paradox in positive organizational change. *Journal of Applied Behavioral Science, 44*, 7–24.

Campbell, J. P., Dunnette, M. D., Lawler, III, E. E., & Weick, K. E. (1970). *Managerial behavior, performance, and effectiveness,* McGraw Hill.

Capaldi, C. A., Dopko, R. L., & Zelenski, J. M. (2014). The relationship between nature connectedness and happiness: a meta-analysis. *Frontiers in Psychology, 5*, 976. doi:10.3389/fpsyg.2014.00976

Capelli, P., Singh, H., Singh, J. V., & Useem, M. (2010). Leadership lessons from India. *Harvard Business Review, 88*(3): 90–97.

Caplan, R. D., & Jones, K. W. (1975). Effects of work load, role ambiguity, and type A personality on anxiety, depression, and heart rate. *Journal of Applied Psychology, 60*(6), 713–719.

Capps, K. (2022, January 14). Can Boston Mayor Michelle Wu tackle homelessness? Bloomberg News. https://www.bloomberg.com/news/articles/2022-01-14/can-boston-mayor-michelle-wu-tackle-homelessness.

Carmeli, A., Ben-Hador, B., Waldman, D. A., & Rupp, D. E. (2009). How leaders cultivate social capital and nurture employee vigor: implications for job performance. *Journal of Applied Psychology, 94*(6), 1553–1561.

Carmeli, A., Brueller, D., & Dutton, J. E. 2009. Learning behaviors in the workplace: The role of high-quality interpersonal relationships and psychological safety. *Systems Research and Behavioral Science, 26*(1), 81–98.

Carmeli, A., & Gittell, J. H. (2009). High-quality relationships, psychological safety, and learning from failures in work organizations. *Journal of Organizational Behavior, 30*(6), 709–729.

Carter, C., Macdonald, A., Ursu, S., Stenger, A., Ho Sohn, M., & Anderson, A. (2000). How the brain gets ready to perform. Presentation at the 30th Annual Meeting of the Society of Neuroscience, New Orleans, November.

Carton, A. M., Murphy, C., & Clark, J. R. (2014). A (blurry) vision of the future: How leader rhetoric about ultimate goals influences performance. *Academy of Management Journal, 57*(6), 1544–1570.

Carver, C. S., Lawrence, J. W., & Scheier, M. F. (1999). Self-discrepancies and affect: Incorporating the role of feared selves. *Personality and Social Psychology Bulletin, 25*(7), 783–792.

Carver, C. S., & Scheier, M F. (1993). Vigilant and avoidant coping in two patient samples. In H. W. Krohne (ed.), *Attention and avoidance: Strategies in coping with aversiveness* (pp. 295–319). Hogrefe & Huber Publishers.

Casti, J. L. (1994). *Complexification: Explaining a paradoxical world through the science of surprise.* Harper Collins.

Cates, J. (2015). The meaninglessness epidemic—a 21st century disease? *Huffington Post.* https://www.huffingtonpost.co.uk/joanna-cates/the-meaninglessness-epide_b_6557760.html.

Cech, E. A. (2021). *The trouble with passion: How searching for fulfillment at work fosters inequality.* University of California Press.

Champniss, G., Wilson, H. N., & Macdonald, E. K. (2015). Why your customers' social identities matter. *Harvard Business Review, 93*(1–2), 88–96.

Chan, A. K. L. (2002). *Mencius: Context and interpretations.* University of Hawai'i Press.

Cavanagh, M., & Grant, A. M. (2018). The solution focused approach to coaching. In E. Cox, T. Bachkirova, & D. Clutterbuck (eds.), *The complete handbook of coaching* (pp. 54–67). Sage.

Chen, E., Brody, G. H., & Miller, G. E. (2017). Childhood close family relationships and health. *American Psychologist, 72*(6), 555–566.

Chen, G., Gullly, S. M., Whiteman, J. A. & Kilcullen, R. N. (2000). Examination of relationships among trait-like individual differences, State-like individual differences, and learning performance. *Journal of Applied Psychology, 85*(6), 835–847.

Cherniss, C. (2010). Emotional intelligence: Towards clarification of a concept. *Industrial and Organizational Psychology: Perspectives on Science and Practice, 3,* 110–126.

Cherniss, C., & Adler, M. (2000). *Promoting emotional intelligence in organizations: Make training in emotional intelligence effective.* American Society of Training and Development.

Cherniss, C. & Boyatzis, R. E. (2013). Using a multi-level theory of performance based on emotional intelligence to conceptualize and develop "soft" leader skills. In Ron Riggio and Sherylle Tan (eds.), *Building Interpersonal Skills in Management Programs* (pp. 53–72). Routledge/Taylor & Francis Group.

Chibanda, D., Weiss, H. A., Verhey, R., Simms, V., Munjoma, R., Rusakaniko, S., Chingono, A., Munetsi, E., Bere, T., Manda, E., Abas, M., & Araya, R. (2016). Effect of a primary care–based psychological intervention on symptoms of common mental disorders in Zimbabwe: A randomized clinical trial. *JAMA, 316*(24), 2618–2626.

Christakis, N. A., & Fowler, J. H. (2009). *Connected: The surprising power of social networks in our lives—how you friends' friends' friends' affect everything you feel, think, and do.* Little, Brown.

Chuang, S. C., & Lin, H. M. (2007). The effect of induced positive and negative emotion and openness-to-feeling in student's consumer decision making. *Journal of Business and Psychology, 22*(1), 65–78.

Cianci, A. M., Klein, H. J., & Seijts, G. H. (2010). The effect of negative feedback on tension and subsequent performance: The main and interactive effects of goal content and conscientiousness. *Journal of Applied Psychology, 95*(4), 618–630.

Clayton, B. (2014). Shared vision in corporate acquisitions. *Frontiers in Psychology, 5*, 1335. https://doi.org/10.3389/fpsyg.2014.01466

Cohen, G. L. (2022). *Belonging: The science of creating connection and bridging divides*. Norton.

Cohen, R., Bavishi, C., & Rozanski, A. (2016). Purpose in life and its relationship to all causes mortality and cardiovascular events. *Psychosomatic Medicine, 78*(2), 122–133.

Colarelli, N. J., & Siegel, S. M. (1966). *Ward H: An adventure in innovation*. Van Nostrand.

Coles, P. A., Corsi, E., & Dessain, V. (2012). On two wheels in Paris: The vélib' bicycle-sharing program (case study). *Harvard Business School Case Study: Harvard Business School NOM Unit Case No. 912-022*, 912–002.

Conger, J., & Kannugo, R. (1998). *Charismatic leadership in organizations*. Sage.

Conley, N. (2018). *Barriers and facilitators of growth in Black entrepreneurial ventures: Thinking outside the black box*. Unpublished doctoral dissertation, Case Western Reserve University.

Connelly, S., Friedrich, T., Vessey, W. B., Klabzuba, A., Day, E. A., & Ruark, G. (2013). A conceptual framework for emotion management in leadership contexts. In R. Riggio and S. Tan (eds.), *Leader interpersonal and influence skills: The soft skills of leadership* (pp. 101–138). Lawrence Erlbaum.

Converse, B. A., Juarez, L. & Hennecke, M. (2019). Self-control and the reasons behind our goals. *Journal of Personality and Social Psychology, 116*(5), 860–883.

Cooperrider, D. L., & Srivastva, S. (1987). Appreciative inquiry in organizational life. In W. A. Pasmore & R. W. Woodman (eds.), *Research in organizational change and development, volume 1* (pp. 129–169). JAI Press.

Cooperrider, D. L., Stavros, J. M., & Whitney, D. (2008). *The appreciative inquiry handbook: For leaders of change*. Berrett-Koehler Publishers.

Corbetta, M., Essen, D. C. V., & Raichle, M. E. (2005). The human brain is intrinsically organized into dynamic, anticorrelated functional networks. *Proceedings of the National Academy of Sciences of the United States of America, 102*(27), 9673–9678.

Cowen, S. & Seifter, B. (2014). *The inevitable city: The resurgence of New Orleans and the future of urban America*. St. Martins Press.

Coy, P. (2007, August 20 & 27). Ten years from now . . . *Business Week,* 42–43.

Crain's New York Business (2014, January 21). Citi bike supplier rides into bankruptcy. Bloomberg News. https://www.crainsnewyork.com/article/20140122/TRANSPORTAT ION/140129956/citi-bike-supplier-rides-into-bankruptcy.

Cross, S., & Simpson, J. (2019). *Under four trees*. Documentary. www.underfourtrees.com.

Crowne, D. P. & Marlowe, D. (1964). *The approval motive*. Wiley.

Cummings, T. G., & Worley, C. G. (2015). *Organization development and change*. Cengage Learning.

Curran, T., Hill, A. P., Appleton, P. R., Vallerand, R. J., & Standage, M. (2015). The psychology of passion: A meta-analytical review of a decade of research on intrapersonal outcomes. *Motivation and Emotion 39*(5), 631–655 (2015).

Cutter, H., Boyatzis, R. E. & Clancy, D. (1977). The effectiveness of power motivation training for rehabilitating alcoholics. *Journal of Studies on Alcohol, 38*(1), 131–141. doi: 10.15288/jsa.1977.38.131.

Dahl, C. J., Wilson-Mendenhall, C. D., & Davidson, R. J. (2020). The plasticity of well being: A training based framework for the cultivation of human flourishing. *Proceedings of the National Academy of Sciences, 117*(51), 32197–32206.

Dailey, C. A. (1971), *Assessment of lives: Personality evaluation in a bureaucratic society*. Jossey-Bass.

Dalton, G., and Thompson, P. (1986). *Novations: Strategies for career development*. Scott Foresman.

Damasio, A. (2019). *The strange order of things: Life, feeling, and the making of cultures*. Vintage.

Damian, R. I., Spengler, M. Sutu, A., & Roberts, B. W. (2018). Sixteen going on sixty-six: A longitudinal study of personality stability and change across 50 years. *Journal of Personality and Social Psychology, 117*(3), 674–695. doi: 10.1037/pspp0000210.

Damon, W., Menon, J., and Cotton Bronk, K. (2003). The development of purpose during adolescence. *Applied developmental science, 7*(3), 119–128.

D'Argembeau, A., Stawarczyk, D., Majerus, S., Collette, F., Van der Linden, M., Feyers, D., Maquet, P., & Salmon, E. (2009). The neural basis of personal goal processing when envisioning future events. *Journal of Cognitive Neuroscience, 22*(8), 1701–1713.

D'Argembeau, A., Stawarczyk, D., Majerus, S., Collette, F., Van der Linden, M., & Salmon, E. (2010). Modulation of medial prefrontal and inferior parietal cortices when thinking about past, present and future selves. *Social Neuroscience, 5*(2), 187–200.

Davidson, R. (2022). The plasticity of well-being: A new framework for emotional intelligence. Presentation at the Biannual Meeting of the Consortium for Research in Emotional Intelligence. Boston.

Davidson, R. J., Jackson, D. C., & Kalin, N. H. (2000). Emotion, plasticity, context, and regulation: Perspectives from affective neuroscience. *Psychological Bulletin, 126*(6), 890–909.

Davidson, R. J., Kabat-Zinn, J., Schumacher, J. R., Rosenkranz, M. A., Muller, D., Santorelli, S. F., Urbanowski, F., Harrington, A., Bonus, K. A., & Sheridan, J. F. (2003). Alterations in brain and immune function produced by mindfulness meditation. *Psychosomatic Medicine, 65*, 564–570.

Davis C. G., Nolen-Hoeksema S., & Larson J. (1998). Making sense of loss and benefiting from the experience: Two construals of meaning. *Journal of Personality & Social Psychology, 75*, 561–574.

Dawes, A. J., Keogh, R., Robuck, S., & Pearson, J. (2022). Memories with a blind mind: remembering the past and imagining the future with aphantasia. *Cognition, 227*, 1–17.

DeCharms, R. (1968). *Personal causation.* Academic Press.

Deci, E. L., & Flaste, R. (1995). *Why we do what we do: Understanding self-motivation.* Penguin.

Deci, E. L., & Ryan, R. M. (2000). The "what" and" why" of goal pursuits: Human needs and the self-determination of behavior. *Psychological Inquiry, 11*(4), 227–268.

DeFilippis, J. (2004). Community control and development: The long view. In J. DeFilippis (ed.), *Unmasking goliath: Community control in the face of global capital.* Routledge.

DeFilippis, J., & Saegert, S. (2012). *The community development reader.* Routledge.

de Haan, E., Gray, D. E., & Bonneywell, S. (2019). Executive coaching outcome research in a field setting: A hear-randomized controlled trial study in a global healthcare corporation. *Academy of Management Learning & Education, 18*(4). https://doi.org/10.5465/amle.2018.0158.

de Haan, E., Molyn, J., & Nilsson, V. O. (2020). New findings on the effectiveness of the coaching relationship: Time to think differently about active ingredients? *Consulting Psychology Journal: Practice and Research, 72*(3), 155–167.

Denny, B. T., Ochsner, K. N., Weber, J., and Wager, T. D. (2014). Anticipatory brain activity predicts the success or failure of subsequent emotion regulation. *Social cognitive and affective neuroscience, 9*(4), 403–411.

Denworth, L. (2023). Synchronized minds: The brains of social species are strikingly resonant. *Scientific American,* July/August, 49–57.

Devine-Wright, P. (2005) Local aspects of UK renewable energy development: Exploring public beliefs and policy implications. *Local Environment, 10*(1), 57–69.

Dhar, U. (2021). Managerial identity development across the age-spectrum from an Ideal Self and values perspective. *Journal of Management Development, 40*(6), 574–583.

Dhar, U. (2022a). *The interplay of emotionally salient developmental experiences, career stages, and the Ideal Self: An index development and survey analysis.* Unpublished doctoral dissertation, Case Western Reserve University.

Dhar, U. (2022b). Managerial coaching: a paradox-based view. *Leadership & Organization Development Journal, 43*(2), 291–301.

Dhar, U., & Boyatzis, R. E. (in press). Development and validation of a scale to measure subjective liminality: Individual differences in the perception of in-betweenness. *Journal of Organization Change Management, 36*(8), 129–140. doi:10.1108/jocm-07-2023-0279

DiBenigno, J. (2022). How idealized professional identities can persist through client interactions. *Administrative Science Quarterly, 67*(3), 1–48.

Dickerson, S. S., & Kemeny, M. E. 2004. Acute stressors and cortisol responses: A theoretical integration and synthesis of laboratory research. *Psychological Bulletin, 130*(3), 355–391.

Dik, B. J., & Duffy, R. D. (2009). Calling and vocation at work: Definitions and prospects for research and practice. *The Counseling Psychologist, 37*(3), 424–450.

Hicks, R. D. (1925). *Diogenes Laertius: Lives of Eminent Philosophers, volume 1.* Translated by R. Hicks. Harvard University Press.

Dixon, M. L., Thiruchselvam, R., Todd, R., & Christoff, K. (2017, June 15). Emotion and the prefrontal cortex: An integrative review. *Psychological Bulletin.* Advance online publication. http://dx.doi.org/10.1037/bul0000096

Docherty, D. W. (2020). Coaching and development as part of a manager–subordinate relationship: A mixed methods study of tools, dynamics, and outcomes. Unpublished doctoral dissertation, Case Western Reserve University.

Doidge, N. (2007). *The brain that changes itself: Stories of personal triumph from the frontiers of brain science.* Viking Press.

Dolnick, E. (2021). *The writing of the gods: The race to decode the Rosetta Stone.* Scribner.

Dooley, K. J. (2004). Complexity science models of organizational change and innovation. In M. S. Poole and A. Van de Ven (eds.), (pp. 354–373). *Handbook of organizational change and innovation.* Oxford Academic Press.

Dose, J. J. (1997). Work values: An integrative framework and illustrative application to organizational socialization. *Journal of Occupational and Organizational Psychology, 70*(3), 219–240.

Dreyfus, C. (2008). Identifying competencies that predict effectiveness of R and D managers. *Journal of Management Development, 27*(1), 76–91.

Drigotas, S. M., Rusbult, C. E., Wieselquist, J., & Whitton, S. W. (1999). Close partner sculptor of the Ideal Self: Behavioral affirmation and the Michelangelo phenomenon. *Journal of Personality and Social Psychology, 77*(2), 293–323.

Driver, M. J. (1982). Career concepts: A new approach to career research. In R. Katz (ed.), *Career issues in human resource management* (pp. 23–32). Prentice-Hall.

Druskat, V. U., & Kayes, D. C. (2000). Learning versus performance in short-term project teams. *Small Group Research, 31*(3), 328–353.

Druskat, V. U., & Wheeler, J. V. (2003). Managing from the boundary: The effective leadership of self-managing work teams. *Academy of Management Journal, 46*(4), 435–457.

Druskat, V., & Wolff, S. (2001). Building the emotional intelligence of groups. *Harvard Business Review, 79*(3), 80–90, 164.

Dukerich, J. M. (2001). Role transitions in organizational life: An identity-based perspective, by Ashforth Blake E. Lawrence Erlbaum Associates, 2001. *Academy of Management Review, 26*, 670–672.

Dukhaykh, S. (2019). The influence of individual, organizational, and contextual factors on Saudi women career commitment and satisfaction in nontraditional occupations. Unpublished doctoral dissertation, Case Western Reserve University.

Dumas, G., Nadel, J., Soussignan, R., Martinerie, J., & Garnero, L. (2010). Inter-brain synchronization during social interaction. *PLOS One, 5*(8), e12166. https://doi.org/10.1371/journal.pone.0012166

Duncan, J., & Owen, A. M. (2000). Common regions of the human frontal lobe recruited by diverse cognitive demands. *Trends Neuroscience, 23*(10), 475–483.

Dunning, D. (2011). The Dunning-Kruger effect: On being ignorant of one's own ignorance. In J. Olson & M. P. Zanna (eds.), *Advances in experimental social psychology*, 247–296. Elsevier.

Durrheim, K., & Foster, D. (1997). Tolerance of ambiguity as a content specific construct. *Personality and Individual Differences, 22*(5), 741–750.

Dutton, J. E. (2003). *Energize your workplace: How to create and sustain high-quality connections at work.* Jossey-Bass.

Dutton, J. E., Frost, P. J., Worline, M. C., Lilius, J. M., & Kanov, J. (2002). Leading in times of trauma. *Harvard Business Review*, January, 54–61.

Dutton, J. E., Roberts, L. M., and Bednar, J. (2010). Pathways for positive identity construction at work: Four types of positive identity and the building of social resources. *Academy of management review, 35*(2), 265–293.

Dutton, J. E., Workman, K. M., & Hardin, A. E. (2014). Compassion at work. *Annual Review of Organizational Psychology and Organizational Behavior, 1*, 277–304.

Dutton, J. E., Worline, M. C., Frost, P. J., & Lilius, J. (2006). Explaining compassion organizing. *Administrative Science Quarterly, 51*(1), 59–96.

Dweck, C. S. (2006). *Mindset: The new psychology of success.* Ballantine Books.

Dyck, L. R. (2018). The impact of resonance and dissonance on effective physician–patient communication. *Individual, Relational, and Contextual Dynamics of Emotions (Research on Emotion in Organizations, Vol. 14)*, (pp. 139–162). Emerald Publishing Limited. https://doi.org/10.1108/S1746-979120180000014015.

Economist. (2023, July 22). Slow puncture: Urban transport meets the venture capital cycle.

Edelman, G. (1987). *Neural Darwinism: The theory of neuronal group.* Basic Books.

Eisenberg, M. E., Berge, J. M., & Neumark-Sztainer, D. (2013). Dieting and encouragement to diet by significant others: Associations with disordered eating in young adults. *American Journal of Health Promotion, 27*(6), 370–377.

Eisenberger, N. I., & Cole, S. W. (2012). Social neuroscience and health: Neurophysiological mechanisms linking social ties with physical health. *Nature neuroscience, 15*(5), 669–674.

Elfenbein, H. A. (2014). The many faces of emotional contagion: An affective process theory of affective linkage. *Organizational Psychology Review, 4(4),* 336–392.

Elton, A., & Gao, W. (2015). Task-positive functional connectivity of the Default Mode Network transcends task domain. *Journal of Cognitive Neuroscience, 27*(12), 2369–2381.

Ely, R. J., Ibarra, H., & Kolb, D. M. (2011). Taking gender into account: Theory and design for women's leadership development programs. *Academy of Management Learning & Education, 10*, 474–493.

Erdi, P. (2008). *Complexity explained.* Springer-Verlag.

Ericsson, K. A., Krampe, R. T., & Tesch-Römer, C. (1993). The role of deliberate practice in the acquisition of expert performance. *Psychological Review, 100*(3), 363–406.

Erikson, E. H. (1985). *The life cycle completed: A review.* Norton.

Erikson, P. S., Perfilieva, E., Bjork-Eriksson, T., Alborn, A-M, Nordburg, C., Peterson, D. A. & Gage, F. H. (1998). Neurogenesis in the adult human hippocampus. *Nature Medicine, 4*, 1313–1317.

Eurostat (2022). How many marriages and divorces took place in 2020? *European Union Statistical Reports.* Brussels.

Eysenick, H. J. (1952). The effects of psychotherapy" An evaluation. *Journal of Consulting Psychology, 16*, 319–324.

Falk, E. B., Morelli, S. A., Welborn, B. L., Dambacher, K., & Lieberman, M. D. (2013). Creating buzz: The neural correlates of effective message propagation. *Psychological Science, 24*(7), 1234–1242.

Fallows, J. (1981). M-16: A bureaucratic horror story: Why the rifles jammed. *Atlantic Monthly*, June.

Fallows, J. (1985). The case against credentialism. *Atlantic Monthly*.

Farrag, M. A. (2022). What are the characteristics of leaders who need to capture followers' hearts and minds? Unveiling the Arab mind. Unpublished doctoral dissertation, Case Western Reserve University.

Feintzeig, R. (2020, January 24). Younger workers feel lonely at the office. *Wall Street Journal*.

Ferber, J. (1999). *Multi-agent systems: An introduction to distributed AI*. Addison-Wesley.

Ferguson, J. K., Willemsen, E. W., & Castañeto, M. V. (2010). Centering prayer as a healing response to everyday stress: A psychological and spiritual process. *Pastoral Psychology, 59*(3), 305–329.

Festinger, L. (1957). *A theory of cognitive dissonance*. Row Peterson.

Fishbein, M. (1979). A theory of reasoned ACXTION: Some applications and Implications. *Nebraska Symposium on Motivation 1979*. University of Nebraska Press.

Fisher, C. D., Minbashian, A., Beckman, N., & Wood, R. E. (2013). Task appraisals, emotions and performance goal orientation. *Journal of Applied Psychology, 98*(2), 364–373.

Fisher, D. M. (2014). Distinguishing between taskwork and teamwork planning in teams: Relations with coordination and interpersonal processes. *Journal of Applied Psychology, 99*(3), 423–436.

Fitzgerald, F. S. (1934). *Tender is the night*. Scribner.

Flanagan, J. C. (1954). The critical incident technique. *Psychological Bulletin, 51*, 327–335.

Fligstein, N., & McAdam, D. (2011). Toward a general theory of strategic action fields. *Sociological Theory, 29*(1), 1–26.

Flores, B. J. (2023). *ATD's organization development handbook*. ATD Press.

Forbes Woman Africa. (2016, October 1). Classes under rain, clouds and trees. *Forbes Africa*. https://www.forbesafrica.com/current-affairs/2016/10/01/class-rain-clouds-trees/

Ford, J. D., & Ford, L. W. (1994). Logistics of identity, contradiction, and attraction in change. *Academy of Management Review, 19*(4), 756–785.

Fowler, J. H., & Christakis, N. A. (2008). Dynamic spread of happiness in a large social network: Longitudinal analysis over 20 years in the Framingham Heart Study. *British Medical Journal, 337*, a2338. doi: https://doi.org/10.1136/bmj.a2338

Fowler, J. H., & Christakis, N. A. (2010). Cooperative behavior cascades in human social networks. *Proceedings of the National Academy of Sciences, 107*(12), 5334–5338.

Fox, M. D., Corbetta, M., Snyder, A. Z., Vincent, J. L., & Raichle, M. E. (2006). Spontaneous neuronal activity distinguishes human dorsal and ventral attention systems. *Proceedings of the National Academy of Sciences, 103*(26), 10046–10051.

Fox, M. D., Snyder, A. Z., Vincent, J. L., Corbetta, M., Essen, D. C. V., & Raichle, M. E. (2005). The human brain is intrinsically organized into dynamic, anticorrelated functional networks. *Proceedings of the National Academy of Sciences of the United States of America, 102*(27), 9673–9678.

Franklin, B. ([1784] 2004). *The autobiography of Benjamin Franklin: Part 2*. Simon & Schuster.

Frazier, L. D., Hooker, K., Johnson, P. M., and Kaus, C. R. (2000). Continuity and change in possible selves in later life: A 5-year longitudinal study. *Basic and applied social psychology, 22*(3), 237–243.

Fredrickson, B. L. (2001). The role of positive emotions in positive psychology: The broaden-and-build theory of positive emotions. *American Psychologist, 56*(3), 218–226.

Fredrickson, B. L. (2009). *Positivity*. Crown.

Fredrickson, B. L., & Branigan, C. (2005). Positive emotions broaden the scope of attention and thought-action repertoires. *Cognition and Emotion, 19*, 313–332.

Fredrickson, B. L., & Losada, M. F. (2005). Positive affect and the complex dynamics of human flourishing. *American Psychologist, 60*(7), 678–686.

French, R. (2001). "Negative capability": Managing the confusing uncertainties of change. *Journal of Organizational Change, 14*(5), 480–492.

French, S. E., & Jack, A. I. (2014). Dehumanizing the enemy: The intersection of neuroethics and military ethics. In D. Whetham (ed.), *The responsibility to protect: Alternative perspectives* (pp. 169–195). Martinus Nijhoff.

Freud, A. (1936). *Ego and the mechanisms of defense*. International Universities Press.

Freud, S. ([1894] 1994). *The neuro-psychosis of defense*. In J. Stachey, A. Frued, & A. Richards (eds.). *Standard edition of the complete works of Sigmund Freud* (pp. 41–61). Hogarth Press.

Freud, S. (1936). *The ego and the mechanisms of defense*. International University Press.

Friedman, R. A., Tidd, S. T., Currall, S. C., & Tsai, J. C. (2000). What goes around comes around: The impact of personal conflict style on work conflict and stress. *International Journal of Conflict Management, 11*(1), 32–55.

Freitas, A. L., & Higgins, E. T. (2002). Enjoying goal-directed action: The role of regulatory fit. *Psychological Science, 13*(1), 1–6.

Frost, P. J. (2003). *Toxic emotions at work: How compassionate managers handle pain and conflict*. Harvard Business School Press.

Frost, P. J., Dutton, J. E., Worline, M. C., & Wilson, A. 2000. Narratives of compassion in organizations. In S. Fineman (ed.), *Emotion in organizations* (pp. 25–45). Sage.

Fruh, S. M., Fulkerson, J. A., Mulekar, M. S., Kendrick, L. A. J., & Clanton, C. (2011). The surprising benefits of the family meal. *Journal for Nurse Practitioners, 7*(1), 18–22.

Fulcher Gutierrez, A. (2017). The impact of emotional intelligence on the leadership of public school superintendents. Unpublished doctoral dissertation, University of Massachusetts Global.

Gaan, N., Malik, S., & Dagar, V. (2023). Cross-level effect of resonant leadership on remote engagement: A moderated mediation analysis in the unprecedented COVID-19 crisis. *European Management Journal.* https://doi.org/10.1016/j.emj.2023.01.004.

Gabaix, X. (2016). Power laws in economics: An introduction. *Journal of Economic Perspectives. 30*(1), 185–206.

Gagnon, L. (2009). Montreal's wheels of fortune. NPR Business, Morning Edition.

Galanter, M., Josipovic, Z., Dermatis, H., Weber, J. & Millard, M. A. (2016). An initial fMRI study on neural correlates of prayer in members of Alcoholics Anonymous. *American Journal of Drug and Alcohol Abuse, 43*(1), 44–54.

Gambhir, G. (2023). *Gautam Gambhir Profile.* https://sports.ndtv.com/cricket/players/563-gautam-gambhir-playerprofile/news. March 4, 2024.

Gamble, B., Tippett, L. J., Moreau, D., & Addis, D. R. (2021). The futures we want: How goal directed imagination relates to mental health. *Clinical Psychological Science,* 9(4), 732–751.

Garber, J. (1995). Defining feminist community: Place, choice, and the urban politics of difference. In J. Garber (ed.), *Gender in urban research*. Sage.

Gecas, V. (1982). *The self-concept. Annual Review of Sociology,* 8, 1–33.

Gersick, C. J. (1991). Revolutionary change theories: A multilevel exploration of the punctuated equilibrium paradigm. *Academy of Management Review, 16*(1), 10–36.

Gianaros, P. J., & Jennings, J. R. (2018). Host in the machine: A neurobiological perspective on psychological stress and cardiovascular disease. *American Psychologist, 73*(8), 1031–1044.

Gibson, C. B., Dunlop, P. D., & Raghav, S. (2020). Navigating identities in global work: Antecedents and consequences of intrapersonal identity conflict. *Human Relations.* https://doi.org/10.1177/0018726719895314

Gilbert, D. T., & Wilson, T. D. (2007). Prospection: Experiencing the future. *Science, 317*(5843), 1351–1354.

Gilbert, K., Mineka, S., Zinbarg, R. E., Craske, M. G., & Adam, E. K. (2017). Emotion regulation regulates more than emotion: Associations of momentary emotion regulation with diurnal cortisol in current and past depression and anxiety. *Clinical Psychological Science 5*(1), 37–51.

Gill, A. (2021, August 25). Economists explain the Taliban. *Wall Street Journal*. Opinion/Commentary Section.

Gilmore, T., Shea, G., & Useem, M. 1997. Side effects of corporate cultural transformations. *Journal of Applied Behavioral Science, 33*, 174–189.

Gintis, H. 2000. Strong reciprocity and human sociality. *Journal of Theoretical Biology, 206*, 169–179.

Gintis, H. 2003. The hitchhiker's guide to altruism: Gene–culture coevolution and the internalization of norms. *Journal of Theoretical Biology, 220*, 407–418.

Gittel, J. H. 2003. *The Southwest Airlines way: Using the power of relationships to achieve high performance*. McGraw-Hill.

Gittell, J. H., Seidner, R., & Wimbush, J. 2010. A relational model of how high-performance work systems work. *Organization Science, 21*(2), 490–506.

Gladwell, M. (2008). *Outliers: The story of success*. Little, Brown.

Goethe, J. W. V. (1806). Prelude to the theater. Part I of *Faustus, a Dramatic Mystery*. Translated in 1835 by John Anster. Longman, Rees, Orme, Brown, Green, and Longman.

Goldsmith, M., & Reiter, M. (2015). *Triggers: Creating behavior that lasts: Becoming the person you want to be*. Crown Business.

Goleman, D. (1998). *Working with emotional intelligence*. Bantam.

Goleman, D. (2003). *Destructive emotions: A scientific dialogue with the Dalai Lama*. Bantam.

Goleman, D., Boyatzis, R., & McKee, A. (2002). *Primal Leadership: Realizing the Power of Emotional Intelligence*. Harvard Business School Press.

Goleman, D. & Davidson, R. (2017). *Altered traits*. Avery.

Golembiewski, R. T. (1986). Contours in social change: Elemental graphics and a surrogate variable for gamma change. *Academy of Management Review, 11*(3), 550–566.

Gollwitzer, P. M., & Sheeran, P. (2006). Implementation intentions and goal achievement: A meta-analysis of effects and processes. *Advances in Experimental Social Psychology, 38*, 69–119.

Good, D. J., Lyddy, C. J., Glomb, T. M., Bono, J. E., Brown, K. W., Duffy, M. K., Baer, R. A., Brewer, J. A., & Lazar, S. W. (2015). Contemplating mindfulness at work: An integrative review. *Journal of Management, 42*(1), 114–142.

Gordon, A. M., Impett, E. A., Kogan, A., Oveis, C., & Keltner, D. (2012). To have and to hold: Gratitude promotes relationship maintenance in intimate bonds. *Journal of Personality and Social Psychology, 103*(2), 257–274.

Gottman, J. M., Murray, J. D., Swanson, C. C., Tyson, R., & Swanson, K. R. (2002). *The mathematics of marriage: Dynamic non-linear models*. MIT Press.

Gouveia, V. V., Vione, K. C., Milfont, T. L., and Fischer, R. (2015). Patterns of value change during the life span: Some evidence from a functional approach to values. *Personality and Social Psychology Bulletin, 41*(9), 1276–1290.

Graen, G. B., & Uhl-Bien, M. (1995). Relationship-based approach to leadership: Development of leader–member exchange (LMX) theory of leadership over 25 years: Applying a multilevel multi-domain perspective. *Leadership Quarterly, 6*, 219–247.

Grant, A. (2016). Personal communication.

Grant, A. M. (2007). Relational job design and the motivation to make a prosocial difference. *Academy of Management Review, 32*(2), 393–417.

Grant, A. M. (2012). Leading with meaning: Beneficiary contact, prosocial impact, and the performance effects of transformational leadership. *Academy of Management Journal, 55*(2), 458–476.

Grant, A. M., & Gino, F. (2010). A little thanks goes a long way: Explaining why gratitude expressions motivate prosocial behavior. *Journal of Personality and Social Psychology, 98*(6), 946–955.

Grant, A. M., & Hofmann, D. A. (2011). Outsourcing inspiration: The performance effects of ideological messages from leaders and beneficiaries. *Organizational Behavior and Human Decision Processes, 116*(2), 173–187.

Graßmann, C., & Schermuly, C. C. (2020). Understanding what drives the coaching working alliance: A systematic literature review and meta-analytic examination. *International Coaching Psychology Review, 15*(2), 99–118.

Graßmann, C., Schölmerich, F., & Schermuly, C. C. (2020). The relationship between working alliance and client outcomes in coaching: A meta-analysis. *Human Relations, 73*(1), 35–58.

Greenaway, K. H., Haslam, S. A., Cruwys, T., Branscombe, N. R., Ysseldyk, R., & Heldreth, C. (2015). From "we" to "me": Group identification enhances perceived personal control with consequences for health and well-being. *Journal of Personality and Social Psychology, 109*(1), 53–74.

Greene, C. M., Morgan, J. C., Traywick, L. S., & Mingo, C. A. (2017). Evaluation of a laughter-based exercise program on health and self-efficacy for exercise. *The Gerontologist, 57*(6), 1051–1061.

Greenwood, R., & Hinings, C. R. (1988). Organizational design types, tracks and the dynamics of strategic change. *Organization studies, 9*(3), 293–316.

Greenwood, R., & Hinings, C. R. (1996). Understanding radical organizational change: Bringing together the old and the new institutionalism. *The Academy of Management Review, 21*(4), 1022–1054. https://doi.org/10.2307/259163.

Griffin, M. A., Parker, S. K., & Mason, C. M. (2010). Leader vision and the development of adaptive and proactive performance: A longitudinal study. *Journal of Applied Psychology. 95*(1), 174–182.

Groopman, J. (2003). *The anatomy of hope: How people prevail in the face of illness.* Random House.

Guastello, S. J. (2007). Non-linear dynamics and leadership emergence. *Leadership Quarterly, 18*(4), 357–369.

Guastello, S. J. (2011). Leadership emergence in engineering design teams. *Nonlinear Dynamics, Psychology, and Life Sciences, 15*(1), 87–104.

Guo, J., Hu, X., Elliot, A. J., Marsh, H. W., Murayama, K., Basarkod, G., Parker, P. D., & Dicke, T. (2023). Mastery-approach goals: A large-scale cross-cultural analysis of antecedents and consequences. *Journal of Personality and Social Psychology, 125*(2), 397–420.

Hackman, J. R., & Oldham, G. R. (1980). *Work redesign.* Addison-Wesley.

Hackman, J. R., & Wageman, R. (2005). A theory of team coaching. *Academy of Management Review, 30* (2), 269–287.

Hackman, R. (2003). Learning more by crossing levels: evidence from airplanes, hospitals and orchestras. *Journal of Organizational Behavior. 24.* 905–922.

Hagen, E. E. (1962). *On the theory of social change: How economic growth begins.* Dorsey Press.

Halt Organization (2022). Divorce rate skyrocketed post Covid-19. . A surge in divorces during lockdown. Halt.org

Halverstadt, L. (2021, June 18). Downtown homelessness is nearing crisis level. *Voices of San Diego.* Downtown Homelessness Is 'Nearing the Crisis Level' | Voice of San Diego.

Hammer, M. & Champy, J. (1993). *Reengineering the corporation: Manifesto for business revolution.* Harper Business.

Handy, C. (1997). *The hungry spirit: Beyond capitalism: A quest for purpose in the modern world.* Hutchinson.

Hanson, R. & Hanson, F. (2018). *Resilient: How to grow an unshakable core of calm, strength, and happiness.* Harmony Press.

Hardin, E. E., & Lakin, J. L. (2009). The integrated self-discrepancy index: A reliable and valid measure of self-discrepancies. *Journal of Personality Assessment, 91*(3), 245–253.

Harkin, B., Webb, T. L., Chang, B. P., Prestwich, A., Conner, M., Kellar, I., Benn, Y., & Sheeran, P. (2016). Does monitoring goal progress promote goal attainment? A meta-analysis of the experimental evidence. *Psychological Bulletin, 142*(2), 198–229.

Harress, C. (2013, December 5). The sad end of Blockbuster Video: The onetime $5 billion company is being liquidated as competition from online giants Netflix and Hulu prove all too much for the iconic brand. *ibtimes.com* The sad end of blockbuster video: The onetime $5 billion company is being liquidated as competition from online giants Netflix And Hulu prove all too much for the iconic brand | IBTimes.

Harter, J. (2020). Historic drop in employee engagement follows record rise. *Gallup.* https://www.gallup.com/workplace/313313/historic-drop-employee-engagement-follows-record-rise.aspx.

Hartz, D. E. (2014). Within their control: Understanding how managers can influence workplace positivity and employee engagement. Unpublished doctoral dissertation, Case Western Reserve University.

Harvey, A. G., Callaway, C. A., Zieve, G. G., Gumport, N. B., & Armstrong, C. C. (2021). Applying the science of habit formation to evidence-based psychological treatments for mental illness. *Perspectives on Psychological Science, 17*(2), 572–589.

Haslam, S. A., & Reicher, S. (2006). Stressing the group: Social identity and the unfolding dynamics of responses to stress. *Journal of Applied Psychology, 91*(5), 1037–1052.

Hatfield, E., Cacioppo, J. T., & Rapson, R. L. (1994). *Emotional contagion.* Cambridge University Press.

Hawkins, J. L., Mercer, J., Thirlaway, K. J., & Clayton, D. A. (2013). "Doing" gardening and "being" at the allotment site: exploring the benefits of allotment gardening for stress reduction and healthy aging. *Ecopsychology, 5*(2), 110–125.

Haybron, D. M., & Tiberius, V. (2012). Normative foundations for well-being policy. *Papers on Economics and Evolution*, No. 1202. Max Planck Institute of Economics.

Hayes, A. M., Feldman, G. C., Beevers, C. G., Laurenceau, J. P., Cardaciotto, L. A., & Lewis-Smith, J. (2007). Discontinuities and cognitive changes in an exposure-based cognitive therapy for depression. *Journal of Consulting and Clinical Psychology, 75*(3), 409–421.

Hayes, A. M., Laurenceau, J. P., Feldman, G. C., Strauss, J. L., & Cardaciotto, L. A. (2007). Change is not always linear: The study of nonlinear and discontinuous patterns of change in psychotherapy. *Clinical Psychology Review, 27*, 715–723.

Hazy, J. K. & Boyatzis, R. E. (2015). Emotional contagion and protoorganizing in human dynamics. *Frontiers in Psychology*, 6. |http://dx.doi.org/10.3389/fpsyg.2015.00806.

Heaphy, E. D., & Dutton, J. E. (2008). Positive social interactions and the human body at work: Linking organizations and physiology. *Academy of Management Review, 33*, 137–162.

Heatherton, T. F., & Weinberger, J. L. (eds.) (1994). *Can personality change?* American Psychological Association.

Heidrich, S. M. (1999). Self-discrepancy across the life span. *Journal of Adult Development, 6*, 119–130.

Henderson, T. L., & Boje, D. M. (2016). *Organizational development and change theory: Managing fractal organizing processes.* Routledge.

Hennigan, A., O'Callaghan, R. M. & Kelly, A. M. (2007). Neurotrophins and their receptors: Roles in plasticity, neurodegeneration and neuroprotection. *Biochemical Society Transactions, 35*, 424–426.

Hershfield, H. E., & Bartels, D. M. (2018). The future self. In G. Oettingen, A. T. Sevincer, & P. M. Gollwitzer (eds.), *The psychology of thinking about the future* (pp. 89–109). Guilford Press.

Higgins, E. T. (1987). Self-discrepancy: A theory relating self and effect. *Psychological Review, 94*, 319–340.

Higgins, E. T. (1997). Beyond pleasure and pain. *American Psychologist, 52*(12), 1280–1300.

Higgins, E. T. (2006). Value from hedonic experience and engagement. *Psychological Review*, *113*(3), 439–460.

Higgins, E. T. (2015). Personal communication.

Higgins, E. T., Klein, R., & Strauman, T. (1985). Self-concept discrepancy theory: A psychological model for distinguishing among different aspects of depression and anxiety. *Social Cognition, 3*, 51–76.

Higgins, M. C., & Kram, K. E. 2001. Reconceptualizing mentoring at work: A developmental network perspective. *Academy of Management Review, 26*(2), 264–288.

Higgins, E. T., Tykocinski, O., & Vookles, J. (1990). Pat- terns of self-beliefs: The psychological significance of relations among the actual, ideal, ought, can, and future selves. In *Self-inference processes: The Ontario symposium vol. 6* (pp. 153–190). Lawrence Erlbaum.

Hikes, D. (2022a). Bike share programs history. A brief history of bike sharing. www.icebike.org.

Hikes, D. (2022b, September 23). The world's surprising top 8 bike share programs. www.icebike.org/bike- share-programs.

Hill, P. J., & Turiano, N. A. (2014). Purpose in life as a predictor of mortality across adulthood. *Psychological Science, 25*(7), 1482–1486. doi: 10.1177/0956797614531799.

Himelstein, L., & Forest, S. A. (1997, February 17).Breaking through: Wise up guys. *Business Week*, 64–70.

Hinn, D., & Kotte, S. (2021). Participating in coaching research? Attitudes of coaches toward coaching research and their impact upon research participation. *Consulting Psychology Journal: Practice and Research*. Advance online publication. http://dx.doi.org/10.1037/cpb0000200

Hitt, M. A., Beamish, P. W., Jackson, S. E., and Mathieu, J. E. (2007). Building theoretical and empirical bridges across levels: Multilevel research in management. *Academy of Management Journal, 50*(6), 1385–1399.

Hobfoll, S. E. (1989). Conservation of resources: A new attempt at conceptualizing stress. *American Psychologist, 44*, 513–524.

Hofstede, G. (1984). *Culture's consequences: International differences in work-related values, 2nd edition*. Sage.

Hogg, M. A. (2008). Social identity processes and the empowerment of followers. In R. E. Riggio, I. Chaleff, & J. Lipman-Blumen (eds.), *The art of followership: How great followers create great leaders and organizations* (pp. 267_276). Wiley.

Holbeche, L. 1996. Peer mentoring: The challenges and opportunities. *Career Development International, 1*(7), 24–27.

Holding, A. C., Moore, E., Moore, A., Verner-Filion, J., Ouellet-Morin, I., & Koestner, R. (2021). When goal pursuit gets hairy: A longitudinal goal study examining the role of controlled motivation and action crisis in predicting changes in hair cortisol, perceived stress, health and depression symptoms. *Clinical Psychological Science. 9*(6), 1214–1221.

Hollander, E. (1958). Conformity, status, and idiosyncrasy credit. *Psychological Review, 65*(2), 117–127.

Hopkins, C. H. (2009 [1951]). *History of the YMCA in North America*. (online edition Cambridge University Press, 2009). Association Press.

Howard, A. (2005). Personal communication.

Howard, A. (2006). Positive and negative emotional attractors and intentional change. *Journal of Management Development, 25*(7), 657–670.

Howard. A. (2009). A theoretical and empirical examination of positive and negative emotional attractors' impact on coaching intentional change. Unpublished doctoral dissertation, Case Western Reserve University.

Howard, A. (2015). Coaching to vision of mid-career dentists. *Frontiers in Psychology, 5*, 1335. doi: 10.3389/fpsyg.2014.01335.

Howard, A. R., & Coombe, D. (2006). National level intentional change: A story of two countries. *Journal of Management Development, 25*, 732–742.

Howard, V. (2017). The rise and fall of Sears. *Smithsonian Magazine.*

Hudson, N. W., & Fraley, R. C. (2015). Volitional personality trait change: Can people choose to change their personality traits? *Journal of Personality and Social Psychology, 109*(3), 490–507.

Huepe, D., & Salas, N. (2013). Fluid intelligence, social cognition, and perspective changing abilities as pointers of psychosocial adaptation. *Frontiers in Human Neuroscience, 7*, Article 287. https://doi.org/10.3389/fnhum.2013.00287.

Hughes, J. R., Keely, J., & Naud, S. (2004). Shape of the relapse curve and ling-term abstinence among untreated smokers. *Addiction, 99*, 29–38.

Hunt, W. A., Barnett, L. W., Walker, J., & Branch, I. G. (1971). Relapse rates in addiction programs. *Journal of Clinical Psychology, 27*(4), 455–456.

Iacoboni, M. (2009). Imitation, empathy, and mirror neurons. *Annual Review of Psychology, 60*, 653–670.

Ibarra, H. (1999). Provisional selves: Experimenting with image and identity in professional adaptation. *Administrative Science Quarterly, 44*(4), 764–791.

Ibarra, H., & Barbulescu, R. (2010). Identity as narrative: Prevalence, effectiveness, and consequences of narrative identity work in macro work role transitions. *Academy of Management Review, 35*(1), 135–154.

Ibarra, H. & Petriglieri, J. L. (2010). Identity work and play. *Journal of Organizational Change Management, 23*(1), 10–25.

Igic, I., Keller, A. C., Elfering, A., Tschan, F., Kalin, W., & Semmer, N. K. (2017). Ten-year trajectories of stressors and resources at work: Cumulative and chronic effects on health and well-being. *Journal of Applied Psychology, 102*(9), 1317–1343.

Inagaki, T. K., & Orehek, E. (2017). On the benefits of giving social support: When, why, and how support providers gain by caring for others. *Current Directions in Psychological Science, 26*(2), 109–113.

Insel, T. R. (1992). Oxytocin: A neuropeptide for affiliation: Evidence form behavioral, receptor autoradiographic, and comparative studies. *Psychoneuroendocrinology, 17*(1), 3–35.

Insel, T. R. (1997). A neurobiological basis of social attachment. *American Journal of Psychiatry. 154*, 726–735.

Inzlicht, M., Schmeichel, B. J., & Macrae, C. N. (2014). Why self-control seems (but may not be) limited. *Trends in Cognitive Sciences, 18*(3), 127–133.

Ito, T. A., Larsen, J. T., Smith, N. K., & Cacioppo, J. T. (1998). Negative information weighs more heavily on the brain: the negativity bias in evaluative categorizations. *Journal of Personality and Social Psychology, 75*(4), 887–900.

Jack, A. I. (in revision, 2024). The brain divides between "material" and "spiritual" forms of understanding. In D. Yaden, & Michiel van Elk (eds.). *The Oxford Handbook of Psychedelic, Religious, Spiritual, and Mystical Experiences* (online edn., Oxford Academic, 22 May 2024), https://doi.org/10.1093/oxfordhb/9780192844064.001.0001.

Jack, A. I. (2014). A scientific case for conceptual dualism: The problem of consciousness and the opposing domains hypothesis. In J. Knobe, T. Lombrozo, & S. Nichols (eds.), *Oxford studies in experimental philosophy (Vol. 1)*, (pp. 173–207). Oxford University Press.

Jack, A. I., Boyatzis, R. E., Khawaja, M. S., Passarelli, A. M., and Leckie, R. L. (2013). Visioning in the brain: An fMRI study of inspirational coaching and mentoring. *Social Neuroscience, 8*(4), 369–384.

Jack, A. I., Dawson, A. J., Begany, K. L., Leckie, R. L., Barry, K. P., Ciccia, A. H., & Snyder, A. Z. (2012). fMRI reveals reciprocal inhibition between social and physical cognitive domains. *NeuroImage, 66C*, 385–401.

Jack, A. I., Dawson, A. J., Norr, M. E. (2013). Seeing human: distinct and overlapping neural signatures associated with two forms of dehumanization. *Neuroimage, 79C*, 313–328.

Jack, A., Friedman, J., Boyatzis, R. E. & Taylor, S. (2016). Why do you believe in God? Relationships between religious belief, analytic thinking, mentalizing and moral concern. *PLOS One, 11*(3), 1–21.

Jack, A. I., Passarelli, A. M., & Boyatzis, R. E. (2023). When fixing problems kills personal development: fMRI reveals conflict between Real and Ideal selves. *Frontiers in Human Neuroscience. 17*, 1128209. doi: 10.3389/fnhum.2023.1128209.

Jaffee, S. R., Hanscombe, K. B., Haworth, C. M., Davis, O. S., & Plomin, R. (2012). Chaotic homes and children's disruptive behavior: A longitudinal cross-lagged twin study. *Psychological Science, 23*(6), 643–650. doi: 10.1177/0956797611431693. Epub 2012 Apr 30. PMID: 22547656; PMCID: PMC3494454.

Jaffe, S. (2019). The road not taken. *The New Republic.* June 24, 2019.

Jagger, M., Richards, K., Watts, C., and Wood, R. (2003). *According to the Rolling Stones.* Chronicle Books.

James, W. (1892). *Principles of psychology.* Henry Holt.

Janig W. (2006). *The integrative action of the autonomic nervous system.* Cambridge University Press.

Janig, W. & Habler, H-J. (1999). Organization of the autonomic nervous system: Structure and function. In O. Appendzeller (ed.), *Handbook of clinical neurology: The autonomic nervous system: Part I: Normal function* (pp. 1–52). Elsevier.

Jensen, A., Ryan, J., Jones, C, & Ackley, M. (2020, December 14). Two cities tried to fix homelessness; Only one succeeded. Cronkite News. https://cronkitenews.azpbs.org/howardcenter/caring-for-covid-homeless/stories/homeless-funding-housing-first.html.

Jóhannesson, H. (2012). Master plan for energy resources in Iceland. *IAIA 12 Conference Proceedings' Energy Future the Role of Impact Assessment 32nd Annual Meeting of the International Association for Impact Assessment 27 May–1 June 2012.* Centro de Congresso da Alfândega. www.iaia.org. Helgi Jóhannesson (iaia.org). doi:10.2316/P.2012.788-022. https://conferences.iaia.org/2012/pdf/uploadpapers/Final%20papers%20review%20process/Jóhannesson,%20Helgi.%20%20Master%20Plan%20for%20Energy%20Resources%20in%20Iceland.pdf.

Johnson, S. K., Garrison, L. L., Hernez- Broome, G., Fleenor, J. W., & Steed, J. L. (2012). Go for the goal(s): Relationship between goal setting and transfer of training following leadership development *Academy of Management Learning & Education, 11*(4), 555–569.

Jolicoeur, L. (2022, June 22). Boston homelessness unsheltered census shelter decrease. GHB News. https://www.wbur.org/news/2022/06/22/boston-homeless-unsheltered-census-shelters-decrease.

Joseph, P. E. (2020). *The sword and the shield: The revolutionary lives of Malcolm X and Martin Luther King, Jr.* Basic Books.

Juarez-Barco, I., & Ehasz, S. F. (in revision, 2024). How professors inspire student engagement: The importance of relational climate. *Frontiers in Psychology.*

Kahn, W. A. 2007. Meaningful connections: Positive relationships and attachments at work. In J. E. Dutton & B. R. Ragins (eds.), *Exploring positive relationships at work: Building a theoretical and research foundation* (pp. 189–206). Lawrence Erlbaum.

Kahneman, D. (2011). *Thinking, fast and slow.* Macmillan.

Kanfer, F. H., & Goldstein, A. P. (eds.). (1991). *Helping people change: A textbook of methods, 4th edition.* Allyn and Bacon.

Kang, Y., Cooper, N., Pandey, P., Scholz, C., O'Donnell, M. B., Lieberman, M. D., Taylor, S. E., Strecher, V. J., Dal Cin, S., Konrath, S., Polk, T. A., Resnicow, K., An, L., & Falk, E. B. (2018). Effects of self-transcendence on neural responses to persuasive messages and health behavior change. *PNAS Proceedings of the National Academy of Sciences of the United States of America, 115*(40), 9974–9979.

Kanov, J. M., Maitlis, S., Worline, M. C., Dutton, J. E., Frost, P. J., & Lilius, J. M. 2004. Compassion in organizational life. *American Behavioral Scientist, 47*(6), 808–827.

Kantabutra, S., & Avery, G. C. (2010). The power of vision: Statements that resonate. *Journal of Business Strategy, 31*(1), 37–45.

Kaplan, S., Bradley, J. C., Luchman, J. N., & Haynes, D. (2009). On the role of positive and negative affectivity in job performance: A meta-analytic investigation. *Journal of Applied Psychology, 94*(1), 162–176.

Kashdan, T. B., Goodman, F. R., McKnight, P. E., Brown, B., & Rum, R. (2023). Purpose in life: A resolution on the definition, conceptual model, and optimal measurement. *American Psychologist.* Advance online publication. https://doi.org/10.1037/amp0001223.

Kashdan, T. B., and McKnight, P. E. (2009). Origins of purpose in life: Refining our understanding of a life well lived. *Psihologijske teme, 18*(2), 303–313.

Katz, B. & Nowak, J. (2017). *The new localism: How cities can thrive in the age of populism.* Brookings Institution Press.

Kauffman, S. (1995). *At home in the universe: The search for laws of self-organization and complexity.* Oxford University Press.

Kayes, D. C. (2006). *Destructive goal pursuit: The Mt. Everest disaster.* Palgrave Macmillan.

Keashly, L. (1997). Emotional abuse in the workplace: Conceptual and empirical issues. *Journal of Emotional Abuse, 1*(1), 85–117.

Kegan, R., & Lahey, L. L. (2009). *Immunity to change.* Harvard Business Review Press.

Kelman, H. C. (1961). Processes of opinion change. *Public Opinion Quarterly, 25*, 57–78.

Kelner, S. P. Jr. (1990). *Interpersonal motivation: Positive, cynical, and anxious.* Unpublished doctoral dissertation, Boston University.

Kelner, S. P. Jr. (2015). Personal communication.

Kemp, A. H., & Guastella, A. J. (2011). The role of oxytocin in human affect: A novel hypothesis. *Current Directions in Psychological Science, 20*(4), 222–231.

Kendall, L. (2016). A theory of micro-level dynamic capabilities: How technology leaders innovate with human connection. Unpublished doctoral dissertation, Case Western Reserve University.

Kennedy, J., Eberhart, R. C., & Shi, Y. (2001). *Swarm intelligence.* Morgan Kaufman Publishers.

Kensinger, E. A. (2007). Negative emotion enhances memory accuracy behavioral and neuro-imaging evidence. *Current Directions in Psychological Science, 16*(4), 213–218.

Keomoungkhoun, N. (2021, August 27). Thanks to this woman, Houston is a leader in housing the homeless. Here's what Dallas can learn. *Dallas News.* https://www.dallasnews.com/news/2021/08/27/thanks-to-this-woman-houston-is-a-leader-in-housing-the-homeless-heres-what-dallas-can-learn/.

Khawaja, M. (2010). The mediating role of positive and negative emotional attractors between psychosocial correlates of doctor-patient relationship and treatment of Type II diabetes. Unpublished doctoral dissertation, Case Western Reserve University.

Kim, E. S., Delany, S. W., & Kubzansky, L. D. (2019). Sense of purpose in life and cardiovascular disease: Underling mechanism and future directions. *Current Cardiology Reports* 21(I11), Article 135. doi: 10.1007/s11886-019-1222-9.

Kim, S., Cho, S., & Park, Y. (2022). Daily microbreaks in a self-regulatory resources lens: Perceived health climate as a contextual moderator via microbreak autonomy. *Journal of Applied Psychology, 107*(1), 60–77.

Kim, S., Park, Y., & Headrick, L. (2018). Daily micro-breaks and job performance: General work engagement as a cross level moderator. *Journal of Applied Psychology, 103*(7), 772–786.

Kim, Y.-H., Chiu, C.-y., & Zou, Z. (2010). Know thyself: Misperceptions of actual performance undermine achievement motivation, future performance, and subjective well-being. *Journal of Personality and Social Psychology, 99*(3), 395–409.

King, M. L. (1963). *"I have a dream": A call to conscience: The landmark speeches of Dr. Martin Luther King, Jr.* Available at http://www.standord.edu/group/King/speeches/address_at_march_on_Washington.pdf.

Kingsbury, L., Huang, S., Wang, J., Gu, K., Golshani, P., Wu, Y. E., & Hong, W. (2019). Correlated neural activity and encoding of behavior across brains of socially interacting animals. *Cell*, *178*(2), 429–446.

Kitayama, S., Berg, M. K., and Chopik, W. J. (2020). Culture and well-being in late adulthood: Theory and evidence. *American Psychologist*, *75*(4), 567–576. doi: 10.1037/amp0000614.

Klein, K. J., Dansereau, F., & Hall, R. J. (1994). Levels issues in theory development, data collection, and analysis. *Academy of Management Review*, *19*(2), 195–229.

Klein, H. J., Wesson, M. J., Hollenbeck, J. R., & Alge, B. J. (1999). Goal commitment and the goal setting process: Conceptual clarification and empirical synthesis. *Journal of Applied Psychology*. *84*(6), 885–896.

Klimchouk, A. (2005, May). Call of the abyss. *National Geographic*, pp. 70–85.

Knowlton, B. J., Mangels, J. A., & Squire, L. R. (1996). A neostratial habit learning system in humans. *Science*, *273* (1996), 1399–1402.

Koenig, H. G. (2012). Religion, spirituality and health: The research and clinical implications. *ISRN Psychiatry*, 278730.

Kok, B. E., Coffey, K. A., Cohn, M. A., Catalino, L. I., Vacharkulksemsuk, T., Algoe, S. B., Brantley, M., & Fredrickson, B. L. (2013). How positive emotions build physical health: perceived positive social connections account for the upward spiral between positive emotions and vagal tone. *Psychological Science*, *24*(7), 1123–1132.

Kok, B. E., & Fredrickson, B. L. (2010). Upward spirals of the heart: Autonomic flexibility, as indexed by vagal tone, reciprocally and prospectively predicts positive emotions and social connectedness. *Biological Psychology*, *85*, 432–436.

Kolb, D. A. (1984). *Experiential learning: Experience as the source of learning and development*. Prentice-Hall.

Kolb, D. A. (2014). *Experiential learning: Experience as the source of learning and development, 2nd edition*. Pearson Education.

Kolb, D. A., & Boyatzis, R. E. (1970a). Goal setting and self-directed behavior change. *Human Relations*, *23*(5), 439–457.

Kolb, D. A., & Boyatzis, R. E. (1970b). On the dynamics of the helping relationship. *Journal of Applied Behavioral Science, 6*(3), 267–290.

Kooij, D. T. A. M., Kanfer, R., Betts, M., & Rudolph, C. W. (2018). Future time perspective: A systematic review and meta-analysis. *Journal of Applied Psychology*, *103*(8), 867–893.

Koopman, J., Lanaj, K., Lee, Y. E., Alterman, V., Bradley, C., & Stoverink, A. C. (2022). Walking on eggshells: A self-control perspective on workplace political correctness. *Journal of Applied Psychology*, *108*(3), 425–445.

Kosfeld, M., Neinrichs, M. Zak, P. J., Fischbacher, U. & Fehr, E. (2005). Oxytocin increases trust in humans. *Nature, 435*, 673–676.

Koslowsky, M., Kluger, A. N., & Reich, M. (2013). *Commuting stress: Causes, effects, and methods of coping*. Springer Science & Business Media.

Kotter, J. (1995). Leading change: Why transformation efforts fail. *Harvard Business Review, 73* (2), 59–67.

Kozinn, A. (1995). *The Beatles*. Phaidon Press.

Krakauer, J. (1997). *Into thin air*. Anchor Books.

Dobrow, S. R., Chandler, D. E., Murphy, W. M., & Kram, K. E. (2012). A Review of Developmental Networks: Incorporating a Mutuality Perspective. *Journal of Management*, *38*(1), 210–242. https://doi.org/10.1177/0149206311415858

Kram, K. E., & Hall, D. T. (1989). Mentoring as an antidote to stress during corporate trauma. *Human Resource Management*, *28*(4), 493–510.

Kreiman, G., Koch, C. & Fried, I. (2000). Imagery neurons in the human brain, *Nature, 408*, 357–361

Kross, E., Verduyn, P., Demiralp, E., Park, J., Lee, D. S., Lin, N., Shablack, H., Jonides, J., & Ybarra, O. (2013). Facebook use predicts declines in subjective well-being in young adults. *PLOS One*, *8*(8), e69841. doi: 10.1371/journal.pone.0069841.

Krueger, J. I., Baumeister, R. F., & Vohs, K. D. (2022). Feeling good without doing good: Comment on Orth and Robins. *American Psychologist*, *77*(1), 18–19.

Kubit, B., & Jack, A. I. (2013). Rethinking the role of the rTPJ in attention and social cognition in light of the opposing domains hypothesis: Findings from an ALE-based meta-analysis and resting-state functional connectivity. *Frontiers in Human Neuroscience*, 7. https://doi.org/10.3389/fnhum.2013.00323.

Kubzansky, L. D., Sparrow, D., Vokonas, P., & Kawachi, I. (2001). Is the glass half empty or half full? A prospective study of optimism and coronary heart disease in the normative aging study. *Psychosomatic Medicine*, *63*, 910–916.

Kulik, A., Desai, N. R., Shrank, W. H., Antman, E. M., Glynn, R. J., Levin, R., Reisman, L., Brennan, T. A., & Choudhry, N. K. (2013). Full prescription coverage versus usual prescription coverage after coronary artery bypass graft surgery: Analysis from the post-myocardial infarction free rx events and economic evaluation (FREE) randomized trial. *Circulation*, *128*, S219–S225.

Ladge, J. J., Clair, J. A., and Greenberg, D. (2012). Cross-domain identity transition during liminal periods: Constructing multiple selves as professional and mother during pregnancy. *Academy of Management Journal*, *55*(6), 1449–1471.

Laff, M. (2007). Women receive less coaching. *Training and Development*, *61*, 18.

Lally, P., Van Jaarsveld, C. H., Potts, H. W., & Wardle, J. (2010). How are habits formed: Modelling habit formation in the real world. *European Journal of Social Psychology*, *40*(6), 998–1009.

Lambert, B., Caza, B. B., Tirnh, E., & Ashford, S. (2020). Individual centered interventions: Identifying what, how and why interventions work in organizational contexts. *Academy of Management Annals*, *16*(2), 508–546. https://doi.org/10.5465/annals.2020.0351

Lapp, C. A., Taft, L. B., Tollefson, T., Hoepner, A., Moore, K., & Divyak, K. (2010). Stress and coping on the home front: Guard and reserve spouses searching for a new normal. *Journal of Family Nursing*, *16*(1), 45–67.

Larsen, J. T., McGraw, A. P. & Cacioppo, J. T. (2001). Can people feel happy and sad at the same time? *Journal of Personality and Social Psychology*, *81*(4), 684–696.

Latham, G. P., & Saari, L. M. (1979). Application of social learning theory to training supervisors through behavioral modeling. *Journal of Applied Psychology*. *64*(3), 239–246.

Latham, G. P., & Seijts, G. H. (2016). Distinguished scholar invited essay: Similarities and differences among performance, behavioral and learning goals. *Journal of Leadership and Organizational Studies*. *23*(3), 225–233.

Lautarescu, A., Craig, M. C., Glover, V. (2019). Prenatal stress: Effects on fetal and child brain development. *International Review of Neurobiology*, *150*, 17–40.

Lawrence, P. & Lorsch, J. (1967). *Organization and environment*. Harvard Business School Press.

Lazarus, R. L. (1991). Cognition and motivation in emotion. *American Psychologist*, *45*(4), 352–367.

Leah, J. (2024). Translating purpose and mindset into positive impact through shared vision, compassion and energy: A comparative study of seven organizations. *Frontiers in Psychology*. 15. https://doi.org/10.3389/fpsyg.2024.1251256

LeDoux, J. (2002). *Synaptic self: How our brains become who we are*. Viking.

Le Duff, C. (2002, February 21). A pile of medals for a positive thinker. *New York Times*, C–17.

Lenz, T. (1998). Neighborhood development: Issues and models. *Social Policy*, *18*(4), 24–30.

Leonard, D. C. (2008). The impact of learning goals on emotional, social, and cognitive intelligence competency development. *Journal of Management Development*, *27*(1), 109–128.

Levenson, R. W. (1992). Autonomic nervous system differences among emotions. *Psychological Science*, *3*(1), 23–27.

Levinson, D. J., Darrow, C. N., Klein, E. B., Levinson, M. H., and McKee, B. (1978). *The seasons of a man's life.* Knopf.

Lewin, K. (1947). Frontiers in group dynamics: Concept, method and reality in social science; equilibrium and social change. *Human Relations,* 1(1), 5–41.

Lewin, A. Y., & Zwany, A. (1976). *Peer nominations: A model, literature critique and a paradigm for research.* National Technical Information Service. Also appeared as Lewin, A. Y., & Zwany, A. (1976). Peer nominations: A model, literature critique and a paradigm for research, *Personnel Psychology, 29,* 423–447.

Lewin, K., Dembo, T., Festinger, L. & Sears, P. S. (1944). Level of aspiration. In J. McV Hunt (ed.), *Personality and behavior disorders* (pp. 333–378). Ronald Press.

Lewis, T., Amini, F., & Lannon, R. (2000). *A general theory of love.* Random House.

Li, S., Krackhardt, D., & Niezink, N. M. D. (2023, January 12). Do your friends stress you out? A field study of the spread of stress through a community network. *Journal of Personality and Social Psychology.* Advance online publication. https://dx.doi.org/10.1037/pspi 0000415.

Lichtenstein, B. B. (2018). Applying the 15 complexity sciences: Methods for studying emergence in organizations. In *Handbook of research methods in complexity science,* (pp. 65–105). Edward Elgar Publishing. doi:10.4337/9781785364426.00037.

Lichtenstein, B. B. (2000). Self-organized transitions: A pattern amid the chaos of transformative change. *Academy of Management Executive, 14*(4), 128–141.

Lieberman, M. D. (2013). *Social: Why our brains are wired to connect.* Crown.

Likert. R. (1967). *The human organization.* McGraw Hill.

Lin, S. H., & Johnson, R. E. (2015). A suggestion to improve a day keeps your depletion away: Examining promotive and prohibitive voice behaviors within a regulatory focus and ego depletion framework. *Journal of Applied Psychology, 100*(5), 1381–1397.

Lindblom, C. E. (1959). The science of "muddling through." *Public Administration Review, 19,* 79–88.

Lippitt, R., Watson, J., & Westly, R. (1958). *The dynamics of planned change.* Harcourt, Brace & World.

Litwin, G. H. & Stringer, R. A., Jr. (1968). *Motivation and organizational climate.* Harvard Business School Press.

Locke, E. A., and Latham, G. P. (1990). *A theory of goal setting and task performance.* Prentice Hall.

Locke, E. A., & Latham, G. P. (2002). Building a practically useful theory of goal setting and task motivation: A 35-year odyssey. *American Psychologist, 57,* 705–717.

Locke, E. A., & Latham, G. P. (2006). New directions in goal-setting theory. *Current Directions in Psychological Science, 15*(5), 265–268.

Locke, E. A., & Latham, G. P. (2009). Has goal setting gone wile or have its attackers abandoned good scholarship? *Academy of Management Perspectives, 23*(1), 17–23.

Locke, E. A., & Latham, G. P. (eds.). (2013). *New developments in goal setting and task performance.* Routledge/Taylor & Francis Group.

Locke, E. A., Shaw, K. N., Saari, L. M., & Latham, G. P. (1981). Goal setting and task performance: 1969–1980. *Psychological Bulletin, 90*(1), 125–152.

Lockwood, P. L., Abdurahman, A., Gabay, A. S., Drew, D., Tamm, M., Husain, M., & Apps, M. A. J. (2021). Aging increases prosocial motivation for effort. *Psychological Science, 32*(5), 668–681. https://doi.org/10.1177/0956797620975781.

Loehr, J., & Schwartz, T. (2001). The making of the corporate athlete. *Harvard Business Review.*

Loehr, J., and Schwartz, T. (2003). *The power of full engagement: Managing energy, not time, is the key to high performance and personal renewal.* Free Press.

Lord, M. (2015). The role of shared vision and a learning culture on committee effectiveness. *Frontiers in Psychology, 5,* 1335. doi: 10.3389/fpsyg.2014.01335.

Lord, R. (2008). Followers' cognitive and affective structures and leadership processes. In R. E. Riggio, I. Chaleff, & J. Lipman-Blumen, *The art of followership: How great followers create great leaders and organizations* (pp. 255–266). Wiley.

Lorenz, E. N. (1963). Deterministic non-periodic flow. *Journal of the Atmospheric Sciences, 20*(2), 130–141.

Luce, M. F., Bettman, J. R., & Payne, J. W. (1997). Choice processing in emotionally difficult decisions. *Journal of Experimental Psychology: Learning, Memory, and Cognition, 23*(2), 384–405. doi:10.1037//0278-7393.23.2.384.

Ludwig, V. U., Brown, K. W., & Brewer, J. A. (2020). Self-regulation without force: Can awareness leverage reward to drive behavior change? *Perspectives in Psychological Science, 15*(6), 1382–1399. doi: 10.1177/1745691620931460.

Lunceford, G. (2017). What is retirement in the 21st century. Unpublished doctoral dissertation, Case Western Reserve University.

Luthans, F., Hodgetts, R. M., & Rosenkrantz, S. A. (1988). *Real managers.* Ballinger Press.

Lyon, A. (2014). Why are normal distributions normal? *British Journal for the Philosophy of Science, 65*(3), 621–649.

Lyubomirsky, S., Sheldon, K. M, & Schkade, D. (2005). Pursuing happiness: The architecture of sustainable change. *Review of General Psychology, 9*(2), 111–131.

Mackenzie, A. (2005). The problem of the attractor: A singular generality between sciences and social theory. *Theory, Culture & Society, 22*(5), 45–65.

Macnamara, B. N., Moreau, D., & Hambrick, D. Z. (2016). The relationship between deliberate practice and performance in sports: A meta-analysis. *Perspectives on Psychological Science, 11*(3), 333–350.

Macy, M. W., & Willer, R. (2002). From factors to actors: Computational sociology and agent-based modeling. *Annual Review of Sociology, 28*(1), 143–166.

Maddi, S. R. (1969–2004). *Personality theories: A comparative analysis, 1st–6th editions.* Dorsey Press.

Magnuson, C. D., & Barnett, L. A. (2013). The playful advantage: How playfulness enhances coping with stress. *Leisure Sciences, 35*(2), 129–144.

Maguire, E. A., Gadian, D. G., Johnsrude, I. S., Good, C. D., Ashburner, J., Frackowiak, R. S. J., & Firth, C. D. (2000). *Proceedings of the National Academy of Sciences.*

Mahon, E., Taylor, S., & Boyatzis, R. (2014). Antecedents of organizational engagement: exploring vision, mood and perceived organizational support with emotional intelligence as a moderator. *Frontiers in Psychology, 5*, 1322. 10.3389/fpsyg.2014.01322.

Mahoney, J. L., Weissberg, R. P., Greenberg, M. T., Dusenbury, L., Jagers, R. J., Niemi, K., Schlinger, M., Schlund, J., Shriver, T. P., VanAusdal, K., & Yoder, N. (2021). Systemic social and emotional learning: Promoting educational success for all preschool to high school students. *American Psychologist, 76*(7), 1128–1142.

Mahony, D. L., Burroughs, W. J., & Lippman, L. G. (2002). Perceived attributes of health-promoting laughter: A cross-generational comparison. *Journal of Psychology: Interdisciplinary and Applied, 136*(2), 171–181.

Mainemelis, C. (2010). Stealing fire: Creative deviance in the evolution of new ideas. *Academy of Management Review, 35*(4), 558–578.

Mainemelis, C., & Ronson, S. (2006). Ideas are born in fields of play: Towards a theory of play and creativity in organizational settings. *Research in Organizational Behavior, 27*, 81– 131.

Maister, L., De Beukelaer, S., Longo, M. R., & Tsakiris, M. (2021). The self in the mind's eye: Revealing how we truly see ourselves through reverse correlation. *Psychological Science, 32*(12), 1965–1978.

Malacrida, C., and Boulton, T. (2012). Women's perceptions of childbirth "choices" competing discourses of motherhood, sexuality, and selflessness. *Gender and Society, 26*(5), 748–772.

Mallaby, S. (2022). *The power law: Venture capital and the making of the new future.* Penguin.

Mandela, N. (1994). *Statement of the president of the African National Congress, Nelson Rolihlahla Mandela, at his inauguration as president of the Democratic Republic of South Africa.* http://www.anc.org.za/ancdocs/speeches/inaugpta.html.

Mandelbrot, B. B., & Hudson, R. L. (2008). *The mis(behaviour) of markets: A fractal view of risk, ruin, and reward.* Profile Books.

Manniz, L., Chadukar, R., Rybicki, L., Tusek, D., and Solomon, O. (1999). The effect of guided imagery on quality of life for patients with chronic tension-type headaches. *Headache: Journal of Head and Face Pain, 39,* 326–324.

Mangelsdorf, J., Eid, M. & Luhmann, M. (2018). Does growth require suffering? A systemic review and meta-analysis on genuine posttraumatic and postecstatic growth. *Psychological Bulletin.* 145(3), 302–338.

Manpower. (2016). *Millennial careers: 2020 vision* surveying 19,000 Millennials from 25 countries. www.manpowergroup.co.uk/wp-content/uploads/2016/05/MillennialsPaper1_2020Vision.pdf.

Marci, C. D., Ham, J., Moran, E. K., & Orr, S. P. (2007). Physiologic correlates of perceived therapist empathy and social-emotional process during psychotherapy. *Journal of Nervous and Mental Disease, 195,* 103–111.

Marek, S., & Dosenbach, N. (2018). The frontoparietal network: Function, electrophysiology, and importance of individual precision mapping. *Dialogues in clinical neuroscience, 20*(2), 133–140.

Marien, H., Custers, R., Hassin, R. R., & Aarts, H. (2012, June 11). Unconscious goal activation and the hijacking of the executive function. *Journal of Personality and Social Psychology.* Advance online publication. doi: 10.1037/a0028955.

Marion, R. (1999). *The edge of organization: Chaos and complexity theories of formal social systems.* Sage.

Marion, R., & Uhl-Bien, M. (2001). Leadership in complex organizations. *Leadership Quarterly, 12*(4), 389–418.

Markus, H., and Nurius, P. (1986). Possible selves. *American Psychologist, 41*(9), 954.

Mars, R. B., Neubert, F. X., Noonan, M. P., Sallet, J., Toni, I., Rushworth, M. F. (2012). On the relationship between the "default mode network" and the "social brain." *Frontiers in Human Neuroscience,* 6. doi: 10.3389/fnhum.2012.00189.

Martinez, H. (2016). *Inspired and effective: The role of the Ideal Self in employee engagement, well being, and positive organizational behaviors.* Unpublished doctoral dissertation, Case Western Reserve University

Martinez, H., Rochford, K., Boyatzis, R., & Rodriguez, S. (2021). Inspired and effective: The role of the Ideal Self in employee engagement, well-being, and positive organizational behaviors. *Frontiers in Psychology 12.* doi: 10.3389/fpsyg.2021.662386.

Maslow, A. H. (1943). A theory of human motivation. *Psychological Review, 50*(4), 370–396.

Maslow, A. H. (1968). *Toward a psychology of being.* Van Nostrand.

Matheny, A. P., Wachs, T. D., Ludwig, J. L., & Phillips, K. (1995). Bringing order out of chaos: Psychometric characteristics of the confusion, hubbub, and order scale. *Journal of Applied Developmental Psychology, 16*(3), 429–444.

Matthews, S. C., Paulus, M. P., Simmons, A. N., Nelesen, R. A., & Dimsdale, J. E. (2004). Functional subdivisions within anterior cingulate cortex and their relationship to autonomic nervous system function. *Neuroimage, 22*(3), 1151–1156.

Matusky, R. (2023). Lean and agile. In B. J. Flores (ed.), *ATD's organization development handbook* (pp. 105–120). ATD Press.

Mayer, J. D., Salovey, P., & Caruso, D. R. (2000). Emotional intelligence meets traditional standards for an intelligence. *Intelligence, 27*(4), 267–298.

McAdams, D. P., & Constantian, C. A. (1983). Intimacy and affiliation motives in daily living: An experience sampling analysis. *Journal of Personality & Social Psychology, 45*(4), 851–861.

McBer & Company. (1985). *Command effectiveness: What it takes to be the best.* Unpublished research report to the US Naval Military Personnel Command.

McCall, A., Wolfberg, A., Ivarsson, A., Dupont, G., Larocque, A., & Bilsborough, J. (2023). A qualitative study of 11 world-class team-sport athletes' experiences answering subjective questionnaires: A key ingredient for "visible" health and performance monitoring? *Sports Medicine, 53*, 1085–1100.

McCaskey, M. (1974). A contingency approach to planning: Planning with goals and planning without goals. *Academy of Management Journal, 17*(2), 281–291.

McCaskey, M. (1977). Goals and direction in personal planning. *Academy of Management Review, 2*(3), 454–462.

McClelland, D. C. (1951). *Personality.* William Sloane Associates.

McClelland, D. C. (1961). *The achieving society.* Van Nostrand.

McClelland, D. C. (1965). Toward a theory of motive acquisition. *American Psychologist, 20*(5), 321–333.

McClelland, D. C. (1973). Testing for competence rather than intelligence. *American Psychologist, 28*(1), 1–40.

McClelland, D. C. (1975). *Power: The inner experience.* Irvington Press.

McClelland, D. C. (1985). *Human motivation.* Cambridge University Press.

McClelland, D. C. (1998). Identifying competencies with behavioral event interviews. *Psychological Science, 9*, 331–339.

McClelland, D. C., Atkinson, J. W., Clark, R. A., and Lowell, E. L. (1953). *The achievement motive.* Appleton-Century-Crofts.

McClelland, D. C., Baldwin, A. L., Bronfenbrenner, U., & Strodtbeck, F. L. (1958). *Talent and society: New perspectives in the identification of talent.* Van Nostrand.

McClelland, D. C., & Boyatzis, R. E. (1982). The leadership motive pattern and long-term success in management. *Journal of Applied Psychology, 67*(6), 737–743.

McClelland, D. C., Floor, E., Davidson, R. J., & Saron, C. (1980), Stressed power motivation, sympathetic activation, immune function, and illness. *Journal of Human Stress, 67,* 737–743.

McClelland, D. C., & Winter, D. G. (1969). *Motivating economic achievement.* Free Press.

McCrae, R. R., & Costa, P. T. (2008). The five-factor theory of personality. In O. P. John, R. W. Robins, & L. A. Pervin (eds.), *Handbook of personality: Theory and research, 3rd edition* (pp. 150–181). Guilford Press.

McEwen, B. S. (1998). Protective and damaging effects of stress mediators. *New England Journal of Medicine, 338*, 171–179.

McGregor, D. (1960). *The human side of enterprise.* McGraw Hill.

McIntyre, K. P., Korn, J. H., & Matsuo, H. (2008). Sweating the small stuff: How different types of hassles result in the experience of stress. *Stress and Health: Journal of the International Society for the Investigation of Stress, 24*(5), 383–392.

McKee, A. (1991). *Individual differences in planning for the future.* Unpublished doctoral Dissertation, Case Western Reserve University.

McKee, A., Boyatzis, R. E. & Johnston, F. (2008). *Becoming a resonant leader: Develop your emotional intelligence, renew your relationships, sustain your effectiveness.* Harvard Business School Press.

McKenna, S. (2016). Highclere Castle: The real-life Downton Abbey. *The Sydney Morning Herald.*

Meek, M. (2004). *Online Extra: Racing to the Center of the Earth.* National Geographic, February. http://ngm.nationalgeographic.com/ngm/0402/online_extra.html.

Meister, I., Krings, T., Foltys, H., Boroojerdi, B., Muller, M., Topper, R., & Thron, A. (2004). Playing the piano in the mind: An fMRI study on music imagery and performance in pianists. *Cognitive Brain Research, 19*(3), 219–228.

Meleady, R., & Crisp, R. J. (2017). Take it to the top: Imagined interactions with leaders elevates organizational identification. *Leadership Quarterly, 28* (5), 621–638.

Menon, V., & D'Esposito, M. (2022). The role of PFC networks in cognitive control and executive function. *Neuropsychopharmacology, 47*(1), 90–103.

Mentkowski, M. & Associates. (2000). *Learning that lasts: Integrating learning, development, and performance in college and beyond.* Jossey-Bass.

Meyer, M. W., & Zucker, L. G. (1989). *Permanently failing organizations.* Sage.

Meijman, T. F., & Mulder, G. (1998). Psychological aspects of workload. In P. J. D. Drenth, H. Thierry, & C. J. de Wolff (eds.), *Handbook of work and organizational psychology: Work psychology vol. 2* (pp. 5–33). Psychology Press.

Mentkowski, M. (2000). *Learning that lasts: Integrating learning, development, and performance in college and beyond.* Jossey-Bass.

Merton, R. K. (1968). *Social theory and social structure.* Free Press.

Michel, J., Owens, E. H., Zengel, S., Graham, A., Nixon, Z., Allard, T., Holton, W., Reimer, P. D., Lamarche, A., White, M., Rutherford, N., Childs, C., Mauseth, G., Challenger, G., & Taylor, E. (2013). Extent and degree of shoreline oiling: *Deepwater Horizon* oil spill, Gulf of Mexico, USA. *PLOS One , 8*(6), e65087. https://doi.org/10.1371/journal.pone.0065087.

Mikulincer, M., & Shaver, P. R. (2007). *Attachment in adulthood: Structure, dynamics, and change.* Guilford Press.

Milkman, K. (2021). *How to change: The science of getting from where you are to where you want to be.* Penguin.

Miller, J. G. (1978). *Kiving Systems Theory: Biuological systems and Social Systems.* McGraw Hill.

Miller, J.G. (1995). Living Systems. Boulder, CO: University of Colorado Press.

Miller, S. C., Kennedy, C. C., DeVoe, D. C., Hickey, M., Nelson, T., & Kogan, L. (2009). An examination of changes in oxytocin levels in men and women before and after interaction with a bonded dog. *Anthrozoös, 22*(1), 31–42.

Miller, S. P. (2014). Next-generation leadership development in family businesses: The critical roles of shared vision and family climate. *Frontiers in Psychology, 5*, 1335. doi:10.3389/fpsyg.2014.01335.

Miller, S. P. (2023). Family climate influences next generation family business leader effectiveness and work engagement. *Frontiers in Psychology, 14.* https://doi.org/10.3389/fpsyg.2023.1110282

Miller, W. R., & C'de Baca, J. (2001). *Quantum change: When epiphanies and sudden insights transform ordinary lives.* Guilford Press.

Ming, D., Chen, Q., Yang, W., Chen, R., Wei, D., Li, W., Qiu, J., Xu, Z. & Zhang, Q. (2015). Examining brain structures associated with the motive to achieve success and the motive to avoid failure: A voxel-based morphometry study. *Social Neuroscience.* doi: 10.1080/17470919.2015.1034377.

Ministry of Industries and Innovation. (2009). Icelandic National Renewable Energy Action Plan for the promotion of the use of energy from renewable sources in accordance with Directive 2009/28/EC and the Commission Decision of 30 June 2009 on a template for the national renewable energy action plans. Ministry of Industries and Innovation. http://www.atvinnuvegaraduneyti.is/media/Skyrslur/NREAP.pdf.

Miron, D., & McClelland, D. C. (1979). The impact of achievement motivation training on small business. *California Management Review, 21*(4), 13–28.

Mogilner, C., Aaker, J. L., & Pennington, G. L. (2008). Time will tell: The distant appeal of promotion and imminent appeal of prevention. *Journal of Consumer Research, 34*(5), 670–681.

Montagne, R. (2014, January 24). Drowning in debt, bike sharing Bixi files for bankruptcy. NPR Morning Edition.

Montijin, N. D., Gerritsen, L., & Englehard, I. M. (2021). Forgetting the future: Emotional improves memory for imagined future events in healthy individuals but not individuals with anxiety. *Psychological Science, 32*(4), 587–597. doi: 10.1177/0956797620972491.

Moretti, M. M., & Higgins, E. T. (1990). Relating self-discrepancy to self-esteem: The contribution of discrepancy beyond actual-self ratings. *Journal of Experimental Social Psychology, 26*(2), 108–123.

Morris, J. H., & Koch, J. L. (1979). Impacts of role perceptions on organizational commitment, job involvement, and psychosomatic illness among three vocational groupings. *Journal of Vocational Behavior, 14*(1), 88–101.

Morrow, C. C., Jarrett, M. Q., & Rupinski, M. T. (1997). An investigation of the effect and economic utility of corporate-wide training. *Personnel Psychology, 50,* 91–119.

Mosing, M. A., Madison, G., Pedersen, N. L., Kuja-Halkola, R., & Ullén, F. (2014). Practice does not make perfect: No causal effect of music practice on music ability. *Psychological Science, 25*(9), 1795–1803.

Mosteo, L. P., Batista-Foguet, J. M., McKeever, J. D., & Serlavos, R. (2016). Understanding cognitive-emotional processing through a coaching process: The influence of coaching on vision, goal-directed energy, and resilience. *Journal of Applied Behavioral Science, 52*(1), 64–96.

Motowidlo, S. J., Packard, J. S., & Manning, M. R. (1986). Occupational stress: Its causes and consequences for job performance. *Journal of Applied Psychology, 71*(4), 618–629.

Muraven, M., & Baumeister, R. (2000). Self-regulation and depletion of limited resources: Does self-control resemble a muscle? *Psychological Bulletin, 126*(2), 247–259.

Murray, H. A. (1938). *Explorations in personality.* Oxford University Press.

Murray, J., Ehlers, A., & Mayou, R. A. (2002). Dissociation and post-traumatic stress disorder: Two prospective studies of road traffic accident survivors. *British Journal of Psychiatry, 180*(4), 363–368.

Muukkonen, M. (2015). The YMCA: A pioneer of organizational innovations. In R. A. Cnaan (ed.), *Cases in innovative nonprofits: Organizations that make a difference* (pp. 209–220). Sage.

Nadler, D. A., & Tushman, M. L. (1977). A diagnostic model for organizational behavior. In J. R. Hackman, E. E. Lawler, & L. W. Porter (eds.), *Perspectives on behavior in organizations* (pp. 85–100). McGraw Hill.

National Commission on the BP Deepwater Horizon Oil Spill and Offshore Drilling. (2011). *Deep Water: The Gulf oil disaster and the future of offshore drilling.* Report to the President of the US. US Government Printing Office.

Natraj, N., & Ganguly, K. (2018). Shaping reality through mental rehearsal. *Neuron, 97*(5), 998–1000.

Neate, R. (2014, June 22). Amazon's Jeff Bezos: The man who wants you to buy everything from his company. *The Guardian.*

Neff, J. E. (2015). Shared vision and family firm performance. *Frontiers in Psychology, 5,* 1335. doi: 10.3389/fpsyg.2014.01335.

Nelson, A. J., & Irwin, J. (2014). Defining what we do—all over again: Occupational identity, technological change, and the librarian/internet-search relationship. *Academy of Management Journal, 57*(3), 892–928.

Nesse, R. M. (1990). Evolutionary explanations of emotions. *Human Nature, 1,* 261–289.

Neuman, G. A., Edwards, J. E., & Raju, N. S. (1989). Organizational development interventions: A meta-analysis of their effects on satisfaction and other attitudes. *Personnel Psychology, 42*(3), 461–489.

Neville, M. (2013). *20 feet from stardom.* Film.

Newman, D. V. (1996). Emergence and strange attractors. *Philosophy of Science,* 63(2), 245–261.

Noe, R. A., and Schmitt, N. (1986). The influence of trainee attitudes on training effectiveness: Test of a model. *Personnel Psychology, 39,* 497–523.

Nowack, K. (2017). Facilitating successful behavior change: Beyond goal setting to goal flourishing. *Consulting Psychology Journal, 69*(3), 153–171.

Oancea, B., Andrei, T., & Pirjol, D. (2017). Income inequality in Romania: The exponential-Pareto distribution. *Physica A: Statistical Mechanics and its Applications,* 469, 486–498.

Obodaru, O. (2012). The self not taken: How alternative selves develop and how they influence our professional lives. *Academy of Management Review, 37*(1), 34–57.

O'Boyle Jr., E., & Aguinis, H. (2012). The best and the rest: Revisiting the norm of normality of individual performance. *Personnel Psychology, 65*(1), 79–119.

O'Brien, E., & Klein, N. (2017). The tipping point of perceived change: Asymmetric thresholds in diagnosing improvement versus decline. *Journal of Personality and Social Psychology, 112*(2), 161–185.

Ochsner, K. N., Beer, J. S., Robertson, E. R., Cooper, J. C., Gabrieli, J. D., Kihsltrom, J. F., & D'Esposito, M. (2005). The neural correlates of direct and reflected self-knowledge. *Neuroimage, 28*(4), 797–814.

O'Connor, A. (1999). Swimming against the tide: A brief history of federal policy in poor communities. In R. F. Ferguson & W. T. Dickens (eds.), *Urban problems and community development* (pp. 11–29). Brookings Institution Press.

O'Connor, G. (2004). *Miracle.* Walt Disney Productions.

Oettingen, G., & Mayer, D. (2002). The motivating function of thinking about the future: Expectations versus fantasies. *Journal of Personality and Social Psychology,* 83(5), 1198–1212. https://doi.org/10.1037/0022-3514.83.5.1198.

Ogilvie, D. M. (1987). The undesired self: SA neglected variable in personality research. *Journal of Personality and Social Psychology, 52*(2), 379–385.

O'Keefe, P. A., Dweck, C. S., & Walton, G. M. (2018). Implicit theories of interest: Finding your passion or developing it. *Psychological Science,* 1–12.

Okubo, A. (1986) Dynamical aspects of grouping: Swarms, schools, flocks and herds. *Advanced Biophysics, 22,* 1–94.

O'Neil, D. A., & Bilimoria, D. (2005). Women's career development phases: Idealism, endurance, and reinvention. *Career Development International, 10*(3), 168–189.

O'Neil, D. A., Hopkins, M. M., & Bilimoria, D. (2015). A framework for developing women leaders: Applications to executive coaching. *Journal of Applied Behavioral Science, 51*(2), 253–276.

Ordonez, L., Schweitzer, M. E., Galinsky, A., & Bazerman, M. (2009). Goals gone wild: How goals systematically harm individuals and organizations. *Academy of Management Perspectives, 23*(1), 6–16.

Oreg, S., Vakola, M., & Armenakis, A. (2011). Change recipients' reactions to organizational change: A 60-year review of quantitative studies. *Journal of Applied Behavioral Science, 47*(4), 461–524.

Orth, U., & Robins, R. W. (2022). The benefits of self-esteem: Reply to Krueger et al. (2022) and Brummelman (2022). *American Psychologist, 77*(1), 23–25.

Osborn, R. N., & Hunt, J. G. J. (2007). Leadership and the choice of order: Complexity and hierarchical perspectives near the edge of chaos. *Leadership Quarterly,* 18(4), 319–340.

Osman, M. McLachlan, S., Fenton, N., Neil, M., Lofstedt, R., & Meder, B. (2020). Learning from behavioral changes that fail. *Trends in Cognitive Sciences, 24*(12), 969–980.

Ostrove, J. M., Stewart, A. J., & Curtin, N. L. (2011). Social class and belonging: Implications for graduate students' career aspirations. *Journal of Higher Education, 82*(6), 748–774.

Overbeke, K., Bilimoria, D. & Somers, T. (2015). The critical role of the "Ideal Self" in the self-selection of next-generation leaders of family businesses. *Frontiers in Psychology,* 5, 1335. doi: 10.3389/fpsyg.2014.01335.

Owen, A. M., McMillan, K. M., Laird, A. R., & Bullmore, E. (2005). N-back working memory paradigm: A meta-analysis of normative functional neuroimaging studies. *Human Brain Mapping, 25*(1), 46–59.

Owens, B. P., Baker, W. E., Sumpter, D. M., & Cameron, K. (2016). Relational energy at work: Implications for job engagement and job performance. *Journal of Applied Psychology, 101*(1), 35–49.

Public Bike System Company. (2022). Bike share programs. www.pbsc.com/blog/2022/01/what-is-a-bike-share-program-and-how-does-it-work

Pardasani, R. (2016). *Resonant leadership and its individual and organizational outcomes: A test of mediation by emotional attractor and resilience.* Unpublished doctoral dissertation, The Management Development Institute.

Park, B. J., Tsunetsugu, Y., Kasetani, T., Kagawa, T., & Miyazaki, Y. (2010). The physiological effects of Shinrinyoku (taking in the forest atmosphere or forest bathing): Evidence from field experiments in 24 forests across Japan. *Environmental Health and Preventive Medicine, 15*(1), 18–26. doi: 10.1007/s12199-009-0086-9.

Park, M., Leahey, E. & Funk, R. J. (2023). Papers and patents are becoming less disruptive over time. *Nature 613,* 138–144.

Parker, P., Hall, D. T., & Kram, K. E. 2008. Peer coaching: A relational process for accelerating career learning. *Academy of Management Learning & Education, 7*(4), 487–503.

Parker, P., Kram, K. E., & Hall, D. T. 2014. Peer coaching. *Organizational Dynamics, 43*(2), 122–129.

Parker, P., Wasserman, I., Kram, K. E., & Hall, D. T. 2015. A relational communication approach to peer coaching. *Journal of Applied Behavioral Science, 51*(2), 231–252.

Parsons, T. (1937). *The structure of social action.* McGraw-Hill.

Parsons, T. & Bales, R. F. (1955). *Family, socialization and interaction process.* The Free Press.

Pascarella, E. T., & Terenzini, P. T. (1991). *How college affects students: Findings and insights from twenty years of research.* Jossey-Bass.

Passarelli, A. M. (2014). *The heart of helping: Psychological and physiological effects of contrasting coaching interactions.* Unpublished doctoral dissertation, Case Western Reserve University.

Passarelli, A. (2015). The neuro-emotional basis of developing leaders through personal vision. *Frontiers in Psychology,* 5, 1335. doi: 10.3389/fpsyg.2014.01335.

Passarelli, A. M., Boyatzis, R. E., & Wei, H. (2017). Assessing leader development: Lessons from a historical review of MBA outcomes. *Journal of Management Education, 42*(1), 55–79.

Passarelli, A., M., & Taylor, S. N. (2023). Coaching for positive leader development: Dynamic balancing of paradoxical forces in intentional change. In Y. Lee & A. Raes (eds.), *A Research Agenda for Positive Leadership* (pp. 1–30). Edward Elgar Publishing.

Passarelli, A. M., Van Oosten, E. B., & Eckert, M. A. (2018). Neuroscience in coaching: Research and practice. In E. Cox, T. Bachkirova, & D. Clutterbuck, *The complete handbook of coaching* (pp. 610–626). Sage.

Passarelli, A., Zeki, D. A., Boyatzis, R. E., Dawson, A. J. & Jack, A. (2014). Coaching with compassion helps you see the big picture: fMRI reveals neural overlap between different styles of coaching and visual attention. Paper presented at the Academy of management Annual Meeting, Philadelphia.

Pearce, C. L., & Ensley, M. D. 2004. A reciprocal and longitudinal investigation of the innovation process: The central role of shared vision in product and process innovation teams (PPITs). *Journal of Organizational Behavior, 25*(2), 259–278.

Pearsall, M. J., & Venkataramani, V. (2014). Overcoming asymmetric goals in teams: The interactive roles of team learning orientation and team identification. *Journal of Applied Psychology.* Advance online publication. http://dx.doi.org/10.1037/a0038315.

Pek, J., Wong, O., & Wong, A. (2018). How to address non-normality: A taxonomy of approaches, reviewed, and illustrated. *Frontiers in Psychology, 9*, 2104. doi: 10.3389/fpsyg.2018.02104.

Petrides, K. V., & Furnham, A. (2001). Trait emotional intelligence: Psychometric investigation with reference to established trait taxonomies. *European Journal of Personality, 17*, 425–448.

Pfeffer, J., & Fong, C. T. (2002). The end of business schools? Less success than meets the eye. *Academy of Management Learning & Education, 1*, 1560–1582.

Pieper, S., Brosschot, J. F., van der Leeden, R., & Thayer, J. F. (2007). Cardiac effects of momentary assessed worry episodes and stressful events. *Psychosomatic Medicine, 69*(9), 901–909.

Pierce, B. (2001) Weihenmayer reaches the top. *The Braille Monitor*, July. http://nfb.org/legacy/BM/BM01/BM0107/bm010702.htm.

Pierson, D. (2008, January 3). The Chicago bears win the 1986 Super Bowl. *Chicago Tribune*.

Pittenger, L. M. (2015). IT professionals: Recipe for engagement. *Frontiers in Psychology, 5*, 1335. doi: 10.3389/fpsyg.2014.01335.

Porges, S. W. (2003). The polyvagal theory: Phylogenetic contributions to social behavior. *Physiology & Behavior, 79*, 503–513.

Porges, S. W., Dussard-Roosevelt, J. A., & Maiti, A. K. (1994). Vagal tone and the physiological regulation of emotion. *Monographs of the Society of Child Development, 59*(2–3), 167–186.

Porter, R. L., & Latham, G. (2013). The effect of employee learning goals and goal commitment on departmental performance. *Journal of Leadership and Organizational Studies, 20*(1), 62–68.

Posner, J., Russell, J. A. & Peterson, B. S. (2005). The circumplex model of affect: An integrative approach to affective neuroscience, cognitive development and psychopathology. *Development and Psychopathology, 17*, 715–734.

Powell, L., Guastella, A. J., McGreevy, P., Bauman, A., & Edwards, K. M. (2019). The physiological function of oxytocin in humans and its acute response to human-dog interactions: A review of the literature. *Journal of Veterinary Behavior: Clinical Applications and Research, 30*, 25–32.

Pratt, M. G., Rockmann, K. W., & Kaufmann, J. B. (2006). Constructing professional identity: The role of work and identity learning cycles in the customization of identity among medical residents. *Academy of Management Journal, 49*(2), 235–262.

Prinzing, M., Le Nguyen, K., & Fredrickson, B. L. (2023). Does shared positivity make life more meaningful? Perceived positivity resonance is uniquely associated with perceived meaning in life. *Journal of Personality and Social Psychology, 125*(2), 345–366.

Prochaska, J. O., DiClemente, C. C., & Norcross, J. C. (1992). In search of how people change: Applications to addictive behaviors. *American Psychologist, 47*(9), 1102–1114.

Prucha, F. P. (1986). *The great father: The United States Government and the American Indians* (abridged edition). University of Nebraska Press.

Przybylski, A. K., Weinstein, N., Murayama, K., Lynch, M. F., & Ryan, R. M. (2012). The Ideal Self at play: The appeal of video games that let you be all you can be. *Psychological Science, 23*(1), 69–76.

Putnam, Robert D. (2000). *Bowling alone: The collapse and revival of American community*. Simon & Schuster.

Qian, X. L., & Yarnal, C. (2011). The role of playfulness in the leisure stress-coping process among emerging adults: An SEM analysis. *Leisure/Loisir, 35*(2), 191–209.

Quinn, J. F. (2015). The effect of vision and compassion upon role factors in physician leadership. *Frontiers in Psychology*, 1335. doi: 10.3389/fpsyg.2014.01335.

Quinn, R. W., & Dutton, J. E. 2005. Coordination as energy-in-conversation. *Academy of Management Review, 30*(1), 36–57.

Ragins, B., Kram, K. (2007). *Handbook of mentoring at work: Theory, research, and practice*. Sage.

Raichle, M. E., MacLeod, A. M., Snyder, A. Z., Powers, W. J., Gusnard, D. A., & Shulman, G. L. (2001). A default mode of brain function. *Proceedings of the National Academy of Sciences, 98*(2), 676–682.

Raichle, M. E. &, Snyder, A. Z. (2007). A default mode of brain function: A brief history of an evolving idea. *NeuroImage, 37*(4), 1083–1090.

Ramani, R. S., Aguinis, H. & Coyle-Shapiro, J. A-M. (2022). Defining, measuring, and rewarding scholarly impact: Mind the level of analysis. *Academy of Management Learning and Education, 21*, 470–486.

Randall, A. K., & Bodenmann, G. (2009). The role of stress on close relationships and marital satisfaction. *Clinical Psychology Review, 29*(2), 105–115.

Randolph, M. (2019). *That will never work: The birth of Netflix and the amazing life of an idea.* Little, Brown.

Reay, T., Goodrick, E., Waldorff, S. B., & Casebeer, A. (2017). Getting leopards to change their spots: Co-creating a new professional role identity. *Academy of Management Journal, 60*(3), 1043–1070.

Reis, H. T., & Gable, S. L. 2002. Toward a positive psychology of relationships. In C. L. M. Keyes, J. Haidt, & M. E. P. Seligman (eds.), *Flourishing: Positive psychology and the life well-lived* (pp. 129–160). American Psychological Association.

Repton, H. (1803). *Observations on the theory and practice of landscape gardening.* T. Bensley for J. Taylor.

Resick, C. J., Lucianetti, L., Mawritz, M. B., Choi, J. Y., Boyer, S. L., & D'Innocenzo, L. (2023). When focus and vision become a nightmare: Bottom-line mentality climate, shared vision, and unit unethical conduct. *Journal of Applied Psychology.* Advance online publication. https://doi.org/10.1037/apl0001111.

Rettie, Dwight F. (1995). *Our national park system.* University of Illinois Press.

Reynolds, C. W. (1987) Flocks, herds and schools: A distributed model. *Computer Graphics, 21*(4), 25–34.

Riess, H. (2018). *The empathy effect: 7 neuroscience based keys for transforming the way we live, love, work and connect across differences.* Sounds True Press.

Riggio, R. E., Chaleff, I. & J. Lipman-Blumen (2008). *The art of followership: How great followers create great leaders and organizations.* Wiley.

Riza, S. D., & Heller, D. (2015). Follow your heart or your head: A longitudinal study of the facilitating role of calling and ability in the pursuit of a challenging career. *Journal of Applied Psychology, 100*(3), 695–712.

Rizzolatti, G., & Sinigaglia, C. (2008). *Mirrors in the brain: How our minds share actions and emotions.* Oxford University Press.

Roberts, B. W., Luo, J., Briley, D. A., Chow, P. I., Su, R., & Hill, P. L. (2017). A systematic review of personality trait change through intervention. *Psychological Bulletin, 143*(2), 117–141.

Roberts, L. M. (2005). Changing faces: Professional image construction in diverse organizational settings. *Academy of Management Review, 30*(4), 685–711.

Roberts, L. M., Dutton, J. E., Spreitzer, G. M., Heaphy, E. D., & Quinn, R. E. (2005). Composing the reflected best self-portrait: Building pathways for becoming extraordinary in work organizations. *Academy of Management Review, 30*(4), 712–736.

Robinson W. S. (1950). Ecological correlations and the behaviour of individuals. *American Sociological Review, 15,* 351–357.

Rokeach, M. (1964). *The three Christs of Ypsilanti: A narrative study of three lost men.* Knopf.

Rokeach, M. (1973). *The nature of human values.* Free Press.

Romanelli, E., & Tushman, M. L. (1994). Organizational transformation as punctuated equilibrium: An empirical test. *Academy of Management Journal, 37*(5), 1141–1166.

Roney, C. J. R., Higgins, T. E., & Shah, J. (1995). Goals and framing: How outcome focus influences motivation and emotion. *Personality and Social Psychology Bulletin, 21*(11), 1151–1160.

Roosevelt, E. (1957). My day. Attributed to her reflections on July 4, 1957 in the *Nevada State Journal*, page 4, column 4. Reno, Nevada.

Rosenberg, D. (2000). *The Cleveland Orchestra story: Second to none.* Gray & Co.

Rosenthal, R., & Jacobson, L. (1968). *Pygmalion in the classroom: Teacher expectation and pupils' intellectual development.* Holt, Rinehart & Winston.

Ross, H. E., Cole, C. D., Smith, Y., Neumann, I. D., Landgraf, R., Murphy, A. Z., & Young, L. J. (2009). Characterization of the oxytocin system regulating affiliative behavior in female prairie voles. *Neuroscience, 162*(4), 892–903. doi: 10.1016/j.neuroscience.2009.05.055. Epub 2009 May 29. PMID: 19482070; PMCID: PMC2744157.

Rothwell, W. J. (2015). Introduction. In W. K. Rothwell, C. S. Anderson, C. M. Corn, C. Haynes, C. H. Park, & A. G. Zaballero (eds.), *Organization development fundamentals: Managing strategic change* (pp. 1–12). ATD Press.

Rothwell, W. J., Anderson, C. S., Corn, C. M., Haynes, C., Park, C. H., & Zaballero, A. G. (2015). *Organization development fundamentals: Managing strategic change.* ATD Press.

Rousseau, D. M. (1985). Issues of level in organizational research: Multi-level and cross-level perspectives. *Research in Organizational Behavior, 7,* 1–38.

Roszel, E. L. (2015). Central nervous system deficits in fetal alcohol spectrum disorder. *The Nurse Practitioner, 40*(4), 24–33.

Rowe, G., Hirsh, J. B., Anderson, A. K., & Smith, E. E. (eds.). (2007). Positive affect increases the breadth of attentional selection. *PNAS Proceedings of the National Academy of Sciences of the United States of America, 104*(1), 383–388.

Rozin, P., & Royzman, E. B. (2001). Negativity bias, negativity dominance and contagion. *Personality and Social Psychology Review, 5*(4), 296–320.

Rubin, Z. (1973). *Liking and loving: An invitation to social psychology.* Holt, Rinehart and Winston.

Runciman, W. G. (1966). *Relative deprivation and social justice: A study of attitudes to social inequality in twentieth-century England.* University of California Press.

Russell, J. A. & Carroll, J. M. (1999). On the polarity of positive and negative affect. *Psychological Bulletin, 125*(1), 3–30.

Ryan, R. M., & Deci, E. L. (2000). Self-determination theory and the facilitation of intrinsic motivation, social development, and well-being. *American Psychologist, 55*(1), 68–78.

Ryan, R. M., & Frederick, C. 1997. On energy, personality, and health: Subjective vitality as a dynamic reflection of well-being. *Journal of Personality, 65*(3), 529–565.

Salter, C. (2000). Hope and dreams. *Fast Company.* September. 178–204.

Sandel, M. J. (2009). *Justice: What's the right thing to do.* Farrar, Straus and Giroux.

Sanfuentes, M., Valenzuela, F., & Castillo, A. (2021). What lies beneath resilience: Analyzing the affective-relational basis of shared leadership in the Chilean miners' catastrophe. *Leadership, 17*(3), 255–277.

Sapolsky, R. M. (2004). *Why zebras don't get ulcers, 3rd edition.* Harper Collins.

Schabram, K. & Heng, Y. T. (2022). How other- and self-compassion reduce burnout through resource replenishment. *Academy of Management Journal, 65,* 453–478.

Schacter, D. L., Addis, D. R., & Buckner, R. L. (20087). Episodic simulation of future events: Concepts, data, and applications. *Annals of the New York Academy of Sciences, 1124,* 39–60.

Schaefer, S. E., & Coleman, E. (1992). Shifts in meaning, purpose, and values following a diagnosis of human immunodeficiency virus (HIV) infection among gay men. *Journal of Psychology & Human Sexuality, 5*(1–2), 13–29.

Schein, E. H. (1978). *Career dynamics: Matching individual and organizational needs.* Addison Wesley.

Schein, E. H. (2010). *Organizational Culture and Leadership,* 4th edn. Wiley.

Schein, E. H., Schneier, I., & Barker, C. H. (1961). *Coercive persuasion: A socio-psychological analysis of the "brainwashing" of American civilian prisoners by the Chinese communists.* Norton.

Schein, E. H., & Van Maanen, J. (2013). *Career anchors: The changing nature of careers self assessment, 4th edition.* Wiley.

Schilbach, L., Eickhoff, S., Rotarskajagiela, A., Fink, G. & Vogeley, K. (2008). Minds at rest? Social cognition as the default mode of cognizing and its putative relationship to the "default system" of the brain. *Consciousness and Cognition, 17,* 457–467.

Schiller, R. A. (1998). The relationships of developmental tasks to life satisfaction, moral reasoning and occupational attainment at age 28. *Journal of Adult Development, 5*(4), 239–254.

Schindler-Rainman, E., & Lippitt, R. (1992). Building collaborative communities. In M. R. Weisbord (ed.), *Discovering common ground: How future search conferences bring people together to achieve breakthrough innovation, empowerment, shared vision, and collaborative action* (pp. 35–44). Berrett-Koehler.

Schmitt, A. (2020). 15 benefits of negative affective states. *The Cambridge handbook of workplace affect.* Cambridge University Press.

Schlegel, R. J., Hicks, J. A., King, L. A., & Arndt, J. (2011). Feeling like you know who you are: Perceived true self-knowledge and meaning in life. *Personality and Social Psychology Bulletin, 37*(6), 745–756.

Schneider, B., & Barbara, K. M. (2014). *The Oxford handbook of organizational climate and culture.* Oxford University Press.

Schulkin, J. (1999). *Neuroendocrine regulation of behavior.* Cambridge University Press.

Schultheiss, O. C. (1999). A neurobiological perspective on implicit power motivation, testosterone, and learning. Paper presented at the 107th American Psychological Association Annual Meeting, Boston, August.

Schultz, C. A. (2005). *Instructional leadership in the elementary school: An investigation of the emotional connectedness between principal and teacher.* Unpublished doctoral dissertation, Loyola University.

Schutz, W. C. (1958). *FIRO: A three-dimensional theory of interpersonal behavior.* Holt, Rinehart, and Winston.

Schwartz, S. H., Caprara, G. V., & Vecchione, M. (2010). Basic personal values, core political values, and voting: A longitudinal analysis. *Political Psychology, 31*(3), 421–452.

Schweizer, T. S. (2006). The psychology of novelty-seeking, creativity and innovation: Neurocognitive aspects within a work-psychological perspective. *Creativity and Innovation Management, 15*(2), 164–172.

Sedikides, C. (1993). Assessment, enhancement, and verification determinants of the self-evaluation process. *Journal of Personality and Social Psychology, 65*(2), 317–338.

Sedikides, C., & Brewer, M. B. (2001). Individual self, relational self, and collective self: Partners, opponents, or strangers? In C. Sedikides & M. B. Brewer (eds.), *Individual self, relational self, and collective self* (pp. 1–4). Psychology Press.

Seeley, W. W., Menon, V., Schatzberg, A. F., Keller, J., Glover, G. H., Kenna, H., Reiss, A. L., & Greicius, M. D. (2007). Dissociable intrinsic connectivity networks for salience processing and executive control. *Journal of Neuroscience, 27,* 2349–2356.

Segerstrom, S. C., & Miller, G. E. (2004). Psychological stress and the human immune system: A meta-analytic study of 30 years of inquiry. *Psychological Bulletin, 130*(4), 601–630.

Segerstrom, S. C., & Sephton, S. E. (2010). Optimistic expectancies and cell-mediated immunity: The role of positive affect. *Psychological Science, 21*(3), 448–455.

Seijts, G. H., & Latham, G. P. (2005). Learning versus performance goals: When should each be used. *Academy of Management Executive, 19*(1), 124–131.

Seijts, G. H., Latham, G. P. O., Tasa, K. and Latham, B. W. (2004). Goal setting and goal orientation: An integration of two different yet related literatures. *Academy of Management Journal, 47*(2), 227–239.

Seligman, M. E. P., & Csikszentmihalyi, M. (2000). Positive psychology: An introduction. *American Psychologist, 55(1),* 5–14.

Seligman, M. E., Railton, P., Baumeister, R. F., & Sripada, C. (2013). Navigating into the future or driven by the past. *Perspectives on Psychological Science, 8*(2), 119–141.

Selye, H. (1974). *Stress without distress.* Signet.

Senge, P. (1990). *The fifth discipline: The art and practice of the learning organization.* Doubleday.

Shackman, A. J., Tromp, D. P. M., Stockbridge, M. D., Kaplan, C. M., Tillman, R. M., & Fox, A. S. (2016). Dispositional negativity: An integrative psychological and neurobiological perspective. *Psychological Bulletin, 142*(12), 1275–1314.

Shakespeare. W. (1599/2004). *Hamlet.*

Sheehy, G. (1995). *New passages: Mapping your life across time.* Random House.

Sheff, D. (1981, January). Interview with john Lennon and Yoko Ono. *Playboy.* 75–78.

Sheldon, O. J., Dunning, D., & Ames, D. R. (2014). Emotionally unskilled, unaware, and uninterested in learning more: Reactions to feedback about deficits in emotional intelligence. *Journal of Applied Psychology, 99*(1), 125–137.

Shepherd, D. A., & Williams, T. A. (2018). Hitting rock bottom after job loss: Bouncing back to create a new positive work identity. *Academy of Management Review 43*(1), 28–49.

Sherif, M., Harvey, O. J., White, B. J., Hood, W. R., & Sherif, C. W. (1961). *Intergroup conflict and cooperation: The Robbers cave experiment (Vol. 10).* University Book Exchange.

Shi, Z., Ma, Y., Wu, B., Wu, X., Wang, Y. & Han, S. (2016). Neural correlates of reflection on actual versus Ideal Self-discrepancy. *Neuroimage, 124,* 573–580.

Shulman, G. L., Corbetta, M., Buckner, R. L., Fiez, J. A., Miezin, F. M., Raichle, M. E., & Petersen, S. E. (1997). Common blood flow changes across visual tasks: II. Decreases in cerebral cortex. *Journal of Cognitive Neuroscience, 9*(5), 648–663.

Silzer, R. (2023). Personal communication.

Siris, E. S., Pasquale, M. K., Wang, Y., & Watts, N. B. (2011). Estimating bisphosphonate use and fracture reduction among US women aged 45 years and older, 2001–2008. *Journal of Bone Miner Research, 26*(1), 3–11.

Sites, R. Chaskin, R. J., & Parks, V. (2007). Reframing community practice for the 21st century: Multiple transition, multiple challenges. *Journal of Urban Affairs, 29*(5), 519–541.

Sliter, M., Kale, A., & Yuan, Z. (2014). Is humor the best medicine? The buffering effect of coping humor on traumatic stressors in firefighters. *Journal of Organizational Behavior, 35*(2), 257–272.

Sluss, D. M., & Ashforth, B. E. (2007). Relational identity and identification: Defining ourselves through work relationships. *Academy of Management Review, 32*(1), 9–32.

Smallwood, J. (2013). Distinguishing how from why the mind wanders: A process occurrence framework for self-generated thought. *Psychological Bulletin, 139*(3), 519–535.

Smallwood, J. & Schooler, J. (2014). The science of mind wandering: empirically navigating the stream of consciousness. *Annual review of psychology, 66.* 10.1146/annurev-psych-010814-015331.

Smith, D., & Holmes, P. S. (2004). The effect of imagery modality on golf putting performance. *Journal of Sport & Exercise Psychology, 26*(3), 385–395.

Smith, K. E., & Pollak, S. D. (2020). Early life stress and development: Potential mechanisms for adverse outcomes. *Journal of Neurodevelopmental Disorders, 12*(1), 34. doi: 10.1186/s11689-020-09337-y. PMID: 33327939; PMCID: PMC7745388.

Smith, M. (2023, October 2). Worker are the unhappiest they've been in 3 years—and it can cost the global economy $8.8 trillion. https://www.cnbc.com/2023/10/02/-employee-happiness-has-hit-a-3-year-low-new-research-shows.html.

Sneed, J. R., & Whitbourne, S. K. (2003). Identity processing and self-consciousness in middle and later adulthood. *Journals of Gerontology Series B: Psychological Sciences and Social Sciences, 58*(6), 313–319.

Snyder, C. R. (2000). The past and possible futures of hope. *Journal of Social and Clinical Psychology, 19*(1), 11–28.

Sommerfeldt, S. L., Schaefer, S. M., Brauer, M., Ryff, C. D., & Davidson, R. J. (2019). Individual differences in the association between subjective stress and heart rate are related to psychological and physical well-being. *Psychological Science, 30*, 1016–1029.

Specht, L., & Sandlin, P. (1991). The differential effects of experiential learning activities and traditional lecture classes in accounting. *Simulations and Gaming, 22*(2), 196–210.

Spencer, L. M. (1988). *Calculating human resource costs and benefits: Cutting costs and improving productivity.* Wiley.

Spencer, L. M. Jr., & Spencer, S. M. (1993). *Competence at work: Models for superior performance.* Wiley.

Spiegel, S., Grant-Pillow, H., & Higgins, E. T. (2004). How regulatory fit enhances motivational strength during goal pursuit. *European Journal of Social Psychology, 34*, 39–54.

Spreng, R. N., & Grady, C. L. (2010).Patterns of brain activity supporting autobiographical memory, prospection, and theory of mind, and their relationship to the default mode network. *Journal of Cognitive Neuroscience, 22*(6), 1112–1123.

Spreng, R. N., Mar, R. A., & Kim, A. S. N. (2008). The common neural basis of autobiographical memory, prospection, navigation, theory of mind and the default mode: A quantitative meta-analysis. *Journal of Cognitive Neuroscience. 12*(3), 489–510.

Spreng, R. N., Stevens, W. D., Chamberlain, J. P., Gilmore, A. W., & Schacter, D. L. (2010). Default network activity, coupled with the frontoparietal control network, supports goal-directed cognition. *Neuroimage, 53*(1), 303–317.

Stanley, M. & Burrow, A. L. (2015). The distance between selves: The influence of self-discrepancy on purpose in life, self and identity. *Currents in Psychology, 14*(4), 441–452.

Steger, M. F. (2012). Experiencing meaning in life: Optimal functioning at the nexus of spirituality, psychopathology, and wellbeing. In P. T. P Wong (ed.), *The human quest for meaning, 2nd edition* (pp. 165–184). Routledge.

Steger, M. F., Oishi, S., & Kashdan, T. B. (2009). Meaning in life across the life span: Levels and correlates of meaning in life from emerging adulthood to older adulthood. *Journal of Positive Psychology, 4*(1), 43–52.

Stets, J. E., & Burke, P. J. (2000). Identity theory and social identity theory. *Social Psychology Quarterly, 63*(3), 224–237.

Stoecker, R. (1997). The CDC model of urban redevelopment: A critique and an alternative. *Journal of Urban Affairs, 19*(1), 1–22.

Stolzer, J. M. (2016). The meteoric rise of mental illness in America and implications for other countries. *European Journal of Counselling Psychology, 4*(2), 228–246. doi:10.5964/ejcop. v4i2.77.

Stone, B. (2013). *The everything store: Jeff Bezos and the age of Amazon.* Little, Brown.

Stone, B., & Hunter, A. (2004). *Race to the center of the Earth.* National Geographic, April. http://ngm.nationalgeographic.com/ngm/caverace.

Storr, A. (1996). *Feet of clay: Saints, sinners, and madmen: A study of genius.* Free Press.

Story, M., & Neumark-Sztainer, D. (2005). A perspective on family meals: Do they matter? *Nutrition Today, 40*(6), 261–266.

Straub, E. (2015). Cohesion, flexibility and the mediating effects of shared vision and compassion on engagement in Army acquisition teams. Unpublished doctoral dissertation, Case Western Reserve University.

Strauss, K., Griffin, M. A., & Parker, S. K. (2012). Future work selves: How salient hoped for identities motivate proactive career behaviors. *Journal of Applied Psychology, 97*(3), 580–598.

Strauss, T. J. (2003). Summa's vision: Comments by Thomas Strauss, president and CEO, Summa Health Systems of Akron, Ohio at the Heart to Heart 10 Anniversary Conference in Akron, April 28.

Super, D. E. (1984). Career and life development. In D. Brown and L. Brooks (eds.), *Career Choice and Development* (pp. 192–234). Jossey-Bass.

Swenson, K., Guskin, E., & Clement, S. (2022, February 24). Majority of DC residents support clearing of homeless encampments, Post poll finds. *Washington Post.* https://www.washing tonpost.com/dc-md-va/2022/02/24/dc-poll-housing-homeless-bowser.

Tabor, J. M. (2010). Blind descent: The quest to discover the deepest place on Earth. Random House.

Tajfel, H. (1974). Social identity and intergroup behavior. *Trends and Developments: Social Science Informs, 13* (2), 65–93.

Tajfel, H. (1982). Social psychology of intergroup relations. *Annual Review of Psychology, 33*(1), 1–39.

Talarico, J. M., Bernstein, D., & Rubin, D. C. (2009). Positive emotions enhance recall of peripheral details. *Cognition and Emotion, 23*(2), 380–398.

Tangney, J. P., Niedenthal, P. M., Covert, M. V., & Barlow D. H. (1998). Are shame and guilt related to distinct self-discrepancies: A test of Higgins's (1987) hypotheses. *Journal of Personality and Social Psychology, 75,* 256–268.

Tarafdar, M., Tu, Q., Ragu-Nathan, B. S., & Ragu-Nathan, T. S. (2007). The impact of techno-stress on role stress and productivity. *Journal of Management Information Problems, 24*(1), 301–328.

Taylor, S. E., Klein, L. C., Lewis, B. P., Gruenewald, T. L., Gurung, R. A., & Updegraff, J. A. (2000). Biobehavioral responses to stress in females: Tend-and-befriend, not fight-or-flight. *Psychological Review, 107*(3), 411–429.

Taylor, S. N., & Hood, J. N. (2011). It may not be what you think: Gender differences in predicting emotional and social competence. *Human Relations, 64,* 627–652.

Taylor, S. N., Passarelli, A. M., & Van Oosten, E. B. (2019). Leadership coach effectiveness as fostering self-determined sustained change. *Leadership Quarterly, 30*(6), Article 101313. https://doi.org/10.1016/j.leaqua.2019.101313.

Tee, E. Y. J., Ashkanasy, N. M., & Paulsen, N. (2013). The influence of follower mood on leader mood and task performance: An affective, follower-centric perspective of leadership. *Leadership Quarterly, 24*(4), 496–515.

Terehkin, R. (2024). Unveiling the power of peer coaching in groups in professional settings. Unpublished PhD dissertation. Case Western Reserve University.

Thaler, R. H., & Sunstein, C. R. (2003). Libertarian paternalism. *American Economic Review, 93*(2), 175–179.

Thaler, R. H., & Sunstein, C. R. (2008). *Nudge: Improving decisions about health, wealth, and happiness.* Penguin.

Thatcher, S. M. B., & Zhu, X. (2006). Changing identities in a changing workplace: Identification, identity enactment, self-verification, and telecommuting. *Academy of Management Review, 31*(4), 1076–1088.

Thom, R. (1975). *Structural stability and morphogenesis: An outline of a general theory of models.* W. A. Benjamin.

Thornton, G. C. III, & Byham, W. C. (1982), *Assessment centers and managerial Performance.* Academic Press.

Thornton, J. C. (2015). Shared vision: Mediating CSR in US food and beverage SMEs. *Frontiers in Psychology, 5,* 1335. doi: 10.3389/fpsyg.2014.01335.

Thrash, T. M., Elliot, A. J., Maruskin, L. A., & Cassidy, S. E. (2010). Inspiration and the promotion of well being: Tests of causality and mediation. *Journal of Personality and Social Psychology, 98*(3), 488–506.

Tichy, N. M. (1983). *Managing strategic change: Technical, political, and cultural dynamics.* Wiley.

Tompson, S., Lieberman, M. D., & Falk, E. B. (2015). Grounding the neuroscience of behavior change in the sociocultural context. *Current Opinion in Behavioral Sciences, 5,* 58–63.

Ton, D., Duives, D. C., Cats, O., Hoogendoorn-Lanser, S., & Hoogendoorn, S. P. (2019). Cycling or walking? Determinants of mode choice in the Netherlands. *Transportation Research Part A: Policy and Practice, 123,* 7–23.

Traynor, W. (2012. Community building: Limitations and promises. In J. DeFilippis & S. Saegert (eds.), *The community development reader* (pp. 209–219). Routledge.

Trithemius, A. J. ([1492] 1974). *In praise of scribes*. Coronado Press.

Tsoukas, H., & Hatch, M. J. (2001). Complex thinking, complex practice: The case for a narrative approach to organizational complexity. *Human Relations, 54*, 979–1013.

Tsui, A. S., & Ashford, S. J. (1994). Adaptive self-regulation: A process view of managerial effectiveness. *Journal of Management, 20*(1), 93–121.

Tuckman, B. W. (1965). Developmental sequence in small groups. *Psychological Bulletin, 63*(6), 384–399.

Turetsky, A. I. (2018). *Making heads and tails of distributional patterns: A value-creation-type and sector-based analysis among private-equity-owned Companies.* Unpublished doctoral dissertation, Case Western Reserve University.

Uchino, B. N., Cacioppo, J. T., & Kiecolt-Glaser, J. K. (1996). The relationship between social support and physiological processes: A review with emphasis on underlying mechanisms and implications for health. *Psychological Bulletin, 119*, 488–531.

Uddin, L. Q., Kelly, A. M. C., Biswal, B. B., Castellanos, F. X., & Milham, M. P. (2009). Functional connectivity of default mode network components: Correlation, anticorrelation, and causality. *Human Brain Mapping, 30*(2), 625–637.

Useem, M., Jordan, R., & Koljatic, M. (2011) How to lead during a crisis: Lessons from the rescue of the Chilean miners. *MIT Sloan Management Review, 53*(1), 49–55.

Vallerand, R. J. (2008). On the psychology of passion: In search of what makes people's lives most worth living. *Canadian Psychology / Psychologie canadienne, 49*(1), 1– 13.

Vallerand, R. J. (2015). *The psychology of passion: A dualistic mode.* Oxford University Press.

Vallerand, R. J., Blanchard, C., Mageau, G. A., Koestner, R., Ratelle, C., Léonard, M., Gagne, M., & Marsolais, J. (2003). Les passions de l'âme: On obsessive and harmonious passion. *Journal of Personality and Social Psychology, 85*, 756–767.

van de Brake, H. J., van der Vegt, G. S., & Essens, P. J. M. D. (2023). More than just a number: Different conceptualizations of multiple team membership and their relationships with emotional exhaustion and turnover. *Journal of Applied Psychology.* Advance online publication. https://doi.org/10.1037/apl0001168.

VandeWalle, D., Brown, S. P., Cron, W. L. & Slocum, J. W. Jr. (1999). The influence of goal orientation and self-regulation tactics on sales performance: A longitudinal field test. *Journal of Applied Psychology, 84*(2), 249–259.

Van der Zee, R. (2015, May 5). How Amsterdam became the bicycle capital of the world. *The Guardian.*

van Hooft, E. A. J. & Noordzij, G. (2009). The effects of goal orientation on job search and reemployment: A field experiment among unemployed job seekers. *Journal of Applied Psychology, 94*(6), 1581–1590.

Van Maanen, J., & Schein, E. 1979. Toward a theory of organizational socialization. *Annual Review of Research in Organizational Behavior, 1*, 209–264.

Van Oosten, E. (2006). Intentional change theory at the organizational level: A case study. *Journal of Management Development, 25*(7), 707–717.

Van Oosten, E. B., Buse, K., & Bilimoria, D. (2017). The leadership lab for women: Advancing and retaining women in STEM through professional development. *Frontiers in Psychology, 8*, Article 2138. https://doi.org/10.3389/fpsyg.2017.02138.

Van Oosten, E. B., McBride-Walker, S. M., & Taylor, S. N. (2019). Investing in what matters: The impact of emotional and social competency development and executive coaching on leader outcomes. *Consulting Psychology Journal: Practice and Research.* Advance online publication. http://dx.doi.org/10.1037/cpb0000141.

Van Overwalle, F. (2011). A dissociation between social mentalizing and general reasoning. *NeuroImage, 54*(2), 1589–1599.

Vazeou-Nieuwenhuis, A., Orehek, E., & Scheier, M. F. (2017). The meaning of action: Do self-regulatory processes contribute to a purposeful life? *Personality and Individual Differences,* 116, 115–122.

Veldhoven, S. V. (2020). Dutch cycling vision. https://www.dutchcycling.nl/images/downloads/Dutch_Cycling_Vision_EN.pdf.

Vetter, C. (2004). Bill Stone in the abyss. *Outside Magazine,* November.

Viana, M. (2000). What's new on Lorenz strange attractors? *The Mathematical Intelligencer,* 22(3), 6–19.

Vincent, J. L., Kahn, I., Snyder, A. Z., Raichle, M. E., & Buckner, R. L. (2008). Evidence for a frontoparietal control system revealed by intrinsic functional connectivity. *Journal of Neurophysiology,* 100(6), 3328–3342.

Volkova-Feddeck, M. (2022). Helping you helping me: Reflections on peer coaching. Unpublished paper. Case Western Reserve University.

Waldinger, R., & Schulz, M. (2023). *The good life: Lessons from the world's longest scientific study of happiness.* Simon & Schuster.

Waldman, D., Reina, C., & Peterson, S. (2014). *A neuroscience perspective of emotions in the formation of shared vision.* Paper presented at the annual meeting of the Academy of Management, Philadelphia.

Walker, R. (2010, June 13). Merit badges and social identity. *New York Times.*

Wall, R. B. (2005). Tai chi and mindfulness-based stress reduction in a Boston public middle school. *Journal of Pediatric Health Care,* 19(4), 230–237.

Wanchisen, B., & Schweinguber, H. A. (2023). Losing, and finding, a home. *Science,* 379(6631), 510.

Ward, A. M. (2016). A critical evaluation of the validity of episodic future thinking: A clinical neuropsychology perspective. *Neuropsychology,* 30 (8), 887–905.

Warr, D. (2018). Shared vision moderates the effect of CEO mindset and emotional intelligence on work engagement and leader effectiveness: Possible antecedents to leadership development. Unpublished Doctoral Dissertation. Case Western Reserve University: Cleveland, OH.

Waterman, R. H., Peters, T. J., & Phillips, J. R. (1980). Structure is not organization. *Business Horizons,* 23(3), 14–26.

Webb T. L., & Sheeran, P. (2006). Does changing behavioral intentions engender behavior change? A meta-analysis of the experimental evidence. *Psychological Bulletin,* 132(2), 249–268.

Wee, E. X. M., & Taylor, M. S. (2018). Attention to change: A multilevel theory on the process of emergent continuous organizational change. *Journal of Applied Psychology,* 103(1), 1–13.

Wegge, J., Schuh, S. C., & van Dick, R. (2012), "I feel bad," "we feel good"?: Emotions as a driver for personal and organizational identity and organizational identification as a resource for serving unfriendly customers. *Stress Health,* 28, 123–136.

Weick, K. E., & Roberts, K. H. 1993. Collective mind in organizations: Heedful interrelating on flight decks. *Administrative Science Quarterly,* 38(3), 357–381.

Weihenmayer, E. (2001). *Touch the top of the world: A blind man's journey to climb farther than the eye can see.* Penguin.

Weinberger, J., & Smith, B. (2011). Investigating merger: Subliminal psychodynamic activation and oneness motivation research. *Journal of the American Psychoanalytic Association,* 59(3), 553–570.

Weisbord, M. (1976). Organizational diagnosis: Six places to look for trouble with or without theory. *Group and Organizational Studies,* 1, 430–447.

Weisbord, M. R. (1992). *Discovering common ground: How future search conferences bring people together to achieve breakthrough innovation, empowerment, shared vision, and collaborative action.* Berrett-Koehler.

Welsh, D. T., Baer, M. D., & Sessions, H. (2019). Hot pursuit: The affective consequences of organization-set versus self-set goals for emotional exhaustion and citizenship behavior. *Journal of Applied Psychology, 1 05*(2), 166–185.

Wheeler, J. V. (2008). The impact of social environments on emotional, social, and cognitive competency development. *Journal of Management Development, 27*(1), 129–145.

White, R. W. (1960). Competence and the psychological stages of development. In M. R. Jones (ed.), *Nebraska Symposium on Motivation: 1960*, vol. 8 (pp. 97–141). University of Nebraska Press.

Whittman, S. (2019) Lingering identities. *Academy of Management Review, 44*(4), 724–745.

Wijewardena, N., Härtel, C. E., & Samaratunge, R. (2017). Using humor and boosting emotions: An affect-based study of managerial humor, employees' emotions and psychological capital. *Human Relations, 70*(11), 1316–1341.

Williams, H. (2008). Characteristics that distinguish outstanding urban principals, *Journal of Management Development, 27*(1), 36–54.

Wilson, E. O. (2000). *Sociobiology: The new synthesis, twenty-fifth anniversary edition.* Harvard University Press.

Wilson, D. S., Hayes, S. C., Biglin, A., & Embry, D. D. (2014). Evolving the future: Toward a science of intentional change. *Behavioral and Brain Sciences, 37*(4), 395–416.

Wilson, K., Senay, I., Duratini, M., Sanchez, F., Hennessy, M., Spring, B., & Albarracin, D. (2015). When it comes to lifestyle recommendations, more is sometimes less: A meta analysis of theoretical assumptions underlying the effectiveness of interventions promoting multiple behavior domain change. *Psychological Bulletin, 141* (2), 474–509.

Winter, D. G., McClelland, D. C., & Stewart, A. J. (1981). *A new case for the liberal arts: Assessing institutional goals and student development.* Jossey-Bass.

Wolfson, M. A., Tannenbaum, S. I., Mathieu, J. E., & Maynard, M. T. (2018). A cross-level investigation of informal field-based learning and performance improvements. *Journal of Applied Psychology, 103*, 14–36.

Wood, G. & Dow, S. (2011). What lessons have been learned in reforming the renewables obligation? An analysis of internal and external failures in UK renewable energy policy, *Energy Policy, 39*(5), 2228–2244.

Wood, W., Mazar, A., & Neal, D. T. (2022). Habits and goals in human behavior: Separate but interacting systems. *Perspectives on Psychological Science, 17*(2), 590–605.

Wrzesniewski, A., McCauley, C., Rozin, P., & Schwartz, B. (1997). Jobs, careers and callings: People's relations to their work. *Journal of Research in Personality, 31*(1), 21–33.

Yammarino, F. J., & Gooty, J. (2019). Cross-level models. In S. E. Humphrey & J. M. LeBreton (eds.), *The handbook of multilevel theory, measurement, and analysis* (pp. 563–585). American Psychological Association.

Yemiscigil, A., Powdthavee, N., & Whillans, A. V. (2021). The effects of retirement on sense of purpose in life: Crisis or opportunity? *Psychological Science, 32*(11), 1856–1864.

Yu, Y., & Zhang Y. (2023). The impact of social identity conflict on planning horizons. *Journal of Personality and Social Psychology, 124*(5), 917–934.

Yuan, M., Zhang, Q., Wang, B., Liang, Y., & Zhang, H. (2019). A mixed integer linear programming model for optimal planning of bicycle sharing systems: A case study in Beijing. *Sustainable Cities and Society, 47*. https://doi.org/10.1016/j.scs.2019.101515.

Zanini, M. (2008). Using power curves to assess industry dynamics. *McKinsey Quarterly, 1*, 1–6.

Zeeman, E. C. (1979). Catastrophe theory. In W. Güttinger and H. Eikemeier (eds.), *Structural Stability in Physics* (pp. 12–22). Springer.

Index

For the benefit of digital users, indexed terms that span two pages (e.g., 52–53) may, on occasion, appear on only one of those pages.

Note: Tables and figures are indicated by an italic *t* and *f* following the page number.

Adventure Consultants Expedition, 11–13
Allegra Expedition, 11–13, 54–55
ambivalence to change, 1
American Management Associations
 (AMA), 135
American Psychological Association, 3
analysis of variance (ANOVA) tests, 240
Analytic Network, 14, 67, 75, 76
antagonistic states, 78
Appreciative Inquiry, 56
Argyris, Chris, 116
Ashakanasy, Neal, 218
assessment challenge, 115
attachment theory, 193, 195, 201, 203
attention in learning, 148
autonomy, 31, 37, 41, 89, 122, 151, 201–2

Behavioral Event Interview (BEI), 126, 129
Big Five Theory, 122
bike-sharing programs, 60
Bjoerndalen, Ole, 172–73
Brain Derived Neurotropic Factor (BNDF),
 72, 196
Brooks, Herb, 20–21
Burns, Robert, 106

calculations in change research, 239
calling in life, 35
career changes, 44
change research
 calculations, 239
 case examples, 241
 dependent variables, 239, 241
 experimentation and practice to mastery,
  245, 249–50
 ICT-specific questions, 243
 Ideal Self and, 243

introduction to, 237–38
 learning agenda and planning, 245, 249
 longitudinal studies and distributions, 238
 multiple *vs.* single sources of data, 240
 in PEA/NEA, 244, 247
 periodicity of change, 44, 214–15, 238–39
 questions and needs in, 238
 Real Self and, 244, 248–49
 resonant relationships and, 246, 250
 social identity groups and, 246, 251–52
 speed of change, 1–2, 80–81, 90–92, 93,
  235, 238–39, 241
 subjects for, 242
 summary of ICT, 247
 velocity of change, 1, 91–92, 238–39
Chilean Mine Disaster (2010), 208–10
coaching dyads, 80
cognitive behavior therapy (CBT), 183
collective action, 87
collective desired change, 50
collectivist cultures, 41, 101, 108, 187
community change
 experimentation and practice to mastery,
  189
 Ideal Self and, 5–6, 59
 multiple levels of, 23
 PEA/NEA tipping points and, 87, 88, 93
 Real Self and, 143–44
 shared planning in, 165
community development corporations
 (CDCs), 24
Compass, Eddie, 211
compassion, 31, 38, 48–49, 74, 237–38. *See
 also* shared compassion
competencies at behavioral level, 124, 126*f*
complex systems, 8, 11, 19–20, 94, 104, 214–
 17, 251

core values, 38
corporate social responsibility (CSR),
        185, 205–6
country change, 23
courage to change, 6
COVID-19 pandemic, 5, 146, 193–94, 229
critical incident interviewing (CII), 126
cross-level communication, 20, 217, 231

Davidson, Richard, 51
deep-caving, 13, 15, 16–17, 162, 208, 249, 250
deep listening, 198
Deepwater Horizon (2010), 210
Default Mode Network (DMN), 14, 33, 34,
        67, 74, 149, 247
defensive protection, 100
dependent variables in change research,
        239, 241
desired change. *See* sustained, desired change
desire *vs.* drive, 31
Dhar, Udayan, xii–xiii, xv–xvi, 44–45
Dickinson, Emily, 40
Diogenes, 107
discontinuous and nonlinear change
        (Principle 3 of ICT), 14, 19, 64, 94–
        95, 97–98, 103, 214–15, 219, 246, 248
discontinuous emergence, 103
displacement, 109–10, 112
Donne, John, 192
Dreyfus, Christine, 177–78
Driver, Michael, 45–46
drive theory, 31
Dukhaykh, Suad, 227–28
Dunnette, Marvin, 125–26
dyads of change, 1, 5, 8–11, 19, 21, 24, 48, 50–
        51, 79, 80, 105, 161*f*, 161

effort in learning, 148
ego defense mechanisms, 7–8, 15, 109, 116,
        144, 226
elitism in social identity groups, 235
Emerson, Ralph Waldo, 40
emotional and social intelligence (ESI)
        competencies, 129–30, 136*f*,
        136, 224–25
emotional contagion, 90–92, 199
emotional intelligence (EI) competencies,
        142, 206
Empathic Network, 14, 34, 67, 75, 76, 195–96
Enteric Nervous System (ENS), 69, 244
expectation effect, 114–15, 139–40

experiential learning theory (ELT), 158–
        59, 173
experimentation and practice to mastery
        (Principle 6 of ICT)
    basic experience of, 169, 170*f*
    change research and, 245, 249–50
    in communities, 189
    feedback role in, 183
    habit formation, 182
    introduction to, 17, 169
    length of time for, 178
    multitasking and, 180
    nudges/nudge theory, 181, 190–91, 245
    in organizations, 185, 188
    PEA/NEA and, 170–73
    peer coaching groups and, 185
    preferred learning modes in, 173
    requirements for, 175
    rhythm and dosage of, 179
    shared vision and, 200
    stealth learning and, 17, 180, 190–91, 250
    in teams, 187
    10,000 hours of practice myth, 176
    training role in, 184
    visualizing as, 172
expert status, 176
Eysenck, Hans, 4

Faux Self, 15, 112, 114, 249
feedback in experimentation and practice,
        183
Fitzgerald, F. Scott, 7
fixed mindset, 79, 157
forecasting model, 29–30, 33, 102
fractal theory, 8, 12*f*, 19–25, 49*f*, 49, 50, 80,
        81*f*, 104, 137*f*, 137, 161*f*, 161, 187,
        188*f*, 207, 208*f*, 213, 214, 215–17,
        216*f*, 250
Franklin, Benjamin, 182
Freud, Anna, 109
Freud, Sigmund, 107, 109
friendship benches, 212
frontoparietal control network (FPCN),
        150, 161–62
Future Search, 22, 56
future time perspective, 33

Gandhi, Indira, 218–19
Gandhi, Mohandas, 87
goal intentions, 158
Goal Setting Theory, 147–48

goal shielding, 37
Goethe, 169
grandparent relationships, 212
Grant, Anthony, 158
gratitude, 74, 90, 93, 203, 204, 250
growth mindset, 79, 157
Guardiola, Pepe, 223–24

habit formation, 182
Hall, Rob, 54
Handy, Charles, 42
Harris Interactive Polling, 3
healthcare dyads, 80
Helping People Change (Boyatzis, Smith and
        Van Oosten), 181–82
heterogeneity, 215
high-quality connections (HQCs), 199
Hock, Dee, 43
Hollander, Edwin, 111, 116
homogeneity, 59–60, 101, 215
hope
    approach and theory of, 40
    humility and, 3
    learning agenda and planning, 154,
        160, 165
    multiple levels of change and, 216, 218–19,
        221, 224, 233–34, 236
    PEA/NEA and, 79, 88–89, 90, 91, 93
    Real Self and, 133
    resonant relationships and, 198, 199, 200,
        202–3, 204, 208
    shared vision and, 18, 27–28, 40, 47, 49–
        50, 51–52, 57–58
    in sustained, desired change, 1, 2, 3–6, 11,
        14, 18, 20, 25, 26
Howard, Anita, xii, xiii, xv–xvii, 82, 149–50
human degree of magnificence, 26
humility and hope, 3
Humphrey, Ronald, 218
*The Hungry Spirit: Beyond Capitalism: A
        Quest for Purpose in the Modern
        World* (Handy), 42
hurricane disasters, 211

Ideal Self (Principle 1 of ICT)
    career changes, 44
    change in, 43
    in change research, 243
    collective desired change and, 50
    community change and, 5–6, 59
    components of, 225

core values and philosophy, 38
desire *vs.* drive, 31
discrepancies between the Real Self and,
        30, 41–42, 117, 132, 157–58
future time perspective, 33
hope and, 40
Ideal Self test, 50, 255
identity and, 39
introduction to, 11, 12*f*, 27–30, 28*f*, 29*f*
in key relationships, 48
life changes, 44
liminal periods, 46
Ought Self and, 6, 39, 41, 70, 85–86, 106–7,
        108, 111, 115–16, 117–18, 132, 139,
        150–51, 174, 225, 227, 244, 245,
        247, 249
overview of, 30
Personal Sustainability Index, 18, 73, 272
prospection and dream, 32
purpose, meaning, calling, 35
salient experiences and, 47
socialization experiences and, 47
transitional periods, 46
Ideal Self test, 50, 255
Immunity to Change Theory (ITC), 181
inclusiveness in social identity groups, 235
independence, 60–62, 87, 89, 215
individual change, 21
Intentional Change Theory (ICT)
    change research summary, 247
    communities of practice and, 23
    comparative narratives and, 11
    defined, 7
    fractal theory, 8, 12*f*, 19–25, 49*f*, 49, 50,
        80, 81*f*, 104, 137*f*, 137, 161*f*, 161, 187,
        188*f*, 207, 208*f*, 213, 214, 215–17,
        216*f*, 250
    multilevelness, 19, 213, 215–17, 225–30
    process and principles, 8, 9*f*, 10*t*, 28*f*
    resonant relationships in each phase of,
        206
    uniqueness of, 25
    See also discontinuous and nonlinear
        change; experimentation and
        practice; Ideal Self; learning agenda
        and planning; multiple levels of
        change; PEA/NEA tipping points;
        Real Self; resonant relationships;
        sustained, desired change
internal rate of return (IRR), 96
Interpersonal experiences, 71, 73

intrapersonal experiences, 70, 72–73
"I-Thou" relationships, 194–95

Jack, Tony, 14, 34, 75
James, William, 27, 95

Kelner, Steve, 160
Kennedy, John F., 218–19
Kenyatta, Jomo, 46
Khan, Akhter Hameed, 189
King, Martin Luther, Jr., 20, 49–50, 51,
        87, 218–19
Klimchouk, Alexander, 13, 163
Kolb, David, 173
Kolkata Knight Riders (KKR), 224
Krubera Team, 13

leader–member exchange (LMX), 199
leadership, 4, 80, 96–98, 97f. See also resonant
        leadership
learning agenda and planning (Principle 5
        of ICT)
    change research and, 245, 249
    community change and, 165
    focusing attention and effort, 148
    goal intentions, 158
    hope and, 154, 160, 165
    introduction to, 16, 146–48, 147f
    Need for Achievement (N-Ach), 16, 122,
        152–59, 183, 194, 241–42
    organizational change and, 164
    PEA/NEA tipping
        points, 148, 158, 164
    performance goal orientation and, 155
    planning approach, 157
    shared planning and, 161
    SMART goals and, 16, 152–59
    stealth learning, 17, 180, 190–91, 250
    sustained effort building, 159
Learning Style Inventory, 173
Lennon, John, 53–54
life changes, 44
limbic resonance, 204–5, 218
liminal periods, 46

Machiavelli, 2–3
magnificence. See human degree of
        magnificence
Mandela, Nelson, 20, 49–50
Massive Open Online Course (MOOC),
        21, 232–33

Master's in Business Administration
        programs, 3–4
McCartney, Paul, 53–54
McCaskey, Michael, 157–58
McClelland, David, 125, 131, 134,
        152, 241–42
McKee, Annie, 158
meaning of life, 35
Me at My Best exercise, 131
medial parietal cortex (MPC), 74–75
medial prefrontal cortex (mPFC), 34–35, 74–
        75, 118, 150, 154, 231
mentoring, 40–41, 171–72, 185, 190–91, 208
Merton, Robert, 225
Michelangelo effect, 53
mid-life crises, 3, 41, 42, 44, 119
Mothers Against Drunk Driving (MADD),
        39–40
multilevelness, 19, 213, 215–17, 225–30
multiple levels of change (Principle 8, 9, 10
        of ICT)
    community change, 23
    dyad level, 21, 161f, 161
    hope and, 216, 218–19, 221, 224, 233–
        34, 236
    individual level, 21, 161f, 161
    introduction to, 19, 214–18, 216f
    multilevelness, 19, 213, 215–17, 225–30
    organizational change, 5, 22, 24, 85, 104,
        164–65, 198, 228
    social identity groups and, 225–30
    team level, 21, 161f, 161
multiple sources of data, 240
multitasking and practice, 180

nagging, 17, 181, 207, 245
National Federation of the Blind, 54–55
Need for Achievement (N-Ach), 16, 122,
        152–59, 183, 194, 241–42
Need for Affiliation, 122, 194
Need for Power, 122, 241–42
Negative Emotional Attractor (NEA). See
        PEA/NEA tipping points
negative emotions, 77
Nerve Growth Factor (NGF), 72, 196
neural networks, 74
neural synchrony, 218
Nkomo Primary School, 20
nucleus accumbens, 35
nudges/nudge theory, 17, 21, 181, 190–91,
        207, 245

obligatory change, 150–51, 249
obsessive passion, 37, 149
Office of Economic Opportunity, 24
operating philosophy, 38
optimism, 40, 41, 77, 78, 122, 244
orbitofrontal cortex (OFC), 35, 154
organizational change
    experimentation and practice in, 185, 188
    multiple levels of, 5, 21, 22, 24, 85, 104,
        161f, 161, 164–65, 198, 228
    PEA/NEA tipping points, 80, 85, 104
    resonant relationships in, 198
    shared planning in, 164
    shared Real Self and, 138
    sustained, desired change in, 5, 22, 24
organizational development (OD), 22, 24,
    50–51, 55, 85, 165, 197–98
organizational psychology, 30–31, 127
other-focused compassion, 74
Ought Self, 6, 39, 41, 70, 85–86, 106–7,
    108, 111, 115–16, 117–18, 132, 139,
    150–51, 174, 225, 227, 244, 245,
    247, 249
oxytocin hormone, 71–72, 120–22, 195–96

Parasympathetic Nervous System (PNS), 13–
    14, 67, 69, 100
Parker, Annise, 92, 166
Passarelli, Angela, xii, xv–xvii, 149–51, 160
Pasteur, Louis, 146
PEA/NEA tipping points (Principle 2 and 3
    of ICT)
    antagonistic states, 78
    awareness of, 65, 66f
    in change research, 244, 247
    collective action and, 87
    in communities, 87
    community change and, 88, 93
    emotional and social contagion, 90–92
    Enteric Nervous System (ENS) and,
        69, 244
    experimentation and practice to mastery,
        170–73
    hope and, 79, 88–89, 90, 91, 93
    intention vs. consequence, 88
    interpersonal experiences and, 71, 73
    intrapersonal experiences and, 70, 72–73
    introduction to, 13, 64, 65f
    learning agenda and planning, 148,
        158, 164
    multiple levels of change and, 19

neural networks and, 74
    in organizations, 80, 83, 85, 104
    overview of, 67, 68t
    Parasympathetic Nervous System (PNS)
        and, 13–14, 67, 69, 100
    positive vs. negative emotions, 77
    protests and riots, 88
    strange attractors and, 65
    to sustained, desired change, 80
    Sympathetic Nervous System (SNS) and,
        13–14, 64, 67, 69, 100, 247
    in teams, 83
peer coaching groups, 185
performance goal orientation, 155
periodicity of change, 44, 214–15, 238–39
Personal Sustainability Index, 18, 73, 272
pessimism, 122
PhD Project, 21
planned change, 22, 85–86
planning change. See learning agenda and
    planning (Principle 5 of ICT)
Positive Emotional Attractor (PEA). See
    PEA/NEA tipping points
positive emotions, 77
positive feedback, 114
posterior cingulate cortex (PCC), 35,
    39, 74–75
power curves, 96–98, 97f
practice/practicing. See experimentation
    and practice to mastery (Principle 6
    of ICT)
preferred learning modes, 173
projection mechanisms, 110
prospection and dream, 32
protest tipping points, 88
psychological well-being, 31, 205
psychotherapy efficacy, 4
punctuated equilibrium, 104
purpose of life, 35
Pygmalion (Shaw), 115

quiet quitting, 36

reaction formation, 109–10, 111, 144, 207
Real Self (Principle 4 of ICT)
    access to, 109
    assessment challenge, 115
    change research and, 244, 248–49
    changing of, 133
    community change and, 143–44
    shared Real Self and, 140, 141f

Real Self (Principle 4 of ICT) (*cont.*)
  competencies at behavioral level, 124, 126*f*
  competency development, 133
  discrepancies between the Ideal Self and,
      30, 41–42, 117, 132, 160
  Faux Self and, 15, 112, 114, 249
  hope and, 133
  individual self concept, 107
  introduction to, 14, 106–7, 107*f*
  multilevel personality theory, 120, 121*f*
  Ought Self and, 106–7, 108, 111, 115–16,
      117–18, 132, 139
  positive feedback issues, 114
  search for, 108, 120
  shared Real Self, 137*f*, 137, 141*f*
  social identity and, 108–9, 110, 111–
      13, 122
  strength and weaknesses, 132
  transference process and, 109–11
reasoned action theory, 21, 95
recursive process, 215
Relational Climate Survey, 275–77
relationships. *See* resonant relationships
      (Principle 7 of ICT)
reminders for change
  nagging, 17, 181, 207, 245
  nudges/nudge theory, 17, 21, 181, 190–91,
      207, 245
Repton, Humphrey, 25
Reputational Effectiveness Survey, 239–40
resonant leadership, 19–20, 199, 205–6,
      210, 213, 214, 216–17, 218–23, 236,
      243, 246, 251. *See also* leadership;
      multilevelness
resonant relationships (Principle 7 of ICT)
  change research and, 246, 250
  as context for life, 192
  creation of context through, 195
  in each ICT phase, 206
  emotional contagion and, 90–92, 199
  with grandparents, 212
  hope and, 198, 199, 200, 202–3, 204, 208
  introduction to, 18, 192, 193*f*
  in organizations, 198
  overall quality of, 205
  qualities of, 198
  resonant leadership, 19–20, 199, 205–6,
      210, 213, 214, 216–17, 218–23, 236,
      243, 246, 251
  shared compassion and, 203
  shared energy and, 204

sustained, desired change and, 207
riot tipping points, 88
Rochford, Kylie, xii–xiii, xv–xvii
role-playing technique, 175
Rolling Stones, 53–54
Roosevelt, Eleanor, 30
rostral anterior cingulate cortex (rACC), 34

Saint-Exupéry, Antoine de, 27
salient experiences, 47
sawtooth effect, 142
scale dependence, 19, 215, 251
self-assessment, 112, 113, 115–16, 129–
      30, 140–42
Self-Assessment and External Assessment
      Questionnaire, 129–30
self-awareness, 74–75, 106, 107–8, 109, 129,
      130, 133, 159, 244, 249
self-control, 32, 36, 79, 100–1, 109, 114, 129,
      130, 150–52, 159, 170, 175, 249
Self-Determination Theory (SDT), 21,
      31, 194
self-efficacy, 41, 101–2, 120, 125, 201, 221–22
self-esteem, 114, 118, 122–23, 132
self-focused compassion, 74
self-image, 108, 112, 114, 119, 122–23, 130,
      132. *See also* Faux Self; resonant
      relationships (Principle 7 of ICT)
self-regulation/self-regulating systems, 67–
      68, 79, 93, 101, 157, 172
Seligman, Martin, 31
Semple, Mandy Chapman, 92
shared compassion, 18, 84–85, 186, 196, 198,
      200, 203, 205–6, 207–8, 209, 210, 213,
      217, 218, 221–22, 231–32, 235, 236,
      250. *See also* compassion
shared energy, 204
shared planning in learning agenda, 161
shared Real Self, 137, 137*f*, 141*f*. *See also*
      Real Self
shared vision
  Appreciative Inquiry and, 56
  bike-sharing programs, 60
  collective desired change and, 50
  core purpose of, 57
  experimentation and practice with, 200
  Future Search, 22, 56
  hope and, 27–28, 40, 47, 49–50, 51–
      52, 57–58
  in organizations, 55
  in pairs, 51

in teams, 53
vision driving and, 51–53, 59
See also Ideal Self
Shaw, George Bernard, 115
single sources of data, 240
SMART goals, 16, 152–59
Smith, Melvin, 233–34
social contagion, 90–92
social identity groups
    (SIGs), 19, 39, 43, 50
change research and, 246, 251–52
elitism *vs.* inclusiveness, 235
multilevelness, 225–30
outside perspective, 228
Real Self and, 108–9, 110, 111–13, 122
transmitting and transforming
    information, 230
socialization experiences, 47
social justice, 24, 87, 92, 165
social learning theory, 21, 91, 175, 181
solution-focused coaching, 52
speed of change, 1–2, 80–81, 90–92, 93, 235,
    238–39, 241
spirituality/spiritual practice, 1, 35, 36, 37–
    38, 39, 49–50, 54, 100
stealth learning, 17, 180, 190–91, 250
Stone, Bill, 13, 162
Strauss, Tomas, 57–58
subjects for change research, 242
sublimation, 109–10, 111–12
survival through change, 2–3, 48, 62, 67–68,
    74, 77, 79–80, 100, 138–39, 209–
    10, 244
sustained, desired change
ambivalence to, 1
change research and, 247
collective desired change, 50
courage to change, 6
curiosity and awe, 6
defensive protection, 100
desire for inclusion, 101
discontinuities, 103
dynamics of, 94
exploration of, 26
hope in, 1, 2, 3–6, 11, 14, 18, 20, 25, 26
human degree of magnificence, 26
humility and hope with, 3
introduction to, 1
in organizations, 5, 22, 24
PEA/NEA tipping points to, 80
possibilities in, 25

power curves and, 96–98, 97*f*
regressive forces and, 98
resonant leadership for, 19–20, 199, 205–6,
    210, 213, 214, 216–17, 218–23, 236,
    243, 246, 251
resonant relationships and, 207
shared planning and, 161
uncertainty and, 102
See also Intentional Change Theory (ICT);
    multiple levels of change
sustained effort building, 159
swallowtail distribution, 96
swarms/swarming, 92
Sympathetic Nervous System (SNS), 13–14,
    64, 67, 69, 100, 247
Szell, George, 58

Task Positive Network (TPN), 13, 14, 33, 64,
    67, 74, 148–49, 164–65, 247
Taylor, Scott, xii, xiii–xiv, xv–xvii, 113, 130
team change
experimentation and practice to mastery,
    187
multiple levels of, 21, 161*f*, 161
PEA/NEA tipping points and, 83
punctuated equilibrium and, 104
shared Real Self and, 137*f*, 137
shared vision in, 53
technological change, 2
10,000 hours of practice myth, 176
Thales of Miletus, 106
Thematic Apperception Test (TAT), 126–
    27, 152–53
tipping points to transitions. *See* PEA/NEA
    tipping points
training in experimentation and practice,
    184
transference process, 109–11
transitional periods, 46
Trebino, Juan, 170
Trithemius, Johannes, 2
t-tests, 240

undergraduate programs, 4
UN World Food Program, 37

Van Oosten, Ellen, 52
velocity of change, 1, 91–92, 238–39
ventromedial prefrontal cortex (vmPFC), 34,
    75, 195–96, 231
victims of change, 2, 45

vision driving, 51–53, 59
visualizing/visualization, 17, 32, 150, 172, 190, 218–19, 245
volition, 3, 27, 31, 41, 95

Weihenmayer, Erik, 11–13, 54–55
Weisel, Elie, 48
Wilkinson, Laura, 172–73
working alliance, 196–97

working groups of experts, 89
Wu, Michelle, 92, 165

YMCA (Young Men's Christian Organization), 58
Yousafzai, Malala, 218–19

Zikhali, Nomusa, 20, 219–21
Zoffer, Jerry, 134